"Examining the Reformation is like examining a beautiful diamond. Every angle reveals something new and invites further inspection. *Celebrating the Legacy of the Reformation* provides the valuable insights of leading Church historians on various facets of the Reformation. I especially appreciate the chapters dedicated to theology, preaching and missions. This is a welcomed addition to the field of Reformation Studies."

 —Daniel L. Akin, president, Southeastern Baptist
  Theological Seminary

"Needed today is a generation of historians committed to Reformation research. Needed more still, however, is a generation of theologians and pastors committed to applying Reformation doctrine to the church today. For that reason, *Celebrating the Legacy of the Reformation* is a welcomed contribution, encouraging Christians across the globe not only to study the Reformation but retrieve its theological heritage. With the Reformation was born a right reading of scripture, one that not only bowed to the authority of scripture itself but recovered its gospel message. As a result, the church experienced new life, eyes opened wide to the free grace God gives to all those who trust in Christ alone. May this volume do the same for the church today."

 —Matthew Barrett, associate professor of Christian theology,
  Midwestern Baptist Theological Seminary

"The Reformation was a watershed event that transformed the life, faith, and practices of the western church in enduring ways. The recent 500th anniversary of Luther's clarion call for church reform was an apt occasion for reflecting on its impact in the past and ongoing legacy today. This book offers a valuable resource for students, scholars, and pastors alike to consider the multifaceted dimensions of the Reformation story within a faith community."

 —Jennifer Powell McNutt, associate professor of theology
  and history of Christianity, Wheaton College

"While focusing on the key aspects of the Reformation—theology, liturgy, catechesis, preaching, missions, and martyrology—this compendium successfully covers both the magisterial and the radical reformations as well as their most famous representatives. One specific purpose appears to have driven authors and editors in putting these contributions together: that of drafting a comprehensive picture of what the Reformation was five centuries ago and what it means to the contemporary world. Their efforts do pertinently reveal the ever new meanings of the half-millennial European Reformations, a complex range of events whose significance is shown here to be far from over. In other words, I have found a new compulsory source for my course in Reformation theology."

 —Corneliu C. Simuț, professor of historical and systematic
  theology, Emanuel University, Romania, and Senior
  Vice-Chancellor Postdoctoral Research Fellow, University
  of Pretoria, South Africa

"Two major questions direct our understanding of the Protestant Reformation: What happened historically? And, what does it mean for us today? *Celebrating the Legacy of the Reformation* accurately draws upon history in order to provide compelling answers regarding current meaning. Whether addressing theology or devotion, preaching or missions, the authors demonstrate why the Reformation still matters: Ultimately, God's Word of justifying grace continues to address every human being at the point of their deepest need. As a scholar and as a Christian, I thus highly commend this work to you."

 —Malcolm B. Yarnell III, research professor of systematic theology,
  Southwestern Baptist Theological Seminary

CELEBRATING

THE LEGACY

OF THE

REFORMATION

CELEBRATING

THE LEGACY

OF THE

REFORMATION

KEVIN L. KING

EDWARD E. HINDSON

BENJAMIN K. FORREST

Editors

Dedication

To Carl Diemer

who has been teaching church history for over forty years,
thank you for instilling passion and distilling wisdom.

To Bruce K. Bell

friend, and fan of the Reformation.

Contents

Foreword

THE CONTINUING IMPACT OF 1517

In 2017 Christians around the world paused to observe and celebrate an historical event a half millennium ago. Even some outside the faith took note of the cultural significance of the posting of academic theses inviting debate over an issue that is hardly understandable for almost all in the twenty-first century. A relatively young Augustinian friar, with a growing reputation as a biblical scholar and churchman, Martin Luther raised questions about the church's teaching and practice of indulgences that brought relief for those suffering temporal punishment for their sins in purgatory. He simply sought debate and clarification of practices that he thought contributed to the appalling crisis of pastoral care plaguing the church of his time.

This seemingly innocent raising of one more issue that was being debated within Western Christendom in the early sixteenth century made a quite unexpected impact on the following five centuries for several reasons. In fact, Luther's theses formed only a sidebar to his redefinition of what it means to be Christian as it had been developing over nearly a decade and would continue to take form during the subsequent four years. His ideas spread remarkably far and, with unprecedented rapidity, because enterprising printers had risked publishing a genre, academic theses, for a wider public. The modest but nonetheless impressive result of that risk led Luther to experiment further with using print as a medium for spreading and testing his emerging thinking on God and on being human. Public communication and societal discourse have never been the same since.

Luther had been taught and trained, in home and school, in cloister and university, in a system of practicing the Christian faith that had been generated three-quarters of a millennium earlier as Christianity came to the northern European masses, often through political decisions of local leaders. Without adequate preachers and catechists, the church could only inadequately implant the biblical message in minds shaped by the structures of the traditional tribal religions of Europe. Biblical names and terms were fit into these structures. These structures presumed that the relationship between human beings and whatever or whomever people believed was or were absolute and ultimate began and was sustained by human initiative. This way of religious thinking presumed that sacred or religious activities please the higher powers or person(s) more than obedience to ethical codes, although such obedience was also necessary in these systems to preserve societal order and harmony. The church took root in this ground with some concessions to this framework for religious thinking. Luther learned that his own adherence to the laws of the church and his participation in its rituals held the key to his relationship with God. He learned that sacred activities conducted by those in holy orders, in the church's hierarchy, were critical for his access to Christ's saving work and favor.

Luther suffered under the honest perception that his performance of both sacral and secular commands from God and church was inadequate to gain God's favor. Several factors came together to alter his understanding of what his identity as a Christian meant. They included 1) the presuppositions of his training in the school of William of Ockham; 2) his own sensitive personality; 3) the pastoral concern that grew out of his personality and was nurtured by his responsibilities as an Augustinian friar for assisting parish priests; 4) the aids for biblical interpretation of the movement today called "biblical humanism;" and 5) his own study of Scripture, a task that not only had become a gratifying habit in the cloister but also was imposed by his call to teach at the University of Wittenberg. These factors caused him to perceive a different definition of being Christian. His biblical studies convinced him that God initiates the relationship between himself and his human creatures and that God maintains that relationship through his address to his people in his Word. That Word conveys the benefits of Christ's death and resurrection to them as it calls them out of rebellion and doubt to trusting in him. Luther's understanding of how language functions, derived from his university training in logic and rhetoric, helped him realize that God's Word does not return to him without doing what God intends to effect through it (Isa 55:10–11) and that the proclaimed gospel is in fact his means of exercising his saving power among sinners (Rom 1:16).

Luther gained an international following, concentrated in the German lands, the Nordic and Baltic lands, and the kingdoms of Poland and Hungary (especially modern Slovakia). Others, however, found his understanding of the justification of the sinner through faith alone in Christ Jesus convincing, but rejected or modified other elements of his teaching. These elements included his belief in the sacramental true presence of Christ's body and blood in the Lord's Supper; the effectiveness of the baptismal promise for delivering forgiveness of sins, life, and salvation; and his distinction of preaching God's law (as primarily a call for repentance) and proclaiming God's gospel (as the gift of his favor through the death and resurrection of Christ).

Under the leadership of Ulrich Zwingli, his disciple Heinrich Bullinger, John Calvin, and his disciple Theodore Beza, along with a host of others, the Reformed tradition developed on the basis of other philosophical presuppositions that led to differing interpretations of some elements of Scripture. Within the Anglican church elements from the thought of John Wyclif and his Lollard followers formed a tradition that also absorbed elements from Luther, Calvin, and other continental reformers. In the Middle Ages transitory reform movements had arisen that embraced the Bible, as opposed to the regulations and practices of the established church, as the authority for faith and life; these groups emphasized the importance of the imitation of Christ and ethical morality rather than observing the ritual practices of the official church as the key to salvation. That turned these groups to an anti-sacramental stance since they saw the sacraments not as expressions of God's promise but as mechanical performances; this also meant they were fiercely anti-clerical. Many of these groups expected the return of Christ and the establishment of his kingdom in the immediate future. In the sixteenth century, the Anabaptists established this vision of reform and the true church on a lasting institutional basis.

The essays in this volume reflect a spectrum of backgrounds and treat a variety of topics that highlight specific aspects of the historical development of the Reformation and its impact in several streams of the Reformation, labeled as they often are today "Reformations." Serious issues divide these authors, and basic commitments make them one. They recognize that any stream of thought undergoes changes over a period of five hundred years. Therefore, they address the question that naturally arises: do insights of the Reformers of the sixteenth-century Reformation contribute to the proclamation of the biblical message today? These essays demonstrate that insights of the sixteenth-century continue to echo in our world of thought at the beginning of the twenty-first century. These authors highlight repeatedly that what we can learn from the writings of the reformers has practical significance for the doctrine and life of contemporary Christians around the world.

In these explorations of what "Reformation" meant in its theological, social, and cultural context, readers will find sensitive and perceptive evaluations of what it means today. From this rich medley of historical investigation and analysis, readers will gain fresh perspectives on the reasons for the development of new sets of issues that shaped the interpretation of both Scripture and traditions and shape applications of the insights of Protestant reformers for life in the church and the world today.

Robert Kolb
Concordia Seminary

Acknowledgments

In the fall of 2017, Liberty University hosted a Reformation Conference to celebrate the 500th anniversary. This conference was generously funded by the provost's office of the university. Special thanks must be given to the university and to Dr. Ron Hawkins who gave so generously. In addition to Dr. Hawkins's leadership, we would also like to thank the entire provost's office for their support in making this such an enjoyable project. This includes Drs. Scott Hicks, Shawn Akers, David Calland, and Ester Warren.

In addition to the provost's office, we would like to thank those who presented at the conference. In addition to those with chapters below we would also like to thank Carl Trueman, Jeffery Anderson, Kevin Clauson, Mark David Hall, Nicholas Higgens, Hannah Schultz, Scott Amos, Leo Percer, Robert Mills, Michael Saffle, Martin Scott Catino, Andrew Stern, Sean Turchin, Benjamin Esswein, Samuel C. Smith, Miles Smith, Joe Super, E. Ray Moore, A. Chadwick Thornhill, Vernon Whaley, Donna Donald, David Wheeler, Cecil Kramer, Thomas Hudgins, and our two student presenters, Caleb Brown and Kevan D. Keane.

Several key people played valuable roles in organizing and executing the conference details: Rebecca Hartman, Ruth Ronk, Josh Erb, and Drs. Carey Roberts, Roger Shultz, and Troy Temple—thank you all! We also want to thank all those at B&H who have helped bring this project to fruition. This includes Jim Baird, Chris Thompson, Sarah Landers, and a host of others. Your partnership in this project and in gospel ministry is greatly appreciated!

Introduction

Let the Hammers Ring: The Legacy of the Reformation for the Church Today and Tomorrow

EDWARD E. HINDSON

The silence was broken as the statement was nailed up for all to see. Every crack of the hammer drove the nails deeper into the wood. It was the point of no return. The world would never again be the same. The course of human history would be changed forever. The written declaration said it all, "Jesus of Nazareth, King of the Jews."[1]

It was nine in the morning in AD 33. Crucifixion was dirty business and the Romans were experts at it. The soldiers laid the prisoners on the crossbeams and tied them down. Then they picked up the long iron spikes, raised their hammers, and began to pound. They drove spikes through the arms of victims, pinning them to the cross.

The steady crack of the hammers could be heard above the screams of the victims and the cries of their relatives. Each strike of the hammers told the condemned there was no hope of release. But, as the hammer sounds rang out against the rocky cliff, one steady voice could be heard above the clamor. "Father, forgive them, for they know not what they do" (Luke 23:34 ESV).

---

[1] The fullest statement is recorded by John (19:19–20), who was the only disciple to witness the crucifixion in person. For variations of the "indictment," cf. Matt 27:37, Mark 15:26, and Luke 23:38. For suggested reconciliation, see William Hendriksen, *Exposition of the Gospel of Luke*, NTC (Grand Rapids: Baker, 1978), 1030–31.

Even in this awful moment, Jesus would pull himself up on the nails and rise above it all. Here at the place of the skull, we see no squirming, squealing victim—no angry, cursing man. Instead, we see the Savior in all his greatness, goodness, and compassion, forgiving his unsuspecting executioners.

So let the hammers ring! In their ugly sound we hear the voice of God shouting. From the very lips of God incarnate comes the one word of hope for all eternity—grace! Grace that is greater than all our sin. Wonderful, marvelous, matchless grace, flowing from the heart of God, reaching out across the cavern of time, planned from the dawn of history before the worlds were ever framed.

John Stott expressed it like this: "Moved by the perfection of his holy love, God in Christ substituted himself for us sinners."[2] R.C. Sproul observed, "On the cross, Jesus does not merely receive the curse of God. He becomes the curse. He is the embodiment of the curse … His is more than a human death; it is an atonement. Christ is the sacrificial lamb."[3]

The Door to the Future

Sixteen centuries later, Martin Luther approached the church doors at Wittenberg on October 31, 1517. He too was carrying the tools that had been used to crucify the Savior: a hammer and nails. He too nailed up an inscription for all to read—his *95 Theses*. Whether he fully realized it at the time, the world in which Luther lived was about to change forever. The hegemony of the Roman Catholic Church had held sway over Europe for more than a thousand years. All of that was about to change. The future would never be the same.

The Protestant Reformation took place at a time when Europe was in transition, with rising nationalism opposing papal claims to universal power. Medieval feudalism was yielding to a new merchant middle class. The Renaissance brought a revival of learning and the printing press disseminated information faster than ever before in human history. It was only a matter of time until the demand for change in the church would be heard throughout the world.

Earlier attempts to reform the church by John Wycliffe in England, Jan Huss in Bohemia, John Wessel in Holland, and the Waldensians in France

---

[2] John R. W. Stott, *The Cross of Christ* (Downers Grove, IL: InterVarsity Press, 1986), 167.
[3] R. C. Sproul, *The Glory of Christ* (Wheaton, IL: Tyndale House, 1990), 149–50.

had been met with vigorous and often violent opposition from the Roman church. By the sixteenth century times were changing. As the Augustinian monk and university professor stood before the church door, little did he realize that he was about to unleash a torrent of passion that had been building in the hearts and minds of Europe's people for centuries.

While the Reformation had numerous social and political aspects, for Martin Luther it was essentially a spiritual revival and ecclesiastical renewal. What began as a protest over indiscriminate sales of indulgences eventually led to a spiritual awakening. Overwhelmed by every human attempt to find salvation, Luther began to discover the significance of the grace of God as he diligently studied the book of Romans. There he found what he believed to be the true gospel of the Christian faith. Rejecting the idea that human effort could bring reconciliation with God, Luther was convinced that the cross of Christ was the only hope for humankind. Thus, he preferred to call himself a "theologian of the cross."[4] Mark Noll observes, "For Luther, in short, to find God was to find the cross."[5]

For the next four years, Luther continued to write, preach, and debate vigorously. During this time, he lectured on Psalms and Hebrews, debated John Eck at Leipzig, and was interviewed by Cardinal Cajetan at Augsburg. As early as 1518 he had developed strong convictions regarding biblical authority (*sola Scriptura*) as the basis of his beliefs and became a champion of *sola fide* (faith alone). His most controversial works appeared in 1520, including *Sermon of the Mass* (dealing with the priesthood of the believer), *Treatise of Good Works* (focusing on salvation by faith), and *On the Papacy at Rome* (in which he called the pope Antichrist).[6]

In April 1521, Luther was summoned by the youthful Emperor Charles V of the Holy Roman Empire to answer charges of heresy at the Diet of Worms, where he declined to recant, boldly stating, "Here I stand,

---

[4] Martin Luther, *Heidelberg Disputation*, trans. Hilton C. Oswald, in *Career of the Reformer I*, vol. 31 of *Luther's Works* (hereafter cited *LW*), ed. Helmut T. Lehmann (Ann Arbor, MI: Concordia, 1958), 35–70.

[5] Mark Noll, *Turning Points*, 3rd ed. (Grand Rapids: Baker, 2012), 158.

[6] Luther appeared to follow the Wycliffite tradition in identifying the pope with the Antichrist. This was also evident in the works of John Calvin, John Gerhard, Francis Turretin, and Robert Barnes. In 1545, just one year before his death, Luther published another even stronger attack against the pope, *Against the Papacy at Rome, Founded by the Devil.* Cf. K.R. Firth, *The Apocalyptic Tradition in Reformation Britain 1530–1645* (Oxford: Oxford University Press, 1979), 11–15; J. M. Headley, *Luther's View of Church History* (New Haven, CT: Yale University Press, 1963), 242–46; Edward E. Hindson, *The Puritans' Use of Scripture in the Development of an Apocalyptical Hermeneutic* (Pretoria: University of South Africa, 1984), 27–33.

may God help me, Amen."[7] It was early evening on April 18, 1521, when Luther insisted, "Unless I am convinced by the testimony of the Scriptures or by clear reason … I am bound by the Scriptures I have quoted and my conscience is captive to the Word of God. I cannot and I will not retract anything, since it is neither safe nor right to go against conscience."[8] Mark Noll suggests, "With these words, Protestantism was born. Luther's conscience was captive to 'the Word of God,' to the living, active voice of Scripture.…With this dramatic statement in the most exalted company a sixteenth-century European could imagine, the foundations of Protestantism were set for all to see: Protestants would obey the Bible before all other authorities."[9]

The Protestant Reformation quickly spread throughout Europe. The sixteenth century alone produced such stalwarts as Philipp Melanchthon, Ulrich Zwingli, John Calvin, Theodore Beza, John Knox, Menno Simons, Balthasar Hubmaier, Heinrich Bullinger, William Tyndale, John Foxe, Hugh Latimer, and Nicholas Ridley. The *classical* Reformation would result in Lutheran, Reformed, and Anglican churches. In the meantime, the *radical*, or Anabaptist, reform sought to take the church back to its New Testament roots, including the separation of church and state, and believer's baptism by immersion. Despite their differences, the Protestant churches believed their theological convictions were based on the Bible as their sole rule of faith and practice.

The Legacy of the Reformation Today

Many of the blessings and benefits of the evangelical faith that we enjoy today are a direct result of the sixteenth-century Reformation. The Bible was loosed from the chains of tyranny. The laity were loosed from the bonds of the clergy. And the Spirit was loosed in the hearts of believers. The immediate result was the renewal, revival, and revitalization of western Christianity, which would ultimately spread across the Atlantic and eventually around the globe.

---

[7] Martin Luther, *Career of the Reformer II*, *LW* 32:113. The editor notes, "These words are given in German in the Latin text upon which this translation is based. There is good evidence, however, that Luther actually said only: 'May God help me!'" Cf. *Deutsche Reichstagsakten, Vol. II: Deutsche Reichstagsakten unter Kaiser Karl V* (Goth, 1896), 587.

[8] *LW* 32:112.

[9] Noll, *Turning Points*, 146–47.

In this study, we will examine the legacy of the Reformation in several areas of spiritual, social, economic, political, ecclesiastical, and missional living. The impetus of the Reformation was a renewed passion for reading, studying, and interpreting the Bible. To the Reformers, if indeed the Bible was the Word of God, then the voice of God must be heard above the voice of man.

The eventual result was a return to the grammatical-historical method of interpretation of the biblical text and expositional preaching of the message of the text. Whereas the sacrament had been the central focus of worship in the medieval church, the focus soon shifted to the preaching of the Word of God. In many churches, the pulpit took precedence over the communion table. The call to faith became more personal, eventually resulting in the great revivals of succeeding centuries.

Evangelistic efforts and the missionary expansion of Christianity eventually took the claims of the gospel to the far-flung regions of the earth. With this expansion came a renewed emphasis on the work of the Spirit to empower the message of the Word. Luther's translation of the Bible into German signaled an avalanche of Bible translations into hundreds of languages. His hymns of praise and worship set a pattern for a whole new emphasis on music in worship.

The pilgrimage of the heart that led the Reformers to examine the Scriptures for themselves resulted in what we identify as the evangelical and reformed churches today. Baptists, Presbyterians, Episcopalians, Lutherans, Methodists, Mennonites, and a host of other denominations owe their existence to those early Reformers who risked their lives for the cause of Christ and the gospel. The successes, struggles, and failures of those recipients of the heritage of the Reformation have shaped our religious beliefs and practices to this very day.

As we face the challenges and opportunities of the twenty-first century, we again may find it necessary to get out the hammers and nails to post our concerns today for the essential truths of a genuine Christian faith. We too may find it necessary to reform timeworn practices, revitalize worship, energize preaching, and inflame evangelistic and missional passions in a global context that will better enable us to "make disciples of all nations" (Matt 28:19).

Here we stand in our generation. God help us. We can do no other than follow the footsteps of our predecessors. Equipped with the tools of modern technology, but armed with the truth of Scripture, the clarity of the gospel, and the power of the Spirit, may we too be used by God to make a difference for the cause of Christ today, tomorrow, and forever.

Bibliography

Bainton, Roland H. *Here I Stand: A Life of Martin Luther*. Nashville: Abingdon, 1950.

Firth, Katherine R. *The Apocalyptic Tradition in Reformation Britain 1530–1645*. Oxford: Oxford University Press, 1979.

Headley, J. M. *Luther's View of Church History*. New Haven: Yale University Press, 1963.

Hindson, Edward E. *The Puritan's Use of Scripture in the Development of an Apocalyptical Hermeneutic*. Pretoria: University of South Africa, 1984.

Kolb, Robert. *Martin Luther: Confessor of the Faith*. New York: Oxford University Press, 2009.

Lull, Timothy, F. *Martin Luther's Basic Theological Writings*. Minneapolis: Fortress Press, 1989.

Luther, Martin. *Luther's Works*. Edited by Jaroslav Pelikan (vols. 1–30) and Helmut T. Lehmann (vols. 31–55). Philadelphia: Muhlenberg Press, 1958.

Noll, Mark. *Turning Points*. 3rd ed. Grand Rapids: Baker, 2012.

Sproul, R. C. *The Glory of Christ*. Wheaton: Tyndale House, 1990.

Stott, John R. W. *The Cross of Christ*. Downers Grove, IL: InterVarsity Press, 1986.

Part I

CELEBRATING THE THEOLOGICAL LEGACY OF THE REFORMATION

What the Reformers Thought They Were Doing[1]

TIMOTHY GEORGE

On October 31, 1517, a thirty-three-year-old German professor named Martin Luther called for a public discussion of the sale of indulgences, and all hell broke loose. The tumult that ignited the Protestant Reformation began in a backwater university town of some two thousand inhabitants: "Little Wittenberg," Luther called it. Wittenberg may have seemed like an outpost at "the edge of civilization,"[2] but it did boast a university, one founded in 1502 by princely and imperial rather than papal authority. That one of its professors would call for academic debate on the commercial trade in papal indulgences, long recognized by reform-minded critics as a major abuse in the church, was not surprising and may even have been predictable. As early as the Fourth Lateran Council (1215), traffic in "indiscriminate and excessive indulgences"[3]—the kind Luther's parishioners were running to buy—had been condemned by the church. The Reformation was born in a crisis of pastoral care. But Luther's act was a spark that ignited a conflagration. One confrontation led to another, and soon Europe was ablaze with edicts, bans, bulls, anathemas, and condemnations. The Ninety-Five Theses were translated, published, and soon were circulating from the Atlantic to the Baltic, from Lisbon to Lithuania.

---

[1] A version of this essay also appears in *Modern Age 59* no. 4 (Fall 2017). Used with permission.
[2] Heinz Schilling, *Martin Luther: Rebel in an Age of Upheaval* (Oxford: Oxford University Press, 2017), 91.
[3] Edward Peters, *A Modern Guide to Indulgences: Rediscovering this Often Misinterpreted Teaching* (Chicago: Hillenbrand Books, 2008), 6.

As we look back to celebrate the legacy of the Reformation, it is remembered, renounced, regretted, celebrated, commemorated, and analyzed from many perspectives. A new emphasis on reforming from below aims to give voice to groups that have been marginalized in much of Reformation historiography until now—women, peasants, dissenters, Jews, and others. There is much to learn from political, social, economic, intellectual, and cultural tellings of the Reformation story. In pursuing such lines of inquiry, however, it is possible to lose sight of what the Reformers themselves thought they were about. What made them tick? How did they understand the movement of which they were a part? The time is long past when one could speak confidently of presenting any slice of the past—much less such a controverted epoch as the Reformation—"just as it really happened" (*wie es eigentlich gewesen*), to cite Leopold von Ranke's summary of the historian's craft.[4]

In recent years, it has become fashionable for historians of the Reformation to use the word in the plural, *Reformations*. The point is clear: there were many diverse streams of renewal and spiritual innovation in the sixteenth century, and these resulted in various and competing patterns of reformation, including Lutheran, Zwinglian, Calvinist, Anglican, Radical, and, not least, Catholic. There was also the reformation of "the common man" (Thomas Müntzer and the revolt of the peasants), the reformation of the princes (religious change led by territorial rulers), the reformation of the cities (reform as part of communal urban advance), the reformation of the refugees (asylum seekers as agents of religious change), and so on. Paul S. Peterson has written of "the short Reformation," a series of events that took place over the course of some fifteen years around the indulgence controversy, in contrast to "the long Reformation," a period stretching back into the later Middle Ages and forward into the age of confessionalization and beyond.[5] Euan Cameron, however, gives a good reason for continuing to speak of *the* Reformation: "The Reformation, the movement that divided European Christianity into Catholic and Protestant traditions, is unique. No other movement of religious protest or reform since antiquity has been so widespread or lasting in its effects, so deep and searching in its criticism of received wisdom, so destructive in what it abolished, or so fertile in what

---

[4] Leopold von Ranke, *Geschichten der romanischen und germanischen Völker von 1494 bis 1535* (Leipzig: Berlag von Dunker und Humblot, 1874), vii.
[5] Paul S. Peterson, *Reformation in the Western World* (Waco, TX: Baylor University Press, 2017), 17–23.

it created."[6] Patrick Collinson gives another reason for retaining the singular use of Reformation: without first discussing *the* Reformation, discourse about other putative reformations would make no sense.[7]

If F. M. Powicke's dictum "A vision or an idea is not to be judged by its value for us, but by its value to the man who had it"[8] is not the whole truth, it at least reminds us that we cannot begin to evaluate the significance of earlier thinkers, especially the Reformers, until we have asked ourselves their questions and listened well to their answers. This chapter will examine four motifs, each of which is central to the self-understanding of the Reformation as glimpsed primarily from Luther's perspective, but with attention to other Reformers as well: the Reformation as *divine initiative*, as *spiritual struggle*, as *ecclesial event*, and as a movement imbued with a *long view of history*. First, however, we shall look at three oft-repeated "myths" about the Reformation.

Three Reformation Myths

Myth 1: "The Reformation divided the church."

The idea that the Reformation divided the church is dated to the sixteenth century. It was the centerpiece in the classic exchange between Cardinal Jacopo Sadoleto and John Calvin in 1539. Calvin and his fellow Reformers, Sadoleto charged, were attempting to tear into pieces the seamless robe of Christ, which not even the pagan soldiers at the foot of the cross had been willing to divide. Calvin's reply was an appeal to antiquity. "All we have attempted has been to renew that ancient form of the church," he claimed. The "church" Calvin had in mind was the one revealed preeminently in Scripture but also evident in the age of Chrysostom and Basil the Great, of Cyprian, Ambrose, and Augustine—the church of the ancient Christian teachers.[9] That the Reformation entailed the rupture of Western Christendom is not in question. But who had left whom, and why, would be debated between Catholics and Protestants for centuries to come.

The fracturing of Christianity, however, did not begin in the sixteenth century. Not to rehearse the many divisions among Christians of the first

---

[6] Euan Cameron, *The European Reformation* (Oxford: Oxford University Press, 2012), 1.

[7] Patrick Collinson, *The Reformation: A History* (New York: Modern Library, 2003), 13–14.

[8] F.M. Powicke, *Stephen Langton: Being the Ford Lectures Delivered in the University of Oxford in Hilary Term 1927* (Oxford: Oxford University Press, 1997), 161. Cf. Timothy George, *Theology of the Reformers* (Nashville: B&H, 2013), 16.

[9] *John Calvin and Jacopo Sadoleto: A Reformation Debate*, ed. John C. Olin (1966; repr., Grand Rapids: Baker, 1976), 46, 62–63.

millennium, but the split between Eastern and Western churches in 1054 left a gaping hole in the unity of the church, one that persisted despite continuing efforts at reconciliation. In the West, the pontificate of Boniface VIII ended with "the Babylonian Captivity," a period of almost seventy years (1309–77) when the papacy was based at Avignon rather than Rome. This was followed by the Western Schism (1378–1417), with its spectacle of two and eventually three popes excommunicating one another, each presiding as the sole vicar of Christ over separate jurisdictions. The crisis of the multipapacy was resolved at the Council of Constance by the election of Pope Martin V in 1417. But the Hussite wars in Bohemia, the suppression of Lollard dissent in England, the persecution of the Waldensians in France and Italy, and of the Alumbrados in Spain continued to mar the image of the church as the seamless garment of Christ.

One way to understand the Reformation is to see it as an effort to overcome the brokenness of the late medieval church. In this view, the Reformation was a movement for Christian unity based on the recovery of a besieged catholicity. Initially, this effort involved leading Catholics (Contarini and Seripando) and Protestants (Melanchthon and Bucer) alike. That this movement to mend ecclesial rifts did not succeed in the sixteenth century, that in fact what Erasmus once called the "worst century since Jesus Christ" ended up more divided at its close than when it began, does not count against the unitive impulses that were present in the Reformation from 1517 on. In an essay published in 1933, Friedrich Heiler declared:

> It was not Luther's idea to set over against the ancient Catholic church a new Protestant creation: he desired nothing more than that the old church should experience an evangelical awakening and renewal, and that the gospel of the sovereign Grace of God should take its place at the centre of Christian preaching and piety. Luther and his friends wished, as they were never tired of emphasizing, to be and to remain Catholic.[10]

---

[10] Friedrich Heiler, "The Catholic Movement in German Lutheranism," in *Northern Catholicism: Centenary Studies in the Oxford and Parallel Movements,* ed. N. P. Williams and Charles Harris (London: SPCK, 1933). Brad S. Gregory attributes many of the "unintended" but baneful effects of the Reformation to the outworking of the fissiparous principle of *sola Scriptura*. See Brad S. Gregory, *The Unintended Reformation: How a Religious Revolution Secularized Society* (Cambridge, MA: Belknap Press of Harvard University, 2012). For a different perspective on the Scripture principle and its consequences, see Paul C.H. Lim, "From the Spirit to the Sovereign to Sapiential Reason: A Brief History of *Sola Scriptura,*" in *The People's Book: The Reformation and the Bible,* ed. Jennifer Powell McNutt and David Lauber (Downers Grove, IL: IVP Academic, 2017), 207–24.

Myth 2: "Luther was the first modern man."

In 1971, the 450th anniversary of Luther's famous "Here I Stand" speech at the Diet of Worms, Reformation scholars from around the world gathered in St. Louis at the Fourth International Congress for Luther Research. The theme of the Congress was "Luther and the Dawn of the Modern Era," and the keynote speaker was Gerhard Ebeling, a leading Luther scholar and former student of Rudolf Bultmann. He reminded his listeners of Hegel's depiction of the Reformation as "the all-illuminating sun, which follows that day-break at the end of the Middle Ages."[11] Hegel attempted to integrate Luther into the history of thought by portraying him as the first great exponent of individual conscience and human freedom. In other words, Luther was a precursor of the Enlightenment. He stood against the authoritarian darkness and superstition of the Middle Ages and so helped his fellow Europeans break through to civilizational maturity. This view of the Reformation was intrinsic to what Herbert Butterfield would later dub the "Whig interpretation of history."[12]

The same theme was taken up by the Scottish savant Thomas Carlyle, who accorded Luther an honored place in his *Heroes and Hero-Worship* (1841), touting his refusal to recant at Worms as "the greatest moment in the Modern History of Men." "Had Luther at that moment done other, it had all been otherwise!" Carlyle surmised. English Puritanism, the French Revolution, European civilization, parliamentary democracy—all this would have been forestalled had Luther faltered. In that moment of crisis, however, "Luther did not desert us."[13] Ralph Waldo Emerson, Carlyle's best American friend, also gave Luther honorable mention in his famous essay on "Self-Reliance." There he stands in the company of other great achievers in history, all of whom were misunderstood in their own day: Pythagoras, Socrates, Jesus, Copernicus, Galileo, and Newton.[14]

With more nuance than Carlyle or Emerson, but along the same trajectory, elite thinkers in the early twentieth century continued to advance

---

[11] *Georg Wilhelm Friedrich Hegel, Sämtliche Werke,* ed. H. Glockner (Stuttgart-Bad Constatt, 1956–65), XI:519. On Hegel as an interpreter of Luther, see Gerhard Ebeling, "Luther and the Beginning of the Modern Age," in *Luther and the Dawn of the Modern Era,* ed. Heiko A. Oberman (Leiden: E. J. Brill, 1974), 11–39.

[12] Herbert Butterfield, *The Whig Interpretation of History* (New York: W. W. Norton, 1965), 13.

[13] William Dallmann, *Luther the Liberator* (Milwaukee, MN: Northwestern Publishing House Print, 1919), 78. See also A. G. Dickens and John Tonkin, *The Reformation in Historical Thought* (Cambridge: Harvard University Press, 1985), 163.

[14] See Ralph Waldo Emerson, *Self-Reliance: An Essay* (Mount Vernon, NY: Peter Pauper Press, 1949).

the idea of the Reformation as the harbinger of modernity, including Max Weber (disenchantment/secularization), Wilhelm Dilthey (individualism/ freedom), and Karl Holl (conscience). In 1923, Adolf von Harnack, a scion of German liberal Protestantism, summed up the progressive optimistic model of understanding the Reformation, "The modern age began along with Luther's Reformation on 31 October 1517; it was inaugurated by the blows of the hammer on the door of the castle church at Wittenberg."[15] These words were written the year of Hitler's failed Beer Hall Putsch. Countervoices there were, including Ernst Troeltsch, who saw the Reformation as more medieval than modern, more authoritarian than liberating, and more transcendental than immanent. Troeltsch had no more personal sympathy than Harnack for the traditional theological construals of the Reformation. For him its "catholicity" was something to be embarrassed about and also something to be transcended and eliminated by the forward march of progressive Protestantism. Nonetheless, Troeltsch rightly saw that the major break in the Christian culture of the West had taken place in the eighteenth century rather than in the sixteenth, with the Enlightenment rather than at the Reformation. In his eyes, the worldview of medieval Catholicism came to be associated with the "Dark Ages," as Petrarch had named the epoch between Augustine and Dante.[16] Another naysayer was Friedrich Nietzsche. Rather than discovering the beginnings of modernity in the Reformation, he saw it as a challenge and a sign of contradiction. If "Luther would have been burned like Huss," he said, "the Enlightenment would perhaps have dawned somewhat earlier and with a more beautiful luster than we can now conceive."[17]

Myth 3: "The Reformation was a German event."

Like most myths, this one has within it an element of truth. Erasmus was the prototypical European, but Luther was a German through and through. His intuitive genius and brilliance with the German language, especially in his translation of the Bible, has had a shaping influence on

[15] Adolf von Harnack, "Die Reformation und ihre Vorstellung," in *Erforschtes und Erlebtes* (Giessen, 1923), 110, quoted in Heinz Schilling, *Martin Luther: Rebel in an Age of Upheaval* (Oxford: Oxford University Press, 2017), 524.

[16] See William J. Bouwsma, "Renaissance and Reformation: An Essay in Their Affinities and Connections," in *Luther and the Dawn of the Modern Era: Papers for the Fourth International Congress for Luther Research*, ed. Heiko Augustinus Oberman (Leiden: E.J. Brill, 1974).

[17] Friedrich Wilhelm Nietzsche, *Human, All Too Human* (1), trans. Gary Handwerk, Complete Works of Friedrich Nietzsche, vol. 3 (Stanford: Stanford University Press, 1995), 164.

German culture to this day. In the nineteenth century, the German Jewish poet Heinrich Heine commended Luther's mastery of his mother tongue by saying that he had the unique ability to scold like a fishwife and whisper like a maiden at the same time.[18]

The Reformation era was an age of transition in many respects. It witnessed, for example, the hastening decline, if not yet the breakup, of the Holy Roman Empire, which was accompanied by the rise of the modern nation-state. While Germany itself would not become a united country until 1871, Luther boldly appealed to the patriotic sentiment of his German people. One of his early polemical tracts, and one of his most influential, was titled "To the Christian Nobility of the German Nation" (1520). Johann Wolfgang von Goethe, Germany's greatest poet, declared that Luther was the one through whom "the Germans first became one *Volk*."[19] Throughout history, the figure of Luther and his words have been co-opted for ideologies of both left and right—including publicists for National Socialism, who during the 1930s republished and disseminated Luther's deplorable and inexcusable writings against the Jews.[20] The fact that Dietrich Bonhoeffer, one of Luther's most fervent disciples in the twentieth century, was arrested for helping Jews escape Hitler's grasp, and later put to death for trying to bring down the Nazi state, shows how complicated the legacy of Martin Luther has been.

For all this, there are good reasons to challenge the myth of the Reformation as an event that happened largely between the Elbe and the Rhine. There was, after all, a French Reformation, a Swiss Reformation, a Dutch Reformation, even a Polish Reformation, and so on. But even if we expand our vision to include all Europe, the gauge is too narrow. From the outset, the Reformation was a global event. In the same month that Luther stood before the emperor at Worms (April 1521), Ferdinand Magellan completed his circumnavigation of the globe in the faraway Philippine Islands. Magellan was a forerunner of the Catholic Reformation, which inspired a new wave of Jesuit-led missionary activity into Latin America, Africa, China, and Japan. The Protestants were soon to follow, with a Calvinist mission to Brazil in the 1550s, more than sixty years before the Pilgrims came to Plymouth.

---

[18] Heinrich Heine, *The Prose Writings of Heinrich Heine,* ed. Havelock Ellis (London: Walter Scott, 1887), 159.

[19] Quoted in Peterson, *Reformation,* 50.

[20] Eric W. Gritsch, *Martin Luther's Anti-Semitism: Against His Better Judgment* (Grand Rapids: Eerdmans, 2012).

Baptist missionary William Carey went to India in the eighteenth century (following in the steps of Moravian and German Pietist pioneers), aiming to extend the work the Protestant Reformers had begun in the sixteenth. He and his helpers translated the Bible into the many languages of India and the East. He established schools (including for girls), taught the doctrine of justification by faith, and worked to reform the many ills of society. Today, as Philip Jenkins has pointed out, the theology and mission of the sixteenth-century Reformers are finding new life in vibrant forms of spiritual revival in Africa, Latin America, and other places in the Global South.[21]

Four Defining Motifs

Since the nineteenth century, Protestant historians have spoken of the formal principle and the material principle of the Reformation. The formal principle refers to the normative authority of Holy Scripture as the determinative rule for Christian faith and life. The material principle defines the central message of grace and forgiveness as taught in the doctrine of justification by faith alone. These two principles do indeed encompass much that the mainstream Protestant Reformers wanted to say against a resurgent Roman Catholicism on the one hand and a proliferating sectarianism on the other. But these two principles must be set in the context of other defining motifs.

Motif 1: The Reformation as Divine Initiative

The religious situation in the early sixteenth century was dynamic and evolving, and one should not overstate either the unity of the Catholic Church prior to the Council of Trent or the internal schisms among the magisterial Protestant Reformers in the same period. Luther, Bucer, Calvin, Cranmer, and even Zwingli (despite his 1529 clash with Luther over the Eucharist) shared many things in common across the geographical and confessional boundaries that set them apart. This common front has often been downplayed for two reasons. On the one hand, there is what we might call today confessional identity politics, a kind of Reformational tribalism and triumphalism; and on the other, secular, political, and nationalist concerns. For example, in 1917 Harnack traced the carnage of the Great War to the sixteenth-century confessional divide between Calvinism and Lutheranism.

---

[21] Philip Jenkins, "What Hath Wittenberg to Do with Lagos? Sixteenth-Century Protestantism and Global South Christianity," in *Protestantism after 500 Years*, ed. Thomas Albert Howard and Mark A. Noll (Oxford: Oxford University Press, 2016), 208–27.

"This war," he wrote, "shows us that the Reformed territories of Western Europe and America stand over against us with a lack of understanding which makes them susceptible to every defamation. We German Protestants are still just as isolated as 300 years ago."[22]

Luther's radical doctrine of justification by faith alone, shared by all the mainstream Reformers, challenged the entire theology of merit that was central to the sacramental-penitential structure of the medieval church. Yet this teaching presupposed an equally radical Augustinian understanding of divine grace. Augustine's doctrine of election, though controversial at times, had never been condemned by the church nor gone completely out of vogue since his death in 430. Nonetheless, it had been modified, qualified, and attenuated, especially in the various salvific schemes of late medieval nominalism. The Reformation can be understood in part as a recovery of Augustine's original emphasis, an acute Augustinianization of Christianity. Augustine's doctrine of grace, with its high predestination theology, was not entirely unfamiliar in the sixteenth century; similar views can be found in the teachings of medieval theologians such as Thomas Aquinas (in his later writings), Gregory of Rimini, and Thomas Bradwardine. The Reformers picked up on this theme and gave it a new airing, however. Augustine's emphasis on divine sovereignty in salvation was the backdrop for the Reformers' more precise soteriological formulation: God's grace, unmerited and unmeritable, justifies sinners through the imputation of the external, "alien" righteousness of Jesus Christ, which is mediated through faith understood as trust, reliance, dependence.[23]

It is tempting for modern interpreters of the Reformation to portray the Reformers as the great activists of their time—sixteenth-century Lenins or Robespierres out to shake the world and overturn kingdoms. But this is not how they themselves saw their work, and we miss something crucial if we do not take with full force the Reformers' own view of the providential direction of their movement. Perhaps with a twinkle in his eye, Luther put it like this:

I simply taught, preached, wrote God's Word; otherwise I did nothing. And while I slept, or drank Wittenberg beer with my friends

---

[22] For more on this statement and its context, see B. A. Gerrish, *The Old Protestantism and the New* (Chicago: University of Chicago Press, 1982), 28.

[23] See George, *Theology of the Reformers.*

Philip [Melanchthon] and [Nicolaus von] Amsdorf, the Word so greatly weakened the papacy that no prince or emperor ever inflicted such losses upon it. I did nothing; the Word did everything.[24]

Elsewhere he wrote, "God has seized me and is driving me, and even leading me on," and, "I am not the one in control. I want to be at peace but I am snatched up and placed in the middle of an uprising."[25]

Calvin was always more reticent than Luther to speak about himself, but he too referred to his embrace of the evangelical faith as "a sudden conversion" by which God subdued his mind and "made it teachable."[26] When, just a few years later, he was set upon by the fiery Guillaume Farel, who threatened the young scholar with a divine curse should he refuse to join the reforming cause in Geneva, Calvin summed up this fateful encounter by declaring, "Thus God thrust me into the game."[27] Calvin was not interested in making Calvinists, nor Luther Lutherans, though some of their followers did promote a kind of hero worship that would have made even Carlyle blush. Closer to the spirit of the Reformation are Calvin's words to the emperor Charles V in 1543:

The restoration of the Church is the work of God, and no more depends on the hopes and opinions of men, than the resurrection of the dead, or any other miracle of that description. It is the will of our Master that his gospel be preached. Let us obey his command, and follow whithersoever he calls. What the success will be it is not ours to inquire.[28]

Motif 2: The Reformation as Spiritual Struggle

At the heart of Reformation spirituality is the experience of the Christian life as conflict, contention, trial, testing, and assault. This is very different from popular models of spirituality today, which present religion as an

---

[24] Martin Luther, "The Second Sermon, March 10, 1522, Monday after Invocavit," in "Eight Sermons at Wittenberg (1522)—*LW* 51:70–100," chap. 28 in *Martin Luther's Basic Theological Writings*, 3rd ed., ed. Timothy F. Lull and William R. Russell (Minneapolis: Fortress Press, 2012), 294.

[25] *WA BR* 1.344, 4–9; no.152. See Eric L. Saak, *High Way to Heaven: The Augustinian Platform between Reform and Reformation, 1292–1524* (Leiden: Brill, 2002), 643.

[26] *CO* 31:13–35. See Bruce Gordon, *Calvin* (New Haven, CT: Yale University Press, 2009), 33–35.

[27] See E. Harris Harbison, *The Christian Scholar in the Age of Reformation* (New York: Charles Scribner's Sons, 1956), 142.

[28] John Calvin, "The Necessity of Reforming the Church," in *Tracts Relating to the Reformation*, trans. Henry Beveridge (Edinburgh: Calvin Translation Society, 1844), 200.

opiate to soothe the pain of life, an aid to self-enhancement and personal fulfillment. The concept of the spiritual life as struggle was certainly present in medieval Christianity, especially in the monastic-mystical tradition by which Luther was so decisively shaped. Luther had inherited the monastic devotional triad of *lectio*, *oratio*, and *contemplatio*, but he intensified and altered it in a distinctive way. He did so by changing the last step from *contemplatio* to *tentatio*, which he rendered in German as *Anfechtung*. This word is often weakly translated as "temptation" in English, but that rendering misses the intensity inherent in the German original. The word *Anfechtung* derives from the world of fencing: a *Fechter* is a fencer or gladiator. A *Fechtboden* is a fencing room. *Anfechtungen* connotes spiritual attacks, bouts of dread, despair, anxiety, and conflicts that overwhelm; its churning rages within the soul of every believer and in the great apocalyptic struggle between God and Satan. The reality of an active devouring Devil (see 1 Pet 5:8) belonged to the mental world Luther inherited. Some of his Catholic adversaries later concocted a story that he was Satan's own progeny, the product of an illicit sexual union between the Devil and his mother, who was portrayed as a promiscuous bath maid. His father, Hans Luther, once suggested that his son's call to the monastic life in the thunderstorm might have been an intervention of the Fiend rather than a summons from God.[29] At every turn, Luther was confronted with the insinuations of Satan, with whom he often carried on a lively dialogue. On one occasion, when the Devil had accused Luther of being a great sinner, he replied: "I knew that long ago. Tell me something new. Christ has taken my sins upon himself and forgiven them long ago. Now grind your teeth."[30]

Luther's struggles, both with himself and with the Evil One, were not a mere phase through which he passed *en route* to his Reformation breakthrough. No, just as repentance was a lifelong process of turning to God again and again, so too conflict and temptation continued until the end of life. Such struggles were essential to becoming a theologian. "For as soon as God's Word takes root and grows in you, the Devil will plague you and make a real doctor of you, and by his attacks will teach you to seek and love

---

[29] For an overview and interpretation of this event see Lyndal Roper, *Martin Luther: Renegade and Prophet* (New York: Random House, 2016), 34–36; Scott Hendrix, *Martin Luther: Visionary Reformer* (New Haven: Yale University Press, 2017), 36–39; Schilling, *Martin Luther*, 71–72.

[30] Quoted in Philip Schaff, *Modern Christianity: The German Reformation*, vol. 6 in *History of the Christian Church* (New York: Charles Scribner's Sons, 1916), 336.

God's Word."[31] As early as his first exegetical lectures on the Psalms (1513), Luther confessed that "I did not learn my theology all at once, but I had to search deeper for it, where my *Anfechtungen* took me. . . . Not understanding, reading, or speculation, but living, nay, rather dying and being damned makes a theologian."[32] In his famous 1525 debate with Erasmus on the freedom of the will, Luther depicts the human person as a horse that is ridden either by God or by the Devil. Thus the ultimate question of life is not "Who are you?" but rather "Whose are you?" To whom do you belong? Who is your Lord? Luther, along with Zwingli and Calvin, was accused of teaching fatalism because of their emphasis on the will's bondage to sin and Satan. But human responsibility is part of the equation, and the focus is on triumph over Satan through Christ's death and resurrection.

Motif 3: The Reformation as Ecclesial Event

Why did the Reformation happen when it did? A number of factors came together to create a perfect storm in the years leading up to and immediately following Luther's posting of his Ninety-Five Theses in 1517. The Fifth Lateran Council, which concluded in that very year, failed to recognize the urgent need for reform in the church. Meanwhile, the New Learning provided scholars with hitherto unavailable textual and philological resources, such as those used by Lorenzo Valla to challenge the authenticity of the so-called Donation of Constantine, a major bulwark of papal authority. In 1516, Erasmus published the first critical edition of the Greek New Testament, which Luther used in drafting his Theses. The invention of the printing press brought about an explosion of knowledge and the expansion of literacy. It resulted in Luther's becoming the world's first bestselling author and Protestantism the first religious mass movement. In addition, the advance of Islam, signaled by the fall of Constantinople in 1453, changed the geopolitical equation for everyone on the other side of the Ottoman armies. In other circumstances, Luther's protest against the abuse of indulgences, his focus on justification by faith alone, and even his appeal to Scripture as the normative authority for faith and practice (which was not an unknown idea) might have been accommodated within recognized ecclesial structures. Luther's doctrine of the church was rooted

---

[31] *LW* 34:286.
[32] *WA TR* 1:146; *WA* 5:163.

in his early study of the Scriptures, and he returned to this topic in the years following his excommunication.

The image of Luther as a rebellious monk pulling down the pillars of the Mother Church and replacing her with his own subjective interpretation of the Bible stems from a misreading of his famous "conscience" speech at the Diet of Worms. Luther did refer to his conscience but in a distinctive way: he declared that his conscience had been captured by the enduring Word of God. When asked to defend his right to challenge the received teaching of the church in which he had been ordained, Luther cited the vow he made when he first became a doctor of theology in 1512, when he swore to preach faithfully and purely and teach "my most beloved Holy Scriptures."[33]

Luther and the Reformers who followed him, including those in the Reformed and Anglican traditions and some of the Anabaptists, were not lonely, isolated seekers of truth asserting "the right of private judgment."[34] They were rather pastors committed to proclaiming God's Word in the company of God's people. As Luther wrote in his 1535 commentary on Galatians:

> This is the reason why our theology is certain: it snatches us away from ourselves and places us outside ourselves, so that we do not depend on our own strength, conscience, experience, person, or works but depend on that which is outside ourselves, that is, on the promise and truth of God, which cannot deceive.[35]

The priesthood of all believers, a distinctive Reformation idea, was set forth in 1520 in Luther's address to the German nobility and its implications spelled out in his popular tract *On the Freedom of the Christian.* This teaching asserted that all Christians, by virtue of their baptism, had direct access to God and enjoyed the same spiritual status as priests, bishops, or popes. There is sanctity in the secular; no calling is intrinsically higher or more spiritual than another. The Reformation doctrine of the priesthood of all believers did not, however, produce modern rugged individualism, the ideology of every tub sitting on its own bottom.[36] Paul Althaus, in *The*

---

[33] *LW* 34:103; *WA* 30/3:386.

[34] Leon O. Hynson, "The Right of Private Judgment," *Asbury Theological Journal* 60, no.1 (Spring 2005): 89–104.

[35] *LW* 26:387; *WA* 40/1:589.

[36] See John Bunyan, *The Pilgrim's Progress* (Chicago: Moody Classics, 2007), 53.

Theology of Martin Luther, rightly places the original meaning of the Reformation in the context of Luther's churchly commitment:

> Luther never understands the priesthood of all believers merely in the "Protestant" sense of the Christian's freedom to stand in a direct relationship to God without a human mediator. Rather he constantly emphasizes the Christian's evangelical authority to come before God on behalf of the brethren and also of the world. The universal priesthood expresses not religious individualism but its exact opposite, the reality of the congregation as a community.[37]

Motif 4: The Reformation as a Movement with a Long View of History

Luther lived in an apocalyptic age, and he shared with many of his contemporaries the belief that the world was running out of time. Sebastian Brant's *The Ship of Fools*, published at Basel in 1494, portrayed society, from the mighty down to the lowly, as a company of fools on board a ship sailing to "Narragonia," the country of fools, and headed for disaster. Four years later, the Nuremberg artist Albrecht Dürer gave an artistic depiction of a similar situation in his *Apocalypse* series. "It is a dramatic sequence—oppressive, alarming in its reality, heralding disaster," wrote the art historian Karl-Adolf Knappe in *Dürer: The Complete Engravings, Etchings, and Woodcuts*. Dürer "ventured to depict never seen, unimaginable things, events outside space and time, thunder and lightning, conflagrations and voices—the alleluias of the blessed and the despairing groans of the damned."[38]

Luther shared the anxieties of his time and understood himself as living at the very edge of history. Nevertheless, there was an eschatological reserve in his thought. Neither he nor Calvin wrote a commentary on the book of Revelation. They both followed Augustine in interpreting the thousand-year reign of Christ in Revelation 20 as already fulfilled in the history of the church rather than pending in the future. Luther thought the thousand years in the vision of John had culminated in the pontificate of Gregory VII (1073–85), with his extravagant claims for papal supremacy. Subsequent

---

[37] Paul Althaus, *The Theology of Martin Luther* (Philadelphia: Fortress Press, 1966), 314.
[38] Karl-Adolf Knappe, *Dürer: The Complete Engravings, Etchings, and Woodcuts* (Secaucus, NJ: Wellfleet Press, nd), xxi.

events, such as the threat of Islam and the Hussite revolt, simply brought the world closer to the finish line.

Although Luther had a keen interest in history and did some sanctified number crunching to determine where he was in the scheme of things, he resisted making too much of such calculations and refused to set a date for the Second Advent. He was neither a meliorist nor a utopian. One could not force God's hand, as both the imperial knights led by Franz von Sickingen and the rebellious peasants led by "the hammer" Thomas Müntzer attempted to do during the tumults of the 1520s. Living at the edge of history did not give license for apocalyptic speculation. Thus when the numerologist Michael Stifel predicted that Christ would return on October 19, 1533, at eight o'clock in the morning, Luther demurred. Still, Luther did believe that the last day was at hand. "For almost all the signs which Christ and the apostles Peter and Paul announced have now appeared, the trees sprout, the Scripture greens and blooms, whether or not we can know the day in just this way does not matter; let another do it better. It is certain that everything is coming to an end."[39] As he grew older, crankier, and more and more ridden with sickness and pain, he came to see the world as the mirror image of himself—an old, gray-haired man. The Reformation had not turned out to be the success he hoped for as a young Reformer in his thirties. But he continued to believe that, to cite one of his favorite Old Testament texts, the Word "shall not return . . . void" (Isa 55:11 KJV).

"If the world should come to an end tomorrow, I will still plant a little apple tree today!" These words have been attributed to Martin Luther, though recent scholarship has shown that they come from a proverb instead. Nonetheless, they capture something of the hopefulness with which he lived and the confidence of the faith in which he died.

Bibliography

Althaus, Paul. *The Theology of Martin Luther.* Philadelphia: Fortress Press, 1966.

Bouwsma, William J. "Renaissance and Reformation." In *Luther and the Dawn of the Modern Era: Papers for the Fourth International Congress for Luther Research,* ed. Heiko A. Oberman. Leiden: E.J. Brill, 1974.

Bunyan, John. *The Pilgrim's Progress.* Chicago: Moody Classics, 2007.

---

[39] *WA DB* 11/II, 124. See Bernhard Lohse, *Martin Luther's Theology* (Minneapolis: Fortress Press, 1999), 335.

Butterfield, Herbert. *The Whig Interpretation of History*. New York: W. W. Norton, 1965.

Calvin, John. "The Necessity of Reforming the Church." In *Tracts Relating to the Reformation*, translated by Henry Beveridge. Edinburgh: Calvin Translation Society, 1844.

_____. *Ioannis Calvini opera quae supersunt Omnia*. Edited by G. Baum, E. Cunitz, and E. Reuss. Brunswick and Berlin: Schwetschke, 1863–1900.

Cameron, Euan. *The European Reformation*. Oxford: Oxford University Press, 2012.

Collinson, Patrick. *The Reformation: A History*. New York: Modern Library, 2006.

Dickens, A. G., and John Tonkin. *The Reformation in Historical Thought*. Cambridge: Harvard University Press, 1985.

Emerson, Ralph Waldo. *Self-Reliance: An Essay*. Mount Vernon, NY: Peter Pauper Press, 1949.

Georg Wilhelm Friedrich Hegel, Sämlliche Werke. Edited by H. Glockner. Stuttgart-Bad Constatt, 1956–65.

George, Timothy. *Theology of the Reformers*. Nashville: B&H, 2013.

Gerrish, B. A. *The Old Protestantism and the New*. Chicago: University of Chicago Press, 1982.

Gritsch, Eric W. *Martin Luther's Anti-Semitism: Against His Better Judgment*. Grand Rapids: Eerdmans, 2012.

Heiler, Friedrich. "The Catholic Movement in German Lutheranism." *Northern Catholicism: Centenary Studies in the Oxford and Parallel Movements,* ed. N. P. Williams and Charles Harris. London: SPCK, 1933.

Heine, Heinrich. *The Prose Writings of Heinrich Heine*. Edited by Havelock Ellis. London: Walter Scott, 1887.

Hynson, Leon O. "The Right of Private Judgment." *Asbury Theological Journal* 60, no. 1 (Spring 2005): 89–104.

Jenkins, Philip. *The Next Christendom*. New York: Oxford University Press, 2002.

_____. "What hath Wittenberg to do with Lagos? Sixteenth-Century Protestantism and Global South Christianity." In *Protestantism after 500 Years*, ed. Thomas Albert Howard and Mark A. Noll. Oxford: Oxford University Press, 2016.

Knappe, Karl-Adolf. *Dürer: The Complete Engravings, Etchings, and Wood-cuts.* New York: Wellfleet Press, 1964.

Luther, Martin. *Martin Luther's Basic Theological Writings.* 3rd ed. Edited by W. R. Russell and T. F. Lull. Minneapolis: Fortress Press, 2012.

_____. *Luther's Works.* Edited by Jaroslav Pelikan, H.T. Lehmann, et al. St. Louis: Concordia Publishing House, 2009.

_____. *D. Martin Luthers Werke. Kritische Gesamtausgabe.* Weimar: Bohlau, 1883–1929.

_____. *D. Martin Luthers Werke. Tischrede.* Weimar: Bohlau, 1883–1929.

Nietzsche, Friedrich Wilhelm. *Human, All Too Human* (1). Translated by Gary Handwerk. Vol. 3 of *The Complete Works of Friedrich Nietzsche.* Stanford: Stanford University Press, 1997.

Peterson, Paul Silas. *Reformation in the Western World: An Introduction.* Waco, TX: Baylor University Press, 2017.

Powicke, F.M. *Stephen Langton: Being the Ford Lectures Delivered in the University of Oxford in Hilary Term 1927.* Oxford: Oxford University Press, 1997.

Saak, Eric L. *High Way to Heaven: The Augustinian Platform Between Reform and Reformation, 1292–1524.* Leiden: Brill, 2002.

Schaff, Philip. *History of the Christian Church.* New York: Charles Scribner's Sons, 1916.

Von Ranke, Leopold. *Geschichten der romanischen und germanischen Völker von 1494 bis 1535.* Leipzig: Reimer, 1824.

2

The Legacy of the Printing Press for the Production and Study of the Bible

BENJAMIN P. LAIRD

Much attention has been devoted in recent centuries to the numerous ways in which the leaders of the Protestant Reformation challenged the teachings and traditions associated with the Roman church and the significant changes the movement brought to society. Often overlooked, however, are the sociological, political, and cultural developments that provided favorable conditions for the advancement of the Reformation. One particularly notable technological development that took place during the eve of the Reformation was the printing press, an instrument that proved to be an especially powerful mechanism for advancing the viewpoints of the Reformers and ultimately the transformation of society.[1] Contemplating recent technological advancements, the renowned English philosopher and scientist Francis Bacon wrote in 1620 that three particular inventions had left an indelible mark on the world: the compass, a device that enabled sailors to navigate the oceans more capably;

---

[1] For a recent study of the various ways in which the printing press influenced Western civilization, see Andrew Pettegree, *The Book in the Renaissance* (New Haven, CT: Yale University Press, 2010). Among other things, Pettegree demonstrates that the invention of the printing press ultimately changed society's reading habits and book culture. While the initial writings produced on the press were largely limited to scholarly and religious works, a variety of popular writings for a wider audience eventually began to be published to satisfy a greatly expanded market. See also Elizabeth Eisenstein, *The Printing Press as an Agent of Change: Communications and Cultural Transformations in Early-Modern Europe*, 2 vols. (Cambridge: Cambridge University Press, 1979).

gunpowder, a substance used to power newly invented weapons on the battlefield; and the printing press, an invention that enabled authors to disseminate their works much more quickly, widely, and economically than had been possible in previous centuries.[2]

The potential usefulness of the printing press to disseminate fresh ideas was not lost on the leaders and supporters of the various movements seeking reform throughout the continent. Those such as Luther who dissented from the authorized teaching and practices of the Roman church were now in possession of a powerful tool that could be used to propagate alternative viewpoints much more widely and with much greater force than was previously possible.[3] As Mark Edwards observes:

> The Reformation saw the first major, self-conscious attempt to use the recently invented printing press to shape and channel a mass movement. The printing press allowed Evangelical publicists to do what had been previously impossible, quickly and effectively reach a large audience with a message intended to change Christianity. For several crucial years, these Evangelical publicists issued thousands of pamphlets discrediting the old faith and advocating the new.[4]

Noting the importance of the media revolution in sixteenth-century Germany and the influence of Luther, Richard Cole writes, "The Reformation itself seems to be almost unthinkable without taking into consideration the printed pages of Luther's sermons, essays, addresses, and biblical translations."[5] As recent Luther biographer Lyndal Roper observes, Luther's "use of print was tactically brilliant: He knew exactly how to forestall censorship and protect his ideas by spreading them as widely as possible, each new work marking yet another radical advance delivered to an audience that was hungry for more....No one had previously used

---

[2] Francis Bacon, *Novum Organum* 1:129 (1620).

[3] It was not Protestants alone who benefited from the invention of the printing press. Interestingly, the first material to be produced on Gutenberg's press was indulgences. As Read Mercer Schuchardt writes, "While it is a historical truism that the printing press helped spread the cure of the Reformation, it needs to be mentioned that it first produced the disease that necessitated the Reformation." Read Mercer Schuchardt, "The Reformation as Media Event," in *The People's Book: The Reformation and the Bible*, ed. Jennifer McNutt and David Lauber (Downers Grove, IL: InterVarsity Press, 2017), 96–97.

[4] Mark U. Edwards Jr., *Printing, Propaganda, and Martin Luther* (Berkeley, CA.: University of California Press, 1994), 1.

[5] Richard Cole, "Reformation Printers: Unsung Heroes," *Sixteenth Century Journal* 15, no. 3 (1984), 327.

print to such devastating effect."[6] In addition to his judicious use of the printing press, the sheer volume of Luther's works circulating among the general populace quickly elevated his status and provided him with a unique platform from which to advance his viewpoints. According to the calculation of Hans-Joachim Köhler, Luther's pamphlets alone added up to a staggering 20 percent of all material published in Germany between the years of 1500 and 1530.[7] Edwards further estimates that during Luther's lifetime, German presses produced five times more of his works than of all his Catholic opponents combined.[8] These statistics, while difficult to validate with absolute certainty, underscore the important role that the printing press played in advancing the causes and ideas of the Reformers.

Although the importance of the printing press in challenging long-standing traditions is widely recognized, much less attention has been given to the ways in which the transition from handwritten manuscripts to printed works influenced how readers of the sixteenth and subsequent centuries encountered and studied the Scriptures.[9] This chapter will briefly demonstrate that in addition to its usefulness in propagating the viewpoints of the Reformers to a wide audience, the printing press also played a significant role in changing and shaping the manner in which readers of the Bible encountered, read, and studied the Scriptures. This invention ultimately led to the popularization of various paratextual features[10] common in modern Bibles, such as verse and chapter divisions and the standardization of a particular arrangement of the biblical writings that differed from the typical order found in Hebrew and Greek manuscripts.

---

[6] Lyndal Roper, *Martin Luther: Renegade and Prophet* (New York: Random House, 2016), 108–09.

[7] Edwards, *Printing*, 1–2.

[8] Edwards, 1.

[9] Perhaps the most notable recent work relating to this subject is Kimberly Van Kampen and Paul Saenger, eds., *The Bible as Book: The First Printed Editions* (New Castle, DE: Oak Knoll, 1999).

[10] The term "paratext" refers to supplemental content included in either handwritten or printed copies of a text that is distinct from the author's original composition or the main body of the writing. In modern works, this may include material such as the publisher's information, table of contents, indices, etc. With respect to biblical writings, examples of paratextual features include chapter and verse divisions, the titles of writings, and subscriptions (short summary statements often found at the end of a writing). It was typical for subscriptions to contain fundamental background information such as the author, provenance, recipients, and perhaps a brief description of the work's key objectives and major themes.

The Paratextual Features in the Bible

Among the paratextual features commonly present in modern editions of the Bible, perhaps none have been as closely associated with the biblical text or as taken for granted as the chapter and verse divisions.[11] Contemporary readers may be surprised to learn that the ubiquitous chapter and verse numbering present in virtually all modern editions are relatively recent innovations. Attempts have been made throughout church history to divide the biblical text into smaller units. A notable example of an earlier attempt is the so-called Eusebian Canons, a division of the four Gospels thought to have originated with Ammonius of Alexandria in the third century and subsequently developed and expanded by the historian Eusebius of Caesarea in the fourth century.[12] The Canons provided readers of the Gospels with a convenient means of cross-referencing various subjects that appear in the Gospel accounts. Nearly 1,200 distinct sections of the Gospels were established, most of which were considerably longer than modern verses yet shorter than modern chapters. In addition to dividing the text of the Gospels into multiple sections, ten tables revealed which Gospels addressed certain topics or recorded certain events. For example, Canon I included accounts or subjects contained in all four Gospels, while Canon II listed content found in the Synoptic Gospels but not the Gospel of John. How widely the Eusebian Canons circulated is unclear; however, they do not appear extensively in manuscripts produced prior to the thirteenth century.

The origin of the standard chapter divisions that appear in modern editions of the Bible is a matter of scholarly debate. Paul Saenger contends that many French scholars prior to the late-nineteenth century were of the persuasion that the divisions originated with Hugh of Saint-Cher, a Dominican biblical scholar who taught in Paris during the mid-thirteenth century. Scholars in England, however, have generally contended that the creation of the divisions was the work of Stephen Langton (1150–1228), a former student and lecturer in Paris who was later appointed Archbishop of Canterbury. As Saenger notes, Langton was recognized as the originator

---

[11] The *ESV Reader's Bible* published by Crossway is an example of a modern edition of the Bible that omits chapter or verse divisions.

[12] Ammonius is believed to have been one of the first to develop a concordance of the Gospels. This concordance was based on Matthew's Gospel with parallel passages from the other Gospels placed alongside the text of Matthew. See Gaspar Ladocsi and Stefan Samulowitz, "Eusebian Canons," in *Encyclopedia of Ancient Christianity Volume 1 A–E* (Downers Grove, IL: InterVarsity Press, 2014), 870–71.

of the divisions by fourteenth-century scholars such as Nicholas Trevet and Ranulf Higden, and ultimately by John Foxe, who credited Langton with the creation of the chapter divisions in the first edition of his *Book of Martyrs*, published in 1563.[13]

A close association between the modern chapter divisions and Langton may be observed in several witnesses from the thirteenth century. In the late nineteenth century, Paulin Martin discovered a manuscript copied around the year 1230 that contained the text of Langton's commentary on the Minor Prophets.[14] The manuscript is unique in that it included spaces within the text in which chapter divisions were placed in red ink. While the manuscript does not prove conclusively that Langton created the divisions—it may be that they were not included by Langton in his original composition—it does provide an early link between Langton and the modern chapter divisions. In addition to this particular manuscript, several witnesses from the thirteenth century indicate that associates of Langton made use of the modern divisions in their compilation of his *Summa* and *Quaestiones*.[15] Prior to 1230, however, manuscripts containing writings attributed to Langton typically omit the chapter divisions or include divisions that are not entirely consistent with those used in modern Bibles. One possible explanation for the inconsistency is that Langton spent much of his adult life devising and revising a system of chapter divisions; this was the viewpoint of Beryl Smalley, who concluded that Langton ultimately devised the standard chapter divisions "at the end of about thirty years of trial and error."[16] It may have also been that Langton was not personally responsible for the chapter divisions but that various systems of chapter divisions in use during the thirteenth century were later inserted into copies of his commentaries and other works. Regardless of the precise role Langton may have played in the development of the divisions, various witnesses from this time period indicate that recognition of a standard set of chapter divisions was a slow process.

---

[13] Paul Saenger, "The Twelfth-Century Reception of Oriental Languages and the Graphic *Mise en page* of Latin Vulgate Bibles Copied in England," in *Form and Function in the Late Medieval Bible*, ed. Eyal Poleg and Laura Light (Leiden: Brill, 2013), 39.

[14] The manuscript has been catalogued as Troyes, Bibliothèque municipale, MS 1046. Langton's commentary was composed in 1203.

[15] Saenger, "Twelfth-Century Reception," 42.

[16] Beryl Smalley, *The Study of the Bible in the Middle Ages*, 1st paperback ed. (Notre Dame, IN: University of Notre Dame Press, 1964), 224.

While many scholars remain convinced that the modern chapter divisions originated with Langton or perhaps those associated with him, some contemporary scholars contend that they emerged as early as the late twelfth century.[17] According to Saenger, no codices of Langton's works have survived that can be conclusively dated before the year 1200.[18] Remarkably, however, several Bibles produced in monastic settings in late twelfth-century England do include chapter divisions similar to those in modern Bibles. Saenger points to five Bibles that originated in the abbey of Saint Albans after around 1180 and the Bible of Stephen Harding, which originated in Burgundy. The oldest of these, Saenger notes, appears to be a Bible produced around 1180 in Saint Albans that is catalogued as MS 48 and currently housed at Corpus Christi College in Cambridge.[19]

Although scholars continue to debate whether the modern chapter divisions are to be attributed to Langton or to an unknown scribe in late twelfth-century Britain, the catalyst for their widespread acceptance may be confidently attributed to their placement in subsequent translations of Scripture that were widely distributed. Roughly two centuries after their creation, the chapter divisions were included in John Wycliffe's English translation, the groundbreaking work first published in 1382.[20] The inclusion of the chapter divisions in the Wycliffe edition ultimately proved to be more than an historical anomaly, as nearly all subsequently produced English translations also incorporated these chapter divisions.

The verse divisions contained in modern editions did not begin to appear in print for more than a century after the chapter divisions first began to circulate. Interestingly, many of the English translations printed in the early sixteenth century included chapter divisions but lacked the verse divisions that customarily appear in modern Bibles. This may be

---

[17] Frans van Liere, "Biblical Exegesis through the Twelfth Century," in *The Practice of the Bible in the Middle Ages: Production, Reception, and Performance in Western Christianity*, ed. Susan Boynton and Diane Reilly (New York: Columbia University Press, 2011), 172–73.

[18] Saenger, "Twelfth-Century Reception," 42.

[19] Saenger, 52.

[20] According to Bruce Metzger, "It is doubtful whether Wycliffe himself took any direct part in the work of translating the Scriptures…. One need not, however, have any qualms about referring to the Wycliffe Bible, for it was under his inspiration that the work was done." Bruce Metzger, *The Bible in Translation: Ancient and Modern English Versions* (Grand Rapids: Baker, 2001), 57.

observed, for example, in the Tyndale Bible (1526),[21] the Coverdale Bible (1535),[22] the Matthew Bible (1537),[23] and the Great Bible (1539).[24]

It is widely believed that the verse divisions that appear in modern translations of the Old Testament were established by the Jewish rabbi Isaac Nathan ben Kalonymus around the mid-fifteenth century in preparation for his work the *Meïr Netib*, an innovative research tool considered by many to be the first concordance of the Hebrew Scriptures.[25] Though groundbreaking in that it helped establish a standardized set of chapter and verse divisions for the Old Testament, Isaac Nathan's verse divisions were not entirely innovative. After adopting the chapter divisions that were by this time well recognized, Isaac Nathan simply divided each chapter into verse divisions that were based on the accent marks devised by the Masoretes, a group of Jewish scribes active primarily between the sixth and tenth centuries. Among other things, the Masoretes are credited with the placement of accent marks (e.g., the *sof pasuq* and *silluq* in the final word of each sentence). While the Masoretes tallied the total number of sentences contained in each section (*parashah*), they were not responsible for devising a universally recognized numbering system for the individual verses.

During the approximate period in which Isaac Nathan devised his system of verse divisions for the Old Testament, attempts were also made to create verse divisions for the New Testament writings. One of the first to do so was by Santes Pagnino (1470–1541), an Italian Dominican and biblical scholar who produced a translation of the entire Bible into Latin in 1528. Despite its novelty—it was the first complete Latin translation of the entire Bible printed during the Renaissance—Pagnino's divisions were not widely adopted and do not correspond with the modern verse divisions. Although his translation

---

[21] The Tyndale Bible is regarded as the first English Bible to have been translated directly from the Hebrew Old Testament and Greek New Testament. At the time of Tyndale's death (c. 1536), the entire New Testament and much of the Old Testament had been translated.

[22] The translation by Miles Coverdale (c. 1488–1569) was the first complete Bible printed in English. It relied heavily upon Tyndale's incomplete translation as well as Luther's German translation.

[23] Published by John Rogers (c. 1505–1555) under the pseudonym Thomas Matthew, the Matthew Bible was essentially a combination of the Tyndale and Coverdale Bibles.

[24] The Great Bible was authorized by Henry VIII for public reading in ecclesiastical settings. Like the Matthew Bible, it was heavily based upon the previous work of Tyndale and Coverdale, the latter of whom oversaw the translation.

[25] A brief history of the *Meïr Netib* is contained in the preface of Alexander Cruden's work *A Complete Concordance to the Holy Scriptures of the Old and New Testament* (Philadelphia: Kimber, Conrad, 1806). Cruden notes that Isaac Nathan began the work in 1438 and completed it in 1448. It was first printed in Venice in 1523 by Daniel Bomberg and later in Basel and Rome.

was widely consulted by scholars engaged in the work of Bible translations (e.g., the Coverdale Bible and the Geneva Bible), the Pagnino version was not extensively read by the general public, perhaps a result of its exceedingly literal style or its association with Michael Servetus, the scientist and controversial theologian who was responsible for republishing the work in 1542.[26]

The eminent Parisian printer Robert Estienne (1503–1559), also known as Stephanus or Robert Stephens, is credited for the creation of the verse divisions in the New Testament that are used in modern translations.[27] As a result of his interest in publishing a biblical concordance that could be used as a study tool for the various Bibles he published, Stephanus came to recognize the need for divisions of the text that were smaller than the chapter divisions that had become popular. As a remedy, Stephanus divided each chapter of the New Testament into the standard verse divisions known today, a task he purportedly accomplished during a trip from Paris to Lyons. An account of this journey has been preserved by his son Henri, who recorded that the divisions were devised *inter equitandum*. Some have interpreted the Latin phrase to mean "while on horseback," a reading which may suggest that the inappropriate or misplaced verse divisions in the New Testament were the unfortunate result of a slip of the pen when Stephanus's horse made an unexpected or erratic movement. Though certainly a humorous interpretation of Henri's account, it is now the opinion of many scholars that his description simply implies that his father completed the project during the course of his journey, perhaps during his breaks and nightly stops.[28] While the concordance was not ultimately published until several decades after his death, Stephanus's verse divisions were incorporated into the fourth edition of his critical edition of the Greek New Testament published in 1551, his French translation of the Bible in 1553,[29] and an edition of the Vulgate published in 1555.[30]

---

[26] After being condemned by the Roman Catholic Church, Servetus was executed in Geneva in 1553 by the city's authorities.

[27] For a study of Robert Estienne's career and legacy, see Elizabeth Armstrong, *Robert Estienne, Royal Printer: An Historical Study* (Cambridge: Cambridge University Press, 1954); DeWitt T. Starnes, *Robert Estienne's Influence on Lexicography* (Austin: University of Texas Press, 2014).

[28] Among others, this conclusion has been made by Bruce Metzger and Caspar Gregory. See Bruce Metzger, *Manuscripts of the Greek Bible: An Introduction to Palaeography* (Oxford: Oxford University Press, 1981), 41n106; Caspar Gregory, *Canon and Text of the New Testament* (New York: Charles Scribner's Sons, 1907), 474.

[29] Earlier editions were published in 1546, 1549, and 1550. See Armstrong, *Robert Estienne*, 136–38.

[30] All three of these volumes were published in Geneva. Stephanus's Latin volume was based on the work of Pagnino (Old Testament) and Calvin's companion Theodore Beza (New Testament).

Shortly after the publication of Stephanus's Greek New Testament and French translation, a little-known theologian named William Whittingham (c. 1524–1579) fled England to escape the reign of Mary I. After a brief period in Frankfurt, Whittingham arrived in Geneva where he worked alongside both John Knox and John Calvin, the latter of whom he was related to through marriage.[31] His work in Geneva was highlighted by the production of an English translation of the New Testament published by the French printer Conrad Badius, a brother-in-law of Stephanus, in 1557. Though not widely known today, Whittingham's translation was monumental given that it was the first English Bible in print to include the verse divisions devised by Stephanus. Shortly after the publication of his New Testament, Whittingham assumed a leading role in the translation of the Geneva Bible, the most widely read English Bible from its publication in 1560 through the early seventeenth century. Like Whittingham's personal translation, the popular Geneva Bible included Stephanus's recently created verse divisions. As a result of the widespread influence of the Geneva Bible, the chapter and verse divisions it contained became inseparably linked in the minds of many readers with the biblical text and were thus included in nearly all subsequent translations of the New Testament, such as the King James Bible in 1611.

Without the use of the printing press, neither the Geneva Bible nor even the King James Bible would have likely played such a decisive role in popularizing the chapter and verse divisions that appear in nearly all modern Bibles. Prior to this landmark invention, readers of Scripture encountered the text only in the form of handwritten manuscripts, each of which contained unique features and characteristics. Rarely was a particular edition of Scripture produced on a large scale by hand.[32] With the invention of the printing press, however, access to editions of the Bible that contained recently created paratextual features such as chapter and verse

---

[31] Whittingham was married to Catherine Jaquemayne, the sister of Calvin's wife, Idelette de Bure. See B.F. Westcott, *General View of the History of the English Bible*, 3rd ed., rev. William Aldis Wright (New York: Macmillan, 1906), 90n1.

[32] The Wycliffe Bible is one notable example of an edition of Scripture in which multiple copies were produced by hand. According to David Daniell, "over 250 manuscripts of all or part [of Tyndale's New Testament] survive today, a larger number than for any other medieval English text." David Daniell, introduction to *The New Testament: A Facsimile of the 1526 Edition*, trans. William Tyndale (Peabody, MA: Hendrickson, 2008), introduction. Despite the large number of copies that were produced, the total number in circulation was quite small compared to the number of copies that were produced of later translations such as the Geneva Bible and the King James Bible.

divisions became available to a much larger audience. The popularity and influence of the major Bible translations produced during the sixteenth and seventeenth centuries thus ensured that the particular verse divisions associated with Isaac Nathan and Stephanus became standard features of virtually all subsequently printed editions of the Bible.

The Arrangement of the Biblical Writings

In addition to popularizing and standardizing notable paratextual features, the printing press also played a role in the establishment of a standard arrangement of the writings contained in both the Old and New Testaments. The traditional order of writings in the Hebrew Bible is built on the threefold division of Law (*Torah*), Prophets (*Nebi'im*), and Writings (*Kethubim*). The precise period when these major divisions began to be recognized is unclear, although references to the Hebrew writings in both canonical and noncanonical sources may indicate that a threefold division was recognized by some during the first century and perhaps even earlier. Possible awareness of these divisions may be observed in first-century texts such as Matt 23:35 (cf. Luke 11:51) and 24:44 as well as Josephus's *Against Apion* (1.8). Prior to the first century, the prologue of the apocryphal work *Sirach* (also known as *Ecclesiasticus*) and 2 Macc 2:13 may also point to an awareness of a threefold division. Nevertheless, not all scholars are convinced that these sources provide conclusive evidence that three specific divisions of the Hebrew Bible were commonly recognized during the first century. Possible allusions or references in these sources to the so-called Writings (*Kethubim*) are understood by some as simply a general reference to various noncanonical Jewish texts or to only a limited portion of the writings that were later recognized as an established literary collection.

Even more difficult than establishing the specific period in which the tripartite collection of Hebrew writings emerged is determining the specific order of the Hebrew books during the first several centuries of the Christian era. Although the sources cited above have been regarded by some scholars as reliable evidence the three major divisions of the Old Testament writings were in fact recognized by the first century, a precise and uniform ordering and arrangement of the individual writings does not appear to have been established by the early centuries of the Christian era. As Edmon Gallagher and John Meade write, "Our sources provide no consistent ordering of books within the third section (the Ketuvim/

Writings), and there are some slight inconsistencies in the ordering of the second division (the Neviim/Prophets), but the Masoretic manuscripts, the Talmudic list, and Jerome's alternative ordering all situate the same books within the three divisions."[33] With respect to the *Ketuvim*, James Sanders has concluded that "the third section of the Jewish canon was not stabilized into its rabbinic, proto-Masoretic form until after the failure of the Bar Kochba revolt" of the second century.[34]

While there is simply insufficient evidence to affirm precisely when a consistent and uniform arrangement of the individual writings in the Hebrew tradition first emerged, recognition of the basic threefold division of the Hebrew Bible did eventually become widespread. This general arrangement, however, was ultimately replaced by a more chronologically influenced sequence in copies of the Greek Septuagint and subsequent Latin texts, most notably the Vulgate. While generally favoring a more chronological arrangement over the tripartite structure of the Hebrew tradition, the ordering of Old Testament writings in the Greek and Latin traditions remained somewhat unsettled. For example, Codex Vaticanus placed the poetic writings prior to the prophets, while this order was reversed in Codex Sinaiticus and Codex Alexandrinus.[35] This divergence largely subsided when printed copies of the Bible began to be produced during the sixteenth century. The printed Bibles commonly followed an arrangement of the Old Testament writings associated with the Septuagint and Vulgate rather than the traditional threefold Hebrew division.

Regarding the New Testament, it is helpful to remember that biblical manuscripts produced prior to the sixteenth century were handwritten and typically included only one major collection of writings, such as the Gospels, the *Praxapostolos* (the collection of Acts and the Catholic Epistles), the Pauline Epistles, or Revelation. Of the nearly 6,000 extant Greek manuscripts catalogued to date, only about sixty may be concluded with reasonable certainty to have once contained the entire New Testament and only

---

[33] Edmon L. Gallagher and John D. Meade, *The Biblical Canon Lists from Early Christianity: Texts and Analysis* (New York: Oxford University Press, 2017), 3. As the authors note, it is difficult to ascertain the precise ordering of the Old Testament books during the period in which the Hebrew writings were transmitted on scrolls rather than codices.

[34] James A. Sanders, "The Stabilization of the Tanak," in *A History of Biblical Interpretation: Volume 1 The Ancient Period*, ed. Alan Hauser and Duane Watson (Grand Rapids: Eerdmans, 2003), 245.

[35] Greg Goswell, "The Order of the Books in the Greek Old Testament," *Journal of the Evangelical Theological Society* 52, no. 3 (2009): 449–66.

about ten of these included the entire Bible.[36] Given the laborious nature of handwriting, the thickness of parchment, and the prohibitive expense often associated with the production of manuscripts, the small percentage of handwritten manuscripts originally containing the entirety of the New Testament should come as little surprise. Most extant Greek manuscripts are thought to have originally included only the four Gospels, although several manuscripts have been determined to have contained two or three of the four New Testament subcollections (e.g., The Gospels and Pauline Epistles). In extant manuscripts which included three subcollections, the book of Revelation is typically omitted. By no later than the fourth century, the four subcollections of New Testament writings began to circulate occasionally in a single codex, essentially forming what is now collectively referred to as the New Testament.[37] However, even after the smaller units began to circulate together in one volume, the vast majority of manuscripts continued to include only one of the four major subcollections, a trend that continued until the invention of the printing press a full millennium later.

Interestingly, numerous Greek manuscripts that include writings from more than one New Testament subcollection do not divide the *Praxapostolos*, but instead juxtapose Acts with the Catholic Epistles while placing this collection immediately before the Pauline Epistles. In fact, the most common arrangement of the New Testament writings found in Greek witnesses produced prior to the sixteenth century followed the sequence Gospels-Acts-Catholic Epistles-Pauline Epistles-Revelation.[38] It has been observed that the placement of the Catholic Epistles prior to the Pauline

---

[36] The precise number of Greek witnesses containing the entire New Testament is difficult to discern, given the fragmentary nature of many manuscripts. See, D. C. Parker, *An Introduction to the New Testament Manuscripts and Their Texts* (Cambridge: Cambridge University Press, 2008), 70; Tomas Bokedal, *The Formation and Significance of the Christian Biblical Canon: A Study in Text, Ritual, and Interpretation* (London: T&T Clark, 2014), 150. David Trobisch suggests that there are 59 such extant manuscripts. David Trobisch, *The First Edition of the New Testament* (New York: Oxford University Press, 2000), 26. Included among the extant Greek manuscripts that presently contain or may be determined to have once contained the entire New Testament are the well-known manuscripts of Codex Sinaiticus (fourth century), Codex Alexandrinus (fifth century), Codex Vaticanus (fourth century), and Codex Ephraemi Rescriptus (fifth century).

[37] The term "New Testament" derives from the Greek καινή διαθήκη, which appears in various passages such as Luke 22:20; 1 Cor 11:25; 2 Cor 3:6; Heb 8:8 and 9:15.

[38] A notable exception to this arrangement is Codex Sinaiticus which places the *Corpus Paulinum* prior to the *Praxapostolos*. However, Sinaiticus still differs from the arrangement found in modern editions of the New Testament given that it places the Pauline Epistles immediately after the Gospels. The arrangement found in Sinaiticus (Pauline Epistles-Acts-Catholic Epistles) may also be observed in manuscripts such as Minuscule 203.

Epistles allows for a canonical reading that is more consistent with the structure of Acts. In this arrangement, the writings of the "Pillar Apostles (cf. Gal 2:9)" of James, Peter, and John—characters dominant in the first half of Luke's narrative—precede the writings of the Apostle Paul, the central character in the second half of the work.[39]

Given the common placement of the Catholic Epistles immediately following Acts in many Greek witnesses, it may be asked what factors eventually led to the placement of these writings between the Pauline Epistles and Revelation in modern English translations. It appears that while the placement of the Catholic Epistles immediately following Acts was common in Greek witnesses, alternative arrangements existed in witnesses of western origin. Of particular significance is Jerome's Vulgate, a Latin translation that placed the Pauline Epistles before the Catholic Epistles. The common arrangement of writings contained in the Vulgate is notable given that it was retained in Desiderius Erasmus's Latin-Greek polyglot of the New Testament, the *Novum Instrumentum omne*, a seminal work first published in 1516 and republished in four subsequent editions.[40] Prior to this publication, the renowned humanist had worked diligently editing the writings of Jerome, a process which ultimately convinced him that an updated and improved translation of the Latin text of the New Testament was needed. Erasmus began his work in 1512 while he was in Cambridge; it was completed four years later and published by Johann Froben in Basel, Switzerland.

The lasting significance of Erasmus's critical edition was not his fresh Latin translation, as monumental as this must have seemed at the time, but the Greek text that it contained. The Greek was included primarily to provide justification for his Latin translation when it differed from the Vulgate, but many have speculated that Froben rushed the publication of the

---

[39] For further background on the early canonical development of the Catholic Epistles, see Darian Lockett, *Letters from the Pillar Apostles: The Formation of the Catholic Epistles as a Canonical Collection* (Eugene: Pickwick, 2017), 103–4.

[40] As David Nienhuis explains, "The Eastern sequence of canonical collections did not ultimately prevail. Other orderings placed Paul after the gospels, and before the CE [Catholic Epistles], and placed Acts at the end of the canon with the Apocalypse (Codex Claromontanus, Apostolic Canon 85, Jerome, Augustine, and Pope Innocent I). The ultimate ordering *Gospels-Acts-Paul-CE-Apocalypse* found several earlier witnesses (Gregory of Nazianzus, Amphilochius, Rufinus, and the North African Councils) and was the sequence ultimately chosen for the Vulgate version that came to dominate the Western church." David Nienhuis, *Not by Paul Alone: The Formation of the Catholic Epistle Collection and the Christian Canon* (Waco, TX: Baylor University Press, 2007), 87.

volume to achieve recognition as the first to publish the Greek text of the New Testament.[41] Regardless of the original motivation for publishing the Greek text, Frans van Liere rightly concludes that Erasmus's work "turned the tables on the authority of the Vulgate" by placing authority on the Greek text rather than a translation.[42]

By modern standards, the scholarship on which Erasmus's Greek text was based was rather unimpressive given that he had access to only a small number of Greek manuscripts during his preparation of the volume, none of which appear to have predated the twelfth century.[43] Despite its imperfections, Erasmus's Latin-Greek New Testament proved to be a landmark publication, quickly becoming the source for several notable translations produced during the Protestant Reformation, including Luther's German Bible and several prominent English translations such as the Tyndale Bible, the Geneva Bible, and the King James Bible.

Because the Greek text contained in Erasmus's Latin translation was included to justify his translation, it followed the order of writings that had become standard in the Vulgate rather than the Greek tradition. The *Praxapostolos* was thus divided with the Catholic Epistles placed between the Pauline Epistles and Revelation rather than after Acts.[44] Erasmus's 1516 Greek-Latin New Testament, the first publication of its kind, was a great boon to the study of the Greek text of the New Testament. Often overlooked, however, is the role that it played in promoting an arrangement of New Testament writings that differed from the arrangement common in the Greek tradition.

---

[41] The Complutensian Polyglot was first printed in 1514. However, publication was delayed until the completion of the Old Testament in 1522. Erasmus's Latin-Greek edition of the New Testament was hastily edited for his standards and rushed to the press. As biographer Roland Bainton notes, "Erasmus was far from satisfied with the entire production and devoted the remainder of his life among other labors to the improvement of this edition." Roland H. Bainton, *Erasmus of Christendom* (Peabody, MA: Hendrickson, 1969), 139.

[42] Frans van Liere, *An Introduction to the Medieval Bible* (Cambridge: Cambridge University Press, 2014), 103.

[43] Based on the Gregory-Aland numbering, these manuscripts included Minuscules 1, 2, 817, 2814, 2815, 2816, and 2817. With the exception of 2814, each manuscript is currently housed at the University of Basel.

[44] Although the Latin Vulgate included the same New Testament writings found in the Greek tradition, it placed the Pauline Corpus immediately following Acts, thus giving greater prominence to the Pauline epistles. In addition to Latin witnesses containing the Vulgate, Jerome's preference for placing the Pauline Epistles prior to the Catholic Epistles may be observed in Jerome, *To Paulinus*, no. 53.9 (*NPNF* 2.6).

The manner and extent to which the customary arrangement of New Testament writings has influenced readers of the New Testament is difficult to ascertain. The Catholic Epistles have never been studied as rigorously or read as widely as the Pauline writings, and their placement after the Pauline Epistles has certainly not encouraged further study or reflection. Some have concluded that the modern arrangement presents the Catholic Epistles as a somewhat disjointed collection of incongruent epistles that are of less importance than the other portions of the New Testament, particularly the Pauline epistles.[45]

Conclusion

During the period of the Protestant Reformation, the recently invented printing press played an important role not only in advancing a variety of theological perspectives, many of which were at odds with the official dogma of the Roman church, but also in influencing how readers encountered and studied the Bible. The printing press was used to solidify and popularize a particular order of the biblical writings as well as a number of paratextual features such as the chapter and verse divisions now common in virtually all modern translations.

The chapter and verse divisions have made the study of Scripture more convenient in many respects. Because a particular numbering system is now universally recognized, a small portion of biblical text can be quickly and precisely identified and located, a great convenience to both scholars and readers. While the divisions have proven to be a helpful tool, readers must be careful not to allow them to divert attention away from a passage's literary context. Modern readers are often prone to intuitively assume these divisions serve as a reliable and even authoritative guide to the structure of a text and the flow of an author's thought. Even a casual reading of Scripture, however, reveals this is not always the case. Given that chapter and verse divisions were not original to the authors of Scripture, readers and interpreters of the biblical text must learn to observe the shape and flow of the

---

[45] Gerd Theissen concluded that the Catholic Epistles serve in part as a corrective to various aspects of Paul's theology. He contends, for example, that the Epistle of James was designed to counter how Paul articulated the relationship between faith and works in his Epistle to the Romans. Gerd Theissen, *The New Testament: A Literary History*, trans. Linda Maloney (Minneapolis: Fortress, 2012), 125–29. This theory, however, runs into challenges relating to chronology (e.g., the early composition of James) and is considered by many biblical scholars to be based on exaggerated claims of contradictions between Paul and the writers of the Catholic Epistles.

larger discourse and how the smaller segments of a text contribute to the larger structure.[46] Sound biblical exegesis is predicated, in part, upon the interpreter's ability to analyze more than the meaning of individual words or even the meaning of individual sentences. It requires, among other things, an awareness of an author's flow of thought and the overarching themes and arguments present throughout the writing. While the various reading aids popularized by the first printed Bibles have certainly served readers of the Bible well for nearly half a millennium, contemporary readers must learn to recognize these features merely as tools of convenience rather than as authoritative guides to reading and interpreting the text.

Bibliography

Armstrong, Elizabeth. *Robert Estienne, Royal Printer: An Historical Study*. Cambridge: Cambridge University Press, 1954.

Bainton, Roland H. *Erasmus of Christendom*. Peabody, MA: Hendrickson, 1969.

Bokedal, Tomas. *The Formation and Significance of the Christian Biblical Canon: A Study in Text, Ritual and Interpretation*. London: T&T Clark, 2014.

Campbell, Constantine. *Advances in the Study of Greek: New Insights for Reading the New Testament*. Grand Rapids: Zondervan, 2015.

Cole, Richard. "Reformation Printers: Unsung Heroes." *Sixteenth Century Journal* 15, no. 3 (1984): 327–39.

Cruden, Alexander. *A Complete Concordance to the Holy Scriptures of the Old and New Testament*. Philadelphia: Kimber, Conrad, 1806.

Daniell, David. Introduction to *The New Testament: A Facsimile of the 1526 Edition*, trans. William Tyndale, vii–xxxii. Peabody, MA: Hendrickson, 2008,

Devey, Joseph, ed. *Novum Organum*. By Francis Bacon. New York: P.F. Collier, 1902.

Edwards, Mark U. *Printing, Propaganda, and Martin Luther*. Berkeley, CA: University of California Press, 1994.

Eisenstein, Elizabeth. *The Printing Press as an Agent of Change: Communications and Cultural Transformations in Early-Modern Europe*. 2 vols. Cambridge: Cambridge University Press, 1979.

---

[46] For an overview of recent trends in the discipline of discourse analysis and how it has been used in the study of the New Testament, see chapters 7 and 8 in Constantine Campbell, *Advances in the Study of Greek: New Insights for Reading the New Testament* (Grand Rapids: Zondervan, 2015), 148–91.

Gallagher, Edmon L., and John D. Meade. *The Biblical Canon Lists from Early Christianity: Texts and Analysis*. New York: Oxford University Press, 2017.

Goswell, Greg. "The Order of the Books in the Greek Old Testament." *Journal of the Evangelical Theological Society* 52, no. 3 (2009): 449–66.

Gregory, Caspar. *Canon and Text of the New Testament*. New York: Charles Scribner's Sons, 1907.

Ladocsi, Gaspar, and Stefan Samulowitz. "Eusebian Canons." In *Encyclopedia of Ancient Christianity Volume 1 A–E*, ed. Angelo Di Berardino. Downers Grove, IL: InterVarsity Press, 2014.

Lockett, Darian. *Letters from the Pillar Apostles: The Formation of the Catholic Epistles as a Canonical Collection*. Eugene: Pickwick, 2017.

Metzger, Bruce. *Manuscripts of the Greek Bible: An Introduction to Palaeography*. Oxford: Oxford University Press, 1981.

_____. *The Bible in Translation: Ancient and Modern English Versions*. Grand Rapids: Baker, 2001.

Nienhuis, David. *Not by Paul Alone: The Formation of the Catholic Epistle Collection and the Christian Canon*. Waco, TX: Baylor University Press, 2007.

Parker, D. C. *An Introduction to the New Testament Manuscripts and Their Texts*. Cambridge: Cambridge University Press, 2008.

Pettegree, Andrew. *The Book in the Renaissance*. New Haven, CT: Yale University Press, 2010.

Roper, Lyndal. *Martin Luther: Renegade and Prophet*. New York: Random House, 2016.

Saenger, Paul. "The Twelfth-Century Reception of Oriental Languages and the Graphic *Mise en page* of Latin Vulgate Bibles Copied in England." In *Form and Function in the Late Medieval Bible*, ed. Eyal Poleg and Laura Light, 31–66. Leiden: Brill, 2013.

Sanders, James A. "The Stabilization of the Tanak." In *A History of Biblical Interpretation: Volume 1 The Ancient Period*, ed. Alan Hauser and Duane Watson, 225–52. Grand Rapids: Eerdmans, 2003.

Schaff, Philip, ed. *A Select Library of the Nicene and Post-Nicene Fathers of the Christian Church*. 14 vols. Reprint ed. Peabody, MA: Hendrickson, 1994.

Schuchardt, Read Mercer. "The Reformation as Media Event." In *The People's Book: The Reformation and the Bible*, ed. Jennifer McNutt and David Lauber, 89–109. Downers Grove, IL: InterVarsity Press, 2017.

Smalley, Beryl. *The Study of the Bible in the Middle Ages*. 1st paperback ed. Notre Dame, IN.: University of Notre Dame Press, 1964.

Starnes, DeWitt T. *Robert Estienne's Influence on Lexicography*. Austin: University of Texas Press, 2014.

Theissen, Gerd. *The New Testament: A Literary History*. Translated by Linda Maloney. Minneapolis: Fortress, 2012.

Trobisch, David. *The First Edition of the New Testament*. New York: Oxford University Press, 2000.

Van Kampen, Kimberly, and Paul Saenger, eds. *The Bible as Book: The First Printed Editions*. New Castle, DE: Oak Knoll Press, 1999.

Van Liere, Frans. *An Introduction to the Medieval Bible*. Cambridge: Cambridge University Press, 2014.

_____. "Biblical Exegesis through the Twelfth Century." In *The Practice of the Bible in the Middle Ages: Production, Reception, and Performance in Western Christianity*, ed. Susan Boynton and Diane Reilly, 157–89. New York: Columbia University Press, 2011.

Westcott, Brooke Foss. *General View of the History of the English Bible*. 3rd ed. Revised by William Aldis Wright. New York: Macmillan, 1906.

The Priesthood of All Believers: Theological Intent and Subsequent Practice

STEPHEN BRETT ECCHER

The events of January 5, 1527, were just as horrific as they were heart-breaking. What took place on that chilly winter day in Zürich would have been unimaginable just a few short years earlier. Following a public trial, the Zürich authorities took Felix Mantz from the Wellenberg prison to a small fishing hut in the middle of the Limmat River. Mantz's hands were bound and secured behind his knees. The executioner then flung the prisoner into the icy cold waters.[1] Throughout the trial and execution, the Swiss Reformer, Huldrych Zwingli, refused to intervene or defend the accused. In fact, Mantz's one-time friend, mentor, and co-laborer in the Zürich Reformation celebrated the execution.[2]

Less than four years earlier, in 1523, Mantz shared in Zwingli's work of reforming the Swiss church. Nevertheless, two days prior to Mantz's execution Zwingli wrote to Johannes Oecolampadius, "The Anabaptist, who should already have been sent to the devil, disturbs the peace of the pious

---

[1] An accounting of Mantz's execution was recorded by Heinrich Bullinger, Zwingli's successor at Zürich. Heinrich Bullinger, *Reformationsgeschichte*, Band II, ed. Johann Jakob Hottinger and Hans Heinrich Vögeli (Frauenfeld: Beyel, 1838), 382.

[2] Zwingli tutored Mantz in the ancient languages of Hebrew, Greek, and Latin from 1522–23. Ekklehard Krajewski, *Leben und Sterben des Zürcher Täuferführers Felix Manz: Über die Anfänge der Täuferbewegung und des Freikirchentums in der Reformationszeit* (Kassel: J. G. Oncken, 1957), 22–23.

people. But I believe, the axe will settle it."[3] Zwingli's final encounters with his former student were nearly as cold as the waters that took Mantz's life. But what had Mantz done to elicit such a callous, deadly rebuke from his erstwhile partner in the gospel? What had gone wrong?

That memorable day was a microcosm of a larger issue that plagued the Reformers during the Reformation. In the mid-1520s especially, the Reformers' efforts were complicated by a logical corollary of their developing theology, which only surfaced through a series of unforeseen events. Reformers like Martin Luther and Huldrych Zwingli once rallied their Reformation movements by casting a new vision for the priesthood of all believers. This doctrine garnered them support by empowering the laity to greater participation in the church's life. But it was entangled with a hermeneutical consequence the Reformers never anticipated. As Luther and Zwingli soon realized, the doctrine had the seeds of schism sown deep within. Sadly, this schism often brought life-and-death consequences for dissenting figures like Felix Mantz.

This chapter explores the development of the doctrine of the priesthood of all believers in the key first-generation Reformers and demonstrates how their theological hope for that doctrine eventually betrayed them in application. The Reformers' understanding of the priesthood of all believers will be elucidated, especially as it was first realized and implemented in a corporate context by Luther and Zwingli in the early 1520s. Attention will then be directed toward those historic circumstances that spiraled this doctrine beyond what the Magisterial Reformers ever foresaw and into radical forms of Reformation outside their control. The Reformers were ultimately forced to reconsider how the priesthood of all believers was to be understood and exercised.

The Magisterial Reformers' decision to permit and promote lay participation in the ecclesiastical discourse of the day came back to haunt them. Their radically democratic understanding of the priesthood of all believers led to a problem of authority as contrasting forms of Reformation emerged. Different readings of Scripture engendered different visions for the church. Once others began to paint ideas outside the hermeneutical lines deemed acceptable to the mainline Reformers, the Reformation reached a tipping point. As those ideas coalesced into the German Peasants' War and the rise

---

[3] Ruth A. Tucker, *Parade of Faith: A Biographical History of the Christian Church* (Grand Rapids: Zondervan, 2015), 267.

of Anabaptism, the Magisterial Reformers' understanding of the priesthood of all believers had to be reconsidered.

Martin Luther's New Understanding of Priesthood

The world Luther was born into was bifurcated, with a strict distinction between clergy and laity, a tradition bequeathed from the medieval period. The clergy were exclusively empowered to oversee religious matters. The laity, which included peasants, princes, and kings, toiled in the less-important temporal estate. The laity's place in society, much like their work, was important, but it paled in comparison to the clergy's elevated status as mediators of the divine. There was an ontological distinction that separated the clergy, whose work was rooted in a spiritual and eternal significance, from all others in society.

Luther sought to change this dualistic cultural anthropology. As early as 1518 Luther started to undercut the clergy/laity divide by his use of the vernacular. Penning his *Explanations of the 95 Theses* in German recast the nature of theological discourse.[4] Luther chose to speak to the people in their own language and on their own terms.[5] His voice was bold and resonated with the concerns of an increasingly dissatisfied and disenfranchised people. Once Luther embraced the vernacular, a pathway toward a new understanding of priesthood became viable.

Of greatest consequence to Luther's recasting of priesthood of believers was the way in which the laity were granted a participatory role in theology. As Ulrike Zitzlsperger has contended, "During the early 1520s the German Reformation gave lay men and women, albeit only briefly, an opportunity to engage actively in religious and current affairs. Some of these lay people saw themselves as mediators between the still rather exclusive theologians and the so called 'common man.'"[6] This shift in religious discourse was revolutionary and empowering. Luther cleverly used his pulpit and the newly realized print medium to persuade the people of his vision for their place in the German church.[7] This strategy provided Luther access to

---

[4] Martin Luther, "Explanations of the Ninety-Five Theses," *LW* 31:83–252.

[5] Latin was the language of theology, the Bible, and the liturgy. Alister E. McGrath, *Reformation Thought: An Introduction*, 4th ed. (Oxford: Wiley-Blackwell, 2012), 15.

[6] Ulrike Zitzlsperger, "Mother, Martyr and Mary Magdalene: German Female Pamphleteers and Their Self-Image," *History* 88, no. 3 (July 2003): 379.

[7] Hans J. Hillerbrand, *The Division of Christendom: Christianity in the Sixteenth Century* (Louisville: Westminster John Knox, 2007), 83.

and influence over the German populace in a way that was unmatched by Rome. It also afforded Luther the chance to help stir the general populace to move beyond their passivity and toward an active reshaping of the faith detached from the unbiblical boundaries of the Roman Curia.[8]

It was not just the language or medium that was empowering to the people; it was Luther's new vision for the priesthood of believers. During the 1520 pamphlet wars, the German Reformer made clear that the clergy/laity divide was a fabricated and oppressive Romanist measure unsupported by Scripture. In his *To the Christian Nobility of the German Nation*, Luther clarified, "There is no true, basic difference between laymen and priests, princes and bishops, between religious and secular."[9] In fact, Luther believed that the papacy's external form of priesthood had its provenance in the devil.[10] Based on a particular reading of 1 Peter 2 and Revelation 5, Luther contended that priesthood was the common property of all Christians. This was rooted in the fact that all Christians share in "one baptism, one gospel, [and] one faith."[11]

Despite the personal value of priesthood to every German, Luther never viewed priesthood through an individualistic lens. Rather, the Christian's right to go before God came with a corporate responsibility.[12] He frequently spoke about the importance of interceding on behalf of others as a crucial obligation of one's priesthood.[13] He also believed that it was incumbent on all Christians to oversee the doctrinal fidelity of the faith community. That the pope presumptively served as the final interpreter of Scripture was "an outrageous fancied fable."[14] Such an authoritative structure was fraught with peril, especially if the church's head was corrupted. Instead, the entire church community had an important role to play in the interpretation of Scripture. If all Christians are priests, then those same priests are both qualified and called to judge matters of the faith correctly.[15]

---

[8] Hans-Joachim Köhler, "Erste Schritte zu einem Meinungsprofil der frühen Reformationszeit," in *Martin Luther: Probleme seiner Zeit*, ed. Volker Press and Dieter Stievermann (Stuttgart: Klett-Cotta, 1986), 246.

[9] Martin Luther, "To the Christian Nobility of the German Nation Concerning the Reform of the Christian Estate," in *LW* 44:129.

[10] Martin Luther, "The Misuse of the Mass," in *LW* 36:138, 142.

[11] Luther, "To the Christian Nobility," in *LW* 44:127.

[12] Timothy George, *Theology of the Reformers*, rev. ed. (Nashville: B&H, 2013), 97.

[13] Paul Althaus, *The Theology of Martin Luther* (Philadelphia: Fortress, 1970), 314.

[14] Luther, "To the Christian Nobility," in *LW* 44:134.

[15] Luther, 44:135.

Accordingly, the important place of the "common person" became a theme woven into the Reformation literature of the early 1520s.[16]

The formative development of Luther's thought on priesthood came in 1520 and 1521. This coincided with his work at the Wartburg Castle to translate the New Testament into his native German tongue. A vernacular Bible was equally scandalous and subversive to Rome as Luther's innovative view of priesthood. Although he understood the risks with each, Luther was unaware that linking the two would light a fuse in the German church. Ironically, the forthcoming explosion of controversy was largely realized through two of his colaborers in Wittenberg, Andreas Karlstadt and Thomas Müntzer. Luther would have plenty to regret about his understanding of the priesthood of believers, once others pushed the doctrine to its logical end. Of greater lament, the tumult that loomed on the German horizon soon ushered in devastating consequences to the peasants once empowered by Luther.

In all his efforts there was a flaw to Luther's approach: he assumed he could control the reading of Scripture. Luther was aware from the outset of the threat of unchecked, rogue interpretations of Scripture. He labored to direct the reading of the Bible, imbedding interpretive guides and restrictions into his vernacular Bible. He knew that one's translation of the Bible served as an interpretation as well.[17] Thus, Luther guided his audience in their reading of the Bible by the very selection, and at times creation, of certain words and phrases in his translation. He implemented Old and New Testament prefaces that directed the reader to view the Bible through his Law/Gospel dialectic.[18] Furthermore, a legion of glosses provided in the margins became a hermeneutical lens through which key theological themes, foundational to Luther's theology, might be impressed on the reader. As Timothy Wengert has stated, "Luther had no place in his vocabulary for a reading of Scripture that excluded commentary."[19] Still, these guides were not enough to curtail the hermeneutical crisis that Luther faced.

---

[16] R. W. Scribner and C. Scott Dixon, *The German Reformation*, 2nd ed. (New York: Palgrave Macmillan, 2003), 49.

[17] Martin Brecht, *Martin Luther: Shaping and Defining the Reformation, 1521–1532*, trans. James L. Schaaf (Minneapolis: Fortress Press, 1990), 50.

[18] Martin Luther, "Prefaces to the Old Testament" and "Prefaces to the New Testament," *LW* 35:235–37, 357–62.

[19] Timothy J. Wengert, *Reading the Bible with Martin Luther: An Introductory Guide* (Grand Rapids: Baker Academic, 2013), 17.

A New Understanding of Priesthood in Zürich

During the early 1520s, Huldrych Zwingli was making Reformation gains in Zürich comparable to those of Luther in Wittenberg. The Word of God and the Christian community were both crucial catalysts to the dramatic changes taking place. From Zwingli's early commitment in 1519 to preach *lectio continua*, through the publication of the Zürich Bible in 1524, the Scriptures helped to reshape the Zürich community.[20] As they had in Germany with Luther, the lay populace played an important role in supporting and promoting Zwingli's reform efforts. Yet, through it all Zwingli was unaware that these guiding forces behind the changes in the Swiss church would soon lead to personal frustrations and a deep schism in his own camp.

Zwingli initially argued for the perspicuity of Scripture. In a 1522 sermon he stressed that all Christians, including the laity, could properly discern and appropriate the wisdom of Scripture. [21] This was not the first instance in which Zwingli demonstrated such a conviction. From the outset of his time at Zürich, he believed that God's truth illumined by his Spirit would pave a path toward change.[22] Reformation would be accomplished principally by means of the Bible's power. Accordingly, the Swiss Reformer loosed the Word through thundering sermons and biblically laden theological treatises at the genesis of his reforming efforts at Zürich. But he was only one man. To multiply the effect of the Word, Zwingli promoted the reading and study of the Bible in lay settings throughout Zürich beginning as early as 1520.[23]

This vision for expanding the Bible's influence in Zürich initially began small. Zwingli surrounded himself with a cadre of vibrant young humanists, whom he trained and loved. Zwingli taught these students how to read the Word, providing interpretive guidance from the beginning. He intended to leverage his students' shared passion for the text as a means of

---

[20] I. L. Snavely Jr., "Ulrich Zwingli (1484–1531)," in *Historical Handbook of Major Biblical Interpreters*, ed. Donald K. McKim (Downers Grove, IL: InterVarsity Press, 1998), 250; and Peter Opitz, "The Authority of Scripture in the Early Zurich Reformation (1522–1540)," *Journal of Reformed Theology* 5, no. 3 (2011): 296–309.

[21] Huldrych Zwingli, "Of the Clarity and Certainty of the Word of God," in *Zwingli and Bullinger*, ed. G.W. Bromiley (Philadelphia: Westminster, 1953), 59–95.

[22] Bruce Gordon, *The Swiss Reformation* (Manchester: Manchester University Press, 2002), 56.

[23] Randolph C. Head, "The Swiss Reformations: Movements, Settlements, and Reimagination, 1520–1720," in *The Oxford Handbook of the Protestant Reformations*, ed. Ulinka Rublack (Oxford: Oxford University Press, 2016), 170–71.

stoking and spreading the flames of change. However, this Reformation fire soon changed direction and Zwingli was burned in the process by those closest to him. Once cherished friends became hated enemies and Scripture was the catalyst for their rift.

At first, the schism that loomed on the horizon was undetectable. Zwingli drew close to figures like Conrad Grebel, Felix Mantz, and Simon Stumpf through their shared study of the Word and their work in the biblical languages.[24] As they searched the depths of Scripture in community, Zwingli's stable of clerical and lay humanists grew in their love for the newly recovered gospel and each other. They took the fruits of their studies into the larger community with two interrelated ends in mind. First, those lay Bible study groups that sprouted up in 1520 were a means of spreading the evangelical gospel. Drawing heavily from Erasmus, Zwingli stressed the Word's work in the inner person as the catalyst toward external morality.[25] Given that Zwingli believed Zürich functioned as a theocracy, he thought these personal changes would soon bear fruit for the community as a whole.[26] Second, giving commoners unfettered access to the Bible allowed Zwingli's Reformation to tap into the rising currents of anticlericalism and further highlight the disconnect that existed between the Catholic clergy and the Bible's pastoral qualifications.[27]

Initially, Zwingli's plan worked flawlessly. In fact, the religious agitation caused by many of his students through their lay home-study groups served as the stimulant that started the Zürich Reformation. The famous Lenten sausage-eating incident, attacks on nearby monasteries, the disruption of sermons, and other anticlerical demonstrations all bolstered Zwingli's reforming efforts in the spring and summer of 1522.[28] Through it all Zwingli maintained his commitment to the lay interpretation of Scripture. In his August 1522 letter to the Bishop of Constance, Zwingli rebutted the notion that only clerics should interpret the Bible. Since all Christians are indwelt by the same Holy Spirit, "even the most ignorant if they are pious ... will understand the Scriptures in the plainest way according to God's purpose . . . . It is not the function of one or two to expound passages of Scripture, but of all

---

[24] Andrea Strübind, *Eifriger als Zwingli: Die frühe Täuferbewegung in der Schweiz* (Berlin: Duncker & Humblot, 2003), 266–70.

[25] W. P. Stephens, *The Theology of Huldrych Zwingli* (Oxford: Clarendon Press, 1986), 13, 15–17.

[26] Robert C. Walton, *Zwingli's Theocracy* (Toronto: University of Toronto Press, 1967).

[27] Carter Lindberg, *The European Reformations*, 2nd ed. (Oxford: Wiley-Blackwell, 2010), 50–51.

[28] Hans-Jürgen Goertz, *The Anabaptists* (London: Routledge, 1996), 8–9.

who believe in Christ."[29] Such a conviction worked well in those early years, but the unintended consequences of this belief loomed.

Priesthood Put to the Test

In a cold twist of irony, some of the people that supported Luther and Zwingli in the early years of the Reformation became their greatest adversaries. The problems for Luther began in late 1521. Cloistered at the Wartburg because of Charles V's imperial ban, Luther was eventually forced to return to Wittenberg because of the agitation caused by Andreas Karlstadt. In Luther's absence, Karlstadt's reading of Scripture began to expand his understanding of priesthood, especially relating to the laity's involvement in the church's life.[30] This belief, coupled with a different *literal* reading of Scripture from Luther, led Karlstadt to argue for changes to the Eucharist. On Christmas 1521, Karlstadt presumptively instituted the first evangelical Mass in Wittenberg when he cast aside the clerical vestments, neglected to elevate the host and placed both the bread and wine into the laity's hands.[31]

Days later, controversy was again stirred by Karlstadt over the removal of images.[32] The iconoclastic destruction that ensued was an affront to Roman Catholics, as well as to Luther.[33] This was not the ordered Reformation Luther had envisioned.[34] Karlstadt's reading of Scripture even began to pervert Luther's doctrine of justification. The radical's emphasis on *Gelassenheit*, or yielding oneself to the commands of God, led him to stress a visible faith. This emphasis not only allowed a visible believers' church to be gathered, but also implied the embrace of believers' baptism.[35] Luther

---

[29] Huldrych Zwingli, "The Zwingli-Grebel Reply to the Bishop's Admonition," in *The Sources of Swiss Anabaptism: The Grebel Letters and Related Documents*, ed. Leland Harder (Scottdale, PA: Herald Press, 1985), 185.

[30] Calvin Augustine Pater, *Karlstadt as the Father of the Baptist Movements: The Emergence of Lay Protestantism* (Toronto: University of Toronto Press, 1984), 66–68.

[31] Amy Nelson Burnett, *Karlstadt and the Origins of the Eucharistic Controversy* (Oxford: Oxford University Press, 2011), 28.

[32] Andreas Karlstadt, "On the Removal of Images," in *The Essential Carlstadt: Fifteen Tracts by Andreas Bodenstein (Carlstadt) from Karlstadt*, ed. E.J. Furcha, Classics of the Radical Reformation (Scottdale, PA: Herald Press, 1995), 101–28.

[33] Lindberg, *European Reformations*, 101–2.

[34] Andrew Pettegree, *Brand Luther: How an Unheralded Monk Turned His Small Town into a Center for Publishing, Made Himself the Most Famous Man in Europe—and Started the Protestant Reformation* (New York: Penguin Press, 2005), 193.

[35] Andreas Karlstadt, "Tract on the Supreme Virtue of Gelassenheit," in *The Essential Carlstadt*, 37–39; and C. Arnold Snyder, *Anabaptist History and Theology: Revised Student Edition* (Kitchener, ON: Pandora Press, 1997), 51–53.

and the magistrates knew that the consequences of Karlstadt's beliefs would be devastating for Germany. Thus, Karlstadt was expelled from Saxony in September 1524, which coincided with the early waves of the German Peasants' War.

From the outset of the peasants' unrest in 1524, Luther lamented that social rebellion was being cloaked in evangelical language.[36] The peasants had misread the Scriptures just as they had misunderstood his view of priesthood.[37] Such was the case for the "Satan of Allstedt," Thomas Müntzer.[38] Luther had encountered Müntzer at Wittenberg amid the *95 Theses* controversy and even promoted him for a preaching post at Zwickau in 1520.[39] However, by 1522 Luther was aghast at Müntzer's belief that the wheat and the chaff were to be separated, most notably through adult baptism.[40] Müntzer's exegesis also left him believing that the apocalypse was nigh. Accordingly, he not only encouraged the princes of Saxony to institute a holy war as part of ushering in God's Kingdom, but also provided the theological justification for the peasants that rose up in Thuringia.[41] The subsequent bloodshed at Mühlhausen, with Müntzer's cowardice amid the peasants' defeat, were enough evidence that dissident spirits of the age must be crushed by the civil authorities.[42] Luther's harsh words of condemnation for the peasants even surprised those in his own camp.[43] However, the peasants had overstepped their bounds under the guise of the newly realized priesthood granted to them by Luther. The peasants' revolt and their poor understanding of priesthood could not be tolerated.

In Zürich, Zwingli faced internal strife in his own camp, partly as a consequence of his championing of priesthood.[44] By the end of 1523,

---

[36] Pettegree, *Brand Luther*, 236.

[37] Martin Luther, "Admonition to Peace," *LW* 46:17–43.

[38] R. Ward Holder, "Revelation and Scripture," in *T&T Clark Companion to Reformation Theology*, David M. Whitford (London: T&T Clark, 2014), 47.

[39] Tom Scott, *Thomas Müntzer: Theology and Revolution in the German Reformation* (London: Palgrave Macmillan, 1989), 9, 13.

[40] Snyder, *Anabaptist History and Theology*, 56, 58.

[41] Thomas Müntzer, "Sermon to the Princes," in *The Collected Works of Thomas Müntzer*, ed. Peter Matheson (Edinburgh: T&T Clark, 1988), 230–52; and Günther Franz, *Der Deutsche Bauernkrieg* (Darmstadt: Hermann Gentner Verlag, 1956), 248–70.

[42] Abraham Friesen, *Thomas Muentzer, A Destroyer of the Godless: The Making of a Sixteenth-Century Religious Revolutionary,* (Berkeley: University of California Press, 1990), 259–63.

[43] Martin Luther, "Against the Robbing and Murdering Hordes of Peasants," *LW* 46:49–55.

[44] John Howard Yoder, *Anabaptism and Reformation in Switzerland: An Historical and Theological Analysis of the Dialogues Between Anabaptists and Reformers* (Kitchener, ON: Pandora Press, 2004), 11–17.

many of Zwingli's students began to turn on him, especially given their dissatisfaction with the pace of reform and his deferral to the authority of the Zürich Council. Over the next year, early waves of persecution, coupled with Zwingli's refusal to heed what they believed were the clear words of Scripture, forced Grebel, Mantz, and others to make an ecclesiological pivot. These future Anabaptists began to embrace a separatist church freed from the entanglements of the civil authorities.[45] According to Zwingli, that step went too far.

Zwingli's growing outrage did not signal a detour from his commitment to lay participation in theological discourse. In fact, quite the contrary was true. After all, the Zürich Council was comprised of theologically untrained laypersons.[46] Given the growing unrest and rise of differing interpretations of Scripture in Zürich, Zwingli cleverly chose a politically expedient path by acquiescing to the civil authorities. This move allowed the Swiss Reformer to exert influence over the city council in the hope of charting a viable path toward reform without steering Zürich into social chaos.[47] Like Luther, Zwingli learned that the civil and ecclesiastical authorities were crucial to overseeing the interpretation of Scripture during the Reformation. The latter provided doctrinal oversight, while the former offered the enforcement required to avoid social disruption. Embracing a "Reformation from above" paradigm was not only preferable but required, given the fragile nature of reform.[48]

As the question of infant baptism arose in 1524, a link with Luther's trouble in Germany materialized when the Swiss radicals, now ostensibly led by Conrad Grebel, contacted both Thomas Müntzer and Andreas Karlstadt. Müntzer encouraged the Zürich radicals to break from the state church. Karlstadt's writings led the Grebel group to defer the baptism of children and to begin considering a non-resistant, sectarian ecclesiology.[49] The tensions in Zürich climaxed with the January 1525 rebaptisms that

---

[45] Stephen Brett Eccher, "A Return to Christ's Kingdom: Early Swiss Anabaptist Understanding and Temporal Application of the Kingdom of God," *Southeastern Theological Review* 5, no. 2 (2014): 207–10.

[46] Gordon, *Swiss Reformation*, 52.

[47] Arnold Snyder, "Word and Power in Reformation Zurich," *Archiv für Reformationsgeschichte (Archive for Reformation History)*81 (1990): 266–67.

[48] Berndt Hamm, "Reformation 'from below' and Reformation 'from above': On the Problem of the Historical Classifications of the Reformation," in *The Reformation of Faith in the Context of Late Medieval Theology and Piety*, ed. Robert J. Bast (Leiden: Brill, 2004), 217–53.

[49] Pater, *Father of the Baptist Movements*, 135–36, 144–46.

shook the community. Given the seditious nature of the action, the Zürich Council moved swiftly to implement civil measures to crush Anabaptism. But the coercive measures aimed at quelling religious dissent produced the opposite result. The more the Swiss Anabaptists faced persecution, the more they read the Scriptures through a lens of oppression.[50] Consequently, the radicals' new vision for the church appeared not only biblically correct, but also justified in its separatism.

Priesthood Reimagined and Restrained

Given the unrest stoked by radical voices in both Wittenberg and Zürich, a modification of the priesthood of all believers was inevitable. Luther and Zwingli worked too hard and believed there was too much at stake to allow their visions for reform to be derailed by dissident agitators. To quell rebellion in their territories, beginning in 1525, both worked to consolidate authority through the civil magistrates and the ordained pastoral office. Modifications were required, but came at a cost to their earlier understandings of the priesthood of all believers and to the very people once empowered by that doctrine.

Luther's support of the German princes took many by surprise. Why had Luther abandoned the peasants when they were so close to the social and religious changes they had collectively envisioned? In truth, the peasants had misunderstood Luther. His strong support of the German princes amid the peasant uprising did not indicate a fundamental shift in the Reformer's thinking. Rather, this continued an already existing belief that civil authorities, who were themselves part of this newly cast priesthood, were uniquely situated to peaceably oversee the German church's transformation.[51] Thus, Luther never wavered on his commitment to a magisterial form of Reformation. What did change during the mid-1520s was Luther's willingness to allow and encourage individuals to read the Bible privately, detached from the Christian community.

Luther once offered words of empowerment and encouragement to the peasants in their reading of God's Word. That all stopped once the unintended consequences of the principle of individual interpretation of Scripture materialized. This shift in Luther was subtle, but clearly directed by concerns for those who followed figures like Karlstadt and Müntzer. On

---

[50] Goertz, *Anabaptists*, 50.
[51] Hamm, "Reformation 'from below,'" 234–35.

a practical level this meant, beginning around 1525, Luther fell silent on promoting lay reading and, more specifically, private interpretation of the Bible.[52] By the time he revised his preface to the New Testament in 1546, he omitted multiple references found in its first version that exhorted the laity to read Scripture.[53] Luther was never one to be muzzled on matters of faith, so his silence was telling.

Luther knew the transformative power of the Bible, but how could the Word be stewarded to avoid the problems that arose in the early 1520s? The answer rested in the consolidation of clerical power in the German church's pastoral office. As Luther made clear in his 1530 exposition of Psalm 82, the "private preaching" and "secret ceremonies", which had fueled much of the religious dissent in the early 1520s were intolerable and must stop.[54] Pastors were to be the primary caretakers of biblical exegesis, given their unique calling. Anticipating that his earlier words on priesthood might be used against him, Luther clarified:

> It does not help their case to say that all Christians are priests. It is true that all Christians are priests, but not all are pastors. For to be a pastor one must be not only a Christian and a priest but must have an office and a field of work committed to him. This call and command make pastors and preachers.[55]

While Luther's new vision for the priesthood of all believers rejected an ontological distinction between the clergy and the laity, the Reformer was pushed by radical sectarians to offer an important qualifier to his position. The office of pastor, because of their unique calling, would be the means through which the corporate interpretation of Scripture should be administrated.[56]

Luther learned a lesson similar to that Zwingli was learning at roughly the same time: the interpretation of Scripture was best left in the hands of pastors educated in hermeneutics and the biblical languages. On those occasions when rivaling figures could not reach an accord on interpretation,

---

[52] Richard Gawthrop and Gerald Strauss, "Protestantism and Literacy in Early Modern Germany," *Past and Present* 104, no. 1 (August 1984): 34.

[53] Gawthorp and Strauss, "Protestantism and Literacy," 34.

[54] Martin Luther, "Exposition of Psalm 82:4," *LW* 13:65.

[55] Luther, 13:65.

[56] Scott Hendrix, "Luther," in *The Cambridge Companion to Reformation Theology*, ed. David Bagchi and David C. Steinmetz (Cambridge: Cambridge University Press, 2004), 46–47.

Luther, citing "the great Emperor Constantine," left the final decision in the hands of the civil magistrates.[57] Constantine's achievement of social harmony in the fourth century stood in stark contrast to the unrest of the German Peasants' War, for which Luther blamed both Karlstadt and Müntzer.[58]

While the German Peasants' War had some impact on the Reformation in Zürich, it was more tangential to Zwingli's reconsideration of the priesthood of all believers than the rise of Anabaptism. Although Zwingli showed a measure of restraint going back to the fall of 1523, once the radicals began questioning infant baptism, Zwingli was forced to act. As it was with Luther, his response required assistance from the civil authorities. On January 21, 1525, Zwingli worked with the Zürich Council to forbid the convening of the same lay study groups he had once encouraged and used for his own ends.[59] Zwingli was shrewd enough to know that laws deterring unsanctioned religious gatherings were not going to be enough. But how was he going to redirect the communal interpretation of Scripture he had once championed at the genesis of his Reformation without remaining susceptible to the rogue readings of Scripture that threatened his Reformation? Here, Zwingli employed two tactics aimed to restore order to the church, while also allowing his reforms to press forward.

First, Zwingli modified the focus of his preaching in response to the Anabaptists. In April 1525, the Swiss preacher interrupted his exposition from the New Testament and began preaching through the Psalms. The timing was hardly coincidental. A return to the Old Testament allowed Zwingli to show that Jesus was ubiquitous in Israel's history, which was a crucial idea undergirding the Reformer's developing covenantal theology.[60] A reformed, covenantal hermeneutic became his biblical means for corroborating long-standing ecclesiastical practices like infant baptism.[61] This preaching shift afforded Zwingli new and innovative ways of combatting the Anabaptists at a delicate moment for the Zürich Reformation.

---

[57] Martin Luther, "Exposition of Psalm 82:4," *LW* 13:63.

[58] Luther, 13:64.

[59] Leonhard von Muralt and Walter Schmid, eds., *Quellen zur Geschichte der Täufer in der Schweiz*, Erster Band (Zürich: Theologischer Verlag Zürich, 1952), 35–36.

[60] Edwin Künzli, "Quellenproblem und mystischer Schriftsinn in Zwinglis Genesis-und Exoduskommentar," *Zwingliana* 9 (1950): 185–207.

[61] Peter A. Lillback, *The Binding of God: Calvin's Role in the Development of Covenant Theology* (Grand Rapids: Baker Academic, 2001), 81–109.

Second, the shift in Zwingli's preaching rota was accompanied by the founding of a school designed to return the responsibility of biblical interpretation back to the hands of learned scholars qualified to handle the biblical text rightly. In June 1525, Zwingli established the Prophezei, a body of humanist elites entrusted to secure the proper interpretation and application of God's Word from the Hebrew Scriptures.[62] The fruits of the Prophezei's exegetical labors were then offered as spiritual fare intended to nourish the Zürich community through the state church pulpits.[63] The Prophezei afforded Zwingli the chance to retain his earlier commitment to a community of biblical interpreters, while at the same time narrowing the scope of that community. Additionally, given that this school was housed in both the Grossmünster and Fraumünster, Zwingli could keep close tabs on the group's conclusions.[64] This school was an ingenious way for Zwingli to implement a "Polizei und Prophezei" agenda whereby a safe path could be charted between the dangerous currents of Catholicism and Anabaptism.[65]

Beyond the practical changes employed by Luther and Zwingli, they attempted to control biblical interpretation through a hermeneutical shift in the 1520s. Here, love (*charitas*) was employed as an interpretive axiom that stressed patience when implementing reforms. Immediately after his return from hiding at the Wartburg, Luther confronted Karlstadt's iconoclastic agitation through his Invocavit sermons. A theme woven through those sermons was the idea that faith working in love required some in Wittenberg to wait on the necessary reforms until others were convinced of and ready for said changes.[66] The washing of the Word over the Wittenberger, not the coercive measures of magistrates, would help the community to slowly realize what the Scriptures prescribed.[67]

Zwingli employed a similar hermeneutical tool through his "rule of faith and love." Although first evidenced during the rise of Anabaptism in late 1524, the most lucid articulation of this rule came in Zwingli's 1527

---

[62] Bullinger, *Reformationsgeschichte*, Band I, 289–90.
[63] Bruce Gordon, "Huldrych Zwingli," *Expository Times* 126, no. 4 (2015): 163.
[64] G. R. Potter, *Zwingli* (Cambridge: Cambridge University Press, 1976), 221.
[65] Werner O. Packull, *Hutterite Beginnings: Communitarian Experiments during the Reformation* (Baltimore: Johns Hopkins University Press, 1999), 23.
[66] Lindberg, *European Reformations*, 103.
[67] Brecht, *Shaping and Defining*, 60.

anti-Anabaptist work, *Elenchus*.[68] Zwingli differentiated between those things that must be abolished immediately and those "things at which fraternal love may wink."[69] Of course, any immediate and substantive changes had to be done under the auspices of the civil authorities.[70] Although Zürich was not Wittenberg and Zwingli's reforms were quite different than Luther's, there was a shared affinity in the formulation of a new understanding of the priesthood of believers that was freeing to the people, yet provided the necessary constraints required to maintain societal peace.

In the end, that peace trumped even the closest of friendships. So, despite his affection for his one-time students, Zwingli, much like Luther, appealed to the civil authorities to address and enforce the boundaries of what was acceptable for the Zürich community. Wearied by the persistence of Anabaptism, Zwingli worked closely with the city council in 1526 to make rebaptism a crime punishable by death, based on a historic link to the Donatist heresy.[71] A personal test of religious toleration versus magisterial Reformation came for Zwingli in January 1527. As Felix Mantz slipped into the chilly waters of the Limmat River, Zwingli's decision, much like his resolve, was clear. The priesthood of believers had its limitations and Mantz had stepped beyond them.

Conclusion

The early 1520s were years of promise and optimism for the Reformers, who were beginning to reap a harvest from their bold, gospel-centered labors. Those exciting years also offered great advancement for the laity, as men and women otherwise marginalized were given a voice in the shifting religious ethos of early modern Europe. But the unique window of speech afforded to the commoners was not without consequence. As evidenced by the German Peasants' War and the rise of Anabaptism, the path forward was not always clear. For all the praise that Luther and Zwingli are given for their theological acumen, their developing views on priesthood are a

---

[68] Huldrych Zwingli, "Zwingli to Lambert and other Brethren in Strasburg, Zurich," in *The Sources of Swiss Anabaptism: The Grebel Letters and Related Documents*, ed. Leland Harder (Scottdale, PA: Herald Press, 1985), 304.

[69] Huldrych Zwingli, "Refutation of the Tricks of the Baptists," in *Ulrich Zwingli (1484–1531): Selected Works*, ed. Samuel Macauley Jackson (Philadelphia: University of Pennsylvania Press, 1972), 142.

[70] Zwingli, 182.

[71] Carlos M. Eire, *Reformations: The Early Modern World, 1450–1650* (New Haven, CT: Yale University Press, 2016), 248.

reminder that their Reformations were fluid and always in flux. They were not systematic, but situational theologians practicing theology with an eye toward the particular concerns of their unique worlds. Often this meant not seeing the logical outcomes of their views. Thus, modifications to their convictions should be expected. This is precisely what happened as Luther and Zwingli reimagined and later restrained priesthood.

As Christians today reflect on the Reformation there is much to be celebrated. However, just as the Reformers helped to reorient the church's doctrine according to Scripture, they also left a complex legacy for modern believers. Contemporary Christians are left in the tenuous position of enjoying the fruit of the Reformers' promotion of *sola Scriptura* and their new vision for the priesthood of all believers, while at the same time living with the reality that those very things led to the fracturing of Protestantism into a myriad of denominations. Not all Christians read the Bible the same way and Protestants no longer cede to the pope to adjudicate such differences. As the drama of the 1520s reminds, this leaves the modern church celebrating that which separates us. It also leaves Christians today returning to the Bible and the timeless endeavor of trying to properly hear and heed God's divine voice. From Luther and Zwingli, we can learn to attend to those current theological decisions whose outcomes we ourselves may not yet be able to see.

Bibliography

Althaus, Paul. *The Theology of Martin Luther*. Philadelphia: Fortress, 1970.

Brecht, Martin. *Martin Luther: Shaping and Defining the Reformation, 1521–1532*. Translated by James L. Schaaf. Minneapolis: Fortress, 1990.

Bullinger, Heinrich. *Reformationsgeschichte*. Band II. Edited by Johann Jakob Hottinger and Hans Heinrich Vögeli. Frauenfeld: Beyel, 1838.

Burnett, Amy Nelson. *Karlstadt and the Origins of the Eucharistic Controversy*. Oxford: Oxford University Press, 2011.

Eccher, Stephen Brett. "A Return to Christ's Kingdom: Early Swiss Anabaptist Understanding and Temporal Application of the Kingdom of God." *Southeastern Theological Review* 5, no. 2 (2014): 203–32.

Eire, Carlos M. *Reformations: The Early Modern World, 1450–1650*. New Haven, CT: Yale University Press, 2016.

Franz, Günther. *Der Deutsche Bauernkrieg*. Darmstadt: Hermann Gentner Verlag, 1956.

Friesen, Abraham. *Thomas Muentzer, A Destroyer of the Godless: The Making of a Sixteenth-Century Religious Revolutionary.* Berkeley: University of California Press, 1990.

Gawthrop, Richard, and Gerald Strauss. "Protestantism and Literacy in Early Modern Germany." *Past & Present* 104, no. 1 (1984): 31–55.

George, Timothy. *Theology of the Reformers.* Rev. ed. Nashville: B&H, 2013.

Goertz, Hans-Jürgen. *The Anabaptists.* London: Routledge, 1996.

Gordon, Bruce. "Huldrych Zwingli." *Expository Times* 126, no. 4 (2015): 157–68.

_____. *The Swiss Reformation.* Manchester: Manchester University Press, 2002.

Hamm, Berndt. "Reformation 'from below' and Reformation 'from above': On the Problem of the Historical Classifications of the Reformation." In *The Reformation of Faith in the Context of Late Medieval Theology and Piety,* ed. Robert J. Bast. Leiden: Brill, 2004.

Head, Randolph C. "The Swiss Reformations: Movements, Settlements, and Reimagination, 1520–1720." In *The Oxford Handbook of the Protestant Reformations,* ed. Ulinka Rublack. Oxford: Oxford University Press, 2016.

Hendrix, Scott. "Luther." In *The Cambridge Companion to Reformation Theology,* ed. David Bagchi and David C. Steinmetz. Cambridge: Cambridge University Press, 2004.

Hillerbrand, Hans J. *The Division of Christendom: Christianity in the Sixteenth Century.* Louisville: Westminster John Knox, 2007.

Holder, R. Ward. "Revelation and Scripture." In *T&T Clark Companion to Reformation Theology,* ed. David M. Whitford. London: T&T Clark, 2014.

Karlstadt, Andreas. "On the Removal of Images." In *The Essential Carlstadt: Fifteen Tracts by Andreas Bodenstein (Carlstadt) from Karlstadt,* ed. E. J. Furcha. Scottdale, PA: Herald Press, 1995.

_____. "Tract on the Supreme Virtue of Gelassenheit." In *The Essential Carlstadt: Fifteen Tracts by Andreas* Bodenstein (Carlstadt) from Karlstadt, ed. E.J. Furcha. Scottdale: Herald Press, 1995.

Köhler, Hans-Joachim. "Erste Schritte zu einem Meinungsprofil der frühen Reformationszeit." In *Martin Luther: Probleme seiner Zeit,* ed. Volker Press and Dieter Stievermann. Stuttgart: Klett-Cotta, 1986.

Künzli, Edwin. "Quellenproblem und mystischer Schriftsinn in Zwinglis Genesis-und Exoduskommentar." *Zwingliana* 9 (1950): 185–207.

Krajewski, Ekklehard. *Leben und Sterben des Zürcher Täuferführers Felix Manz: Über die Anfänge der Täuferbewegung und des Freikirchentums in der Reformationszeit.* Kassel: J. G. Oncken, 1957.

Lillback, Peter A. *The Binding of God: Calvin's Role in the Development of Covenant Theology.* Grand Rapids: Baker Academic, 2001.

Lindberg, Carter. *The European Reformations.* 2nd ed. Oxford: Wiley-Blackwell, 2010.

Luther, Martin. "Admonition to Peace." In vol. 46 of *Luther's Works,* ed. Helmut T. Lehman. Philadelphia: Fortress Press, 1967.

————. "Against the Robbing and Murdering Hordes of Peasants." In vol. 46 of *Luther's Works,* ed. Helmut T. Lehman. Philadelphia: Fortress, 1967.

————. "To the Christian Nobility of the German Nation Concerning the Reform of the Christian Estate." In vol. 44 of *Luther's Works,* ed. Helmut T. Lehman. Philadelphia: Fortress, 1966.

————. "Explanations of the Ninety-Five Theses." In vol. 31 of *Luther's Works,* ed. Helmut T. Lehman. Philadelphia: Fortress, 1957.

————. "Exposition of Psalm 82:4." In vol. 13 of *Luther's Works,* ed. Jaroslav Pelikan. Philadelphia: Fortress, 1956.

————. "The Misuse of the Mass." In vol. 36 of *Luther's Works,* ed. Helmut T. Lehman. Philadelphia: Fortress, 1959.

————. "Prefaces to the Old Testament." In vol. 35 of *Luther's Works,* ed. Helmut T. Lehman. Philadelphia: Fortress, 1960.

————. "Prefaces to the New Testament." In vol. 35 of *Luther's Works,* ed. Helmut T. Lehman. Philadelphia: Fortress, 1960.

McGrath, Alister E. *Reformation Thought: An Introduction.* 4th ed. Oxford: Wiley-Blackwell, 2012.

Müntzer, Thomas. "Sermon to the Princes." In *The Collected Works of Thomas Müntzer,* ed. Peter Matheson. Edinburgh: T&T Clark, 1988.

Opitz, Peter. "The Authority of Scripture in the Early Zurich Reformation (1522–1540)." *Journal of Reformed Theology* 5, no. 3 (2011): 296–309.

Packull, Werner O. *Hutterite Beginnings: Communitarian Experiments during the Reformation.* Baltimore: Johns Hopkins University Press, 1999.

Pater, Calvin Augustine. *Karlstadt as the Father of the Baptist Movements: The Emergence of Lay Protestantism.* Toronto: University of Toronto Press, 1984.

Pettegree, Andrew. *Brand Luther: How an Unheralded Monk Turned His Small Town into a Center for Publishing, Made Himself the Most Famous Man in Europe—and Started the Protestant Reformation.* New York: Penguin Press, 2005.

Potter, G. R. *Zwingli.* Cambridge: Cambridge University Press, 1976.

Scott, Tom. *Thomas Müntzer: Theology and Revolution in the German Reformation.* London: Palgrave Macmillan, 1989.

Scribner, R. W., and C. Scott Dixon. *The German Reformation.* 2nd ed. New York: Palgrave Macmillan, 2003.

Snavely, I. L., Jr., "Ulrich Zwingli (1484–1531)." In *Historical Handbook of Major Biblical Interpreters,* ed. Donald K. McKim. Downers Grove, IL: InterVarsity Press, 1998.

Snyder, C. Arnold. *Anabaptist History and Theology: Revised Student Edition.* Kitchener, ON: Pandora Press, 1997.

_____. "Word and Power in Reformation Zurich." *Archiv für Reformationsgeschichte (Archive for Reformation History)* 81 (1990): 263–85.

Stephens, W. P. *The Theology of Huldrych Zwingli.* Oxford: Clarendon Press, 1986.

Strübind, Andrea. *Eifriger als Zwingli: Die frühe Täuferbewegung in der Schweiz.* Berlin: Duncker & Humblot, 2003.

Tucker, Ruth A. *Parade of Faith: A Biographical History of the Christian Church.* Grand Rapids: Zondervan, 2015.

Von Muralt, Leonhard, and Walter Schmid. *Quellen zur Geschichte der Täufer in der Schweiz.* Erster Band. Zürich: Theologischer Verlag Zürich, 1952.

Walton, Robert C. *Zwingli's Theocracy.* Toronto: University of Toronto Press, 1967.

Wengert, Timothy J. *Reading the Bible with Martin Luther: An Introductory Guide.* Grand Rapids: Baker Academic, 2013.

Yoder, John Howard. *Anabaptism and Reformation in Switzerland: An Historical and Theological Analysis of the Dialogues between Anabaptists and Reformers.* Kitchener, ON: Pandora Press, 2004.

Zitzlsperger, Ulrike. "Mother, Martyr and Mary Magdalene: German Female Pamphleteers and Their Self-Image." *History* 88, no. 3 (2003): 379–92.

Zwingli, Huldrych. "Of the Clarity and Certainty of the Word of God." In *Zwingli and Bullinger,* ed. G.W. Bromiley. Philadelphia: Westminster, 1953.

_____. "Refutation of the Tricks of the Baptists." In *Ulrich Zwingli (1484–1531): Selected Works*, ed. Samuel Macauley Jackson. Philadelphia: University of Pennsylvania Press, 1972.

_____. "The Zwingli-Grebel Reply to the Bishop's Admonition." In *The Sources of Swiss Anabaptism: The Grebel Letters and Related Documents*, ed. Leland Harder. Scottdale, PA: Herald Press, 1985.

_____. "Zwingli to Lambert and other Brethren in Strasburg, Zurich." In *The Sources of Swiss Anabaptism: The Grebel Letters and Related Documents*, ed. Leland Harder. Scottdale, PA: Herald Press, 1985.

John Calvin and Penal Substitutionary Atonement

PAUL OWEN

In his book, *Calvin and the Atonement*, Robert Peterson states, "Calvin is not the first person to formulate the legal/penal view of the atonement. . . . But it belongs to Calvin to have given to the penal substitutionary doctrine of the atonement a compelling statement."[1] Richard Phillips describes "the penal, substitutionary doctrine" of the atonement as:

> Jesus died as the substitute for sinners before God—suffering vicariously in our place and as our representative—and . . . he died to suffer the wrath of God that we deserve and to pay the penalty for our sins under the divine justice of God's law.[2]

In a modern defense of penal substitution we find this definition slightly augmented with the claim that Christ, "took our sin and guilt upon himself and died a cursed death, suffering in his human nature the infinite torment of the wrath and fury of his Father."[3] The same volume clarifies that to maintain a consistent form of penal substitutionary atonement, it is necessary, not only to assert that the Son of God vicariously bore *the consequences* of human guilt on the cross, but that he did so, as one to

---

[1] Robert A. Peterson, *Calvin and the Atonement*, rev. ed. (Fearn, Ross-shire, Scotland: Mentor, an imprint of Christian Focus Publications, 2009), 89.

[2] Richard D. Phillips, "Penal Substitutionary Atonement and Its 'Non-Violent' Critics," in *Precious Blood: The Atoning Work of Christ*, ed. Richard D. Phillips (Wheaton: Crossway, 2009), 207–08.

[3] Steve Jeffrey, Michael Ovey, and Andrew Sach, *Pierced for Our Transgressions: Rediscovering the Glory of Penal Substitution* (Wheaton, IL: Crossway, 2007), 104.

whom *the guilt itself* was actually imputed, for according to the authors, "if Christ was not guilty before God even by imputation, then God *unjustly* punished an innocent man."[4] The logic of this doctrine is widely conceded among modern advocates of penal substitutionary atonement. The purpose of this chapter is to explore whether or not John Calvin understood penal substitutionary atonement with the same modern nuances theologians readily accept today: the notion that the guilt for our sin was imputed to Christ, and that he, therefore, became on the cross the just object of God's wrath, which undergirds the notion that he was punished by the Father in our place. Stated in this manner, I am confident that Calvin did not hold to such an atonement theory, and would have found it objectionable. In fact, I don't think this theory of the atonement enters the mainstream of Reformed theological discourse until the seventeenth century, as a developed response to Socinianism.[5]

What exactly am I denying in this essay? 1) I am denying that Calvin believed the actual guilt of our sin was transferred to Christ, making Christ truly guilty in the sight of God, and so for a limited time the object of God's personal wrath; 2) I am denying that Calvin believed the cross involved a transaction in which the divine wrath was actually poured out on the Son in our place and so propitiated the divine wrath; 3) I am denying that Calvin taught that the Father punished his own Son in our place on the cross, as the necessary means of propitiating God's wrath. My goal here is to examine four places where, had Calvin held to such notions, we might expect to find them among his commentaries: 2 Corinthians 5:21; Jesus's cry of abandonment from the cross; Romans 3:25–26; and Galatians 3:13.

2 Corinthians 5:21: "He made the one who did not know sin to be sin for us, so that in him we might become the righteousness of God" (CSB). At first glance, Calvin could appear to teach the penal substitutionary atonement theory. He says of the phrase "to be sin for us": "What, on the other hand, is denoted by *sin*? It is the guilt on account of which we are arraigned at the bar of God. As, however, the curse of the individual was of old cast upon the victim, so Christ's condemnation was our absolution."

---

[4] Jeffrey, Ovey, and Sach, 179.

[5] Cf. Paul Helm, *Calvin at the Centre* (Oxford: Oxford University Press, 2010), 182–95; and Carl R. Trueman, "Post-Reformation Developments in the Doctrine of the Atonement," in Phillips, *Precious Blood*, 189–203.

And further down he adds: "How are we righteous in the sight of God? It is assuredly in the same respect in which Christ was a sinner. For he assumed in a manner our place, that he might be a criminal in our room, and might be dealt with as a sinner, not for his own offences, but for those of others, inasmuch as he was pure and exempt from every fault, and might endure the punishment that was due to us—not to himself."[6] However, these comments are equally open to two readings.

Calvin could be saying that Christ assumed our "guilt" only in the sense that he voluntarily agreed to take our place and suffer the consequences for sin that we actually deserved; in which case, his "punishment" would then entail the suffering that Jesus endured as a consequence of that substitution for sinners. None of this requires "guilt" to effect the actual transference of the Father's objective hostility toward sinners to Christ on the cross, nor the subsequent definition of "punishment" as the Father's direction of his own punitive wrath toward the Son. The "punishment" of the Son in our place does not automatically include the "punishing" of the Son. Calvin does not speak of Christ becoming guilty (by imputation or otherwise), but only of Christ suffering in our place *as though* ("in a manner") he were guilty of our offenses. It is one thing to bear the burden of another's guilt, quite another to actually bear the guilt itself.[7]

Matthew 27:46 (Psalm 22:1): Lest one think we are splitting hairs, it may be instructive to examine Calvin's comments on Jesus's words on the cross (quoting Psalm 22:1) in Matthew 27:46 and parallels: "My God, my God, why have you abandoned me?" Does Calvin believe that God actually

---

[6] John Calvin, *Commentary on the Epistles of Paul to the Corinthians: Volume Second*, trans. John Pringle (Calvin Translation Society; repr. Grand Rapids: Baker, 2005), 242.

[7] I do not believe this is an anachronistic distinction, especially in light of Calvin's comments on Jesus's cry of abandonment from the cross (see below). There he says that by "faith" Jesus "beheld the presence of God, of whose absence he complains," which clearly means that God *did not* in fact condemn or abandon the Son on the cross, but only allowed him to have the "perception" or "natural feeling" of divine "estrangement." Calvin says that even in his despair Jesus continued "to be assured by faith that God was reconciled to him." While Jesus suffered the consequences and felt the agony of our divine abandonment, he was not, in fact, himself abandoned. That is exactly the distinction for which I'm arguing. To this we could add the comments of Calvin on Galatians 3:13 (also below): "For how could he reconcile the Father to us, if he had incurred his hatred and displeasure?" Nobody in Calvin's day (or at any other stage of church history) suggested that Jesus had actually committed any sins, so that is not what Calvin is denying—to do so would be to slay a nonexistent dragon. Rather, Calvin is taking pains to deny that the cross involved a transaction of such a nature that the Son actually became the substituted object of the divine hatred, which is something one might be tempted to think in light of the depth of Jesus's suffering and sacrifice in the place of guilty sinners. My argument is that Calvin was trying to make it clear that he was not intending to say what some advocates of penal substitutionary atonement now insist upon as essential to the doctrine of the atonement.

turned away from and became hateful toward his Son on the cross? Only if Calvin's view of the cross entails such elements does he rightfully belong among the adherents of penal substitutionary atonement. But he teaches nothing of the sort. What Calvin does say about this scene is: 1) The cross was a display of the righteous judgment of God toward sinners, which Jesus endured on their behalf. Calvin sees this in the eclipse of the sun at the sixth hour, for, "it was an astonishing display of the wrath of God that he did not spare even his only begotten Son, and was not appeased in any other way than by that price of expiation."[8] But it is one thing for the Son to willingly undergo the judgment of God in the place of guilty and condemned sinners, it is another thing to say that the Son was actually guilty and condemned by God on the cross, something which Calvin denies. 2) As for the cry of despair itself, Calvin is at pains to deny what advocates of penal substitutionary atonement affirm, that the Father actually forsook and became wrathful toward his Son. Calvin says,

> Though the perception of the flesh would have led him to dread destruction, still in his heart faith remained firm, by which he beheld the presence of God, of whose absence he complains. . . . Therefore, the perception of God's estrangement from him, which Christ had, as suggested by natural feeling, did not hinder him from continuing to be assured by faith that God was reconciled to him.[9]

In other words, Jesus's cry of abandonment was simply an expression of his weakness, uttered in the depths of despair and human misery, which had to be overcome by the confession of faith.[10] This is a far cry from the interpretation of Jesus's words one will hear in expositions of penal substitutionary atonement. For example, advocates of penal substitution have

---

[8] John Calvin, *Commentary on a Harmony of the Evangelists, Matthew, Mark, and Luke,* vol. 3, trans. William Pringle (Calvin Translation Society; repr. Grand Rapids: Baker, 2005), 316–17.

[9] Calvin, 318–19.

[10] Some take Jesus's cry of abandonment to mean that the forsaken Son continued to trust God in spite of his abandonment. It is certainly possible to read the scene that way. But that is not the burden of my argument; that burden being to show *what Calvin thought* about the topic and how it differs from some advocates of penal substitutionary atonement. Calvin could not be more clear in his discussion that he views the abandonment of the Son as only one of subjective perception, not an *actual* abandonment. Calvin affirms that Jesus continued to have with him the "presence of God," and that by faith he continued to be assured that "God was reconciled to him" while dying on the cross. Calvin says God was always present with the Son, always reconciled to the Son, and never inimical or angry toward him, even during the darkest moments of Christ's suffering. In this I am *in complete agreement* with Anthony Lane (see n. 15), one of the foremost Calvin scholars of our day.

said, "The juxtaposition of the darkness with Jesus's cry of abandonment suggests that . . . God's judgment was falling on his Son as he died as a substitute, bearing the sins of his people."[11] In a footnote on the same page the authors make even more explicit their disagreement with any interpretations of this scene that would deny Jesus's citation from the psalm was, "intended to describe the experience of God-forsakenness."[12]

And yet Calvin explicitly does deny this. He says that Jesus was only speaking out of his frail human perspective, and that in fact God did not forsake or abandon him on the cross. Calvin speaks of the divine abandonment as "the perception of the flesh," and "the perception of God's estrangement" as only what was "suggested by natural feeling." At the same time he insists that Christ's faith still "beheld the presence of God" and that he was still assured "that God was reconciled to him." Calvin goes on to read Jesus's adaptation of the words of the psalmist in the following manner: "[Jesus] begins by saying that he betakes himself to God as *his God*, and thus by the shield of faith he courageously expels that appearance of *forsaking* which presented itself on the other side. In short, during this fearful torture his faith remained uninjured, so that, while he complained of being forsaken, he still relied on the aid of God as at hand."[13] Calvin insists that Jesus only had a subjective perception of being forsaken during his moment of weakness, though he never was objectively abandoned by his Father on the cross. The logic of the modern penal substitutionary atonement depends precisely on the notion that the Father did become wrathful toward his Son on the cross and in an objective relational sense "turned away" from him, and that it was this objective relational break between Father and Son that caused Jesus to cry out in despair with the words of the psalm. That is the opposite of Calvin's reading, which is also clarified in the *Institutes*. Commenting on this same scene at the cross, Calvin writes, "Yet we do not suggest that God was ever inimical or angry toward him. How could he be angry toward his beloved Son, 'in whom his heart reposed'? How could Christ by his intercession appease the Father toward others, if he were himself hateful to God?"[14]

---

[11] Jeffrey, Ovey, and Sach, *Pierced for Our Transgressions*, 72.
[12] Jeffrey, Ovey, and Sach, 72n93.
[13] Calvin, *Harmony of the Evangelists*, 319.
[14] John T. McNeill, ed., *Calvin: Institutes of the Christian Religion in Two Volumes* (Philadelphia: Westminster, 1960), 2.16.11. All quotes from the *Institutes* in this chapter are from this edition.

Calvin specifically denies that when Jesus cried out with the words of Psalm 22, we should take this as though somehow the Son had even for a few moments become hateful to God, or that God had become angry toward him.[15] Clearly Calvin did not believe what is required as the premise for such claims, that the actual guilt of sinners was imputed to Christ so that he could become something he was not prior to that point—namely the party whom God held personally responsible for the sins of all those for whom he was the substitute. There is a real difference between saying that on the cross Christ as our substitute endured the penalty we deserved to pay for our sins, and saying that on the cross Christ became the guilty substitute on whom God's personal hostility toward sinners was exhausted. The former is the view of Calvin; the latter is the view of the modern penal substitutionary atonement theory.[16]

Romans 3:25 is a classic penal substitutionary atonement text: "God presented him as an atoning sacrifice in his blood, received through faith, to demonstrate his righteousness, because in his restraint God passed over the sins previously committed." Penal substitutionary atonement advocates see here the sins of the world, which went unpunished in the era before the cross, called into question God's justice, until their penalty was executed on Christ on the cross (thus demonstrating God's justice to the world). But is this how Calvin reads the passage?

Calvin does not see "blood" sacrifice as the satisfaction of divine justice through punishment, but as the means of expiation (with propitiation as the effect of our cleansing). He says, "What Paul especially meant here is no doubt evident from his words; and it was this,—that God, without having regard to Christ, is always angry with us,—and that we are reconciled to him when we are accepted through his righteousness. . . . And he

---

[15] Cf. Anthony Lane on *Institutes*, 2.16.10–11: "Christ felt himself to be forsaken by God and experienced the effects of God's wrath, but the Father was not actually hostile toward him (11). Calvin holds the nuanced position that Christ's death appeased God's wrath (10), but that the Father was never actually angry toward his beloved Son (11)." Anthony N. S. Lane, *A Reader's Guide to Calvin's Institutes* (Grand Rapids: Baker, 2009), 93. And on 2.16.6: "*Neither here nor anywhere else does Calvin speak of God punishing Christ.* He holds to Christ's role in bearing the consequences of our sin without imperiling the unity of the Father and the Son" (p. 93, italics added).

[16] Cf. Henri Blocher, "The Atonement in John Calvin's Theology," in *The Glory of the Atonement*, ed. Charles E. Hill and Frank A. James III (Downers Grove, IL: IVP, 2004), 283–88. For more on this line of reasoning, cf. Anthony Lane on Calvin's position, which avoids saying that God literally "punished" Christ in our place, and Paul Helm on the important contrast between John Calvin's position on the atonement and the later view of John Owen with respect to how Christ's death relates to God's justice (both cited in this discussion).

mentioned 'blood,' because by it we are cleansed."[17] Calvin does not say, "because by it God's wrath was satisfied."

It is important to note how Calvin handles the use of the word "restraint" in Rom 3:25. First look at J. I. Packer's exposition: "This 'passing over' of sins in 'forbearance' was not, indeed, forgiveness, but postponement of judgment only; nevertheless, it prompts a question. . . . If he allows sinners to continue unpunished, does he not himself come short of perfection in his office as Judge of the world?"[18] Packer sees the question here as the execution of justice upon sinners, which is then answered by the punitive suffering of Christ.

Now hear Calvin, who thinks Paul is talking about the actual forgiveness of sins which sinners enjoyed even in the old dispensation: "He adds, that this remission was through forbearance; and this I take simply to mean gentleness, which has stayed the judgment of God, and suffered it not to burst forth to our ruin, until he had at length received us into favour."[19] What Packer sees as a postponing of judgment until it should be meted out on Christ in accordance with the demands of strict justice, Calvin sees as the patient working out of redemptive history until the types and shadows of the old economy found their fulfillment in the grace of the cross. Calvin says of the relationship between the "atoning sacrifice" and the passing over of the "sins previously committed" in verse 25: "Though this passage is variously explained, yet it seems to me probable that Paul had regard to the legal expiations, which were indeed evidences of a future satisfaction, but could by no means pacify God."[20] So whereas Calvin links propitiation to the ritualistic forgiveness available under the Mosaic types, Packer links propitiation to the suspended punishment of the sins of the world. And whereas Calvin sees in the "forbearance" of God a rationale for the divine forgiveness of Old Testament saints before Christ came, Packer sees only the enjoyment of common grace by sinners: "The point here is that though human beings were, and had been from time immemorial, every bit as bad as Romans 1 depicts them, God had not at

---

[17] John Calvin, *Commentaries on the Epistle of Paul the Apostle to the Romans*, trans. John Owen (Calvin Translation Society; repr. Grand Rapids: Baker, 2005), 143.

[18] J. I. Packer "The Heart of the Gospel," in J. I. Packer and Mark Dever, *In My Place Condemned He Stood: Celebrating the Glory of the Atonement* (Wheaton: Crossway, 2008), 39 [29–52].

[19] Calvin, *Epistle to the Romans*, 145.

[20] Calvin, 144.

any time since the flood made it his principle to deal publicly with the race as it deserved."[21]

The reason Packer can only see common grace in the *forbearance*, and not remission of sins, is because he sees propitiation in this passage as the display of the justice of God's holy wrath against sin, whereas Calvin sees propitiation as the fulfillment of the types of God's grace hinted at in the Levitical sacrifices. Calvin sees in this verse the enactment of the saving grace of God through expiatory sacrifice—with the propitiation of divine wrath being the effect of faith, rather than the effect of a punitive display of cosmic judgment. To quote again from Calvin: "God is propitious to us as soon as we have our trust resting on the blood of Christ; for by faith we come to the possession of this benefit."[22] But what of verse 26? "God presented him to demonstrate his righteousness at the present time, so that he would be righteous and declare righteous the one who has faith in Jesus." Packer explains the meaning as follows: "Our sins have been punished; the wheel of retribution *has* turned; judgment *has* been inflicted for our ungodliness—but on Jesus, the lamb of God, standing in our place. In this way, God is just—and the justifier of those who put faith in Jesus."[23] Calvin has no consciousness of such themes in the passage, and posits God's righteousness in terms of the goodness of God's character, which is then communicated to believers in justification: "for God by no means keeps his riches laid up in himself, but pours them forth upon men. Then the righteousness of God shines in us, whenever he justifies us by faith in Christ."[24] Whereas Calvin sees a profound continuity between God's righteousness in the cross and in the justification of sinners, Packer sees mostly a contrast.

Galatians 3:13 is the final text for comparison in this brief analysis: "Christ redeemed us from the curse of the law by becoming a curse for us, because it is written, **Cursed is everyone who is hung on a tree.**" Here there is no getting around the fact that on the cross, Jesus suffers the penalty that God justly inflicts on sinners, and of course Calvin's commentary reflects that. But did our Lord suffer that penalty as an innocent substitute, whose obedient sacrifice on behalf of the guilty was sanctified by the

---

[21] Packer, "Heart of the Gospel," 39.
[22] Calvin, *Epistle to the Romans*, 143.
[23] Packer, "The Heart of the Gospel," 40.
[24] Calvin, *Epistle to the Romans*, 146.

infinite dignity of his person as the God-man, thus making satisfaction for the sins of the world—a classical satisfaction model? Or did Christ's sacrifice include the actual assumption of human guilt, so that his substitution entailed not simply the voluntary payment of the penalty for our sin on the part of the Son, but the necessary execution of the penalty, and complete exhaustion of the wrathful justice of God the Father on the Son in the place of every sin of every sinner for whom the Son of God suffered—more or less the view we find later in the Puritan John Owen?[25]

In commenting on this text, Calvin is careful to qualify in what sense Christ was and was not cursed by the Father. What is important in Calvin's atonement model (in the mold of Anselm) is what Christ did on the cross to compensate for the offense of sinners, and that involved his voluntary assumption of their penalty in order to pay what he did not owe. In this sense, the cross was merely a culmination of "the whole course of his obedience."[26] But for the later penal substitutionary atonement model, what is important is what the cross provides God the Father the opportunity to do, which is to exact from the innocent substitute the just penalty incurred by each and every sin committed by those for whom Christ offered the sacrifice. The penal substitutionary atonement model requires the Father to impose on the Son the same penalty which would have been executed on the guilty sinners for whom Christ was the surety.

John Owen, in the preface to his "Dissertation on Divine Justice," lists Calvin as being among those who differ with him on the question of God's justice and how it relates to the necessity of punishment.[27] As Paul Helm has noted, for Owen, "the atonement is primarily an act of divine justice making mercy possible—whereas with Calvin the atonement is an act of divine mercy that is consistent with justice."[28] Those who, like Calvin, regard the atonement as an Anselmian payment of satisfaction, see Christ offering to God the merits of his innocent suffering as the substitute for the punishment of sinners; whereas those who, like Owen, see the atonement

---

[25] According to Packer: "Anselm's *Cur Deus Homo?* which largely determined the medieval development, saw Christ's *satisfactio* for our sins as the offering of compensation or damages for dishonor done, but the Reformers saw it as the undergoing of vicarious punishment (*poena*) to meet the claims on us of God's holy law and wrath (i.e., his punitive justice)." J. I. Packer, "What Did the Cross Achieve? The Logic of Penal Substitution," in Packer and Dever, *In My Place Condemned*, 54.

[26] Calvin, *Institutes*, 2.16.5.

[27] John Owen, preface to *A Dissertation on Divine Justice*, in *The Works of John Owen: Volume X* (Johnstone & Hunter; repr. Edinburgh: Banner of Truth, 1967), 488.

[28] Helm, *Calvin at the Centre*, 194.

as the necessary punitive exaction of the same penalty deserved by sinners, are driven to the conclusion of having Christ become the actual recipient of the divine hostility itself. This is where Owen parts company with Calvin, and this is where the modern penal substitutionary atonement theory begins. We see this clearly in Owen's dispute with Twisse in his *Dissertation*. Twisse agrees that God punished the Son, in the sense that the Son suffered the punishment sinners deserved to receive, but he refuses to say that this substitution entailed becoming the recipient of the divine hatred itself. "God forbid that we should say he ever hated" his own "most holy Son," Twisse gasps. Owen, however, refuses to draw back from this, and draws a distinction between the Son in himself and the Son in union with the sinful elect: "though God hated not his Son when he punished him, personally considered, he however hated the sins on account of which he punished him (and even himself, substitutively considered, with respect to the effect of sin), no less than if they had been laid to any sinner."[29] Owen is very clear: God hated his own Son on the cross because of the sins which were there imputed to him.

In Calvin's comments on Galatians 3:13, it is clear that he would have agreed with Twisse, and not with Owen. Calvin asks, "For how could he reconcile the Father to us, if he had incurred his hatred and displeasure?"[30] For Calvin, Christ on the cross endured objectively the divine wrath against sin, but subjectively as an innocent sacrifice who was entirely pleasing to the Father at every moment of his suffering. For Owen, Christ *necessarily* became hateful to the Father on the cross, because the divine "displeasure" itself was part of the penalty God had to mete out on the Son to satisfy the demands of his own strict justice. This explains why the Savoy Declaration (of which Owen was one of the chief architects) makes subtle changes to the Westminster Confession in the fourth article pertaining to *Christ the Mediator*. Whereas the Westminster Confession is content to say that in his mediatory office, Christ endured "most grievous torments immediately in his soul, and most painful sufferings in his body," the Savoy Declaration adds, "and underwent the punishment due to us, which we should have borne and suffered, being made sin and a curse for us, enduring most grievous torments immediately *from God* in his soul,

---

[29] Owen, *Dissertation on Divine Justice*, 553.
[30] John Calvin, *Commentaries on the Epistles of Paul to the Galatians and Ephesians* (Calvin Translation Society; repr. Grand Rapids: Baker, 2005), 92.

and most painful sufferings in his body" (italics added).[31] Here, and not in the theology of John Calvin, lies the Reformed origin of the modern penal substitutionary atonement theory.

Conclusion

The purpose of this chapter has been to explore the topic of the atonement in one of the Protestant tradition's most revered theological luminaries: the Great Reformer of Geneva, John Calvin. Although Calvin is sometimes cited by advocates of penal substitution as a voice in support of their theory, there is reason to call that judgment into question. On the point where penal substitution is most distinctive and theologically groundbreaking (the objective imputation of human guilt to Christ on the cross), Calvin seems to demur. That does not automatically make the theory wrong. Sometimes over the course of centuries new questions are asked of the biblical materials that bring clarity of articulation with respect to particular theological points, and this could well be the case here. Perhaps new ways of thinking about justification as involving the imputation of righteousness to the guilty sinner led to more precise formulations regarding the nature of the satisfaction made for us on the cross. Even if Calvin did not express himself with the same clarity on these questions that modern Protestants would wish, it could still be argued that penal substitutionary atonement is the consistent expression of the basic theological trajectory of the Reformation. Perhaps Owen was a better interpreter of Calvin's thought than was Calvin himself!

I continue to have reservations about the way penal substitution has come to be expressed in modern evangelical theology, and believe we might want to allow voices like Calvin's to enter the conversation and moderate our language. It seems to me there is an equivocation taking place between guilt and the consequences of guilt. There can be no doubt that Jesus suffered on the cross *as though* he were actually guilty of sin, but this seems to dissolve too quickly into the actual assumption of the guilt for sin. Does that not reproduce the misunderstanding of the onlookers in Isaiah 53:4, who "regarded him stricken, struck down by God, and afflicted"? Adequate

---

[31] Citations taken from Philip Schaff, ed., *The Creeds of Christendom: Volume III: The Evangelical Protestant Creeds* (Harper and Row 1983; repr. Grand Rapids: Baker, 1993), 620–21; and "Of Christ the Mediator," chapter 8 in "The Savoy Declaration of Faith and Order 1658," Center for Reformed Theology and Apologetics http://reformed.org/master/index.html?mainframe=/documents/Savoy_Declaration/index.html, accessed April 19, 2018.

satisfaction for the sins of the world is due, not to the depth or extent of Christ's suffering being calculated as the cumulative weight and misery of collective guilt, but rather to the innocence and infinite dignity of his person, and the voluntary nature of his sacrifice for us.[32]

On a related note, I think we have to be very careful not to drive a wedge between the "active" obedience of the life of Jesus and the "passive" obedience of his death. Isaiah 53, whatever its meaning, cannot be limited to the darkness of a few hours of Christ's earthly suffering. When did our Lord begin to be a "man of suffering" (Isa 53:3)? I am confident this began at the moment of his earthly incarnation, so that we can say with the Heidelberg Catechism, in answer to Question 37: "That he, all the time he lived on earth, but especially at the end of his life, sustained in body and soul, the wrath of God against the sins of all mankind that so by his passion, as the only propitiatory sacrifice, he might redeem our body and soul from everlasting damnation; and obtain for us the favor of God, righteousness, and eternal life." Whatever it means to "sustain the wrath of God" must be applicable to the entirety of Jesus's incarnate existence during the period of his humility (Phil 2:5–8), and we know that Jesus did not live his earthly existence out of fellowship with his Father and as the object of God's personal displeasure.[33]

---

[32] Here, some may object and argue that I am pitting things against each other which do not require opposition. I agree that one can sincerely affirm the infinite dignity of the person of the Son of God, and simultaneously affirm that God's justice was necessarily satisfied by the exacting of the punishment due to sinners through the imputation of their sins to Jesus on the cross (the gist of penal substitutionary atonement). What I am pointing out, however, is that a proper consideration of the dignity of the substitute who made satisfaction for our sins on the cross implicitly does away with *the need for* precisely the sort of exacting of punishment which is entailed in penal substitutionary atonement. The dignity of Jesus's person on the cross, voluntarily suffering and dying there for sinners, is itself *already more than abundant compensation* for the sins of the whole world; there does not then need to be *added* to this a measuring out of the exact quantity of all the sins of the elect to be expiated by the punishment of Jesus. We are dealing with matters of theological inference, and I understand that good Christians can differ on these questions. I highly respect the learned gifts of John Owen, J. I. Packer, and other modern advocates of penal substitutionary atonement.

[33] "By the term passion we are to understand the whole humiliation of Christ, or the obedience of his whole humiliation, all the miseries, infirmities, griefs, torments and ignominy to which he was subject, for our sakes, from the moment of his birth even to the hour of his death, as well in soul as in body." Zacharias Ursinus, *The Commentary of Zacharias Ursinus on the Heidelberg Catechism*, trans. G. W. Williard (Columbus, OH: G. W. Williard, 1851), 212.

Bibliography

Blocher, Henri. "The Atonement in John Calvin's Theology." In *The Glory of the Atonement*, ed. Charles E. Hill and Frank A. James III, 279–303. Downers Grove, IL: IVP, 2004.

Calvin, John. *Commentary on a Harmony of the Evangelists, Matthew, Mark, and Luke, Volume 3*. Translated by William Pringle. Calvin Translation Society, 1845. Reprint, Grand Rapids: Baker, 2005.

_____. *Commentary on the Epistles of Paul to the Corinthians, Volume 2*. Translated by John Pringle. Calvin Translation Society, 1848. Reprint, Grand Rapids: Baker, 2005.

_____. *Commentaries on the Epistle of Paul the Apostle to the Romans*. Translated by John Owen. Calvin Translation Society, 1849. Reprint, Grand Rapids: Baker, 2005.

_____. *Commentaries on the Epistles of Paul to the Galatians and Ephesians*. Calvin Translation Society, 1854. Reprint, Grand Rapids: Baker, 2005.

Helm, Paul. *Calvin at the Centre*. Oxford: Oxford University Press, 2010.

Jeffrey, Steve, Michael Ovey, and Andrew Sach. *Pierced for Our Transgressions: Rediscovering the Glory of Penal Substitution*. Wheaton, IL: Crossway, 2007.

Lane, Anthony N. S. *A Reader's Guide to Calvin's Institutes*. Grand Rapids: Baker, 2009.

McNeill, John T., ed. *Calvin: Institutes of the Christian Religion*. 2 vols. Philadelphia: Westminster, 1960.

Owen, John. *A Dissertation on Divine Justice*. In *The Death of Christ*. Vol. 10 of *Works of John Owen*. Johnstone & Hunter, 1850–53. Reprint, Edinburgh: Banner of Truth, 1967.

Packer, J. I., and Mark Dever. *In My Place Condemned He Stood*. Wheaton, IL: Crossway, 2008.

Peterson, Robert A. *Calvin and the Atonement*. Fearn, Ross-Shire, Scotland: Mentor, an imprint of Christian Focus Publications, 2009.

Phillips, Richard D. "Penal Substitutionary Atonement and Its 'Non-Violent' Critics." In *Precious Blood: The Atoning Work of Christ*, ed. Richard D. Phillips, 205–25. Wheaton, IL: Crossway, 2009.

Schaff, Philip, ed. *The Evangelical Protestant Creeds*. Vol. 3 of *The Creeds of Christendom*. Harper and Row, 1983. Reprint, Grand Rapids: Baker, 1993.

Trueman, Carl R. "Post-Reformation Developments in the Doctrine of the Atonement." In *Precious Blood: The Atoning Work of Christ*, ed. Richard D. Phillips, 179–204. Wheaton, IL: Crossway, 2009.

Ursinus, Zacharias. *The Commentary of Zacharias Ursinus on the Heidelberg Catechism*. Translated by G. W. Williard. Columbus, OH: G. W. Williard, 1851.

Part II

CELEBRATING THE DEVOTIONAL LEGACY OF THE REFORMATION

◇ **5** ◇

Retrieving the Reformation
for the Flourishing
of Evangelical Spirituality

NATHAN A. FINN

During the Vietnam and Watergate eras, spirituality was all the rage among middle-class Americans.[1] Much of this interest took the form of alternative spiritualities that were rooted in Eastern mysticism and came to be identified with the New Age movement. Orthodox Christians across the ecclesial spectrum also evidenced a growing interest in spirituality, though instead of turning to the East, they typically looked to the Christian past and advocated a renewed emphasis on classical spiritual disciplines such as contemplative prayer, Scripture meditation, fasting, and silence and solitude. In the early 1970s, Roman Catholic seminaries began to stress the importance of spiritual formation for future clergy, and Protestants soon adopted this same language. Among evangelicals, a loosely defined spiritual formation movement was taking shape by the end of that decade, inspired by Richard Foster's influential book *Celebration of Discipline* (1978).[2] The

---

[1] The emergence of the spiritual formation movement among North American evangelicals is discussed in greater detail in Nathan A. Finn and Keith Whitfield, "The Missional Church and Spiritual Formation," in *Spirituality for the Sent: A New Vision for the Missional Church*, ed. Nathan A. Finn and Keith Whitfield (Downers Grove, IL: IVP Academic, 2017), 17–27; and Nathan A. Finn, "What in the World is Holiness? Christian Spiritualities in the Modern World," in *Biblical Spirituality*, Theology in Community, ed. Christopher Morgan (Wheaton, IL: Crossway, expected publication date: June 30, 2019).

[2] Foster's book has sold more than a million copies and is currently in its third edition. See Richard J. Foster, *Celebration of Discipline: The Path to Spiritual Growth*, 3rd ed. (San Francisco: Harper San Francisco, 2002).

years following witnessed a proliferation of writings, conferences, and ministries dedicated to spiritual formation from a broadly evangelical perspective.

What follows is an exercise in spiritual theology, specifically a preliminary retrieval of certain Reformation emphases for the sake of the flourishing of evangelical spirituality. The remainder of the chapter is divided into two main parts. The first defines key terms and makes an initial attempt to move beyond mere description toward prescription. The second, larger part deals with a cluster of reformational concepts that have a direct bearing on evangelical spirituality. The intention is to foster conversation, debate, and, Lord willing, some "iron sharpening" among evangelicals engaged in broader discussions about the nature and goals of spiritual formation.

Defining the Terms

Scholars and thoughtful ministry practitioners will recognize that the opening paragraph of this chapter is fraught with words that elude easy definitions. What is "spirituality"? What does "spiritual formation" mean and how does it relate to the doctrine of sanctification? What is an "evangelical"? Good questions, all. This section offers some working definitions of these terms for readers who need to orient themselves to the discussion.

Spirituality is a broad concept that sometimes is applied to all religions, and other times separated from religion completely.[3] Though many claim to be "spiritual, but not religious," this chapter is concerned with self-consciously religious understandings of spirituality. According to Alister McGrath, "Spirituality concerns the quest for a fulfilled and authentic religious life," as these concepts are defined by a particular religion like Christianity.[4] Even when used in a distinctively Christian way, the term is notoriously difficult to define, in part because some use the phrase descriptively while others opt for more prescriptive usage.[5] Challenges notwithstanding, for the purposes of this chapter Christian spirituality is the

---

[3] Robert Wuthnow, *After Heaven: Spirituality in America since the 1950s* (Berkley, CA: University of California Press, 1998); Robert C. Fuller, *Spiritual, But Not Religious: Understanding Unchurched America* (New York: Oxford University Press, 2001).

[4] Alister E. McGrath, *Christian Spirituality* (Malden, MA: Blackwell, 1999), 2.

[5] On the history of the word "spirituality" and the difficulties in defining it, see Glen G. Scorgie, "Overview of Christian Spirituality," in *Dictionary of Christian Spirituality*, ed. Glen G. Scorgie (Grand Rapids: Zondervan, 2011), 27–32; T. R. Albin, "Spirituality," in *New Dictionary of Theology*, ed. Sinclair B. Ferguson, David F. Wright. and J. I. Packer (Downers Grove, IL: IVP Academic, 1988), 656–58; Philip Sheldrake, *Spirituality and History: Questions of Interpretation and Method* (New York: Crossroad, 1992), 32–56.

Christian's experiential relationship with the triune God, through faith in Jesus Christ, manifested through the full range of the believer's convictions, attitudes, priorities, and actions. A less-technical definition is the experience of what Dallas Willard and Richard Foster have often called the "with-God life."[6]

Spiritual formation is closely related to sanctification, though the latter is a more explicitly doctrinal concept. Sanctification speaks to a believer's gradual growth in godliness, "the Spirit-empowered process begun at regeneration and competed at glorification that increasingly conforms the believer's inner and outer life to the image of Christ."[7] Spiritual formation addresses the process of sanctification, including priorities and practices conducive to spiritual growth. Thus, Jeffrey Greenman defines spiritual formation as "our continuing response to the reality of God's grace shaping us into the likeness of Jesus Christ, through the work of the Holy Spirit, in the community of faith, for the sake of the world."[8] To make progress in sanctification is to be formed spiritually, to grow in godliness, to become increasingly holy. Generally, ministry practitioners focus their attention on spiritual formation (sometimes also called "Christian formation"), while theologians give more emphasis to the doctrine of sanctification. Both are key facets in Christian spirituality.

Evangelical has proven to be almost impossible to define, sometimes even among those who self-identify as evangelicals.[9] Others have written extensively on debates over evangelical identity, so for the purposes of this chapter, it is enough to note, as with previously discussed terms, that some opt for descriptive accounts while others prefer more prescriptive definitions. The most widely used descriptive approach is found in historian David Bebbington's "quadrilateral" of evangelical distinctives: biblicism, conversionism, crucicentrism (cross-centeredness), and activism.[10]

---

[6] For example, see Richard J. Foster, "The With-God Life," Renovaré (website), July 25, 2016, accessed September 1, 2017, https:renovare.org/articles/the-with-god-life.

[7] Steve L. Porter, "Sanctification," in *Dictionary of Christian Spirituality*, 734.

[8] Jeffrey P. Greenman, "Spiritual Formation in Theological Perspective: Classical Issues, Contemporary Challenges," in *Life in the Spirit: Spiritual Formation in Theological Perspective*, ed. Jeffrey P. Greenman and George Kalantzis (Downers Grove, IL: IVP Academic, 2010), 24.

[9] For an introduction to this discussion, see Mark A. Noll, "What is 'Evangelical'?" in *The Oxford Handbook of Evangelical Theology*, ed. Gerald R. McDermott (New York: Oxford University Press, 2013), 19–32.

[10] David W. Bebbington, *Evangelicalism in Modern Britain: A History from the 1730s to the 1980s* (London: Routledge, 1992), 1–19.

Bebbington suggests that these four emphases have been universally present among evangelicals from the early 1700s to the present day. Historians, social scientists, and journalists especially look to Bebbington's quadrilateral when studying evangelicals, particularly evangelical thought. Even those who reject Bebbington's paradigm as incomplete, insufficient, or too simplistic recognize that his approach is the standard that others must accept, contest, or expand.[11]

Theologians appreciate the descriptive usefulness of Bebbington's quadrilateral, but often desire to see a greater emphasis on prescription. While Bebbington describes the general contours of the evangelical *is*, when it comes to the evangelical *ought*, there is room for sometimes-heated debate within each of his four evangelical distinctives. In the book *Four Views on the Spectrum of Evangelicalism*, Albert Mohler advocates what he calls "confessional evangelicalism."[12] Confessional evangelicals understand evangelicalism to be a gospel-centered renewal movement that enjoys considerable continuity with the Reformation and the Great Tradition of Christian orthodoxy from the early church to the present. Confessional evangelicals believe that evangelicalism ought to be a movement with a strong theological core rather than one with fuzzy commitments and porous boundaries. In Mohler's understanding, not all who claim the label are authentic evangelicals because of significant discontinuities in matters of doctrine historically affirmed by self-confessed evangelicals.

Since this chapter is intended to be prescriptive rather than descriptive, it assumes a more confessional understanding of evangelical identity. Thus, we might define evangelicalism as an interdenominational renewal movement within Protestantism that bases doctrine and practice upon a fully trustworthy Scripture; affirms historic Christian orthodoxy as taught in Scripture and passed down in the best of the Christian theological tradition; treasures the saving work of Jesus Christ in his perfectly obedient life, substitutionary death, and victorious resurrection; emphasizes that human salvation is found only through personal faith in Jesus Christ;

---

[11] See the contributions to "Roundtable: Re-Examining David Bebbington's 'Quadrilateral Thesis,'" *Fides et Historia* 47, no. 1 (Winter/Spring 2015): 47–96.

[12] R. Albert Mohler Jr., "Confessional Evangelicalism," in *Four Views on the Spectrum of Evangelicalism*, ed. Andrew David Naselli and Collin Hansen, Counterpoints: Bible and Theology, ed. Stanley N. Gundry (Grand Rapids: Zondervan, 2011), 68–96. Greg Thornbury's "classic evangelicalism" offers a similar perspective, drawn from the influence of evangelical theologian Carl Henry, a thinker who also significantly influenced Mohler. See Gregory Alan Thornbury, *Recovering Classic Evangelicalism: Applying the Wisdom and Vision of Carl F. H. Henry* (Wheaton, IL: Crossway, 2013).

and champions intentional evangelism as central to all forms of Christian mission. The remainder of this chapter will draw upon select reformational emphases and put them in service to construct a healthy evangelical spirituality that is in continuity with the best of the various Reformation traditions.

Reformation Resources for Evangelical Spirituality
Sola Scriptura: The Supreme Authority for Spirituality

Sola Scriptura, Latin for "Scripture alone," is the belief that the Bible alone is the supreme authority in all matters of faith and practice. According to Kevin Vanhoozer, for Luther and the other Reformers, "Scripture alone contains all things necessary for salvation, communicates them effectively, compels one's conscience, determines doctrinal truth, and commands the church's allegiance above all other earthly powers and authorities, including councils and popes."[13] *Sola Scriptura* is sometimes called the "formal principle" of the Reformation because it was the doctrine that provided the authoritative first principle for every other Reformation conviction. Though the various Reformers disagreed among themselves on any number of issues, all agreed that the church of Rome had drifted morally and theologically in the late-medieval era because of its refusal to affirm biblical teachings in some areas and its elevation of extra-biblical traditions in other areas.[14]

Sola Scriptura does not mean the Bible is the *only* authority—a misunderstanding of the principle that is sometimes cleverly called "solo *Scriptura*."[15] This form of thoroughgoing biblicism is rooted in Enlightenment understandings of human autonomy, which elevates commonsense readings of Scripture, downplays the noetic effects of sin on hermeneutics, and elevates the role of private interpretation. Though common among American evangelicals, especially Baptists and others with Free Church sensibilities, this view rejects the role of the church as an interpretive community and identifies almost all tradition as a distraction from sound doctrine.

---

[13] Kevin J. Vanhoozer, *Biblical Authority after Babel: Retrieving the* Solas *in the Spirit of Mere Protestant Christianity* (Grand Rapids: Baker Academic, 2016), 111.

[14] For two overviews that adopt a multiple reformations perspective, see Carter Lindberg, *The European Reformations*, 2nd ed. (London: Wiley-Blackwell, 2010); and Carlos M. N. Eire, *Reformations: The Early Modern World, 1450–1650* (New Haven, CT: Yale University Press, 2016).

[15] Vanhoozer, *Biblical Authority after Babel*, 120–21; Keith A. Mathison, "A Critique of the Evangelical Doctrine of Solo *Scriptura*," chap. 8 in *The Shape of Sola Scriptura* (Moscow, ID: Canon Press, 2001).

While the Anabaptists arguably embraced a similar form of biblicism, most Reformers believed the supreme authority of Scripture is compatible with a critical appropriation of church tradition. They regularly appealed to church councils, cited the writings of patristic and medieval theologians, and drafted their own confessional standards and catechisms.

Martin Luther publicly articulated his commitment to *sola Scriptura* in his famous speech before the Diet of Worms in 1521:

> Since then Your Majesty and your lordships desire a simple reply, I will answer without horns and without teeth. Unless I am convinced by Scripture and plain reason—I do not accept the authority of popes and councils, for they have contradicted each other—my conscience is captive to the Word of God. I cannot and will not recant anything, for to go against conscience is neither right nor safe. God help me. Amen.[16]

For Luther, the authority of popes and councils could not be on par with Scripture, which was a common assertion of late-medieval Catholicism, because these authorities contradicted themselves and Scripture. According to Luther, "nothing except the divine words are to be the first principles for Christians. All human words are conclusions drawn from them and must be brought back to them and approved by them."[17] Furthermore, "In all articles, the foundation of our faith must be God's Word alone, and without God's Word there can be no article of faith."[18] Luther valued tradition, and elsewhere he commended what he considered the best of the Great Tradition to his followers.[19] But Scripture is our final authority, and tradition is only valuable insofar as it is consistent with that authority. Luther did not reject catholicity in his advocacy of *sola Scriptura*; he rejected Catholic departures from authentic catholicity due to elevating tradition over Scripture.[20]

---

[16] Quoted in Roland H. Bainton, *Here I Stand: A Life of Martin Luther* (Nashville: Abingdon, 2013), 182.

[17] Ewald M. Plass, ed., *What Luther Says*, vol. 1 (St. Louis: Concordia, 1959), 87–88.

[18] Plass, 405.

[19] See Luther's "On the Councils and the Church" (1539), in *LW* 41:3–178.

[20] See David Yeago, "The Catholic Luther," in *The Catholicity of the Reformation*, ed. Carl E. Braaten and Robert W. Jenson (Grand Rapids: Eerdmans, 1996), 13–34; and Mathison, *Shape of Sola Scriptura*, 95–102.

The same could be said of John Calvin. While Luther was a topical theologian whose writings were either shaped by controversies or pressing pastoral concerns, Calvin was more systematic in his approach. In Book One of his *Institutes of the Christian Religion*, Calvin argues, contrary to late-medieval Catholicism, that the Scripture created the church rather than the church creating the Scripture. Thus, the Scripture is of greater authority than tradition because the former predates the latter:

> Hence the Scriptures obtain full authority among believers only when men regard them as having sprung from heaven, as if there the living words of God were heard.... But a most pernicious error widely prevails that Scripture has only so much weight as is conceded to it by the consent of the church. As if the eternal and inviolable truth of God depended upon the decision of men.[21]

Furthermore, Calvin answers Catholic claims that tradition and church are equal in authority by citing from the Apostle Paul:

> He testifies that the church is "built upon the foundation of the prophets and apostles" [Eph 2:20]. If the teaching of the prophets and apostles is the foundation, this must have had authority before the church began to exist.... Thus, while the church receives and gives its seal of approval to the Scriptures, it does not thereby render authentic what is otherwise doubtful or controversial. But because the church recognizes Scripture to be the truth of its own God, as a pious duty it unhesitatingly venerates Scripture.[22]

Though Calvin also valued church tradition—arguably more than Luther—he agreed with Luther that the Bible is the only final authority for faith and practice.[23] The confessional standards adopted during the Reformation reinforced and codified the Reformers' belief in *sola Scriptura*. In the preface to the *Augsburg Confession* (1530), addressed to Emperor Charles V, the Lutheran princes state, "We offer, in this matter of religion, the Confession of our preachers and of ourselves, showing what manner

---

[21] John Calvin, *Institutes of the Christian Religion*, trans. Ford Lewis Battles, ed. John T. McNeil (Louisville, KY: Westminster-John Knox, 1960), I.vii.1.

[22] Calvin, I.vii.2.

[23] For more on Calvin's catholicity, see Anthony N. S. Lane, *John Calvin: Student of Church Fathers* (Edinburgh: T&T Clark, 1999).

of doctrine from the Holy Scriptures and the pure Word of God has been up to this time set forth in our lands, dukedoms, dominions, and cities, and taught in our churches."[24] In addition to appealing to the authority of Scripture, the Augsburg Confession also explicitly states that tradition is subservient to the gospel and denies that the church has any authority to promote practices that contradict the gospel as it is proclaimed in the Word of God.[25] The Lutheran *Formula of Concord* (1577) is even more explicit, opening with an unambiguous affirmation of *sola Scriptura*:

> We believe, teach, and confess that the sole rule and standard accord-ing to which all dogmas together with [all] teachers should be esti-mated and judged are the prophetic and apostolic Scriptures of the Old and of the New Testament alone, as it is written Ps. 119:105: Thy Word is a lamp unto my feet and a light unto my path. And St. Paul: Though an angel from heaven preach any other gospel unto you, let him be accursed, Gal. 1:8.
>
> Other writings, however, of ancient or modern teachers, what-ever name they bear, must not be regarded as equal to the Holy Scrip-tures, but all of them together be subjected to them, and should not be received otherwise or further than as witnesses, [which are to show] in what manner after the time of the apostles, and at what places, this [pure] doctrine of the prophets and apostles was preserved.[26]

Reformed confessions of the era also affirm *sola Scriptura*. For example, the *Second Helvetic Confession* (1536) confesses of Scripture:

> We believe and confess the canonical Scriptures of the holy prophets and apostles of both Testaments to be the true Word of God, and to have sufficient authority of themselves, not of men. For God himself spoke to the fathers, prophets, apostles, and still speaks to us through the Holy Scriptures.
>
> And in this Holy Scripture, the universal Church of Christ has the most complete exposition of all that pertains to a saving faith, and also to the framing of a life acceptable to God; and in this respect it

---

[24] "The Augsburg Confession: Preface to the Emperor Charles V," The Book of Concord (website), accessed September 2, 2017, http://bookofconcord.org/augsburgconfession.php.

[25] "Augsburg Confession," Articles 7 and 28.

[26] "Epitome of the Formula of Concord: Comprehensive Summary, Rule, and Norm," The Book of Concord (website), accessed September 2, 1017, http://bookofconcord.org/fc-ep.php.

is expressly commanded by God that nothing either be added to or taken from the same.[27]

The *Second Helvetic Confession* follows up in its second chapter by applying *sola Scriptura* to biblical interpretation, church councils, and human traditions.[28] The *Belgic Confession* (1563) also clearly affirms *sola Scriptura* in its fifth and seventh articles:

> We receive all these books and these only as holy and canonical, for the regulating, founding, and establishing of our faith. And we believe without a doubt all things contained in them—not so much because the church receives and approves them as such but above all because the Holy Spirit testifies in our hearts that they are from God, and also because they prove themselves to be from God. For even the blind themselves are able to see that the things predicted in them do happen.
>
> We believe that this Holy Scripture contains the will of God completely and that everything one must believe to be saved is sufficiently taught in it.… Therefore we must not consider human writings—no matter how holy their authors may have been—equal to the divine writings; nor may we put custom, nor the majority, nor age, nor the passage of times or persons, nor councils, decrees, or official decisions above the truth of God, for truth is above everything else. For all human beings are liars by nature and more vain than vanity itself. Therefore we reject with all our hearts everything that does not agree with this infallible rule, as we are taught to do by the apostles.[29]

If the Reformers are correct that Scripture is the final authority for faith and practice, this necessarily includes spirituality. Evangelical spirituality must be Word-centered. In terms of personal spiritual formation, evangelicals must prioritize knowing and applying the Scriptures through regular Bible reading, meditation, and memorization. This often comes intuitively to evangelicals. Many observers note that the "daily quiet time" of Bible reading and prayer is one of the most distinguishing evangelical spiritual

---

[27] Chapter 1, "The Second Helvetic Confession," accessed September 2, 2017, http://www.ccel.org/creeds/helvetic.htm.

[28] Chapter 2, "The Second Helvetic Confession."

[29] "Article 5: The Authority of Scripture" and "Article 7: The Sufficiency of Scripture," The Belgic Confession, Christian Reformed Church (website), accessed September 4, 2017, https://www.crcna.org/welcome/beliefs/confessions/belgic-confession.

practices.[30] Though having a daily quiet time is not sufficient in and of itself to nurture one's growth in holiness, regular Bible intake is nevertheless an important discipline to cultivate. For this reason, most evangelical manuals on spiritual disciplines include one or more chapters dedicated to devotional, reflective reading of Scripture for the sake of spiritual formation.[31]

Scripture also plays an important role when it comes to evangelical corporate spirituality, which is expressed primarily through public worship. Paul encouraged his pastoral protégé, Timothy, to "give your attention to public reading, exhortation, and teaching" (1 Tim 4:13). Elsewhere, Paul charged Timothy to "preach the word; be ready in season and out of season; rebuke, correct, and encourage with great patience and teaching" (2 Tim 4:2). When the earliest churches gathered, believers "devoted themselves to the apostles' teaching" (Acts 2:42), their prayers were filled with quotations and allusions to the Old Testament (Acts 4:24–30), and their songbook included "psalms, hymns, and spiritual songs" (Eph 5:19). The earliest Christian worship gatherings were saturated with the Word of God read, proclaimed, sung, and prayed. The same should be true of evangelical worship today, in all its many varieties. Though liturgies vary from church to church, the purpose of public worship should be to invite worshipers into the narrative arc of the Scriptures, forming them into a Word-centered people who rightly love God and neighbor (Matt 22:34–40).[32]

Because of a thin understanding of biblical authority, many self-confessed evangelicals engage in spiritual practices with non-Christian roots.[33] For example, some believers are enamored with moralistic self-

---

[30] David Parker, "Evangelical Spirituality Reviewed," *Evangelical Quarterly* 63, no. 2 (1991): 128, 130–32. See also Alister McGrath, *Beyond the Quiet Time: Practical Evangelical Spirituality* (Grand Rapids: Baker, 1996; repr., Vancouver, British Columbia: Regent College Press, 2003).

[31] For example, see John Ortberg, "An Undivided Life: the Practice of Reflection on Scripture," chap. 11 in *The Life You've Always Wanted: Spiritual Disciplines for Ordinary People*, 2nd ed. (Grand Rapids: Zondervan, 2009); Donald Whitney, "Bible Intake (Parts 1 and 2)," chaps. 2–3 in *Spiritual Disciplines for the Christian Life*, 2nd ed. (Colorado Springs: NavPress, 2014); Philip Nation, "From the Head to the Heart: the Practice of Bible Study," chap. 3 in *Habits of our Holiness: How the Spiritual Disciplines Grow Us Up, Draw Us Together, and Send Us Out* (Chicago: Moody, 2016); and David Mathis, "Hear His Voice (Word)," part 1 in *Habits of Grace: Enjoying Jesus through the Spiritual Disciplines* (Wheaton, IL: Crossway, 2016).

[32] For more on the place of Scripture in shaping the church's worship, see Bryan Chapell, *Christ-Centered Worship: Letting the Gospel Shape Our Practice* (Grand Rapids: Baker Academic, 2009); Mike Cosper, *Rhythms of Grace: How the Church's Worship Tells the Story of the Gospel* (Wheaton, IL: Crossway, 2013); and James K. A. Smith, "What Story Are You In? The Narrative Arc of Formative Christian Worship," chap. 4 in *You Are What You Love: The Spiritual Power of Habit* (Grand Rapids: Brazos, 2016).

[33] The next three paragraphs are adapted from Nathan A. Finn, "The Dangers of Postmodern Spirituality," *Expositor* 4 (March/April 2015): 38–41.

help books that are plagued by a low view of sin, a high estimation of natural human virtue, and traditionally Eastern ideas such as panentheism or even pantheism. Celebrity spiritual gurus Oprah Winfrey, Dr. Oz, and Dr. Phil enjoy wide followings among evangelicals, even though their spiritual insights are often sub-Christian or even anti-Christian.[34] Though often inspired by noble health concerns, many believers embrace techniques such as transcendental meditation and yoga with little consideration for the spiritual assumptions that undergird these practices. Some even gravitate to horoscopes and other superstitious practices that claim to offer some special insight into God's will for their lives. Evangelicals should not pursue spiritual health using tools that conflict with the teachings of Scripture.

Even more troubling than evangelicals dipping into alternative spiritualities is the confusion sometimes evidenced in embracing suspect forms of ostensibly Christian spirituality. For many evangelicals, the belief that something is helpful spiritually is apparently all that matters, even if the practice has no scriptural basis. Many "Christian living" books are little more than baptized versions of the same anthropocentric material available in the self-help section of the local secular bookstore. When surveying bestselling Christian books that are purportedly aimed at spiritual growth, one finds any number of soul-deadening heresies, including redefinitions of the Trinity, antinomianism (a rejection of God's moral commands), an implicit universalism, and alleged visits to heaven during near-death experiences.[35] Christian self-help books routinely adopt an optimistic view of human nature that has little place for human depravity, especially when wed to the "prosperity gospel" of health and wealth.[36]

Sometimes, even thoughtful proponents of spiritual formation fail to adequately root spiritual practices in the supreme authority of Scripture. Some forms of contemplative prayer, notably centering prayer, are rooted in anthropocentric forms of mysticism that downplay the distinctions

---

[34] Kathryn Lofton, *Oprah: The Gospel of an Icon* (Berkeley: University of California Press, 2011).

[35] One young boy whose story inspired a bestselling evangelical book about a near-death visit to heaven has since admitted the account was fabricated. The publisher subsequently pulled the book from shelves. See Sarah Eekhoff Zylstra, "The 'Boy Who Came Back from Heaven' Retracts Story," *Christianity Today* (January 15, 2015; updated January 21, 2015), http://www.christianitytoday.com/news/2015/january/boy-who-came-back-from-heaven-retraction.html.

[36] For an historical study of the prosperity gospel, see Kate Bowler, *Blessed: A History of the American Prosperity Gospel* (New York: Oxford University Press, 2013). For a critique from a confessional evangelical perspective, see David W. Jones and Russell S. Woodbridge, *Health, Wealth, and Happiness: How the Prosperity Gospel Overshadows the Gospel of Christ* (Grand Rapids: Kregel Academic, 2011).

between God and his human creatures.[37] Some extreme forms of fasting smack more of medieval legalism than biblical sorrow for sin and longing for the kingdom. Silence and solitude, when divorced from prayer and Scripture meditation, may have many benefits, but are not inherently beneficial to one's spiritual health.[38] Religious pilgrimages—even those treated as evangelical tourism—can be captive to superstitious notions that echo the medieval belief that some places are more holy than others. The Reformers would never assume that all practices at times identified with the Christian tradition are automatically spiritually beneficial. After all, sacerdotalism, priestly celibacy, purgatory, and indulgences were all part of the tradition of Western Christendom by the time of the Reformation, and each was rejected by the Reformers for being inconsistent with the teachings of Scripture. Whichever emphases and practices evangelicals embrace for the sake of spiritual formation should be deeply rooted in the Scriptures, which are our supreme authority for faith and practice.

Sola Gratia, Sola Fide, Solus Christus: The Ground of Spirituality

The Reformers energetically championed the supreme authority of Scripture in all matters of faith and practice, in part because a correct approach to Scripture helped safeguard other important beliefs they feared had been undermined or even rejected within late-medieval Catholicism. No belief was more important than the gospel, the announcement that sinful humans can be reconciled with their Creator, through faith in Jesus Christ, based on his saving acts in his perfectly sinless life, atoning death on the cross, and victorious resurrection from the grave. Three reformational principles directly addressed aspects of the gospel: *sola gratia* (grace alone), *sola fide* (faith alone), and *solus Christus* (Christ alone). The reformers believed that salvation is by grace alone, through faith alone, in Christ alone. This approach to the gospel challenged the medieval consensus that salvation is a combination of faith and godly works that flow from that

---

[37] Centering prayer has been popularized by the Trappist monks William Meninger, Basil Pennington, and especially Thomas Keating, though part of its appeal is that it is a strategy that is reproducible among non-Catholics and even theoretically non-Christians. For an evangelical critique of centering prayer, see James Wilhoit, "Contemplative and Centering Prayer," *Journal of Spiritual Formation and Soul Care* 7, no. 1 (Spring 2014): 107–17.

[38] Robert L. Plummer, "Are the Spiritual Disciplines of 'Silence and Solitude' Really Biblical?" *Journal of Spiritual Formation and Soul Care* 2, no.1 (Spring 2009): 101–12.

faith, especially the seven sacraments, through which grace was believed to be imparted to the faithful.

Luther embraced these reformational principles gradually, beginning with *sola fide*, a position he came to between 1513 and 1519, as he was teaching the Scriptures at the University of Wittenberg.[39] Prior to this time, Luther struggled with the legalistic aspects of late-medieval Catholicism, unsure of whether he had been obedient enough to merit God's grace. His study of Rom 1:16–17 changed his entire spiritual outlook: "For I am not ashamed of the gospel, because it is the power of God for salvation to everyone who believes, first to the Jew, and also to the Greek. For in it the righteousness of God is revealed from faith to faith, just as it is written: **The righteous will live by faith**." In his 1520 treatise *The Freedom of a Christian Man*, Luther promoted his mature view of justification, arguing, "Therefore it is clear that, as the soul needs only the Word of God for its life and righteousness, so it is justified by faith alone and not any works; for if it could be justified by anything else, it would not need the Word, and consequently it would not need faith."[40]

Luther continued to develop his view of justification for the remainder of his life, tying *sola fide* and *solus Christus* to *sola gratia* and making fine distinctions between the law (God's commands) and the gospel (God's promises). In his 1525 debate with Erasmus over free will, Luther tied Erasmus' view to works righteousness while identifying his position with that of the Apostle Paul. For Luther, "justification by the grace of God" must be "free and apart from works."[41] The "righteousness of faith" is based upon "God's favorable regard and his 'reckoning' on the basis of grace."[42] Luther believed Erasmus treated faith like a work, confusing law and gospel and opening the door to legalism. In the *Smalcald Articles* of 1537, Luther summed up his view of salvation by grace alone, through faith alone, in Christ alone:

1. *That Jesus Christ, our God and Lord, died for our sins, and was raised again for our justification*, Rom. 4:25.
2. *And He alone is the Lamb of God which taketh away the sins of the world*, John 1:29; *and God has laid upon Him the iniquities of us all*, Is. 53:6.

---

[39] Herman Selderhuis refers to this period as Luther's "reformational development." See Herman Selderhuis, *Martin Luther: A Spiritual Biography* (Grand Rapids: Crossway, 2017), 84.

[40] Martin Luther, *Three Treatises*, 2nd rev. ed. (Minneapolis: Fortress, 1970), 280.

[41] Timothy Lull, ed., *Martin Luther's Basic Theological Writings* (Minneapolis: Fortress, 1989), 182.

[42] Lull, 182.

3. *Likewise: All have sinned and are justified without merit [freely, and without their own works or merits] by His grace, through the redemption that is in Christ Jesus, in His blood,* Rom. 3:23f.

4. Now, since it is necessary to believe this, and it cannot be otherwise acquired or apprehended by any work, law, or merit, it is clear and certain that this faith alone justifies us as St. Paul says, Rom. 3:28: *For we conclude that a man is justified by faith, without the deeds of the Law.* Likewise 3:26: *That He might be just, and the Justifier of him which believeth in Christ.*

5. Of this article, nothing can be yielded or surrendered [nor can anything be granted or permitted contrary to the same], even though heaven and earth, and whatever will not abide, should sink to ruin. *For there is none other name under heaven, given among men whereby we must be saved,* says Peter, Acts 4:12. *And with His stripes we are healed,* Is. 53:5. And upon this article all things depend which we teach and practice in opposition to the Pope, the devil, and the [whole] world. Therefore, we must be sure concerning this doctrine, and not doubt; for otherwise all is lost, and the Pope and devil and all things gain the victory and suit over us.[43]

Through the influence of Luther and his colleagues, justification by faith in Christ alone and its implications, such as a distinction between law and gospel and the imputation of Christ's righteousness, remained at the heart of Lutheran theology and spirituality.[44] For their part, Reformed theologians also embraced these principles, with some modifications at times in terms of emphasis, and codified them in their own confessional standards.[45]

This reformational emphasis on the gospel remains a crucial building block in the spiritual DNA of modern evangelicals. Healthy spirituality is both Word-centered *and* gospel-centered. If evangelical spirituality is to be consistently gospel-centered, careful attention must be paid to what the

---

[43] "The Smalcald Articles: Part 2, Article 1: The First and Chief Article," The Book of Concord (website), accessed September 8, 2017, http://bookofconcord.org/smalcald.php.

[44] Steven D. Paulson, *Lutheran Theology*, Doing Theology (London: T&T Clark, 2011), 35–60; Bradley Hanson, *Grace that Frees: The Lutheran Tradition*, Traditions of Christian Spirituality (Maryknoll, NY: Orbis, 2004), 47–63.

[45] See Joel R. Beeke, *Living for God's Glory: An Introduction to Calvinism* (Grand Rapids: Reformation Trust, 2008), chapters 3–11; and R. Michael Allen, *Reformed Theology*, Doing Theology (London: T&T Clark, 2010), chapters 3–5.

gospel is and the role it plays in spiritual growth. As D. A. Carson argues, "Questions as to the nature of spirituality, the purpose of the putative experience of the transcendent, the nature of the God who is the ultimate source of the experience, the locus of the revelation he has given of himself, and the techniques and forms by which we may ostensibly know him better, must be brought to the test of the gospel."[46] Simply put, if evangelicals are really a people of the gospel, as their name suggests, then the gospel must function as the hermeneutic of evangelical spirituality.

Spirituality is an important form of practical theology, and like all forms of evangelical theology, it must reflect a biblical and reformational understanding of justification by grace alone through faith alone in Jesus Christ alone. Like the Reformers, evangelicals must be clear about the distinction between law and gospel, commands and promises. Justification is the ground of sanctification. Confusing the relationship between these categories leads to the same sort of legalism that Luther and the other Reformers were countering in their own era.[47] In the economy of the kingdom, every indicative ("do this") commanded of the Christian is grounded in the imperative ("done that") promised when we respond in faith to the gospel. Luther counseled his followers to remember their baptism as a way to remain centered in their spiritual life.[48] Evangelicals might consider regularly reminding themselves of the gospel for the same purpose.[49]

Spiritual disciplines should always be practiced in the context of a personal relationship with God through faith in Christ, never as a means to gain or keep a relationship with God. In the latter approach, spiritual disciplines become a substitute for one's faith, even if implicitly and unintentionally so. As Donald Whitney argues, "Spiritual Disciplines are practices *derived from the gospel, not divorced from the gospel.* When the Disciplines are rightly practiced, they take us deeper into the gospel of Jesus and its

---

[46] D. A. Carson, "When is Spirituality Spiritual? Reflections on Some Problems of Definition," *Journal of the Evangelical Theological Society* 37, no. 3 (September 1994): 391.

[47] For doctrinal accounts of this relationship, see G. C. Berkouwer, "'Sola Fide' and Sanctification," chap. 2 in *Faith and Sanctification*, Studies in Dogmatics (Grand Rapids: Eerdmans, 1952); and Michael Allen, "Justification and Sanctification," chap. 7 in *Sanctification*, New Studies in Dogmatics (Grand Rapids: Zondervan, 2017). For a more practical exposition, see David Powlison, *How Does Sanctification Work?* (Wheaton, IL: Crossway, 2017).

[48] Luther, *Three Treatises*, 193.

[49] For years, the late Jerry Bridges advocated the spiritual practice of "preaching the gospel to yourself every day" in his many books. For example, see Jerry Bridges, *The Gospel for Real Life: Return to the Liberating Power of the Cross* (Colorado Springs, CO: NavPress, 2002), 9.

glories, not away from it as though we've moved on to more advanced levels of Christianity."[50] David Mathis agrees, noting, "It is the grace of God that gives us his 'means of grace' for our ongoing perseverance and growth and joy this side of the coming new creation. And the grace of God inspires and empowers the various habits and practices by which we avail ourselves of God's means."[51] Spiritual disciplines are not ends unto themselves. Rather, they are practices that till the soil of our heart, better preparing us to receive the nourishing rain of God's sanctifying grace.

If spiritual disciplines are to be gospel centered—that is to say, properly *evangelical*—they should naturally connect to the promises of the gospel. Scripture study, meditation, and memorization ought to be reflective reading about where a passage fits into the larger story of the gospel and its implications for living in light of the gospel. Prayer and fasting ought to include claiming the promises of the gospel and longing for the final victory of that gospel when Christ's kingdom is consummated in its fullness. Evangelism is sharing the good news through words for the salvation of the lost through the gospel's power, while service is illustrating the good news through deeds for the promotion of human flourishing in the gospel's image. Corporate worship should communicate the gospel through public reading of Scripture, preaching of the Word, communal prayer and praise, and celebration of the Lord's Supper, all of which proclaim the gospel publicly to the community of faith as well as visiting unbelievers. Spiritual disciples should never be practiced as if the gospel is simply the message that jumpstarts our Christian life, to be left behind soon for deeper truths. The gospel is the announcement that we respond to in faith (justification), the motivation that fuels our ongoing growth in that faith (sanctification), and the promise that our faith will reach its ultimate destination (perseverance, glorification). This is the gospel context of authentic evangelical spirituality.

Other Reformational Insights

The classical "*solas*" are certainly not the only reformational resources that evangelicals should retrieve in service to a renewed evangelical spirituality. They are certainly foundational because of their emphasis on Scripture (our final authority) and the gospel (our only hope for redemption). However, other doctrines and emphases should also be brought to bear on

---

[50] Whitney, *Spiritual Disciplines*, 8.
[51] Mathis, *Habits of Grace*, 23–24.

evangelical spirituality. Many theologians in the Calvinist tradition have argued that God not only shows special grace to believers in his acts of redemption, but he exercises common grace toward all his human creatures through his acts of creation and providence. Though an important theme in Calvin's thought, this view of common grace has been especially developed by the Dutch Reformed theologian Abraham Kuyper and his followers.[52] In his common grace, God displays his glory and delights in human affairs, which ultimately point to him, even when unbelievers fail to see how Christ is Lord in every sphere of life.[53]

The priesthood of all believers is another key reformational resource for shaping evangelical spirituality. Drawing on the biblical teaching that God's people are a "kingdom of priests and a holy nation" (Ex 19:6; 1 Pet 2:9), the priesthood of all believers is the belief that every Christian is called and equipped to minister to others in every sphere in which he or she participates. Kevin Vanhoozer has argued that the priesthood of all believers "amounts to a virtual sixth *sola*: *sola ecclesia* (church alone)," by which he means, "*the church alone is the place where Christ rules over his kingdom and gives certain gifts for the building of his living temple.*"[54] Luther advocated the priesthood of all believers in his 1520 treatises *The Babylonian Captivity of the Church* and *To the Christian Nobility of the German Nation.* The doctrine was subsequently embraced by all the major Reformation traditions, each of which sought to counter the Roman Catholic understanding of the priesthood as a special class of Christian that helped mediate God's grace to the common people through the sacraments.[55] The Free Church tradition, and especially the Baptists, made the priesthood of all believers a major emphasis, tying the principle to both ecclesiology and mission.[56]

---

[52] For Calvin's views, see Herman Bavinck, "Calvin and Common Grace," in *Calvin and the Reformation*, ed. William P. Armstrong (Grand Rapids: Revell, 1909), 99–130; and Herman Kuiper, *Calvin on Common Grace* (Grand Rapids: Smitter Book, 1928). For Kuyper on common grace, see Abraham Kuyper, *Lectures on Calvinism* (Grand Rapids: Eerdmans, 1931); Kuyper, *Common Grace: God's Gifts for a Fallen World*, Collected Works in Public Theology, vol. 1 (Bellingham, WA: Lexham Press, 2016).

[53] Richard J. Mouw, *He Shines in All That's Fair: Culture and Common Grace* (Grand Rapids: Eerdmans, 2001).

[54] Vanhoozer, *Biblical Authority after Babel*, 29. Emphasis in original.

[55] Cyril Eastwood, *The Priesthood of All Believers: An Examination of the Doctrine from the Reformation to the Present Day* (1960; repr., Eugene, OR: Wipf and Stock, 2009).

[56] For Baptist interpretations of the priesthood of all believers, see Timothy George, "The Priesthood of all Believers and the Quest for Theological Integrity," *Criswell Theological Review* 3 (Spring 1989): 283–94; and Malcolm B. Yarnell III, "The Priesthood of Believers: Rediscovering the Biblical Doctrine of Royal Priesthood," in *Restoring Integrity in Baptist Churches*, ed. Thomas White, Jason G. Duesing, Malcolm B. Yarnell III (Grand Rapids: Kregel Academic, 2007), 221–44.

When a Reformed understanding of common grace is coupled with the priesthood of all believers, these emphases have much to offer evangelical spirituality. Christian spirituality is lived out in every aspect of life, all of which is under Christ's lordship and is intended to glorify God; the secular is the sacred. Evangelicals should draw upon common grace insights from the social sciences as they reflect on the nature of spiritual flourishing, even as they appeal to Scripture as their final authority for faith and practice.[57] Evangelical spirituality should be missional because every Christian should spread the gospel in word and live out the implications of the gospel in deed, in every vocation and sphere of life, for the sake of promoting human flourishing among both believers and unbelievers.[58] Those called to the vocation of pastor should equip the saints for these works of ministry (Eph 4:12). Evangelical spirituality should never be *worldly* (1 John 2:15–17), but it should always be *earthy*—practical, edifying, and accessible to everyday believers from all walks of life. Spiritual formation should help shape every aspect of the believer's life and practice, bringing all of the Christian life into conformity with Christ's lordship. [59]

Yet another Reformation-era theme draws, not from the Magisterial Reformers, but from the evangelical Anabaptists such as the Swiss Brethren and Mennonites.[60] The Anabaptists affirmed a believer's church where membership was seen as a covenantal commitment restricted to those who gave evidence of regeneration. In service to their believer's church commitments, the Anabaptists rejected infant baptism, emphasized individual liberty of conscience, practiced redemptive church discipline, and rejected territorial church arrangements that blurred the distinction between church and state. Despite considerable persecution at the hands of Magisterial Reformers and Catholics alike, the Anabaptists were also the great evangelists of the Reformation era because of their belief that regeneration was

---

[57] For an example of Kuyperian engagement with psychology that fruitfully influences evangelical spirituality, see Eric L. Johnson, *God and Soul Care: The Therapeutic Resources of the Christian Faith* (Downers Grove, IL: IVP Academic, 2017).

[58] See Finn and Whitfield, *Spirituality for the Sent*; Steven Garber, *Visions of Vocation: Common Grace for the Common Good* (Downers Grove, IL: IVP Academic, 2014); Uche Anizor and Hank Voss, "Worship, Work and Witness: The Practices of the Royal Priesthood," chap. 5 in *Representing Christ: A Vision for the Priesthood of All Believers* (Downers Grove, IL: IVP Academic, 2016).

[59] Craig G. Bartholomew, "The Need for Spiritual Formation," chap. 12 in *Contours of the Kuyperian Tradition: A Systematic Introduction* (Downers Grove, IL: IVP Academic, 2017).

[60] The classic study of evangelical Anabaptism is William R. Estep, *The Anabaptist Story: An Introduction to Sixteenth-Century Anabaptism*, 3rd ed. (Grand Rapids: Eerdmans, 1996).

prerequisite to church membership.[61] Though scholars continue to debate the degree of influence, seventeenth-century Baptists embraced most of these same emphases as the earlier Anabaptists, though the Baptists placed greater emphasis on believer's baptism by immersion and developed a more robustly covenantal ecclesiology.[62]

A final reformational theme is the importance of corporate worship. Many of the Reformers were interested in public worship; they wrote hymns, prepared liturgies, and fought over what practices were and were not appropriate for worship.[63] However, the Church of England became especially identified with the centrality of public worship.[64] The defining document of the English Reformation was not a treatise on justification or predestination, but rather a liturgical guidebook: Thomas Cranmer's *Book of Common Prayer*, published in 1549 and revised periodically thereafter.[65] The Church of England valued the formative power of liturgy, though efforts to meticulously prescribe worship led to the rise of Puritanism after Elizabeth I took the throne in 1558. While the English Reformers preached Protestant views of justification, faith, and grace, most of them also maintained a greater emphasis on the Lord's Supper as the central act of public worship. In many ways, the English Reformation was a thoroughly liturgical reformation wherein the corporate spirituality of public worship shaped the individual spirituality of believers.

The Anabaptist emphasis on a believer's church, coupled with the English Reformation's commitment to the formative power of public

---

[61] Thieleman J. van Braght's 1660 treatise *The Martyr's Mirror* is the most noteworthy account of early Anabaptist martyrs. The text is available online at http://www.homecomers.org/mirror/contents.htm (accessed September 13, 2017). While the Anabaptists were exemplary in this regard, they were by no means the only Reformation movement committed to evangelism and church planting. For a fine essay that challenges the erroneous thesis that the Reformers were unconcerned with missions, see Ray Van Neste, "The Mangled Narrative of Missions and Evangelism in the Reformation," chap. 13 in this book.

[62] See Malcolm B. Yarnell III, *The Anabaptists and Contemporary Baptists: Restoring New Testament Christianity* (Nashville: B&H Academic, 2013); and James A. Patterson, "Anabaptist Kinship Revisited: Implications for Baptist Origins and Identity," chap. 2 in *Reformation 500: How the Greatest Revival Since Pentecost Continues to Shape the World Today*, ed. Ray Van Neste and J. Michael Garrett (Nashville: B&H Academic, 2017), 31–44.

[63] Carlos M. N. Eire, *War Against the Idols: The Reformation of Worship from Erasmus to Calvin* (New York: Cambridge University Press, 1989).

[64] Horton Davies, *Worship and Theology in England: From Cranmer to Baxter and Fox, 1534–1690* (1961; repr., Grand Rapids: Eerdmans, 1996).

[65] Brian Cummings, *The Book of Common Prayer: The Texts of 1549, 1559, and 1662* (New York: Oxford University Press, 2011); Alan Jacobs, *The Book of Common Prayer: A Biography* (Princeton, NJ: Princeton University Press, 2013).

worship, can be synthesized to provide an intentionally communal shape to evangelical spirituality. Spiritual formation should be a community project that is best experienced as a life of discipleship lived out in the fellowship of a local church that understands itself to be a community of disciples.[66] Even among evangelicals who retain infant baptism, meaningful church membership should provide the venue for corporate spirituality as believers walk together under the lordship of Jesus Christ.[67] Individual spiritual disciplines should be reinforced by the corporate disciplines that are experienced in community, especially public worship. For this reason, believers should not forsake regularly assembling with other believers (Heb 10:25). Though churches will vary in their liturgical practices, all evangelicals should take seriously the role that the preaching of the Word and the celebration of the Lord's Supper play in shaping the spiritual life of its members, since one proclaims the gospel in words and the other pictures the gospel in a shared meal.[68] Evangelical spirituality should be deeply rooted in the local church, which in turn should be ground zero for worship, witness, and service.

Conclusion

This chapter has discussed key aspects of reformational thought that should be retrieved for the sake of renewing evangelical spirituality. Evangelical spirituality should be tethered to the supreme authority of Scripture and grounded in the reformational commitment to salvation by grace alone, through faith alone, in Christ alone. These commitments are foundational to Protestant and evangelical identity.[69] Evangelicals should learn from the Anabaptist understanding of the believer's church and the Church of England's emphasis upon public worship, which together will help give an ecclesial shape to evangelical spirituality. This is important, since evangelicals have often been

---

[66] James C. Wilhoit, *Spiritual Formation as if the Church Mattered: Growing in Christ through Community* (Grand Rapids: Baker Academic, 2008); C. Arnold Snyder, *Following in the Footsteps of Christ: The Anabaptist Tradition* (Maryknoll, NY: Orbis, 2004).

[67] Mark Dever, *Nine Marks of a Healthy Church*, 3rd ed. (Wheaton, IL: Crossway, 2013).

[68] Thomas R. Schreiner and Matthew R. Crawford, eds., *The Lord's Supper: Remembering and Proclaiming Christ Until He Comes*, New American Commentary Studies in Bible and Theology (Nashville: B&H Academic, 2010); see especially chapters 11–13.

[69] For an excellent consensus statement that articulates the beliefs of "Mere Protestant" Christianity, endorsed by several hundred evangelicals (including the author), see "A Reforming Catholic Confession," accessed September 13, 2017, http://reformingcatholicconfession.com/.

criticized as having an underdeveloped ecclesiology.[70] Evangelical spiritual formation should also incorporate insights from a Reformed understanding of common grace and the Protestant doctrine of the priesthood of all believers, which will help foster a missional spirituality that fuels evangelical witness and service. Bebbington and others point out that evangelicals are an inherently activist people. The near goal of this reformational retrieval is an evangelical spirituality that is Word-centered in its foundation, gospel-driven in its focus, ecclesial in its shape, and missional in its orientation. The long-term *telos* of this spiritual vision is that evangelical believers "may be filled with the knowledge of his will in all wisdom and spiritual understanding, so that you may walk worthy of the Lord, fully pleasing to him: bearing fruit in every good work and growing in the knowledge of God" (Col 1:9b–10). As the final of the five classic "*solas*" of the Reformation declares, *soli Deo gloria*!

Bibliography

Allen, Michael. *Sanctification*. New Studies in Dogmatics. Grand Rapids: Zondervan, 2017.

————. *Reformed Theology*. Doing Theology. New York: T&T Clark, 2010.

Anizor, Uche, and Hank Voss. *Representing Christ: A Vision for the Priesthood of All Believers*. Downers Grove, IL: IVP Academic, 2016.

Bainton, Roland H. *Here I Stand: A Life of Martin Luther*. Nashville: Abingdon, 2013.

Bartholomew, Craig G. *Contours of the Kuyperian Tradition: A Systematic Introduction*. Downers Grove, IL: IVP Academic, 2017.

Bavinck, Herman. "Calvin and Common Grace." In *Calvin and the Reformation*. Grand Rapids: Revell, 1909.

Bebbington, David W. *Evangelicalism in Modern Britain: A History from the 1730s to the 1980s*. London: Routledge, 1992.

Beeke, Joel R. *Living for God's Glory: An Introduction to Calvinism*. Grand Rapids: Reformation Trust, 2008.

Berkouwer, G. C. *Faith and Sanctification*. Studies in Dogmatics. Grand Rapids: Eerdmans, 1952.

Bowler, Kate. *Blessed: A History of the American Prosperity Gospel*. New York: Oxford University Press, 2013.

---

[70] John G. Stackhouse Jr., ed., *Evangelical Ecclesiology: Reality or Illusion?* (Grand Rapids: Baker Academic, 2003); Mark Husbands and Daniel J. Treier, eds., *The Community of the Word: Toward an Evangelical Ecclesiology* (Downers Grove, IL: IVP Academic, 2009).

Braaten, Carl E., and Robert W. Jenson, eds. *The Catholicity of the Reformation*. Grand Rapids: Eerdmans, 1996.

Bridges, Jerry. *The Gospel for Real Life: Return to the Liberating Power of the Cross*. Colorado Springs, CO: NavPress, 2002.

Calvin, John. *Institutes of the Christian Religion*. 2 vols. Edited by John T. McNeil. Translated by Ford Lewis Battles. Louisville, KY: Westminster-John Knox, 1960.

Carson, D. A. "When is Spirituality Spiritual? Reflections on Some Problems of Definition." *Journal of the Evangelical Theological Society* 37, no.3 (September 1994): 381–94.

Chapell, Bryan. *Christ-Centered Worship: Letting the Gospel Shape Our Practice*. Grand Rapids: Baker Academic, 2009.

Cosper, Mike. *Rhythms of Grace: How the Church's Worship Tells the Story of the Gospel*. Wheaton, IL: Crossway, 2013.

Cummings, Brian. *The Book of Common Prayer: The Texts of 1549, 1559, and 1662*. New York: Oxford University Press, 2011.

Davies, Horton. *Worship and Theology in England: From Cranmer to Baxter and Fox, 1534–1690*. 1961. Reprint Grand Rapids: Eerdmans, 1996.

Dever, Mark. *Nine Marks of a Healthy Church*. 3rd ed. Wheaton, IL: Crossway, 2013.

Eastwood, Cyril. *The Priesthood of All Believers: An Examination of the Doctrine from the Reformation to the Present Day*. Eugene, OR: Wipf and Stock, 2009.

Eire, Carlos M. N. *Reformations: The Early Modern World, 1450–1650*. New Haven, CT: Yale University Press, 2016.

_____. *War Against the Idols: The Reformation of Worship from Erasmus to Calvin*. New York: Cambridge University Press, 1989.

Estep, William R. *The Anabaptist Story: An Introduction to Sixteenth-Century Anabaptism*. 3rd ed. Grand Rapids: Eerdmans, 1996.

Ferguson, Sinclair B., David F. Wright, and J. I. Packer, eds. *New Dictionary of Theology*. Downers Grove, IL: IVP Academic, 1988.

Finn, Nathan A. "The Dangers of Postmodern Spirituality." *Expositor* 4 (March/April 2015): 38–41.

_____. "What in the World is Holiness? Christian Spiritualities in the Modern World." In *Biblical Spirituality*, ed. Christopher Morgan. Wheaton, IL: Crossway, 2019.

Finn, Nathan A., and Keith Whitfield, eds. *Spirituality for the Sent: A New Vision for the Missional Church*. Downers Grove, IL: IVP Academic, 2017.

Foster, Richard J. *Celebration of Discipline: The Path to Spiritual Growth*. 3rd ed. San Francisco: Harper San Francisco, 2002.

Fuller, Robert C. *Spiritual, But Not Religious: Understanding Unchurched America*. New York: Oxford University Press, 2001.

Garber, Steven. *Visions of Vocation: Common Grace for the Common Good*. Downers Grove, IL: InterVarsity Press, 2014.

George, Timothy. "The Priesthood of all Believers and the Quest for Theological Integrity." *Criswell Theological Review* 3 (Spring 1989): 283–94.

Greenman, Jeffrey P., and George Kalantzis, eds. *Life in the Spirit: Spiritual Formation in Theological Perspective*. Downers Grove, IL: IVP Academic, 2010.

Gritsch, Eric W., ed. *Church and Ministry III: Luther's Works*. Vol. 41. St. Louis: Concordia, 1966.

Hanson, Bradley. *Grace that Frees: The Lutheran Tradition*. Traditions of Christian Spirituality. Maryknoll, NY: Orbis, 2004.

Husbands, Mark, and Daniel J. Treier, eds., *The Community of the Word: Toward an Evangelical Ecclesiology*. Downers Grove, IL: IVP Academic, 2009.

Jacobs, Alan. *The Book of Common Prayer: A Biography*. Princeton, NJ: Princeton University Press, 2013.

Johnson, Eric L. *God and Soul Care: The Therapeutic Resources of the Christian Faith*. Downers Grove, IL: IVP Academic, 2017.

Jones, David W., and Russell S. Woodbridge. *Health, Wealth, and Happiness: How the Prosperity Gospel Overshadows the Gospel of Christ*. Grand Rapids: Kregel Academic, 2011.

Kuiper, Herman. *Calvin on Common Grace*. Grand Rapids: Smitter Book, 1928.

Kuyper, Abraham. *Common Grace: God's Gifts for a Fallen World*. Vol. 1: The Historical Section. Edited by Jordan J. Ballor and Stephen J. Grabill. Translated by Nelson D. Kloosterman and Ed M. van der Maas. Bellingham, WA: Lexham Press, 2016.

————. *Lectures on Calvinism*. Grand Rapids: Eerdmans, 1931.

Lane, Anthony N.S. *John Calvin: Student of Church Fathers*. Edinburgh: T&T Clark, 1999.

Lindberg, Carter. *The European Reformations*. 2nd ed. London: Wiley-Blackwell, 2010.

Lofton, Kathryn. *Oprah: The Gospel of an Icon*. Berkley, CA: University of California Press, 2011.

Lull, Timothy, ed., *Martin Luther's Basic Theological Writings*. Minneapolis: Fortress, 1989.

Luther, Martin. *Three Treatises*. Minneapolis: Fortress, 1970.

Mathis, David. *Habits of Grace: Enjoying Jesus through the Spiritual Disciplines*. Wheaton, IL: Crossway, 2016.

Mathison, Keith A. *The Shape of Sola Scriptura*. Moscow, ID: Canon Press, 2001.

McDermott, Gerald R., ed. *The Oxford Handbook of Evangelical Theology*. New York: Oxford University Press, 2013.

McGrath, Alister E. *Christian Spirituality*. Malden, MA: Blackwell, 1999.

_____. *Beyond the Quiet Time: Practical Evangelical Spirituality*. Vancouver, BC: Regent College Press, 2003.

Mouw, Richard J. *He Shines in All That's Fair: Culture and Common Grace*. Grand Rapids: Eerdmans, 2001.

Naselli, Andrew David, and Collin Hansen, eds. *Four Views on the Spectrum of Evangelicalism*. Counterpoints: Bible and Theology. Grand Rapids: Zondervan, 2011.

Nation, Philip. *Habits of our Holiness: How the Spiritual Disciplines Grow Us Up, Draw Us Together, and Send Us Out*. Chicago: Moody, 2016.

Ortberg, John. *The Life You've Always Wanted: Spiritual Disciplines for Ordinary People*. 2nd ed. Grand Rapids: Zondervan, 2009.

Parker, David. "Evangelical Spirituality Reviewed." *Evangelical Quarterly* 63, no. 2 (1991): 123–48.

Patterson, James A. "Anabaptist Kinship Revisited: Implications for Baptist Origins and Identity." In *Reformation 500: How the Greatest Revival Since Pentecost Continues to Shape the World Today*, ed. Ray Van Neste and J. Michael Garrett. Nashville: B&H Academic, 2017.

Paulson, Steven D. *Lutheran Theology*. London: T&T Clark, 2011.

Phillips, Charlie. "Roundtable: Re-Examining David Bebbington's 'Quadrilateral Thesis.'" *Fides et Historia* 47, no. 1 (Winter/Spring 2015): 47–96.

Plass, Ewald M., ed. *Giving.* Vol. 1 of *What Luther Says.* St. Louis: Concordia, 1959.

Plummer, Robert L. "Are the Spiritual Disciplines of 'Silence and Solitude' Really Biblical?" *Journal of Spiritual Formation and Soul Care* 2, no. 1 (Spring 2009): 101–12.

Powlison, David. *How Does Sanctification Work?* Wheaton, IL: Crossway, 2017.

Schreiner, Thomas R., and Matthew R. Crawford, eds. *The Lord's Supper: Remembering and Proclaiming Christ Until He Comes.* Nashville: B&H Academic, 2010.

Scorgie, Glen G., ed. *Dictionary of Christian Spirituality.* Grand Rapids: Zondervan, 2011.

Selderhuis, Herman. *Martin Luther: A Spiritual Biography.* Grand Rapids: Crossway, 2017.

Sheldrake, Philip. *Spirituality and History: Questions of Interpretation and Method.* New York: Crossroad, 1992.

Smith, James K. A. *You Are What You Love: The Spiritual Power of Habit.* Grand Rapids: Brazos, 2016.

Snyder, C. Arnold. *Following in the Footsteps of Christ: The Anabaptist Tradition.* Maryknoll, NY: Obis, 2004.

Stackhouse Jr., John G. ed., *Evangelical Ecclesiology: Reality or Illusion?* Grand Rapids: Baker Academic, 2003.

Thornbury, Gregory Alan. *Recovering Classic Evangelicalism: Applying the Wisdom and Vision of Carl F. H. Henry.* Wheaton, IL: Crossway, 2013.

Vanhoozer, Kevin J. *Biblical Authority after Babel: Retrieving the Solas in the Spirit of Mere Protestant Christianity.* Grand Rapids: Baker Academic, 2016.

Whitney, Donald. *Spiritual Disciplines for the Christian Life.* 2nd ed. Colorado Springs, CO: NavPress, 2014.

Wilhoit, James C. *Spiritual Formation as if the Church Mattered: Growing in Christ through Community.* Grand Rapids: Baker Academic, 2008.

_____. "Contemplative and Centering Prayer." *Journal of Spiritual Formation and Soul Care* 7, no. 1 (Spring 2014): 107–17.

Wuthnow, Robert. *After Heaven: Spirituality in America since the 1950s.* Berkley, CA: University of California Press, 1998.

Yarnell, Malcolm B., III. "The Priesthood of Believers: Rediscovering the Biblical Doctrine of Royal Priesthood." In *Restoring Integrity in Baptist*

Churches, ed. Thomas White, Jason G. Duesing, and Malcolm B. Yarnell III, 221–44. Grand Rapids: Kregel Academic, 2007.

_____. *The Anabaptists and Contemporary Baptists: Restoring New Testament Christianity*. Nashville: B&H Academic, 2013.

Zylstra, Sarah Eekhoff. "The 'Boy Who Came Back from Heaven' Retracts Story," *Christianity Today*. January 15, 2015; updated January 21, 2015. http://www.christianitytoday.com/news/ 2015/january/boy-who-came-back-from-heaven-retraction.html.

Luther's Theology of the Cross
as a Model for Sanctification

JOHN MCKINLEY

Martin Luther distinguished two ways of doing theology, based on how theologians view the cross and suffering. Luther's analysis of the theology of glory and the theology of the cross has been pressed into various uses, primarily with a focus on God's involvement in our suffering. The aim of this chapter is to take Luther's way of doing theology according to the cross as a model for God's providence in progressive sanctification. This is not a normal application, but it is surprisingly fruitful in making sense of God's works in sanctification and the Christian's response for engaging with those works.

Luther's claim that God is to be understood according to the cross and suffering means if we are to live with God, then we must be dependent upon his work for everything—whatever our vocation may be. The allure of a theology of glory is that effort brings fruit and locates our success within our work; however, a theology of the cross reorients this economy by locating success ultimately in the work of Christ through his chosen vessels.

Two Theologies of Sanctification

Theology of Glory

According to Luther, the way of glory takes the cross as God's provision to help humanity in our shortcomings. We may progress to righteousness with God by the help of his grace. Because of the cross, glorious good works are possible for the Christian, and the advance in moral self-improvement may thereby proceed. Gerhard Forde explains: "The hallmark of a theology of glory is that it will always consider grace as something of a supplement to whatever is left of human will and power."[1] The humiliation, weakness, foolishness, and suffering of the cross are viewed as an unfortunate necessity to deal with the mess of sin. The theology of glory looks to the cross for revelation of God's love and grace to provide what was needed for salvation, without looking at how God works in the humiliation of the cross.[2] Like Moses asking to see God's glory, and Philip asking Jesus to show the disciples the Father, the theologian of glory aspires to see God through his works and the natural theology of creation.[3] People assume that God's glory can be seen and understood rationally. We can scrutinize the deeper meaning of God's ways and attributes, and the science of the cross. What remains, then, is for us to respond to God's provisions of grace in daily life by obedience. We thus live to honor God by the glory of our good works. Despite the original human failure of Adam and Eve when they acted independently of God, the theology of glory persists in making room for human effort alongside God's works. Such a rational theology makes sense to us because it is built from our attempt to make sense of God and his ways.[4] The theology of glory is inspired by divine revelation instead of receiving and being confronted by revelation. Paul Althaus gives this summary: "The theology of glory seeks to know God directly in his obviously divine power, wisdom, and glory.... The theology of glory leads man to stand before God and strike a bargain on the basis of his ethical achievement in fulfilling the law."[5] I will argue in this chapter that the theology of glory is too commonly pervasive in evangelical faith and practice. The weakness of this glory approach is that evangelicals often remain stuck in their self-sufficiency either through trying to change themselves in self-sanctification,

---

[1] Gerhard O. Forde, *On Being a Theologian of the Cross: Reflections on Luther's Heidelberg Disputation, 1518* (Grand Rapids: Eerdmans, 1997), 16.

[2] Forde, 73–76.

[3] Kari Kopperi, "Theology of the Cross," chap. 8 in *Engaging Luther: A (New) Theological Assessment*, ed. Olli-Pekka Vainio (Eugene, OR: Wipf and Stock, 2010), 164.

[4] "Theologians of glory create a god in their own image and a picture of the human creature after their own longings. Neither corresponds to reality, Luther claimed." Robert Kolb, "Luther on the Theology of the Cross," *Lutheran Quarterly* 16 (2002): 448. "A theology of glory always leaves the will in control. It must therefore seek to make its theology attractive to the supposed 'free will.'" Forde, *Theologian of the Cross*, 9.

[5] Paul Althaus, *The Theology of Martin Luther*, trans. Robert C. Schultz (Philadelphia: Fortress, 1966), 27.

or through maintaining their independence from God, as if real changes of progressive sanctification were not necessary.

Theology of the Cross

In contrast to the theology of glory, the theology of the cross takes suffering and the cross as the model of God's work in the world. Luther argued, "Because men misused the knowledge of God through works, God wished again to be recognized in suffering. … Now it is not sufficient for anyone, and it does him no good to recognize God in his glory and majesty, unless he recognizes him in the humility and shame of the cross."[6] God alone is the operator in salvation, with no room for the human but to respond in the humility of faith. The cross shows that God works through suffering positively and with mysterious brilliance, not merely as a messy means to a glorious end. The cross shows that salvation occurs only by God's action on humanity, and through the goods of weakness and suffering, with no human contributions to the project. God's chosen work by the cross unmasks all illusions of glory in human initiatives to do good things in the world, as if these were a credit or resource in the progress of sanctification. The complete failure of the human project was demonstrated in Israel's history, and in the church subsequently, to the degree that even with God's grace to help, humanity cannot advance in righteousness. In the cross, God shows who he is. God's wisdom and power are displayed as what humanity considers insane foolishness and disgraceful weakness (1 Cor 1:18–31). In the cross and suffering, God shows how he works— pains and strains are God's curriculum of beneficial suffering for greater conformity to Christ. To know God in truth, people require God's so-called *alien work*: "God needs to take the first step, depriving the human being of his self-confidence. Luther even states that God makes man into nothing (*nihil*)."[7] The theology of the cross is a way of knowing God and his works properly, without regard for human glory in good works or the hubris that we could see God's glory according to our rationalistic and metaphysical speculations. Failing to see all things according to the cross and suffering

---

[6] *Heidelberg Disputation,* Proof for Thesis 20, trans. and ed. Harold J. Grimm, in Martin Luther, *Luther's Works* (hereafter cited LW), *Vol. 31: Career of the Reformer I,* ed. Helmut T. Lehman (Philadelphia: Fortress Press, 1957), 52–53.

[7] Kopperi, "Theology of the Cross," 158. The categories of God's *alien work* is paired with *proper work* by Luther. These will be defined and explained under the heading Thesis 4.

results in a warped vision of human efforts that effectively displace God's works, as in the theology of glory.

Luther's analysis is a broad vision for how to do theology and how to know God according to the cross and suffering; the narrow application of this vision is our concern here, especially as we consider sanctification in the daily Christian life. We will explore how a theology of the cross better undergirds the daily pursuit of Christian maturity, compared to the alternative of a theology of glory. Gerhard Forde observes that underlying Luther's *Heidelberg Disputation* is the question about relating to God: "What advances sinners on the way of righteousness before God?"[8] The focus of this chapter is built on the *Heidelberg Disputation* because of the clarity and focus it provides as we explore how this theology of the cross advances people on the way of righteousness before God as we journey from justification to glorification by way of sanctification.[9]

The theology of the cross is a shocking alternative to the common idea that Christian growth progresses through human efforts to obey God's requirements, with God's help. Evangelicals of the twenty-first century commonly embrace the same warped vision of sanctification that Luther identified as the theology of glory. Luther built his case that God's project, instead of being a program of advancing ourselves by good works, is to make sinners righteous according to God's works in the cross and suffering. Thus, the focus here will redirect Luther's concern for justification to progressive sanctification, which will take place in two steps.[10] First, we will explore the prevalence of a theology of glory in evangelical faith and practice, evidenced by four manifestations in common evangelical culture; and second, we will examine how the theology of the cross can become a model available to the church for discerning God's work in progressive sanctification.

When pastors and theologians lament about the so-called sanctification gap in evangelical Christianity, they would benefit from reading Luther's

---

[8] Forde, *Theologian of the* Cross, 23.

[9] For additional treatment on Luther's theology of the cross, see Walther von Loewenich, *Luther's Theology of the Cross*, trans. Herbert J. A. Bouman (Minneapolis: Augsburg, 1976).

[10] For others who have noted this application, see Kopperi, "Theology of the Cross," 172: "God's alien work is not a singular episode in the salvation process, but it is a continuous experience in Christian life. A Christian always remains a sinner and therefore he is confronted with God's alien and proper work every day." Also Kolb, "Luther on Theology of the Cross," 458: "The theology of the cross enables God's children to understand the shape of life as God has planned it for them, following Christ under the cross."

critique of the theology of glory.[11] Christian attempts at self-sanctification will always fail, Luther wrote, because they depend on human effort. Obedience to law does not bring righteousness because the human will, acting self-sufficiently, twists even our obedience into pride and independence from God.[12] Theologians in more recent time have noted various misapplications in the evangelical pursuit of sanctification, each of which is actually a version of the theology of glory.

Manifestation 1: Moralistic Therapeutic Deism

One expression of the theology of glory in American Christianity is the so-called Moralistic Therapeutic Deism that was recently identified by a national study of youth and religion in the United States.[13] This expression of the theology of glory is based on the evidence that several hundred teens gave in interviews with sociologists. The study exposed the reality that the faith Christian teens had learned from the adults surrounding them at home and church was a theology that communicated God is distant and uninvolved, but expects various moral requirements that we might in turn have good lives. This theology yields a view of sanctification as simply one's efforts to be a good person by obeying God, with God's help, if you want it, through prayer and other religious devotion. Moralistic therapeutic deism is the symptom of many American churches practicing a theology of glory: we can understand God and figure out a formula for living with him by staying out of his way; our job is to maintain our morality of good works and enjoy daily life. This faith ignores God's agenda for radical transformation of the disciple into conformity with Jesus.[14] This version of the theology of glory prizes human self-sufficiency to be a good person through doing good works and assenting to a few minimal aspects of Christian faith (while missing the reality of actually knowing God).

---

[11] Richard Lovelace, "The Sanctification Gap," *Theology Today*, 29, no. 4 (1973): 364. "There seemed to be a sanctification gap among Protestants, a peculiar conspiracy somehow to mislay the tradition of spiritual growth and to concentrate on side issues."

[12] LW 31:39, 40, 48–52. The first three theses in the *Heidelberg Disputation* introduce the problem of so-called good works that hinder the Christian from engaging with God because we commonly trust in our own works instead of God's works.

[13] Christian Smith and Melinda Lundquist Denton, *Soul Searching: The Religious and Spiritual Lives of American Teenagers* (New York: Oxford University Press, 2005).

[14] Dallas Willard labeled the distorted evangelical faith in America a "gospel of sin management," according to which "[t]ransformation of life and character is no part of the redemptive message." *The Divine Conspiracy* (New York: HarperCollins, 2001), 41.

Manifestation 2: Prosperity Theology

Another aspect of the theology of glory is the attempt to avoid suffering through good works, a trait that finds a modern echo in the American invention of prosperity theology. Here is Luther's critique: "Thesis 21. A theologian of glory calls evil good and good evil. A theologian of the cross calls the thing what it actually is." In the proof for this thesis, Luther charges that theologians of glory "call the good [suffering] of the cross evil and the evil of a [human virtuous] deed good."[15] Luther has earlier argued that good works are evil when we trust in them, because our trust in them blocks us from relying on God's works.[16] Forde explains: "We depend on and glory in our works, and we call these self-serving deeds good. Suffering, we insist, is bad. If it comes upon us we immediately begin to wonder if we have failed somehow in our works."[17] In the theology of glory, people judge by appearances of things, and so they misunderstand everything—especially those things which are governed by the economy of the Kingdom of God, in which weak are strong, poor are rich, and those that mourn are comforted.

Likewise, in prosperity theology we see the same agenda of superficial judgment by appearances calling all suffering bad, since suffering is assumed to be the opposite of well-being. Jesus rebuked the crowd for the same problem: "Do not judge according to appearance, but judge with righteous judgment" (John 7:24).[18] Paul rebuked the Christians at Corinth for misjudging his suffering as a discredit to his authority as an apostle (2 Cor 10–12). As a theology of glory that misunderstands suffering, "the prosperity gospel tries to solve the riddle of human suffering. It is an explanation for the problem of evil. It provides an answer to the question: Why me?"[19] The answer to "Why me?" in prosperity theology is that by our

---

[15] *LW* 31:53. Forde explains that the proper translation should be "theologian" even though the American Edition of *Luther's Works* has "theology of glory" and "theology of the cross."

[16] *LW* 31:43. Thesis 3 and its proof: "*Although the works of man always seem attractive and good, they are nevertheless likely to be mortal sins.* Human works appear attractive outwardly, but within they are filthy, as Christ says concerning the Pharisees in Matt. 23." The superficial attractiveness of these good works tempts people to make idols of themselves so they trust in their own works instead of trusting in God's works to save them: "To trust in works ... is equivalent to giving oneself the honor and taking it from God ... and to adore oneself as an idol" (*LW* 31:46, proof for Thesis 7).

[17] Forde, *Theologian of the Cross*, 83.

[18] All translations of biblical passages in this chapter are taken from the NASB.

[19] Kate Bowler, "Death, the Prosperity Gospel and Me," Opinion, *New York Times*, February 13, 2016, https://www.nytimes.com/2016/02/14/opinion/sunday/death-the-prosperity-gospel-and-me.html.

effort and obedience to God, people can avoid suffering and receive blessings. Kate Bowler explains the essential prosperity idea: "God grants health
and wealth to those with the right kind of faith. ... Follow these rules, and
God will reward you."[20] Salvation is now in the Christian's hands to avoid
pain and difficulty through optimistic belief. Sanctification is reduced to
the appearances of material well-being, while eclipsing God's agenda for
substantial change through discipleship to Jesus. Thus we have a second
manifestation of the theology of glory in contemporary American faith and
practice.

Manifestation 3: Cheap Grace

The theology of glory is not just an American problem, since we can
also see the avoidance of the cross and suffering in Bonhoeffer's critique of
cheap grace in the early twentieth century. He argued that German Lutherans had sidestepped the call to discipleship by saying that they would be
adding works to God's grace, if they tried to live righteously. Like prosperity theology, cheap grace is a way to maintain a Christian's independence
from God through the principle of correct belief—no radical changes of
one's life are necessary and are thus happily avoided. Both errors are strategies to escape God's demands of discipleship through costly grace—heavy
with the cost of God's Son and the disciple's whole life.[21]

Bonhoeffer's antidote of costly discipleship follows the same lines of the
theology of the cross: discipleship entails suffering with Jesus in daily life.[22]
Cheap grace as a theology of glory fails to see God's action on the Christian,
that the job of sanctification cannot be finished by mere human effort to
believe in God's grace (a spurious belief, cf. Jas 2:14–26). Instead, costly
grace and the theology of the cross see properly that "[t]he cross is laid on
every Christian"[23] as a work of God, and that "[s]uffering ... is the badge
of true discipleship."[24] Salvation is a gift, but we must pay a price to share
in Christ's death by allowing God to kill all our illusions of self-sufficiency.
Along with prosperity theology and moralistic therapeutic deism, cheap
grace shows the prevalence of the theology of glory. These versions are alike

---

[20] Bowler.
[21] Dietrich Bonhoeffer, *The Cost of Discipleship*, trans. R.H. Fuller, rev. Irmgard Booth (New York: Touchstone, 1995), 49. "When he spoke of grace, Luther always implied as a corollary that it cost him his own life."
[22] Bonhoeffer, 87.
[23] Bonhoeffer, 89.
[24] Bonhoeffer, 91.

in the way that Christians hide out from sanctification through avoiding the demands of the cross and the reality of suffering as the model of God's works to produce our discipleship.

Manifestation 4: Diligent Moralism

A fourth version of the theology of glory errs to the opposite side of moral performance that Luther targeted directly. The most dangerous theology of glory is the illusion that a Christian can advance in righteousness through obedient moral performance of God's requirements. Evangelicals commonly affirm the gift of justification by faith, and then proceed to work at earning their worthiness before God through personal diligence in progressive sanctification.[25] Diligence may take the forms of spiritual disciplines, church ministry, and the activism of evangelism, missions, and social justice or mercy ministries. While the diligent moralist may look more religious than other Christians who seem to be putting in little or no effort at good works, Paul's rebuke to the Galatians attacks the hard worker: "Having begun by the Spirit, are you now being perfected by the flesh?" (Gal 3:3). The problem is trust in human actions as the basis of one's maturity before God. John Coe defines the moralist as attempting "to grow oneself by being good in the power of the self, to live the moral life in autonomy from the transformative power of the Spirit."[26] The appearance of many good works can be a cover for the unchanged reality of the Christian who persists in self-reliance for self-righteousness. Like the farce of the emperor's new clothes in the folktale, moralists may be optimistic about the value of their activism, but belief alone does not make progressive sanctification a reality; for this is an end that only God can produce (Eph 2:10; 1 Thess 5:23–24).

Moralism is a failure of sanctification because human autonomy, first asserted by Adam and Eve, is the very illusion of self-sufficiency.[27] The human being was not created to make choices independently of God, so

---

[25] John Coe, "Resisting the Temptation of Moral Formation: Opening to Spiritual Formation in the Cross and the Spirit," *Journal of Spiritual Formation & Soul Care* 1, no. 1 (2008): 54–78. Coe's solution to the problem he analyzes is retraining the conscience through spiritual disciplines to open to the Spirit's work on the heart (67, 76–77). For me, this solution is too near to becoming just another program of doing by the diligent Christian. Instead, I urge that we must despair of our initiatives entirely and "be still" to respond to God's operations on us. Perhaps we miss these operations if we focus on the spiritual exertions of religious people as the venue of God's works instead of attending to the grit and pinch of our troubles in daily life.

[26] Coe, 56.

[27] Coe, 61.

Luther argued that self-sufficient attempts at good works are mortal sins, deadly to our salvation.[28] This is an echo of Jesus, who warned that the self-righteous scribes and Pharisees were a danger to themselves (Matt 23:25–28) and others (Luke 11:44) because the illusion of moral performance eclipses one's sense of need for God's work (Luke 18:9–17). The Pharisees show us human love for glory in our good works (Matt 6:2, 5, 16). We are tempted to trust in these works instead of trusting in God's works. We are tempted to prefer our glory rather than God's suffering and accomplishment of righteousness for us, which is the only righteousness that avails before God. As Luther wrote: "Thesis 25. He is not righteous who does much, but he who, without work, believes much in Christ."[29] The cross leaves no room for the glory of human works.

Human Glory vs. the Cross

The theology of glory is natural and common to human optimism about capacities for good, albeit with the help of justifying grace and other props; the theology of the cross shocks our ears. The theologian of glory puts the law and effort to use for personal advance in righteousness while imagining he is honoring God. Thus, a *practicing* theologian of glory might add many disclaimers to attribute God's grace powering her works, but no amount of footnoting to credit God will erase the evidence of our innate glory hunger.[30]

Sanctification requires that God displaces our attempts at self-reliance with the reality of our dependence on him. Repeated assertion of human initiatives for good works cannot advance the Christian in righteousness since our need is for increased dependence. Self-sufficiency expressed in good works is actually avoiding God, a return to the flesh. For this reason, Luther attacked the theology of glory for exalting a contribution of the human will for good works as "mortal sins" (Thesis 3), and he swept aside the illusion of people having any ability for good apart from God acting through them (Theses 13–18).[31] The alternative Luther offered is that we

---

[28] LW 31:39. "Thesis 3. Although the works of man always seem attractive and good, they are nevertheless likely to be mortal sins." Luther adds that the works are not mortal only when we fear that they may be mortal sins!

[29] LW 31:40.

[30] The emphasis on practicing here is to clarify that all believers practice their theologies and thus are practical theologians, even if they have not theologized about this reality in their life.

[31] LW 31:40.

turn away from looking at human capacities to see instead the cross and suffering. This is a better and more biblical way forward, as we look to the cross for God's action in the life of the Christian and a model for understanding God's work of sanctification.

Sanctification According to the Cross

How is the theology of the cross a model of progressive sanctification? The lens of the cross and suffering opens our vision to see God at work conforming us to Jesus by means of everyday strains and pains. This is a better model of sanctification because it recognizes God as the one who sanctifies us by his workmanship (Eph 2:10), with our role properly diminished to engaging with his initiatives. This model meaningfully draws a close connection between Jesus and the Christian through the cross and suffering that is God's curriculum for us all. The lens invites us to see God's work in everyday strains and pains on the way to forming us to love, hope, and faith.

The theologian of the cross sees and embraces God's work, however ugly, foolish, and repulsive it may appear to us at first. Luther understood that God's chosen method to operate through the cross and suffering means that these are absolute goods. They are not simply absolute goods in the case of Jesus, but for the Christian also in God's work of progressive sanctification. To this conclusion, Luther's proposal can be developed into five theses about sanctification: 1) the cross evidences God's good use of suffering; 2) the cross is the curriculum for sanctification; 3) the cross redeems pain and suffering; 4) the cross crucifies our ongoing attachments to sin; and 5) the cross forms Christ's death and life in us.

Thesis 1: The Cross Evidences God's Good Use of Suffering

The cross, and Jesus's life, show that God puts suffering to good use. Thus, the theologian of the cross is undeterred by the apparent public relations problem of a *good* God whose children experience some of the harshest and most painful events of history (e.g., Job, Israel, Jesus, Paul, Christian martyrs). With the cross clearly having been "predetermined" by God (Luke 22:22; Acts 2:23; 4:27–28), we must say that all Jesus's suffering occurred by God's design and are a supreme good.[32] Suffering that results from evil

---

[32] I will support this claim later in the chapter. A parallel is Joseph's revelation that his brothers' evil act to enslave him was benevolently intended by God (Gen 45:7–8; 50:20).

choices is paradoxically good in God's plan and useful to bring good results. This is mysterious, like the use of chemotherapy and radiation to poison cancer while healing a patient, or a surgeon cutting a patient to heal her of a harmful tumor. Luther explained that the cross is our model for understanding God's paradoxical works of using suffering for positive purposes:

> *Thesis 21. A theologian of glory calls evil good and good evil. A theologian of the cross calls the thing what it actually is.* This is clear: He who does not know Christ does not know God hidden in suffering. Therefore, he prefers [good] works to suffering, glory to the cross, strength to weakness, wisdom to folly, and, in general, good [works that people do] to evil [of suffering that God orchestrates]. These are the people whom the apostle calls "enemies of the cross of Christ" (Phil 3:18), for they hate the cross and suffering and love works and the glory of works. Thus, they call the good of the cross evil and the evil of a deed good. God can be found only in suffering and the cross, as has already been said. Therefore, the friends of the cross say that the cross is good and works are evil.[33]

The cross was ordained by God to include betrayal, injustice, murder, rejection, and suffering the wrath of God. Clearly, these episodes of suffering had value as Jesus was to be the suffering servant: paying for our sins, breaking the power of sin, death, and the devil, accommodating himself to the vulnerability of his people, revealing the true good of suffering in God's universe, and, above all else, extending the maximum of God's self-giving love to us.

In view of the wisdom, goodness, and providence of God, we can assume that each moment of pain that Jesus endured had value for his mission, that all his suffering was ordained for many good purposes. We know that Jesus "learned obedience from the things which He suffered" (Heb 5:8), and that he became merciful and faithful as a human high priest. His competency as the Mediator depends on his lifelong suffering, "since He Himself was tempted in that which He has suffered, He is able to come to the aid of those who are tempted. ... [He is] One who has been tempted in all things as we are" (Heb 2:17–18; 4:14–15). Christians typically think of Jesus's suffering on the cross as his portion of pain, but his entire human

---

[33] LW 31:53. As noted earlier at n16, I follow Forde's translation of "theologian of glory" and "theologian of the cross" for Thesis 21.

life was a divine curriculum of attempted assassinations, material poverty, demonic attacks, false accusations, public mockery and humiliation, betrayal to his enemies by a disciple, abandonment by friends and family, and a lifetime of temptations to sin against which he always fought.[34]

God's use of suffering for Jesus seems wrong; his goodness is hidden beneath the harshness of his methods, so such use may not seem to fit with a loving God. We rationally would expect that a God of goodness would only use painless means to bring out the good results he desires in us. A God who loves the world and kindly provides for all sorts of creatures also afflicts people ferociously by means of natural disasters, diseases, demonic malice, and the full array of human evils—always with good purposes in view (cf. Gen 45:7–8; 50:20; Rom 8:28–29). Occasions of suffering throughout the Bible are clearly attributed to God's hand (Exod 4:11, Job, the cross, etc.) without apology, even if the suffering was caused by demonic or human choices. God is not a doer of evil, but he does orchestrate the materials of his creatures' evil variously for purposes of justice against evil (as in the curses of Genesis 3 and the flood of Genesis 6), for warning against worse outcomes (Luke 13:1–5), or to position his people for events of salvation (as with Joseph's enslavement and unjust imprisonment in Egypt).[35] We see in the case of Job that God limits evil that does not suit his purposes, and in Jesus's life the crowd was thwarted many times from assassinating Jesus because God's plan was to bring him to the cross. Accordingly, we may say that God is in control of everything that occurs, good and bad (Exod 4:11) for good results that he brings about despite and by means of the evil and suffering that creatures cause. The assurance for the Christian is that God has promised to bring all suffering to a permanent end when he establishes the new creation (Rev 21:4). God uses suffering on the large scale of bringing his original creation to perfection, and on the small scale of bringing the rebel sinner to voluntary union with him as a saint (see Thesis 2, below). The cross shows us how to see God's complicated involvement, working in strange ways to show his love to sinners, and working in

---

[34] For the argument that Jesus was tempted throughout his earthly life, see John E. McKinley, *Tempted for Us: Theological Models and the Practical Relevance of Christ's Impeccability and Temptation,* Paternoster Theological Monographs (Milton Keynes, UK: Paternoster, 2009).

[35] More could be said to explain the complicated operations of God's providence to permit and use evil and the resulting suffering for his good purposes at the end of the day. At least one benefit of the theology of the cross for the so-called theological problem of evil is that we have a clear case of God ordaining a cluster of evil acts that were intended by God for good results while remaining real evils for which the evildoers will be judged (cf. Judas's sense of his own guilt when he hanged himself).

mysterious ways to transform sinners into lovers of God. In Luther's words: "Thesis 28. The love of God does not find, but creates, that which is pleasing to it. The love of man comes into being through that which is pleasing to it."[36] The cross and Jesus's life of suffering show that God typically works by putting suffering to good use.

Thesis 2: The Cross is the Curriculum for Sanctification

The curriculum for making Jesus to be the suffering servant is the same for conforming the Christian to Jesus. Seeing God's works in the cross, we can translate this reality to God's involvement in a Christian's pain. God's use of suffering to form Jesus in his mission has double value to form Christ in others, making them to be suffering servants. Paradoxically, salvation in Christ involves people in becoming like him, with a life in the pattern of suffering "in His steps" (1 Pet 2:21–25). Christians are united to Jesus, so they will endure what he endured of hatred and persecution (John 15:20), and learn as he did the obedience of faith through suffering (Heb 5:8). Discipleship is the Christian's response to "deny himself, and take up his cross daily" (Luke 9:23) in the lived metaphor of crucifixion. This lifelong death of self-sufficiency cannot be done to ourselves, as if we could self-starve, immolate, mortify, or otherwise punish our old self into sanctified conformity to Jesus. The ascetics in church history attempted this posture in their own quest for sanctification, but instead created another manifestation of glory related to diligent moralism. This, however, does not work. Instead, crucifixion is a method of death that must be done to the victim, with the victim's willing participation ("If anyone wishes to come after Me, he must deny himself, and take up his cross daily and follow Me," Luke 9:23). Jesus suffered crucifixion to end his earthly life, and so must we, dying deaths of our self-assertion throughout each day. For our sakes, Jesus denied himself the safety of avoiding the cross ("yet not as I will, but as You will," Matt 26:39). The same call is thrust upon us in choices large and small that entail suffering the death of our independence, self-sufficiency, autonomy, self-righteousness, and self-protection.

In Romans 6:4–6, Paul explains "the flesh" and "the old self" as a continuing problem for the believer that is solved through union with Christ for death and resurrection:

---

[36] LW 31:41.

Therefore we have been buried with Him through baptism into death, so that as Christ was raised from the dead through the glory of the Father, so we too might walk in newness of life. For if we have become united with Him in the likeness of His death, certainly we shall also be in the likeness of His resurrection, knowing this, that our old self was crucified with Him, in order that our body of sin might be done away with, so that we would no longer be slaves to sin.

The Christian practice of water baptism dramatizes a believer's experience of union with Christ.[37] Luther took the connection between water baptism and sharing in Jesus's death to be a daily experience throughout one's life, not merely a one-time initiation—that baptism pictured a daily dying of the Christian's attachment to sin (self-sufficiency, "the old Adam"):

[Baptism...] is simply the slaying of the old Adam and the resurrection of the new man, both of which actions must continue in us our whole life long. Thus, a Christian life is nothing else than a daily Baptism, once begun and ever continued.[38]

[Baptism] indicates that the Old Adam in us should by daily contrition and repentance be drowned and die with all sins and evil desires....By baptism we have been made to share in Christ's death and resurrection.[39]

Defeated and dealt with in principle by the cross, the flesh, "Old Adam," as a power still pulls at the Christian to live contrary to the Spirit in the habitual and familiar ways of sin (Gal 5:17). The enslaving power of sin before conversion now continues to drag as weakened and invisible tentacles of perpetual evil in the modes of pride, coveting, lying, and so on that we are warned against in the Bible. Such a multifaceted and maladaptive personal condition must be crucified and allowed to die. The crucifixion has already begun (we "have been baptized into His death," Rom 6:3), but killing by crucifixion is not instantaneous completion as with beheading or hanging. Notice that crucifixion is a drawn-out death that sometimes

---

[37] While a possible interpretation of Romans 6 is reference to Spirit baptism, I think water baptism is more likely because of Paul's reference to water baptism as union with Christ in Galatians 3:26–28, where he connects baptism and clothing language ("put on Christ") and repeats the idea of union with Christ by this clothing metaphor in Romans 13:14; Colossians 3:10–12; Ephesians 4:24.

[38] Martin Luther, "The Large Catechism," in *The Book of Concord the Confessions of the Evangelical Lutheran Church*, trans. and ed. Theodore G. Tappert (Philadelphia: Fortress, 1959), 446.

[39] Martin Luther, *Luther's Small Catechism* (St. Louis: Concordia, 1986), 210–11.

takes many days. Death does not come quickly without leg breaking (or, in Jesus's case, suffering something extra not visible to observers: the wrath of God). People could remain alive while enduring crucifixion for a few days. A spear thrust to the chest in Jesus's case was a confirmation that death had finally occurred.

Death by crucifixion also comes with some cooperation of the victim, by contrast to other executions in which the victim is entirely passive and one's life is cut off or ripped out in sudden violence. The crucified one progressively submits to death on the cross, just as we see Jesus yielding up his spirit while the two men hanging alongside him persisted in struggling against their deaths and had their legs broken to end their resistance (since they did not embrace the cross).

What prevents the crucified one from dying? His own efforts to remain alive by continuing to support himself for gulps of breath. Only when he is exhausted will the man surrender to death. You cannot crucify yourself, but you can choose either to resist the cross or to embrace the death a cross inflicts (through asphyxiation). Disciples of Jesus must each voluntarily "take up his cross daily and follow [Him]" (Luke 9:23). We must actively surrender to God's works that kill our familiar adaptive mechanisms (the flesh). We must submit to the crucifixion in daily life. In this way, the metaphor of crucifixion is our lifelong suffering of God's sanctification.[40] This metaphor offers a good fit with other statements that the afflictions and daily suffering of this life are how we follow Jesus's path of suffering to glory (Rom 8:17–18) and part of God's work to conform us to the image of his Son (Rom 8:28–29). He progressively exhausts our attempts to live from the flesh, our self-sufficiency, and God progressively defeats our illusions of our ability to do anything apart from him.

For the Christian, the metaphor of crucifixion is a severe and *imitatio Christi* model of God's work to sanctify us progressively through union with Christ. We die and live with him because he is our new identity and reality, even as we are his virtual body (1 Cor 6:15). We are made to share in Jesus's sufferings of all sorts (1 Pet 4:13) and on the way to sharing in his liberty from sin and death that plague us now. The lens of the cross and

---

[40] The metaphor of crucifixion for God's work of sanctification is similar to the metaphor of smelting precious metals from ore, often translated as "testing" as in Proverbs 17:3, cf. Isaiah 48:10, "I have refined you ... I have tested you in the furnace of affliction," and 1 Peter 1:7, "the proof of your faith, being more precious than gold ... even though tested by fire."

suffering for seeing God's works allows us to see why we suffer. The curriculum for making Jesus to be the suffering servant is the same for conforming the Christian to Jesus and forming Jesus in the Christian (Gal 4:19).

Thesis 3: The Cross Redeems Pain and Suffering

Suffering that God uses for sanctification includes everyday strains and pains. God's providence exerted to sanctify people by means of suffering after Jesus's pattern is clear in Romans 8:28–29, where the context of chapter 8 deals with assurance of God's care in the midst of "the sufferings of this present time" (v. 18) to explain what Paul means by "all things":

> And we know that God causes all things to work together for good to those who love God, to those who are called according to His purpose. For those whom He foreknew, He also predestined to become conformed to the image of His Son, so that He would be the firstborn among many brethren.

The assurance is given many times to energize the Christian's joy and assurance of God's care when suffering "various trials" (James 1:2–6), "momentary, light affliction" (2 Cor 4:17), "tribulations" (Rom 5:3–5), and "a thorn in the flesh" (2 Cor 12:7–10). Apart from union with Christ and the theology of the cross, these assurances and the paradoxical outcomes of Christian joy amid all sorts of troubles make no sense at all. Seeing them through the lens of the cross enables us to embrace God's works more profitably than if we tell ourselves that these troubles are just the problem of evil to be endured patiently, but with little real purpose in God's hands.[41]

Living in the West with religious freedom and abundant material prosperity, we have the tendency to distinguish suffering of everyday strains and pains from religious suffering, the trouble that is caused by explicit witness to Jesus. According to this distinction of religious suffering, the hundred or so references to suffering and affliction in the New Testament are commonly assumed to be limited to the troubles specifically incurred as part of Christian witness (e.g., persecution for preaching the gospel, martyrdom). I appreciate the severity of abuse that many Christians around the world

---

[41] Or, according to prosperity theology, we might be tempted to read troubles as punishments for failures in obedience. Instead, even if we do commit sins that cause us pain, this suffering is not the punishment for sin (only Hell is that). Jesus propitiated God's wrath for all our sin; suffering for our sins in our lives is better seen as consequences provided to warn us off further self-destruction (Gal 6:7–8). We are our own cautionary tale.

continue to suffer because of their identification with Jesus, starting with the imprisonment of Peter and John for preaching about Jesus (Acts 4) and the assassination of Stephen (Acts 7). Clearly, Christians share in persecutions and hatred after the pattern of what Jesus suffered because they bear witness to Jesus. Nonetheless, for every Christian, suffering as a result of bearing witness to Jesus is not the only sort of pain that has value and afflicts people for Christ's sake.

For every Christian, all suffering is religious suffering, providentially, since by these troubles God is attacking our self-sufficiency to increase dependence on him. By "all suffering," I mean all the everyday strains and pains, in a range from mild to severe, including physical, psychological, and social distresses. For example, one Christian is afflicted with a life-long and unwanted same-sex attraction; another battles against heterosexual lust in recovery from a pornography addiction of a decade earlier; one endures imbalances of hormones that incline him to depression; another faces cancer with a sequence of painful therapies by surgery, radiation, and chemotherapy; and another suffers daily with chronic back pain. All troubles and frustrations are the afflictions due to sin in a world that is hostile to God and life (which pains provoke us to hope for God's renewal of all things, as in Rom 8:18–25; Rev 21–22). All people suffer these large and small strains in daily life, to varying degrees (some people have troubles much worse than others). These examples of suffering include sins committed by people against others, the consequences of our own sins, demonic afflictions (2 Cor 12, Luke 4), and the chaos of earthquakes, diseases, harsh weather, psychological disturbances, and physiological maladies. Notice how many times suffering is described in the New Testament with vague terms so that we might see the full range of our everyday strains and pains according to this theology of God's paradoxical and providential works for our sanctification: "a thorn in the flesh" (2 Cor 12:7); "various trials" (Jas 1:2; 1 Pet 1:6); "afflicted in every way" (2 Cor 4:8); "our tribulations" (Rom 5:3); "our weaknesses" (Heb 4:15), "discipline" (Heb 12:5–14). When we consider the idea of the cross and suffering as the lens of God's work in sanctification, we see that the suffering that God uses includes everyday strains and pains to make suffering servants. Since the goal in sanctification is conformity to Jesus (Rom 8:28–29), and since Jesus was a suffering servant (Heb 5:8), then at least some of the goal in sanctification is to become a suffering servant like Jesus was for us—a vessel through whom God does his works. Everyday troubles are effective to that goal, as daily experiences of cross bearing. Jesus suffered on our behalf, and as the model for what we are to become in relationship with him. Suffering and troubles are inevitable for everyone in life, but for the Christian these are repurposed by God to be worthwhile for sanctification.

Thesis 4: The Cross Crucifies Our Ongoing Attachments to Sin

God orchestrates suffering as a scalpel to remove the effects of sin that obstruct us from God. He makes us to suffer for our independence from him and all attempts to live from ourselves instead of through reliance on him. Suffering makes us stop and look to him who can stop our suffering but chooses not to. We are forced by pain and trouble to look at what God is doing, to question how he wants us to respond, and to receive his emptying, grinding, and humbling works operating on us. These are the seemingly unattractive and evil acts of God, his strange, "unusual work" (Isa 28:21) by which "he humbles us thoroughly, making us despair, so that he may exalt us in his mercy, giving us hope."[42] Luther explained the theology of the cross as a model for how God relates to people paradoxically by using suffering to attack our perpetual reliance on good works:

> ...through the cross works are dethroned and the old Adam, who is especially edified by works, is crucified. It is impossible for a person not to be puffed up by his good works, unless he has first been deflated and destroyed by suffering and evil until he knows that he is worthless and that his works are not his but God's.[43]

We could not see this unless God had pointed to the parallel of discipleship as taking up one's cross *daily* (Luke 9:23), meaning some sort of devastation must be done to us *every day*. The cross and suffering are God's attack on human illusions of self-sufficiency through reliance on good works for some glory or merit before God, as Luther explained:

> He who has not been brought low, reduced to nothing through the cross and suffering, takes credit for works and wisdom and does not give credit to God. He thus misuses and defiles the gifts of God. He,

---

[42] LW 31:44. Proof for Thesis 4, "*Although the works of God always seem unattractive and appear evil, they are nevertheless really eternal merits.*"

[43] LW 31:53. Proof for Thesis 21.

however, who has emptied himself through suffering no longer does works but knows God works through him. He knows that it is sufficient if he suffers and is brought low by the cross in order to be annihilated all the more.[44]

Since our primary problem is self-sufficiency, the removal of our attachment to the flesh cannot be done by our initiative. God must do the surgery on us, and suffering is his scalpel. This painful and devastating work that seems to attack the believer is termed by Luther God's "alien work" (Isa 28:21) of affliction that is paired with God's "proper work" of assurance and formation. Both are elements of God's work for salvation. The so-called alien works of God hurt, but they also heal us from the more painful problem of ongoing independence from God's care. In commentary on Psalm 2, Luther explained the paradox of God's attack on his people to conquer our stubborn resistance to him. In shocking terms, Luther wrote:

> He is the God of life and salvation and this is His proper work, yet, in order to accomplish this, He kills and destroys. These works are alien to Him, but through them He accomplishes His proper work. For He kills our will that His may be established in us. He subdues the flesh and its lusts that the spirit and its desires may come to life.[45]

God's alien work is to tear down the disciple in preparation for his so-called proper work of filling and working through people by God's own agenda, conforming them to Jesus. God's alien works include the use of suffering to attack our self-sufficiency. Radical change is needed that we cannot do by our initiatives in religious exertions. Neither will talk therapy displace the old self. God creates change through suffering to defeat our illusion of self-sufficiency and all attachments to the flesh. God also creates change through suffering to develop our humble dependence on God and receptivity to his love for us. Why is suffering the necessary approach to our condition? Because our situation is intractable as personal identity wrapped up in the flesh, our very self-identity, God can only change us through attack and trauma that defeats moralism and convinces us to rely on him instead of ourselves. God succeeds in emptying us of our fears, illusions about ourselves, false ideas about him, and our trust in the glory

---

[44] LW 31:55. Proof for Thesis 24.
[45] *LW* 14:335, quoted in Forde, *On Being a Theologian*, 88.

of our works. This emptying is the alien work to make possible his so-called proper work of filling us with his Spirit, leading us in life with him, and exerting his love through us. According to the thesis of the cross and suffering, God puts suffering to use to attack obstructions in us. This is his work of loving us to make us receptive to him.

Thesis 5: The Cross Forms Christ's Death and Life in Us

God's alien and proper works accomplish our conformity to Jesus in faith, hope, and love. Luther identified faith, hope, and love as virtuous conditions that are only possible through suffering, meaning they are divinely accomplished, not humanly wrought: "Other virtues may be perfected by doing; *but faith, hope, and love, only by suffering,* by suffering I say, that is, *by being passive under the divine operation.*"[46] The theology of the cross as a model means paradoxically that God saves through suffering in Christ and Christians. Jesus suffered *for* them; Christians now suffer *with* him because they exist in real union with him, experiencing "the fellowship of His sufferings, being conformed to His death" so that they might also "attain to the resurrection from the dead" (Phil 3:10–11) *with* him. God's alien works tear believers down; God's proper works build believers up, conforming them to Christ. Faith, hope, and love are the practice of personal engagement with God, particularly as a paradox in which the Christian holds to God and his promises in the face of circumstances that appear to contradict the reality and goodness of God, such as when people suffer horribly. Faith, hope, and love are possible without suffering, but Luther's claim is that these virtues are *perfected* through suffering; that is, in the context of troubles, faith, hope, and love are brought to fullness. Similarly, God's response to Paul about his thorn in the flesh was that "power is perfected in weakness" (2 Cor 12:9), an echo of the meaning Paul explained earlier in the letter as the value of the many dimensions of his suffering to display God's power unmistakably: "We have this treasure in earthen vessels [vulnerability to suffering], so that the surpassing greatness of the power will be of God and not from ourselves" (2 Cor 4:7). When Paul and those with him should have felt crushed, despair, forsaken, and been destroyed by their afflictions, their ongoing faith, hope, and love was clearly evidence of God's power active in them. Troubles in life are

---

[46] Martin Luther, *Operationes in Psalmos, 1519–1521,* WA 5.176.1, quoted and translated in Forde, *Theologian of the Cross,* 86n17. Emphasis in Forde's quote.

the dark background against which faith, hope, and love appear all the brighter, since suffering requires that we trust in, depend on, and engage with God more heavily than at other times in life.

Luther interpreted faith, hope, and love as the formation that God presses toward in the believer, after stripping away the obstructions, particularly our ongoing illusion that we can do good things on our own:

> Wherefore, let this be your standard rule: wherever the holy scriptures command good works to be done, understand that it forbids you to do any good work by yourself, because you cannot; but to keep a holy Sabbath unto God, that is, a rest from all your works, and that you become dead and buried and permit God to work in you. Unto this you will never attain, except by faith, hope, and love; that is, by a total mortification of yourself (Col. 3:5) and all your own works.[47]

Luther would rebuke us if we imagined that the mortification was something we could do. As in crucifixion, we cannot mortify our flesh, our desires for sin and independence; we submit to God's alien works exerted graciously on us. Any supposed religious success at faith, hope, and love through our efforts would resurrect our illusion of self-sufficiency. Our vision of progressive sanctification must be according to the cross, a work that we cannot do or even add to. God alone must do it, his proper work to fill and form us in Christ, and we voluntarily embrace his gift.

Going beyond Luther's claim that faith, hope, and love are perfected through suffering, we may see further that they specify the meaning of conformity to Jesus, the goal of our sanctification. These virtues are not personal exertions, but the shape of Jesus's *modus operandi* that God forms progressively in the Christian. The triad of faith, hope, and love in 1 Corinthians 13:13 is well known; since their meaning is not told in this passage, I suggest a brief biblical theology of their meaning, drawing from Luther's definitions for the terms. Normally, Christians read the meanings as *faith* is trust in God, *hope* is expectation of eschatological promises, and *love* is the ongoing life in relationships.[48] I suggest that we can see in the three a summary of Jesus's life as God's aim of sanctification for the Christian.

---

[47] Martin Luther, *Operationes in Psalmos*, 277, WA 5.169.14–19, quoted in Forde, *Theologian of the Cross*, 109.

[48] Gordon D. Fee, *The First Epistle to the Corinthians* (Grand Rapids: Eerdmans, 1987), 650. Paul's point in citing these three is to mark their permanence as a contrast to the temporary manifestation of so-called spiritual gifts in the church.

First, while faith is normally synonymous with trust or belief, we can see a dimension of faith as humility, that is, faith as opposed to works of merit (Eph 2:8–9), and the believer's posture of abject emptiness before God, like a child (any truly good works that we do are the result of God's workmanship, Eph 2:10). This meaning of faith as humility is less a cognitive thing than "the faith" as a set of beliefs (Acts 14:22), or exerted faith as reliance on God's promise to save (Rom 14:22). Faith as humility is a condition and consequence of God's long work to tear down self-sufficiency and empty out all that is within us that gets in God's way and obstructs us from enjoying God. Interpreting Luther's view of humility, Forde writes, "Humility is always something done to us. Humility in this context means precisely to be reduced to the position where we claim *absolutely nothing*."[49] For Luther, faith and humility were closely connected: "This is the faith that saves…. This faith is the humility which turns its back on its own reason and its own strength."[50] Jesus exemplifies this humility as the servant washing his disciples' feet, and by not counting the right to be honored as God as something to be grasped (Phil 2:6–11). His model of humility to serve others is the shape of a Christian's life. Like him, we are brought low and serve others, not from exertion, but from God moving us because we trust only in him and not in our own movements. While it is right to think of faith as our reliance on God, I suggest the aspect of faith as humility is a mode of operating in daily life as the result of God's works, and a mode that Jesus exemplified thoroughly for us. This sort of faith as humility comes clearly into view when we look at ourselves through the cross to see we are nothing in ourselves, and anything we have is a gift received from God (1 Cor 4:7). John the Baptist's view of himself as a humble servant to Jesus's mission is the paradigm for every Christian: "He must increase, but I must decrease" (John 3:30).

Second, "hope" is normally an eschatological reach to God's promises, but there is also a connotation of existential dependence. We see in Jesus a continual dependence on his Father's initiative enabling him to do anything. Jesus's teaching, exorcisms, and other works were exerted by God's Spirit through him (John 14:10; Acts 2:22). As the Messiah, he functioned as the Man-of-the-Spirit, the human king empowered by the Holy Spirit

---

[49] Forde, *Theologian of the Cross*, 62. The italic emphasis is Forde's.

[50] Martin Luther, *Early Theological Works*, ed. and trans. James Atkinson, Library of Christian Classics 16 (Philadelphia: Westminster, 1962), 289, quoted in Forde, *Theologian of the Cross*, 62.

to be the suffering servant for the people. The simple summary of his life of faithful dependence is John 17:4, "I glorified You on the earth, having accomplished the work which You have given Me to do." Jesus's dependence on the Spirit of God for leading and empowering his daily life choices is also the model for Christian dependence on God. Instead of independence and the delusion of autonomy, Christians can be "led by the Spirit" (Rom 8:14) and "filled with the Spirit" (Eph 5:18) so that their choices are moved by God, living under God's influence, and thereby operate as godly. Conformity of our choices to God's will is one clear outcome of sanctification (Rom 12:2; Phil 2:12–13). Instead of living year to year by inviting God to guide our major decisions, God's intention seems to be that we would be open to his leading in all our choices that he wants to be involved in—even decisions that seem very insignificant or trivial to us. How do I spend the next two hours of discretionary time? God might have an interest in that decision and a desire to direct our focus.

The Spirit-filled life is to be led by God in the daily experience of small, mundane choices. God is sometimes in the storm or the earthquake (e.g., Acts 4:31), but more typically he comes near to his people in the still, small voice, like a shepherd speaking to his sheep (John 10:26–30). We may recall that Jesus did everything as a man that God wanted him to do, and nothing that God did not want him to do (John 5:30; 8:28). This dependence is a reliance on God to lead in everything, just as we have an example of the Spirit leading Jesus around in the wilderness (Luke 4:1–14). Hope of living properly and pleasingly to God rests on God as the director involved in our choices. We can know we are doing what he wants when we have done things at his leading. Thus, we hope in God's guidance instead of relying on our own lights and twisted motivations. Similar to faith as humility, hope as dependence is a mode of operating in daily life with God; we cannot do it, but God forms this disposition in us.

Third, love as *agape*, self-giving for the benefit of others, is beyond human ability as we might attempt to operate independently of God.[51] We might imagine that we can love others and respond to God with the love he looks for in us, but at best these frail and short-lived movements are sentimental; at worst they are self-serving performance. The love that God envisions for us is not possible for us to give to others or in return to him.

---

[51] Leon Morris, *Testaments of Love: A Study of Love in the Bible* (Grand Rapids: Eerdmans, 1981), 128.

Such *agape* of self-giving must be done by God, so that we, having been engaged by his love, give ourselves, as a consequence of his love, to others and to his purposes. Our love is like quickly failing battery power of good will and service, but we are made to be vessels of God's love, like a lightning rod conveying voltage from God himself. As we continue to live and love from ourselves, we will not be able to live and love from God's distinct sort of love. Luther helpfully distinguished human love from God's love:

> *Thesis 28. The love of God does not first discover but creates what is pleas-ing to it. The love of man comes into being through attraction to what pleases it.* ...Rather than seeking its own good, the love of God flows forth and bestows good. Therefore sinners are attractive because they are loved; they are not loved because they are attractive. For this reason the love of man avoids sinners and evil persons. Thus Christ says: "For I came not to call the righteous but sinners" [Matt.9:13].... This is the love of the cross, born of the cross, which turns in the direction where it does not find good that it may enjoy, but where it may confer good upon the bad and needy person. "It is more blessed to give than to receive" [Acts 20:35], says the Apostle.[52]

The formation of human love in response to being loved by God is shown in Luke 7:36–50. The woman who washed Jesus's feet "loved much" (v. 47) as the consequence of having been loved much by God in forgiving her many sins. The love of her service to Jesus parallels his love to us, which is a parallel of God's love. Thus does God achieve the Christian's conformity to Christ in love, as with faith and hope, by working through suffering and troubles that we all face in this life. The theology of the cross is God's way of doing things to engage the rebel creature and transform that one into a trusting child who enjoys God as Father, just like Jesus.[53]

Bibliography

Althaus, Paul. *The Theology of Martin Luther*. Translated by Robert C. Schultz. Philadelphia: Fortress, 1966.

Bonhoeffer, Dietrich. *The Cost of Discipleship*. Translated by R.H. Fuller. Revised by Irmgard Booth. New York: Touchstone, 1995.

---

[52] LW 31:57. Proof for Thesis 28.

[53] I am indebted to Keith Poppen for helping me understand Luther's grip on God's works, and how the theology of the cross connects with progressive sanctification.

Bowler, Kate. "Death, the Prosperity Gospel and Me." *New York Times*. Opinion. February 13, 2016.

Coe, John. "Resisting the Temptation of Moral Formation: Opening to Spiritual Formation in the Cross and the Spirit." *Journal of Spiritual Formation & Soul Care* 1, no. 1 (2008): 54–78.

Fee, Gordon D. *The First Epistle to the Corinthians*. Grand Rapids: Eerdmans, 1987.

Forde, Gerhard O. *On Being a Theologian of the Cross: Reflections on Luther's Heidelberg Disputation, 1518*. Grand Rapids: Eerdmans, 1997.

Kolb, Robert. "Luther on the Theology of the Cross." *Lutheran Quarterly* 16 (2002): 443–66.

Kopperi, Kari. "Theology of the Cross." In *Engaging Luther: A (New) Theological Assessment*, ed. Olli-Pekka Vainio, 155–72. Eugene, OR: Wipf and Stock, 2010.

Lovelace, Richard. "The Sanctification Gap." *Theology Today* 29, no. 4 (1973): 363–69.

Luther, Martin. *Heidelberg Disputation, 1518*. In *Luther's Works, Vol. 31: Career of the Reformer I*, ed. and trans. by Harold J. Grimm, 35–70. Philadelphia: Fortress Press, 1957.

_____. *Psalm 2*. In *Luther's Works, Vol. 14: Selected Psalms II*, edited by Jaroslav Pelikan, 313–49. St. Louis: Concordia, 1958.

_____. "The Large Catechism." In *The Book of Concord: The Confessions of the Evangelical Lutheran Church*, trans. and ed. by Theodore G. Tappert. Philadelphia: Fortress, 1959.

_____. *Luther's Small Catechism*. St. Louis: Concordia, 1986. No translator given.

_____. *Early Theological Works*. Edited and translated by James Atkinson. Library of Christian Classics 16. Philadelphia: Westminster, 1962. Quoted in Gerhard O. Forde, *On Being a Theologian of the Cross: Reflections on Luther's Heidelberg Disputation, 1518*, 62. Grand Rapids: Eerdmans, 1997.

_____. *Operationes in Psalmos, 1519–1521*. In *D. Martin Luthers Werke: Kritische Gesamtausgabe*, 5. Weimar: Hermann Böhlaus Nachfolger, 1981. Quoted in Gerhard O. Forde, *On Being a Theologian of the Cross: Reflections on Luther's Heidelberg Disputation, 1518*, 86n17. Grand Rapids: Eerdmans, 1997.

McKinley, John E. *Tempted for Us: Theological Models and the Practical Relevance of Christ's Impeccability and Temptation.* Paternoster Theological Monographs. Milton Keynes, UK: Paternoster, 2009.

Morris, Leon. *Testaments of Love: A Study of Love in the Bible.* Grand Rapids: Eerdmans, 1981.

Smith, Christian, and Melinda Lundquist Denton. *Soul Searching: The Religious and Spiritual Lives of American Teenagers.* New York: Oxford University Press, 2005.

Von Loewenich, Walther. *Luther's Theology of the Cross.* Translated by Herbert J. A. Bouman. Minneapolis: Augsburg, 1976.

Willard, Dallas. *The Divine Conspiracy.* New York: HarperCollins, 2001.

Theodore Beza, Latin Poetry, and Personal Worship

MICHAEL SPANGLER

This chapter will approach the Reformation's legacy of personal worship from an unexpected angle, Latin poetry. Readers might question what poetry has to do with worship, and how a dead language could stimulate a life of Christian devotion. But as we explore the Latin poetry of Theodore Beza, the answers to these will become increasingly clear. For Beza, writing Latin poetry was an important part of his personal devotion to Christ and promoting such devotion among God's people.

The Protestant Poet

Theodore Beza is most well known as the colleague of John Calvin in Geneva. Like Calvin, Beza labored tirelessly for the establishment of Christ's church, especially in France. After Calvin's death in 1564, Beza served as his successor, defending, consolidating, and expanding the reforming work of his brother and father in the faith until his own death forty-one years later, in 1605. But though Beza was a Reformer, theologian, pastor, educator, and churchman, he was also from the beginning of his life to its end a poet.

Born in 1519 in France, Beza began his literary training at age nine in the house of the famous Protestant humanist, Melchior Wolmar. Beza called his arrival at Wolmar's home a "second birthday" and for many years afterward praised his teacher for the serious formation he gave him in the ancient authors, including the ancient poets. Beza later wrote to Wolmar,

"There was no worthy writer I did not sample, whether Greek or Latin, in the seven years I lived with you."[1]

After his time with Wolmar, Beza went on to study law, but he spent the better part of his school day pursuing his love of literature with a circle of like-minded friends.[2] Beza published his first collection of Latin poems to great acclaim in 1548: it featured a great variety of poems, and even included a few racy love songs to an anonymous mistress named Candida.[3]

Beza, however, came to regret his youthful bohemian literary life, when the Lord in his kindness converted him to Christ and to the evangelical faith. He fled France for Geneva in 1548, only months after he published his first poetry book. He renounced the indiscretions in his published poems, became estranged from his former poet-friends,[4] and would continue throughout his adult life to have to defend himself against criticisms of his early excesses.[5] What he never renounced, however, was his gift and interest in writing poetry. Though Beza was truly a new man—with new desires, a new home, and a new career—he was still Theodore Beza, the poet, and he remained so throughout his long life.[6] Indeed, the last years of his literary life were marked by even greater poetic production than the first: in 1550, he published *Abraham Sacrificing*, the first neo-Classical verse drama ever written in French.[7] He contributed over one hundred French

---

[1] Author translation from the Latin quoted in Scott M. Manetsch, "Psalms before Sonnets: Theodore Beza and the Studia Humanitatis," in *Continuity and Change: The Harvest of Late Medieval and Reformation History: Essays Presented to Heiko A. Oberman on His 70th Birthday*, ed. Robert James Bast, Andrew Colin Gow, and Heiko Augustinus Oberman (Leiden: Brill, 2000), 400n2. His statement here means that according to his own testimony he had studied all the best works of Latin and Greek literature by the time he was sixteen.

[2] Kirk M. Summers, "Theodore Beza's Classical Library and Christian Humanism," *Archiv für Reformationsgeschichte* 82, no. jg (1991), 195.

[3] Theodore Beza, *A View from the Palatine: The Iuvenilia of Théodore de Bèze*, ed. Kirk M. Summers (Tempe: Arizona Center for Medieval and Renaissance Studies, 2001).

[4] Manetsch, "Psalms before Sonnets," 401.

[5] Summers, "Beza's Classical Library," 202.

[6] A number of recent works have sought to explore the interplay between the roles of poet, pastor, and theologian in the life of Theodore Beza. Three notable monographs are: Alain Dufour, *Théodore de Bèze: Poète et Théologien* (Geneva: Librairie Droz, 2009); Julien Goeury, *La muse du consistoire: Une histoire des pasteurs poètes des origines de la Réforme jusqu'à la révocation de l'édit de Nantes* (Geneva: Librairie Droz, 2016); and Kirk M. Summers, *Morality After Calvin: Theodore Beza's Christian Censor and Reformed Ethics* (Oxford: Oxford University Press, 2016). Especially in light of such excellent studies, it would seem that not only has Richard Muller's labor to break down the wall between "scholastic" and "humanist" been successful—see especially "Calvin and the 'Calvinists': Assessing Continuities and Discontinuities between the Reformation and Orthodoxy, Part 2," in *After Calvin : Studies in the Development of a Theological Tradition* (Oxford: Oxford University Press, 2003), 81–102—but also, poetry is beginning to be taken seriously in the study of historical theology.

[7] Summers, "Beza's Classical Library," 204.

psalms to the Genevan Psalter, the completed edition of which was published in 1562.[8] In 1580, he published his *Icons*, a collection of pictures and poems praising various Reformers, educators, and magistrates; in 1584, a Latin metrical version of the Song of Songs;[9] in 1591, *Cato the Christian Censor*, a collection of small Latin poems warning various types of sinners;[10] in 1595, a collection of biblical songs in French; and finally, in 1597, a deluxe edition of his Latin poetry, which included many poems from the original book he published before his conversion in 1548.[11] In addition to these works, he wrote verse for special occasions and would sometimes even conclude letters to friends with a short Latin poem.[12]

Therefore, while it is most appropriate to speak of Beza as a Protestant Reformer, churchman, and theologian, we do not have a complete picture of the man without also recognizing that he was a Protestant poet. And indeed, that title not only seems appropriate to us as we look back on his lifetime of poetic work: it also describes well how his contemporaries viewed him.

As we approach Beza's book of Latin psalms, we will first consider a poem included in the introduction, in which an anonymous admirer, calling himself a "reverent reader," praises Beza for his many gifts.[13] In the first seventeen lines, the author combines images from Psalms 1 and 2: the stalwart Reformer is compared to a large aged tree whose well-fixed roots hold him firm against the wild winds, pagan Jupiter, false religion, kings, criticism, and even death, for in all these things he has made up his mind, "to worship the eternal Christ while tyrants rage in vain" (*Aeternum invitis Christum celebrare tyrannis*). He moves on in lines 18–22 to describe Beza's outstanding gifts (*egregias dotes*), first of which is his gift of poetry.

---

[8] On the Genevan Psalter, see Pierre Pidoux, Clément Marot, and Théodore de Bèze, *Le psautier huguenot du XVIe siècle* (Bâle, Switzerland: Édition Baerenreiter, 1962).

[9] On this version and the controversy that ensued after its publication, see Max Engammare, "Licence poétique versus métrique sacrée. La polémique entre Bèze et Génébrard au sujet des Psaumes et du Cantique des Cantiques (1579–86). Première partie," in *Théodore de Bèze (1519–1605)*, ed. Irena Dorota Backus (Geneva: Librairie Droz, 2007); and Max Engammare, "Licence poétique versus métrique sacrée (II)," *Revue de l'histoire des religions* 226, no. 1 (2009): 102–25.

[10] The *Cato* is the subject of Summers, *Morality After Calvin*.

[11] *Theodori Bezae Vezelii Poemata varia* (Geneva: Estienne, 1597).

[12] Manetsch, "Psalms before Sonnets," 413–16. For a complete list of Beza's works, see Fréderic Gardy, *Bibliographie des Oeuvres Théologiques, Littéraires, Historiques et Juridiques de Théodore de Bèze* (Geneva: Librairie Droz, 1960).

[13] Prefatory poems, in *Psalmorum Davidis et aliorum prophetarum libri quinque, argumentis et Latina paraphrasi illustrati, ac etiam vario carminum genere Latine expressi* (Geneva: Eustache Vignon, 1579), n.p.

Your virtues, if I may, now let me tell:	*Quid memorem egregias dotes? si forte libebit*
You tread with skill the Muses' secret paths,	*Carmine secretos Musarum insistere calles,*
And win the laurel crown of every age.	*Dignus qui aeterna cingaris tempora lauro,*
Indeed, in Latin, Greek, and even French	*Praecipue Ausoniis, Graiis, Gallisque Camenis*
You tuned great David's lyre to sweetly play,	*Davidicos aptare modos, et nablia sacra*
And justly earned the name of holy bard.[14]	*Aggressus, sacri merito fers nomina vatis*

Beza, according to his devotee, became the master of the ancient pagan Muses, which are referred to by two Latin names, *Musae* and *Camenae*. He was like Virgil, a poet laureate, and like Homer, a bard, but unlike them in the most important way: he was a *holy* bard, the word *sacri* given special emphasis by its placement well before the noun *vatis*. Beza, according to his fellow poet, mastered and transformed pagan models in his poetry. But lest we think Beza was only a poet, we read in lines 23–25 of another outstanding gift—that of preaching. The best of ancient oratory yields the rostrum to him: lines 23–25 make it clear that even Cicero bows to him, together with Cethegus, an ancient orator whom Cicero called "the marrow of Persuasion."[15] Furthermore, we read in lines 26–28 of Beza's ability as a philosopher and interpreter of Aristotle and Plato. Then, as if in response to a potential objection, lines 29–31 remind us how and why Beza, the Christian, made such free use of pagan poetry, pagan rhetoric, and pagan philosophy. In line 28, we read that Beza made the ancients "serve for holy ends," and therefore he first purged them of unholiness. And therefore, we read in lines 29–31:

And yet you give no thought to pagan talk	*Nec vero ipse probas id quod gens barbara garrit,*
That boasts of light but ends in darkest sin,	*Docta sequi tenebras, et cassa vivere luce,*
And eloquently stifles godliness.[16]	*Et studia et Musas pietati offundere nubem.*

---

[14] The author's translations offered in this chapter are free renderings into English verse that attempt to capture the poetic character of the original. The whole poem and translation are in Appendix 1, p. 317.

[15] Cicero, *Brutus* 15. This epithet for Cethegus is originally from Ennius.

[16] Manetsch, in "Psalms before Sonnets," 409–12, describes in detail Beza's serious criticism of the errors and dangers of pagan thought, a criticism that seemed to sharpen as he aged.

Thus, we see that for Beza, poetry and theology were not enemies. In fact, Beza's vocation as classical Latin poet was an important means of fulfilling his vocation as Protestant Reformer. Good poetry served the purposes of good theology. And indeed, Beza's poetic learning made his godliness all the more beautiful, as lines 32–37 describe, using the image of a diamond ring:

Instead, as when a diamond fitly set	*Sed veluti ridenti adamas circumdatus auro*
Shines even brighter in its nest of gold,	*Purior apparet, maiori exitque nitore,*
Yet dull appears when chained in lead or steel,	*Quam plumbi durive inclusus carcere ferri,*
So godly love and virtue, when they rest	*Sic verae pietatis amor, sic incluta virtus,*
Within a learned heart, a well-schooled soul,	*Siquando docto resident in pectore, miros*
What harmony then rings, what light shines forth!	*Edunt concentus, maioraque lumina pandunt.*

According to his anonymous admirer, Beza's life of literary cultivation, of poetic excellence, was the beautiful setting in which the diamond of a Christian life shone most brightly.

Beza's Latin Psalms

This "double light" of poetry and piety is particularly visible in one of Beza's greatest, though least known, poetic achievements: a Latin metrical translation of the biblical Psalms.[17] The work took him nearly two decades to complete.[18] In it Beza wrote a distinct Latin metrical version for all 150 psalms, with the exception of twenty-two distinct settings for each of the sections of Psalm 119. He used in all forty-seven different types of Latin meter, most of which he borrowed from ancient Roman poetry. To put it

---

[17] *Psalmorum libri quinque.* Both Margaret Duncumb, "The Latin Psalm Paraphrases of Théodore de Bèze," in *Théodore de Bèze (1519–1605)*, ed. Irena Backus (Geneva: Librairie Droz, 2007), 381–87; and Hippolyte Aubert et al., eds., *Correspondance de Théodore de Bèze* (Geneva: Librairie Droz, 1960–present) XX.104 contain histories of the editions that followed in 1580, 1581, 1593, and 1594. Besides these two short studies and a few mentions in broader treatments of Beza and Buchanan (see below), there has been very little work devoted to this book, and to my knowledge no comprehensive study or critical edition. What Dufour wrote in 2009 still applies: "Ces paraphrases en vers latins, pourtant fort igénieuses, sont aujord'hui totalement oubliées [These paraphrases in Latin verse, though quite ingenious, are today totally forgotten]," *Théodore de Bèze*, 195.

[18] According to Kirk Summers, the Latin Psalms first began appearing in 1551, two years after his conversion; "Beza's Classical Library," 202n42. Duncumb records the first published collection as that of six psalms in 1566; "Latin Psalm Paraphrases of de Bèze," 382.

simply, he made David and Asaph sound like Virgil and Catullus. The title reads in English: "The Psalms of David and other prophets, in five books, explained through summaries and a Latin paraphrase, and also rendered into Latin with various poetic meters." As the title explains, the book featured four tiers of translation for each psalm. First came a prose summary or argument, then in two columns, an interpretive paraphrase and a literal rendering of the Hebrew.[19] But for our purposes, we will focus on the main attraction of the book: the settings in Latin meter.[20]

It should be noted, however, that Beza was not unique in this endeavor. There were many in his day laboring to translate the Psalms into Latin verse: rendering biblical books, and especially the Psalms, into Latin meter was a popular pastime of educated Europeans, whether Protestant or Catholic.[21]

---

[19] In the preface, p. vi, Beza testified that he wrote the summaries and paraphrases himself, but the translation he lightly adapted from Heinrich Möller. Margaret Duncumb searches for possible Latin psalm translations from which Beza wrote his paraphrases, "Psalm Paraphrases of De Bèze," 387–93. However, if we take Beza's description of his own process at face value, he in fact wrote them himself with great labor (*magno studio*), helped by commentaries of the most learned theologians, and often intentionally departing from his own earlier French version. Note that though "paraphrases" is the most common term used today to describe verse translations like Beza made, Beza himself used the word to describe his expanded, interpretive prose version. The verse settings, in Beza's mind, were the psalms themselves, literally "pressed out" into Latin verse (*versibus expressi*). Roger P. H. Green argues that the word "paraphrase" for this genre may obscure the authors' intention of conformity to the original, "Poetic Psalm Paraphrases," in *Brill's Encyclopaedia of the Neo-Latin World*, ed. Philip Ford, Jan Bloemendal, and Charles Fantazzi (Leiden: Brill, 2014), 461.

[20] A small number of works have focused on the reception of Beza's paraphrases and arguments. For example, Anthony Gilby (c. 1510–1585) made an English translation of Beza's prose versions, *The Psalmes of David, Truely Opened and explained by Paraphrasis Set foorth in Latine by Theodore Beza and Faithfully Translated into English* (London: J. Harison & H. Middleton, 1580) (cited in Gosselin, below, 37n24), which influenced Mary Sydney's English metrical Psalm versions, on which see Margaret Hannay, "Re-Revealing the Psalms: Mary Sidney, Countess of Pembroke, and Her Early Modern Readers," in *Psalms in the Early Modern World*, ed. Linda Phyllis Austern and Kari Boyd McBride (Routledge, 2016), 228; and Rivkah Zim, *English Metrical Psalms: Poetry as Praise and Prayer, 1535–1601* (Cambridge: Cambridge University Press, 2011), 158. Also, Edward A Gosselin argues in "David in Tempore Belli: Beza's David in the Service of the Huguenots," *Sixteenth Century Journal* 7, no. 2 (October 1976): 31–54, that Beza's Latin arguments reveal his views on resistance to ungodly kings. It should also be noted that, since the paraphrases were the labor of the same mind that wrote the poems but are easier to read, they assist remarkably in understanding Beza's verses. Note also that in the same year Beza published an edition with the Latin verse psalms only, and the following year an edition in French, but with the Genevan psalms in place of the Latin metrical psalms: Max Engammare, "Licence poétique versus métrique sacrée. Première partie," 488–89.

[21] Roger Green describes the immense appeal of the genre: "This form of poetry, at once devotional and intellectual, meditative and literary, combining at its best careful biblical interpretation and judicious emulation of the classical poets, engrossed writers and readers for at least two hundred years." In "Poetic Psalm Paraphrases," 461. See also Johannes A. Gaertner, "Latin Verse Translations of the Psalms: 1500–1620," *Harvard Theological Review* 49, no. 4 (1956): 271–305; W. Leonard Grant, "Neo-Latin Verse-Translations of the Bible," *Harvard Theological Review* 52, no. 3 (1959): 205–11; and Véronique Ferrer and Anne Mantero, eds., *Les paraphrases bibliques aux XVIe et XVIIe siècles: actes du colloque de Bordeaux des 22, 23 et 24 septembre 2004* (Geneva: Librairie Droz, 2006).

Nor was Beza alone among the Protestants as a Latin poet. Luther loved writing a good Latin poem, and some of his Latin poetic satire cut quite sharply.[22] His colleague Melanchthon published even more Latin verse, including a few settings of the Psalms.[23] And John Calvin published one poem in Latin, a hymn of the victory of Jesus Christ over the forces of the papacy.[24] Thus, Beza's psalms are not a fluke of eccentric personal genius, but rather a particularly notable example from among the common labors of educated sixteenth-century Christians.

Beza's setting of Psalm 2 will serve well as an example of the whole work. This psalm is set in the meter called the phalaecian hendecasyllable, which is most well known as the favorite meter of Catullus, an ancient Roman poet who, not unlike young Beza, had a reputation for loose living. It is a driving, syncopated rhythm. In English the first two verses read as follows:

Nations rage! Where does such a madness come from?	*Gentium furor unde tantus hic est?*
Why in vain are the peoples so in uproar?	*Sic frustra populos tumultuari?*
Why do kings, so incited, hasten quickly?	*Sic reges properare concitatos?*
Why 'gainst God and together 'gainst the head of	*Sic una inque Deum inque praepotentis*
The great King, by the Lord with oil anointed,	*Regis a Domino caput perunctum,*
Godless deeds such as these do rulers foment?	*Facta haec impia principes movere?*

The effect of the Latin, which I have attempted to convey in the English, is not entirely unlike modern rap or spoken word poetry. The rest of the poem can be found in Appendix 1, and in reading it one can feel how the driving rhythm matches the driving, insistent message of this psalm, that the Father has placed his Son, Jesus Christ, on the throne of the ages, and therefore his enemies will all be destroyed, and he and all who trust in him will never be moved. Beza's setting captures well the

---

[22] See especially Carl P. E. Springer, "Luther's Latin Poetry and Scatology," *Lutheran Quarterly* 23, no. 4 (2009).

[23] See Manfred P. Fleischer, "Melanchthon as Praeceptor of Late-Humanist Poetry," *Sixteenth Century Journal* 20, no. 4 (1989): 559–80.

[24] Calvin, *Epinicion Christo cantatum* (Geneva: Girard, 1544). For an English review of a Dutch book on this poem and its composition, see Harry Boonstra, "Loflied En Hekeldicht: De Geschiedenis van Calvijn's Enige Gedicht: Het Epinicion Christo Cantatum van 1 Januari 1541," *Calvin Theological Journal* 22, no. 2 (November 1987): 324–26.

Psalm's message, and it marshals poetic power for the sake of spiritual power. Such was the purpose of all Beza's Latin psalms: that those who read them might, as God commands in Psalm 2, come on their knees and surrender to the Son, embracing Jesus Christ and freely loving him. One great goal of these psalms, and of all of Beza's poetry, as we will now see in detail, was personal worship.

Latin Poetry for Personal Worship

To understand how Beza used his poetry for personal worship, we will first consider Beza's own testimony of what his Latin psalms did for him, and what he expected them to do for others. In the dedicatory letter to this book of Latin psalms, he expressed three related purposes for his work.[25] First, Beza expressed concern that Christians often missed the true meaning of the Psalms because of poor translations on the one hand and poor interpretation on the other, citing as troubling examples Jerome's Vulgate and Augustine's commentary on the Psalms. His careful attention to the Hebrew and to modern scholarly interpretation would, he intended, give Christians a more accurate Psalter, and therefore help them enjoy it with greater spiritual fruit. Because of the great need for accuracy in biblical interpretation, Beza praised the blessings of Renaissance humanism, describing the "gift of the three languages" (Latin, Greek, and Hebrew), "poured out again from heaven upon the church" as something like a new Pentecost. He warned, however, against scholars who worked merely for personal gain and not for the good of God's people. The point of theological study, Beza insisted, was usefulness to the church of Christ.

Second, Beza described the process by which he came to write Latin psalms. Encouraged especially by Calvin, he began to write rhythmic, rhymed French settings of the Psalms for use in public worship, completing the work of Clement Marot to produce what became the enormously popular Genevan Psalter. The motivation to translate the Psalms again into Latin, however, was less ecclesiastical and more personal. In Beza's words, "Afterward, more and more delighted by reading and reflecting on them [that is, the French Psalms], I tried also to turn a few into Latin meters, not of course because I thought I could in any way attain to the

---

[25] Except where otherwise noted, citations in this paragraph and the two that follow it are from *Psalmorum libri quinque*, dedicatory epistle, and translations are by the author.

dignity of the Holy Spirit, but so that by fixing what I had read more deeply in my soul, the exercise would do me good." This line is perhaps the clearest evidence that for Beza, the original and primary purpose of writing his Latin psalms was for his own spiritual devotion. It would not be a stretch to say that the same motivation lay behind all Beza's poetic writing. He said as much in a letter he wrote at seventy-seven years old to encourage a young noblewoman who showed literary promise: "If you continue to write poetry, your soul will receive consolation from it, and it will lift you higher and more devoutly toward heaven than you could have imagined possible."[26]

Third, in returning to Beza's preface, it is clear that he wanted edification not only for himself, but also for others, that they might enjoy the spiritual benefit that he had received from his Latin psalms. This is why, ultimately, he published them, despite some hesitation. Not many years before, the great Scottish Latin poet, George Buchanan, had published his own Latin psalms—the first edition was printed in Beza's backyard in Geneva!—and Beza knew he could not hold a candle to Buchanan's greatness.[27] Indeed, Buchanan's psalms became the most popular Latin metrical Psalter of all time.[28] Beza nonetheless published his versions, encouraged by "the counsel of certain excellent and very learned men," that even if they had to stand in the shadow of Buchanan's glory, they would still be received, in his words, as "not unpleasing, nor entirely unprofitable." And the profit he hoped to gain by his literary labors was above all, in Beza's mind, for the body of Christ: "I will be greatly satisfied," he wrote, "if my work is not useless for the church." And from all we can tell, Beza was satisfied by the response from his fellow believers. In testimony of this we read a number of praise poems, like poetic book blurbs, which other famous Christian poets of Beza's day had prepared before publication for placement in Beza's book: one written in Hebrew, two in Greek, and four in Latin. The words of Beza's fellow Genevan pastor-poet, Antoine de la Faye, represent those of all:

---

[26] Manetsch, "Psalms before Sonnets," 415.

[27] George Buchanan, *Poetic Paraphrase of the Psalms of David = Psalmorum Davidis paraphrasis poetica*, ed. Roger Green (Genève: Librairie Droz, 2011), 26.

[28] On the reception of Buchanan's Psalms, see Buchanan, *Poetic Paraphrase*, 84–91.

O Beza, to what heights you transport
   me:
To heaven high I'm raised, and by
   your lead,
I walk and pick good fruit from fields
   of stars...

Throughout the age to come,
   succeeding sons
Shall praise this learned man, who
   taught our race
To cling to God and serve him with
   our minds.[29]

Quo me, Beza, rapis? Caelos subuectus
   in altos
Sydereas iam nunc, te duce, carpo vias.

Venturi Bezam laudent per secla
   nepotes,
Mortales doctum iungere mente Deo.

Conclusion

Perhaps Beza's Latin poetry may not transport all its modern readers quite high enough to "pick good fruit from fields of stars," but at the least, we can see clearly from de la Faye's poem that Beza did succeed in his goal of stirring up other Christians to personal love and devotion. For Beza, and for those who read his work, Latin poetry was an excellent motivation for personal worship. Especially in the form of translations of the biblical psalms, Beza's Latin verse was a means for God's people more and more to learn to serve God with their minds, as well as with their heart, soul, and strength. Godly literature, and especially godly poetry, was a great help for godly living.

If we move for a moment from Beza's day to ours, this kind of "literary piety" is not as strange as it may sound to twenty-first century ears. Every Christian, no matter his level of education, should recognize the value of poetry for piety. The Psalms are a good example: faithful Christian parents the world over labor to inscribe ancient Hebrew verse in expert vernacular translations on the souls of their children, even from their cradles: "The Lord is my shepherd, I shall not want...." We also find poetry in the psalms, hymns, and spiritual songs that we sing in corporate worship. As in the Reformation, so today "liturgical poetry" sinks deep into our hearts and rises into our memory and out of our mouths throughout the week, borne along by familiar tunes and moving rhythms. In this way the work of some of the church's most learned and literate minds, such as Isaac Watts,

---

[29] *Psalmorum libri quinque*, prefatory poems. Author's translation.

Charles Wesley, and even some medieval monks,[30] becomes the daily meditation of all. It is not too strong to say that poetry is an integral part of Christianity. Therefore, we should never set book learning and liberal arts over against warm Christian devotion. Poetry, in a sense, is the crown of both, which shows they belong together. God forbid by opposing learning and devotion we are left with unbelieving literacy or illiterate Christianity. Beza did repent of his early poetic sins, but nonetheless went on to use his poetic skill to help himself and others to worship and glorify God.

Beza's work is not only an argument for the appreciation of poetry, but also for the learning of Latin. Latin is a useful and, sadly, much-neglected tool for the development of wholesome Christian piety. It was the major language of Christianity from the early Middle Ages until well after the Reformation, over one thousand years. Without Latin, no one can read Beza's psalms, Calvin's *Institutes*, Luther's *The Freedom of a Christian*; or for that matter, Aquinas's *Summa Theologiae* or Augustine's *Confessions*. Indeed, without Latin we are unable to communicate with the greatest of our fathers in the faith who lived before the eighteenth century. To say we have English translations today is to miss the fact that someone had to know Latin to translate them, and that a large majority of historic Latin works (like Beza's psalms) are still untranslated. The need to read is not the only reason to learn Latin. Indeed, it must always be subordinate to another need, the need for which Beza wrote his Latin psalms: the need to worship. Now, corporate worship in Latin would for most people be entirely unprofitable (cf. 1 Cor 14:9), but even so, Latin will always be, for those with the proper gifts and education, a great help for private devotion. A skilled Latinist has a direct connection with the minds and hearts of some of the godliest men that have ever lived. Through Latin, we feel Augustine's anguish over the sins of his youth, Luther's passion to deliver God's people from bondage to dead works, Calvin's profound humility and zeal for pure worship. And indeed, through Latin, the poetry that inflamed Beza with love for Christ, consoling his soul and lifting him higher and more devoutly toward heaven than he could have imagined possible, might do the same for the children of the Reformation today.

---

[30] The modern church still sings a wealth of Latin poetry from late antiquity and the middle ages, especially through the translations of John Mason Neale, e.g., "Of the Father's Love Begotten," "O Come, O Come, Emmanuel," "All Glory, Laud, and Honor," and "Jerusalem the Golden."

Bibliography

Beza, Theodore. *A View from the Palatine: The Iuvenilia of Théodore de Bèze.* Edited by Kirk M. Summers. Tempe, AZ: Arizona Center for Medieval and Renaissance Studies, 2001.

_____. *Correspondance de Théodore de Bèze.* Edited by Hippolyte Aubert, Alain Dufour, Béatrice Nicollier, and Reinhard Bodenmann. Geneva: Librairie Droz, 1998.

_____. *Psalmorum Davidis et aliorum prophetarum libri quinque, argumentis et Latina paraphrasi illustrati, ac etiam vario carminum genere Latine expressi.* Geneva: Eustache Vignon, 1579.

_____. *Theodori Bezae Vezelii Poemata varia.* Geneva: Estienne, 1597.

Boonstra, Harry. "Loflied En Hekeldicht: De Geschiedenis van Calvijn's Enige Gedicht: Het *Epinicion Christo Cantatum* van 1 Januari 1541." *Calvin Theological Journal* 22, no. 2 (November 1987): 324–26.

Buchanan, George. *Poetic paraphrase of the Psalms of David = Psalmorum Davidis paraphrasis poetica.* Edited by Roger Green. Genève: Librairie Droz, 2011.

Calvin, John. *Epinicion Christo cantatum.* Geneva: Girard, 1544.

Dufour, Alain. *Théodore de Bèze: Poète et Théologien.* Geneva: Librairie Droz, 2009.

Duncumb, Margaret. "The Latin Psalm Paraphrases of Théodore de Bèze." In *Théodore de Bèze (1519–1605)*, ed. Irena Dorota Backus, 381–400. Geneva: Librairie Droz, 2007.

Engammare, Max. "Licence poétique versus métrique sacrée. La polémique entre Bèze et Génébrard au sujet des Psaumes et du Cantique des Cantiques (1579–86). Premiére partie." In *Théodore de Bèze (1519–1605)*, ed. Irena Dorota Backus. Geneva: Librairie Droz, 2007.

_____. "Licence poétique versus métrique sacrée (II)." *Revue de l'histoire des religions* 226, no. 1 (2009): 102–25.

Ferrer, Véronique, and Anne Mantero, eds. *Les paraphrases bibliques aux XVIe et XVIIe siècles: actes du colloque de Bordeaux des 22, 23 et 24 septembre 2004.* Geneva: Librairie Droz, 2006.

Fleischer, Manfred P. "Melanchthon as Praeceptor of Late-Humanist Poetry." *Sixteenth Century Journal* 20, no. 4 (1989): 559–80.

Gaertner, Johannes A. "Latin Verse Translations of the Psalms: 1500–1620." *Harvard Theological Review* 49, no. 4 (1956): 271–305.

Gardy, Fréderic. *Bibliographie des Oeuvres Théologiques, Littéraires, Historiques et Juridiques de Théodore de Bèze*. Geneva: Librairie Droz, 1960.

Gilby, Anthony. *The Psalmes of David, Truely Opened and explained by Paraphrasis Set foorth in Latine by Theodore Beza and Faithfully Translated into English*. London: J. Harison & H. Middleton, 1580.

Goeury, Julien. *La muse du consistoire: Une histoire des pasteurs poètes des origines de la Réforme jusqu'à la révocation de l'édit de Nantes*. Geneva: Librairie Droz, 2016.

Gosselin, Edward A. "David in Tempore Belli: Beza's David in the Service of the Huguenots." *Sixteenth Century Journal* 7, no. 2 (October 1976): 31–54.

Grant, W. Leonard. "Neo-Latin Verse-Translations of the Bible." *Harvard Theological Review* 52, no. 3 (1959): 205–11.

Green, Roger P. H. "Poetic Psalm Paraphrases." In *Brill's Encyclopaedia of the Neo-Latin World*, edited by Philip Ford, Jan Bloemendal, and Charles Fantazzi, 461–69. Leiden: Brill, 2014.

Hannay, Margaret. "Re-Revealing the Psalms: Mary Sidney, Countess of Pembroke, and Her Early Modern Readers." In *Psalms in the Early Modern World*, ed. Linda Phyllis Austern and Kari Boyd McBride. Routledge, 2016.

Manetsch, Scott M. "Psalms before Sonnets: Theodore Beza and the Studia Humanitatis." In *Continuity and Change: The Harvest of Late Medieval and Reformation History: Essays Presented to Heiko A. Oberman on His 70th Birthday*, ed. Robert James Bast, Andrew Colin Gow, and Heiko Augustinus Oberman, 400–416. Leiden: Brill, 2000.

Muller, Richard A. "Calvin and the 'Calvinists': Assessing Continuities and Discontinuities between the Reformation and Orthodoxy, Part 2." In *After Calvin: Studies in the Development of a Theological Tradition*, 81–102. Oxford University Press, 2003.

Pidoux, Pierre, Clément Marot, and Théodore de Bèze. *Le psautier huguenot du XVIe siècle*. Basel: Édition Baerenreiter, 1962.

Springer, Carl P. E. "Luther's Latin Poetry and Scatology." *Lutheran Quarterly* 23, no. 4 (2009), 373–87.

Summers, Kirk M. *Morality After Calvin: Theodore Beza's Christian Censor and Reformed Ethics*. Oxford University Press, 2016.

_____. "Theodore Beza's Classical Library and Christian Humanism." *Archiv für Reformationsgeschichte* 82, no. jg (1991): 193–208.

Zim, Rivkah. *English Metrical Psalms: Poetry as Praise and Prayer, 1535–1601*. Cambridge University Press, 2011.

Part III

CELEBRATING THE LEGACY OF REFORMATION CATECHESIS AND PREACHING

8

The Confessing Church

JOSEPH PIPA, JR.

From its inception, the Reformation used confessions and catechisms to summarize and promulgate its doctrinal and practical understanding of the Christian faith.[1] Luther produced two catechisms and early Lutherans summarized their faith in the Augsburg Confession. Calvin produced two catechisms: the continental Reformed three: the Belgic Confession, the Heidelberg, and the Canons of Dordt. The British church produced first the Thirty-Nine Articles and then the Westminster Confession of Faith and the Larger Catechism and Shorter Catechism, while the English Baptists produced the London Confession.

A significant portion of evangelical Christianity rejects the use of creeds and confessions. This rejection is built on the assertion that creeds are man-made additions to Scripture, and the Bible alone is sufficient to guide us; in this rejection they confessionalize the reasoning for rejecting creeds and confessions with the dictum, "No creed but the Bible, no confession but Jesus." In this chapter, I will seek to demonstrate the scriptural commands for the church to make and use creeds; to explain something of their purpose; and to show how we are to make a biblical, theological confession. This conviction is rooted in Paul's final advice to Timothy as he said, "Hold on to the pattern of sound teaching that you have heard from me, in the faith and love that are in Christ Jesus. Guard the good deposit through the Holy Spirit who lives in us" (2 Tim 1:13–14).

---

[1] The first part of this is adapted from my chapter "Great Things He Hath Taught Us," in *Onward Christian Soldiers*, ed. Don Kistler (Morgan, PA: Soli Deo Gloria Publications, 1999), 249–70.

The term "creed" is derived from the Latin *credo*, meaning "I believe." A personal or corporate creed states what one believes and what is important for belief in one's context. Hence, the statement, "No creed but the Bible" is a personal creed in which the adherent is saying, "I believe: neither I nor the church need a 'creed'; the Bible alone is sufficient to guide me."

Throughout history, the church has used creeds to summarize what she believed the Bible taught. Her creeds and confessions gave a precise summary of cardinal doctrines (The Apostles' Creed) or a detailed refutation and articulation of a particular truth under attack (The Nicene Creed). R.L. Dabney defined a creed:

> [I]t is a summary statement of what some religious teacher or teachers believe concerning the Christian system, stated in their own uninspired words. But they claim that these words fairly and briefly express the true sense of the inspired words. The church records several creeds of individual Christian teachers; but the creeds of the modern Protestant world are documents carefully constructed by some church courts of supreme authority in their several denominations, or by some learned committee appointed by them, and then formally adopted by them as their doctrinal standard.[2]

Creeds, catechisms, and confessions differ in form. A creed usually consists of a series of succinct statements expressed as "I (we) believe"; a catechism uses questions and answers to teach the truth contained in the creed; and a confession normally is a more detailed exposition of the truth. In the remainder of this chapter, I shall refer to creeds, catechisms, and confessions by the general term "creeds."

The Biblical Basis for Creeds

Having defined what we mean by creeds, let us first explore their biblical justification. In 2 Tim 1:13–14, God commands the use of creeds. We find here a twofold command: "Retain the standard of sound words," and "Guard the treasure . . . entrusted to you" (NASB). Many opponents of creeds argue that they detract from the sufficiency of Scripture. On the contrary,

---

[2] Robert L. Dabney, *The Doctrinal Contents of the Confession: Its Fundamental and Regulative Ideas and the Necessity and Value of Creeds* (Greenville, SC: Greenville Presbyterian Theological Seminary, 1993), 13–14.

Scripture teaches us to make and use creeds. In these two verses Paul gives Timothy a twofold summary of his message. First, he referred to the "standard of sound words" (NASB). Sound words express the truths taught by Scripture. Words are the expression of truth that Timothy received from Paul, who was taught directly by Christ. The term "sound" means true and accurate. Hence, these are the doctrines that give life: "If you point these things out to the brothers and sisters, you will be a good servant of Christ Jesus, nourished by the words of the faith and the good teaching that you have followed" (1 Tim 4:6).[3]

Paul communicated the necessary truths of the faith to Timothy in a summary he calls "standard" or "form." The word Paul uses is a compound form of the word that we translate "type" (*tupos*; *hupotuposis*). Paul uses *tupos* in Rom 6:17: "But thanks be to God that though you were slaves of sin, you became obedient from the heart to that *form of teaching to which you were committed*" (NASB, emphasis added). The content of the gospel was given to the Roman Christians by Paul in a summary statement, a form. In 1 Tim 1:16 he uses *hupotuposis* to mean "example." Paul says he is an "example" of one who received God's mercy and patience. In non-biblical Greek, the term is used for the sketch of a painter or architect. In Moulton and Milligan's lexicon, they give the meaning "sketch in outline, summary account."[4] Arndt and Gingrich say that in 2 Tim 1:13 it means "standard."[5] Writing on verse 13, E. K. Simpson says,

> We have had *hupotuposis* in I Tim. 1:16.... Whatever may be its precise sense there, the signification of a *summary, outline*, which Galen assigns to the word, best tallies with this context. Sextus Empiricus repeatedly uses it in that acceptation. If so, it presents yet another sign that epitomes of the Christian faith were beginning to pass current. *Logoi* in the plural would naturally mean *propositions* in such a connection."[6]

---

[3] See George W. Knight, *The Pastoral Epistles: A Commentary on the Greek Text* (Grand Rapids: Eerdmans, 1992), 89 (cf., 1 Tim 1:10; 6:3; 2 Tim 4:3; Tit 2:7).

[4] James Hope Moulton and George Milligan, *The Vocabulary of the Greek Testament* (Grand Rapids: Eerdmans, 1974), 661.

[5] W. Arndt and F. Gingrich. *A Greek-English Lexicon of the New Testament and Other Early Greek Literature* (Chicago: University of Chicago Press, 1967), 856.

[6] E. K. Simpson, *The Pastoral Epistles: The Greek Text with Introduction and Commentary* (London: Tyndale Press, 1954), 127.

Thus Paul declared that he had given to Timothy a form or pattern of apostolic doctrine. He is not referring to the entirety of his inspired corpus, but to the summary that he entrusted to Timothy. This interpretation is reinforced in the parallel command in verse 14, when he speaks of the "entrusted treasure." In other words, this form or pattern of sound doctrine is a treasure that Paul entrusts to the guardianship of Timothy. Paul refers to a specific summary that he has entrusted to Timothy. In 2 Tim 2:2 he refers to this stewardship and he commands Timothy to entrust it to others: "What you have heard from me in the presence of many witnesses, commit to faithful men who will be able to teach others also."

Paul, therefore, was referring to a summary of apostolic doctrine that he had given to Timothy. Paul described this summary in other places as "the traditions" (e.g., 1 Cor 11:2; 2 Thess 2:15; 2 Thess 3:6). For example, to the church of Corinth, Paul writes, "Now I praise you because you remember me in everything and *hold fast to the traditions* just as I delivered them to you" (11:2, emphasis added). And to the church at Thessalonica, "So then, brothers and sisters, stand firm and *hold to the traditions you were taught, whether by what we said or what we wrote*" (2 Thess 2:15). Interestingly, the taught traditions were not simply those doctrines he revealed in the Epistles, but also those doctrines he taught them verbally (the summary of the apostolic message).[7]

What Paul commands in 2 Tim 1:13–14 is reinforced by Scripture's own use of creeds. In Deut 6:4 we find the great confession, repeated to this day in the synagogue: "Listen, Israel: The Lord our God, the Lord is one." Paul quoted a number of creeds. For example, in 1 Tim 3:16: "By common confession, great is the mystery of godliness: He who was revealed in the flesh, was vindicated in the Spirit, seen by angels, proclaimed among the nations, believed on in the world, taken up in glory" (NASB). The term translated in the NASB "common confession" literally means "confessedly," emphasizing that it was a common agreement or commitment.[8] With respect to the statement itself, Knight argues that it appears to be a statement of the apostolic church, either a hymn or a creed, although we cannot

---

[7] As an important note, these traditions differ from the traditions taught later by the Roman Catholic Church. Roman Catholic traditions are not summaries of biblical doctrine, but rather teachings added to the teaching of the Bible; thus, I would reject the authority of these non-apostolic "traditions."

[8] Knight, *Commentary*, 182.

be certain.[9] Regardless of its use, Paul quotes it here as a creedal summary, common to the church. In 2 Tim 2:11–13, Paul delivered one of his trustworthy statements: "This saying is trustworthy: For if we died with him, we will also live with him; if we endure, we will also reign with him; if we deny him, he will also deny us; if we are faithless, he remains faithful, for he cannot deny himself." Knight suggests that this was a creedal statement that originated in Rome:

> We can only offer a probable answer to the question of the origin of the saying. Since 2 Timothy was written from Rome, then it is possible that the church in Rome developed the first line by reflection on Romans 6 and by utilizing Rom. 6:8 in a contracted form. This is probable not only because of this link but also because the idea of dying with Christ is more fully developed in Romans 6 than anywhere else in the NT. Since Romans 6 relates death with Christ to baptism, it would be appropriate to conjecture that the saying was used in connection with confession of faith at the time of baptism. The third line seems to reflect Jesus' words in Mt. 10:33 and Lk. 12:9, cast here into the mold of the other lines. No very close similarity exists between the second and fourth lines and other NT statements. Thus one can only say that two likely sources have had their impact on the saying, and that the other lines were added as necessary when converts were confessing their faith and receiving baptism.[10]

Paul clearly used creeds, and we can add to the exegetical argument a number of other inferential reasons. First, every Bible translation is to a degree what the translator believes the Bible teaches. By the nature of translation, no translation of the Hebrew and Greek text is neutral. Translation involves interpretation that involves faith commitments. R.L. Dabney wrote,

> All Protestants believe that Holy Scripture should be translated into the vernacular tongues of the nations. Only the Greek and Hebrew are immediately inspired; the translators must be uninspired. Therefore

---

[9] Knight, 182,183; cf. August Wiesinger, *Biblical Commentary on St. Paul's Epistles to the Philippians, to Titus, the First to Timothy* (Edinburgh: T&T Clark, 1858), 420.

[10] Knight, 408. For a detailed discussion see George W. Knight, *The Faithful Sayings in the Pastoral Letters* (Grand Rapids: Baker Book House, 1979). Knight suggests that these "faithful sayings" function also as summaries of Apostolic teaching.

these versions are uninspired human expositions of the divine origi-
nals. Wycliffe's version, Luther's, Tyndal's are but their human beliefs
of what the Hebrew and Greek words are meant by the Holy Spirit to
signify. These translators might have said with perfect truth, each one,
'These renderings into English or German are my *credo*.' The church
which uses such a translation for the instruction of her people and
the settlement of even her most cardinal doctrines is using a creed of
human composition; and those whom exclaim, 'The Holy Scriptures
themselves are our only and our sufficient creed,' put themselves in a
ridiculous attitude whenever they use a vernacular translation of the
Scriptures, for that which they profess to hold as their creed is still but
an uninspired human exposition.[11]

For an example, let us compare the NASB's translation of Acts 16:34
with that of the ESV. The NASB says, "And he brought them into his house
and set food before them, and rejoiced greatly, having believed in God with
his whole household." The ESV, "Then he brought them into his house and
set food before them. And he rejoiced along with his entire household that
he had believed in God." The NASB translates the verse to give the impression that he and his household believed; the ESV, that he believed and he
and his household rejoiced that he believed. In this case, the ESV is a more
accurate translation of the Greek.

A second example is the NASB's translation of Mark 7:4: "(... and
when they come from the market place, they do not eat unless they
cleanse themselves; and there are many other things which they have
received in order to observe, such as the washing of cups and pitchers and
copper pots)." The ESV adds the words "and dining couches." Here we
have a textual decision. The UBS Greek Testament, which the NASB follows
fairly regularly, includes the term for dining couches. In this instance, the
NASB translators do not follow the preferred reading while the ESV does.
The reason is apparently that the term translated "washing" in verse 4
is *baptismus* (see reference in NASB). If *baptismos* always is to be understood as immerse, then the dining couches would have been immersed.
Theological convictions color translation just as they influence the codi-
fication of creeds and confessions. For this reason, the Westminster Confession of Faith teaches, with respect to the original Hebrew and Greek

---

[11] Dabney, *Contents of the Confession*, 16,17.

versions, that the final arbiter is the Scriptures "so as, in all controversies of religion, the church is finally to appeal unto them."[12] Furthermore, every sermon is the preacher's creed about what the text of the sermon says and means. The Bible commands us to preach (2 Tim 4:2), and thus commands our confessionalization of the Scriptures that our parishioners may know and understand the meaning and significance of Scripture. Again quoting Dabney:

> Beyond question, God has ordained, as a means of grace and indoctrination, the oral explanation and enforcement of divine truths by all preachers. Thus Ezra (Neh 7:8) causes the priests to "read in the book the law of God distinctly, and give the sense, and cause them to understand the reading." Paul commanded Timothy (2 Tim 4:2) to "reprove, rebuke, exhort with all long-suffering and doctrine." He, as an apostle of Christ, not only permits, but commands, each uninspired pastor and doctor to give to his charge his human and uninspired expositions of what he believes to be divine truth, that is to say, his creed. If such human creeds, when composed by a single teacher and delivered orally, *extempore* [without elaborate preparation], are proper means of instruction for the church, by the stronger reason must those be proper and scriptural which are the careful, mature, and joint productions of learned and godly pastors, delivered with all the accuracy of written documents. He who would consistently banish creeds must silence all preaching and reduce the teaching of the church to the recital of the exact words of Holy Scripture without note or comment.[13]

Creeds properly created, which have been handed down to us from faithful churchmen, protect us from the tyranny of eccentric and heretical ideas of the individual, expressed in a sermon. Proverbs is clear that there is safety found in many counselors (11:14). Hence, rather than violating the sufficiency of Scripture, we see that Scripture requires the use of creeds. Creeds do not challenge the authority of the Bible, but are simply the summary of what the church believes the Bible teaches. With respect to this point Samuel Miller declared,

---

[12] *The Westminster Confession of Faith*, 1.8.
[13] Dabney, *Contents of the Confession*, 17.

A church creed professes to be, as was before observed merely an epit-ome, or summary exhibition of what the Scriptures teach. It professes to be deduced from the Scriptures, and to refer to the Scriptures for the whole of its authority. Of course, when any one subscribes it, he is so far from dishonoring the Bible, that he does public homage to it. He simply declares, by a solemn act, how he understands the Bible—in other words, what doctrines he considers it as containing.

...I beg the privilege of declaring, for myself, that, while I believe with all my heart that the Bible is the word of God, the only perfect rule of faith and manners, and the only ultimate test in all contro-versies; it plainly teaches, as I read and believe, the deplorable and total depravity of human nature; the essential divinity of the Savior; a Trinity of persons in the Godhead; justification by the imputed righ-teousness of Christ; and regeneration and sanctification by the Holy Spirit, as indispensable to prepare the soul for heaven. These I believe to be the radical truths which God has revealed in his word; and while they are denied by some, and frittered away or perverted by others who profess to believe that blessed word, I am verily persuaded they are the fundamental principles of the plan of salvation.[14]

The Westminster Confession of Faith rightly defined the relation of creeds to the Scripture: "The supreme judge by which all controversies of religion are to be determined, and all decrees of councils, opinions of ancient writers, doctrines of men, and private spirits, are to be examined, and in whose sentence we are to rest, can be no other but the Holy Spirit speaking in the Scripture."[15]

The Practical Purpose of Creeds

Having determined then the biblical warrant for creeds, let us see what the Bible teaches about the use of creeds or their purpose. In 2 Tim 1:13–14 we learn that the creed is to serve as an apt summary of the orthodox faith for communion and understanding. The command to "retain" (NASB) means to "hold," to keep as a special possession. When we hold it, it serves as our standard of communion and communication.

---

[14] Samuel Miller, *Doctrinal Integrity: On the Utility and Importance of Creeds and Confessions and Adherence to our Doctrinal Standards* (Dallas: Presbyterian Heritage Publications, 1989), 30–31.

[15] *Confession of Faith*, 1.10.

First, it serves as a standard for communion. One of the primary functions of a creed is to promote unity within the church. Amos asks the question, "Do two men walk together unless they have made an appointment [agreement]?" (3:3 NASB). We cannot walk together, unless we are agreed. Think how useful it is for the congregation and those who visit the congregation to know what the church believes and is going to teach and preach. For this reason, in the Dutch and German Reformed Churches, they refer to their confessional statements as The Three Forms of Unity. The church is not adding to the Bible, but saying, "We believe this is what the Bible teaches. If you are going to join with us, you need to be aware of these things." Miller wrote, "But they [the church] simply consider it as a list of the leading truths which the Bible teaches, which, of course, all men ought to believe, because the Bible does teach them; and which a certain portion of the visible Church catholic agree in considering as a formula, by means of which they may know and understand one another."[16] In all creedal churches, the office bearers express their unity by subscribing to the doctrines agreed on in the creed. This commitment guarantees doctrinal harmony. Dabney says, "If a church is to have any honest testimony, something else is needed as a test of harmony in beliefs, a candid explanation in other terms, which, though human, have not been misconstrued."[17] Such churches do not declare that those who do not agree with us in all these doctrines are not churches as long as they agree on the commonly accepted doctrines of evangelical Christianity, but this is the basis for *our* fellowship. Again quoting Dabney:

> But we recognize as other denominations in the sacramental host all who teach the fundamental doctrines and uphold the morals of Christ's gospel. We believe that the visible unity whereby God is to be glorified is to be found in the faithful recognition of each other's sacraments, orders and church discipline (limited to admonition and spiritual penalties), by each denomination in the church catholic; and not in a fusion and amalgamation of all into one visible ecclesiastical body; a result only made feasible by one or the other criminal alternative, popery or broad churchism.[18]

---

[16] Miller, *Importance of Creeds*, 6.
[17] Dabney, *Contents of the Confession*, 20.
[18] Dabney, 15–16.

Some object that the use of creeds to promote communion actually binds the conscience, by forcing people to conform. I would point out that in Presbyterian communions, individual members are not required to subscribe to a creed. They are received on the basis of a creditable profession of faith. All who hold to the basic doctrines of the evangelical faith may be communicant members. But even here unity is protected, since they will be aware through the church's creed of what she confesses and teaches. They will agree to expose themselves to that teaching and in no way to oppose it in the fellowship.

Furthermore, the church is a voluntary organization. We do not live in a country where we may only belong to one church. None, therefore, is bound to submit to any particular creed, unless that individual unites with that church freely. Samuel Miller points out:

> It will not, surely, be denied by anyone, that a body of Christians have a right, in every free country, to associate and walk together upon such principles as they may choose to agree upon, not inconsistent with public order.... They have no right, indeed, to decide or to judge for others, nor can they compel any man to join them. But it is surely their privilege to judge for themselves, to agree upon the plan of their own association, to determine upon what principles they will receive other members into their brotherhood, and to form a set of rules which will exclude from their body those with whom they cannot walk in harmony.[19]

The creed also aids the church in the communication of the truth. This use involves both interpretation and instruction. Because they summarize the teaching of the Bible, creeds are a great tool to use in the interpretation of Scripture. Evangelical Christians believe that Scripture interprets Scripture and that the Bible does not contradict itself. Creeds, confessions, and catechisms give a consensus on the major truths of the Bible. As people learn the catechism, for example, it gives them a grid by which to interpret the Bible. Westcott said, with respect to the Apostles' Creed:

> Such a summary as the Apostles' Creed serves as a clue in reading the Bible. It presents to us the salient features in the revelation which earlier experience has proved to be turning points of spiritual knowledge.

---

[19] Miller, *Importance of Creeds*, 35.

It offers centres, so to speak, round which we may group our thoughts, and to which we may refer the lessons laid open to us. It keeps us from wandering in by-paths aimlessly or at our will, not by fixing arbitrary limits to inquiry but by making the great lines along which believers have moved from the first.[20]

For example, we read in 1 Sam 15:11 that God regretted making Saul king. The immediate impression is that God had changed his mind. But the young child instructed in the Shorter Catechism definition of God knows that God is unchangeable and that his decree is irrevocable.[21] So, while not yet grasping the exact meaning of the language, even the young reader, trained in the catechism, will avoid false interpretation.

Closely connected to interpretation is instruction. What more efficient way to give young Christians a compendium of the faith than by teaching them the catechism and confessions of the church. In the Act approving the Westminster Larger Catechism, The General Assembly of the Scottish Presbyterian Church in 1648 commended this catechism as "a rich treasure for increasing knowledge among the people of God."[22] Warfield points out the educational value of the catechism in a story about D. L. Moody. When Moody was visiting a friend in London, a young man called on Moody to ask a number of questions. One had to do with prayer. "What is prayer?" he said, "I can't tell what you mean by it!" While Moody was talking with the young man, the nine- or ten-year-old daughter of Moody's host was coming down the stairs. Her father called her and asked her to explain to the gentleman what prayer is. As the story goes,

Jenny did not know what had been going on, but she quite understood that she was now called upon to say her Catechism. So she drew herself up, and folded her hands in front of her, like a good little girl who was going to 'say her questions,' and she said in her clear childish voice: 'Prayer is an offering up of our desires unto God for things agreeable to his will, in the name of Christ, with

---

[20] Brooke Foss Westcott, *The Historic Faith: Short Lectures on the Apostles' Creed* (London: Macmillan, 1893), 22–23.

[21] *Westminster Shorter Catechism*, questions 4, 7.

[22] Church of Scotland, *The Confession of Faith; The Larger and Shorter Catechisms, with the Scripture Proofs at Large* (Glasgow: Free Presbyterian Publications, 1985), 128.

confession of our sins and thankful acknowledgement of his mercies.' 'Ah! That's the Catechism!' Moody said, 'thank God for that Catechism.'[23]

In addition to serving as an apt summary of the orthodox faith for communion and communication, creeds serve as an instrument for defending the faith. Paul commends this use in 2 Tim 1:14, with the imperative "Guard." This is a militant term. Jude commands us to contend for the faith (Jude 3). The faith is under attack and the church is entrusted with the responsibility to defend it. Paul says, in 1 Tim 3:14–15, "I write these things to you, hoping to come to you soon. But if I should be delayed, I have written so that you will know how people ought to conduct themselves in God's household, which is the church of the living God, the pillar and foundation of the truth." Part of the responsibility entailed in being a pillar and support is the defense of the truth. For example, many of you have experienced a visit from a Mormon or Jehovah's Witness cultist, who, when asked "Do you believe that Jesus is the Son of God?" answered yes. Thus you must clarify your question. Do you mean he is eternally God, equal with God the Father? Do you deny that he was created? Throughout the history of the church, creeds have served this purpose. Originally, the church developed creeds to guard against error. They continue to serve this purpose. What better way to expose the error of a Mormon or Jehovah's Witness than using the question and answer of the Westminster Shorter Catechism, "Who is the Redeemer of God's elect? The only Redeemer of God's elect is the Lord Jesus Christ, who, being the eternal Son of God, became man, and so was, and continueth to be, God and man in two distinct natures, and one person, forever."[24] Shepherds and teachers of the church must guard the truth and guard the church, because false teachers will arise, "and distort the truth to lure the disciples into following them" (Acts 20:30).

---

[23] Benjamin B. Warfield, *Selected Shorter Writings*, vol. 1 (Nutley, NJ: Presbyterian and Reformed Publishing, 1976), 382–83.

[24] *Westminster Shorter Catechism*, question 21.

Conclusion

Some object to the use of creeds because at times their adherents hold to them in an arrogant, browbeating manner. In 2 Tim 1:13–14, Paul teaches us how to use our creeds. He commands us in verse 13 to hold the form "in the faith and love that are in Christ Jesus." Note there should be no dichotomy between vital faith in Christ and creedal orthodoxy. If our creed is biblical, it will point us to Jesus Christ as the Savior of sinners. We will hold to our creed and express its truth in a way that acknowledges that sincere Christians will not agree with us on every point. We will contend for the truth with love for God and our neighbor. Moreover, our creeds will direct our attention to the beauty and glory of the triune God. The grand purpose of doctrine is that we might know and serve God. Therefore, the church will make her confession with praise and adoration. Thus, we hold to our creeds and confessions evangelically. The doctrines summarized in our creeds are to this end, and we should use them accordingly.

Moreover, as we learn in verse 14, we are to hold to and guard the truth spiritually, "Guard ... through the Holy Spirit." Here we learn that our creeds are not clubs by which we cudgel others to accept our position. We are to guard the good deposit in dependence upon the Holy Spirit. He alone will cause men and women to understand and embrace the truth we love. Paul reminds us in 2 Tim 2:24–26 to teach the truth patiently: "The Lord's servant must not quarrel, but must be gentle to everyone, able to teach, and patient, instructing his opponents with gentleness. Perhaps God will grant them repentance leading them to the knowledge of the truth. Then they may come to their senses and escape the trap of the devil, who has taken them captive to do his will."

We have seen that God teaches the church to use creeds from an experimental commitment to and defense of the faith. Creeds are a rich treasure entrusted to us. When we use them humbly, evangelically, and in dependence on the Holy Spirit, they give us a basis for communion and communication of the truth of the Bible. They serve as a litmus test to protect the church and the truth entrusted to her. Rather than replacing Scripture, they are scriptural in origin and content. I count myself blessed to be a member of a confessing church that adheres to a thorough creed.

Bibliography

Arndt, W., and F. Gingrich. *A Greek-English Lexicon of the New Testament and Other Early Greek Literature*. Chicago: University of Chicago Press, 1967.

Dabney, Robert L. *The Doctrinal Contents of the Confession: Its Fundamental and Regulative Ideas and the Necessity and Value of Creeds*. Greenville, SC: Greenville Presbyterian Theological Seminary, 1993.

Knight, George W., III. *The Faithful Sayings in the Pastoral Letters*. Grand Rapids: Baker, 1979.

_____. *The Pastoral Epistles: A Commentary on the Greek Text*. The New International Greek Text Commentary. Grand Rapids: Eerdmans, 1992.

Miller, Samuel. *Doctrinal Integrity: On the Utility and Importance of Creeds and Confessions and Adherence to our Doctrinal Standards*. Dallas: Presbyterian Heritage Publications, 1989.

Moulton, James Hope, and George Milligan. *The Vocabulary of the Greek Testament*. Grand Rapids: Eerdmans, 1974.

Pipa, Joseph A., Jr. "Great Things He Hath Taught Us." In *Onward Christian Soldiers*, ed. Don Kistler. Morgan, PA: Soli Deo Gloria Publications, 1999.

Simpson, E. K. *The Pastoral Epistles: The Greek Text with Introduction and Commentary*. London: Tyndale Press, 1954.

Warfield, Benjamin B. *Selected Shorter Writings*. Vol. 1. Edited by John E. Meeter. Nutley, NJ: Presbyterian and Reformed, 1976.

Westcott, Brooke Foss. *The Historic Faith: Short Lectures on the Apostles' Creed*. London: Macmillan, 1893.

Wiesinger, August. *Biblical Commentary on St. Paul's Epistles to the Philippians, to Titus, the First to Timothy*. Edinburgh: T&T Clark, 1858.

9

Reformed Confessions and Confessional Faithfulness

ROGER SCHULTZ

In 1528, the ministers of East Friesland issued a new reformational Confession of Faith, made necessary because of accusations of heresy by Catholic opponents. As stated in the preface, the ministers hoped to show all "that they despise neither God's Word nor the sacraments, as they are falsely accused."[1] Sometimes called the "first Protestant confession," the East Friesian Confession stood at the beginning of a confessional revolution that lasted a century, until 1648.[2] This chapter will examine reformed confessions[3] (particularly the Westminster Standards and their acceptance) during this era of confessional revolution, as well as the confessional applications, and related issues of confessional subscription.[4]

Over time, Reformed Christians have sought to preserve, promote and perpetuate the great confessional truths of their heritage, although this

---

[1] "East Friesland Preachers' Confession (1528)," in *Reformed Confessions of the 16th and 17th Century in English Translation*, ed. James T. Dennison Jr. (Grand Rapids: Reformation Heritage, 2008), 1:44–45.

[2] "East Friesland Preachers' Confession."

[3] While there are common themes in Lutheran and Reformed confessions, Reformed standards were more dynamic. See Alasdair I. C. Heron, "Calvin and the Confessions of the Reformation," *HTS Theological Studies* 70, no. 1 (June 2014): 1–5; http://www.scielo.org.za/scielo.php?script=sci_arttext &pid=S0259-94222014000100013. See also the excellent new collection of Reformed documents: James T. Dennison Jr., ed., *Reformed Confessions of the 16th and 17th Century in English Translation*, 4 vol. (Grand Rapids: Reformation Heritage, 2008–2014).

[4] I am particularly interested in reception and subscription, seen from the perspective of the subscription debates in the Presbyterian Church in America in the 1990s. See David W. Hall, ed., *The Practice of Confessional Subscription* (Lanham, MD: University Press of America, 1995).

has come with varying degrees of success.[5] The questions related to the preservation and passing of the faith have continuing relevance—for families, churches, and faith-based institutions, and so it is with this intent in mind that we will examine how the Reformation provided a legacy of faith through confession and catechism. In turn, I hope that in looking back, we might move forward, preserving and teaching the theological heritage committed to us from "faithful men who [were] able to teach others also" (2 Tim 2:2).

The Confessional Revolution

The Confessional Revolution of the Reformation was geographically widespread. From East Friesland to Constantinople, from Scotland to Poland, there was an eagerness to confess and own the Reformation faith. This included the confessions of individuals, of ecclesiastical bodies, of cities, of collections of cities, of nations, of United Kingdoms, and even an international Synod. Someone has noted, "[F]or both Catholic and Protestant the sixteenth century was an era characterized by faith speaking through the composition of their respective confessions of faith."[6] These new confessions had an apologetic function. Protestants sought to defend their positions and share their testimonies. Facing persecution, Reformation Protestants shared their faith earnestly and confidently. Some of the new Protestants would give their lives for the truths of the Reformation. When a copy of the *Belgic Confession* (1561) was sent to Philip II, petitioners said that they were willing to "offer their backs to stripes, their tongues to knives, their mouths to gags, and their whole bodies to the fire, well knowing that those who follow Christ, must take His cross and deny themselves." A few years later, the author of the *Belgic Confession*, Guido de Bres, died a martyr's death.[7]

Doctrinal formulations were evangelical in tone, stressing personal faith in Jesus Christ. The famous first question of the *Heidelberg Catechism* (1563) asks, "What is your only comfort in life and death?" The

---

[5] My operating conviction, which was part of the practical nature of the conference for which this paper was generated, is that the doctrinal truths of the Protestant Reformation are biblically anchored and have continuing relevance for the church.

[6] Peter Lillback, "Confessional Subscription among Sixteenth Century Reformers," in *The Practice of Confessional Subscription*, ed. David Hall (Lanham, MD: University Press of America, 1995), 33.

[7] Joel Beeke and Sinclair Ferguson, eds., *Reformed Confessions Harmonized* (Grand Rapids: Baker, 1999), ix.

answer begins: "That I am not my own, but belong with body and soul, both in life and in death, to my faithful Saviour Jesus Christ. He has fully paid for all my sins with his precious blood. . . ."[8] The Heidelberg Catechism was widely circulated and translated into dozens of languages.[9] Its warm, irenic spirit and first-person confessional tone is a hallmark of the Reformation faith.

Confessions stressed their historic Orthodoxy. Reformation documents typically referenced traditional symbols of the church: the Apostles' Creed, Lord's Prayer, and Ten Commandments. *The Catechism of Pierre Viret* (1558), for instance, asks, "What are the chief points contained in this faith?" Answer: "They are briefly summarized in the little summary called the Apostles' Creed, by which the faithful in the church have always made confession of their faith."[10] Half the questions in the *Westminster Shorter Catechism* involve the Ten Commandments and Lord's Prayer, as do 40 percent of the questions in the *Westminster Larger Catechism*.

New confessions also, not surprisingly, stressed the doctrinal distinctives of the Reformation. These included the authority of Scripture, justification by faith alone, and a repudiation of the papacy. Of particular interest was the meaning and role of the sacraments, territory much contested between Catholics, Lutherans, the Reformed, and Anabaptists. The authority of Scripture is clearly expressed in the first chapter of the *Westminster Confession of Faith*, a mature statement of Reformation theology. *The Second Helvetic Confession* (1566), a much-earlier Swiss standard, also emphasized the Bible in its first chapter on "The Holy Scriptures Being the True Word of God." The Swiss passion for Scripture is likewise obvious in the statement on the Civil Magistrate: "Let him, therefore, hold the Word of God *in his hands*, and look that nothing be taught contrary thereunto. In like manner, let him govern the people, committed to him of God,

---

[8] "Lord's Day 1," Heidelberg Catechism, accessed September 10, 2017, http://www.heidelberg-catechism.com/en/lords-days/1.html. The full answer reads: "That I am not my own, but belong with body and soul, both in life and in death, to my faithful Saviour Jesus Christ. He has fully paid for all my sins with his precious blood, and has set me free from all the power of the devil. He also preserves me in such a way that without the will of my heavenly Father not a hair can fall from my head; indeed, all things must work together for my salvation. Therefore, by his Holy Spirit he also assures me of eternal life and makes me heartily willing and ready from now on to live for him."

[9] Roger Schultz, "Heidelberg Catechism," in *The Popular Encyclopedia of Church History*, ed. Ed Hindson and Dan Mitchell (Eugene, OR: Harvest House, 2013).

[10] Pierre Viret, *The Catechism of Pierre Viret (1558)*, trans. R. A. Sheats (Lausanne: Zurich Publishing, 2017), 19.

with good laws, made according to the Word of God *in his hands...*"[11] The Reformation emphasis on *sola Scriptura* had both theological and practical applications.

Confessional Applications

New confessional statements had a variety of applications, sometimes conflicting, overlapping and evolving. It is interesting to see how this new Reformation theology was expressed and used. Peter Lillback has argued for distinct stages of confessional development.[12] In the early stage of "*Confessional Conception*," for instance, statements were *confessional* ("to express one's faith"), *apologetic* ("to defend one's faith"), *fraternal* ("to establish common ground and unity"), and *pedagogic* ("to teach the youth and new converts"). This first stage was largely positive and affirming.

The middle stage, "*Confessional Consolidation*," Lillback argues, emphasized *uniformity* ("to standardize doctrine in an ecclesiastical context"), *orthodoxy/heterodoxy* (requiring one to reveal his faith as "sound or erroneous"), *qualifications* ("to enable one to enter leadership offices in the Church"), and *definitions* ("to distinguish one religious viewpoint over and against another"). Confessional standards, here, became more structured and settled.

The mature stage of "*Confessional Confrontation*," finally, involved statements that were *polemical* ("to attack a divergent theological viewpoint"), *restrictive* ("to prevent the advance of a divergent theological viewpoint"), and *coercive* ("to compel another into submission in regard to doctrine or practice"). There is something rigid and unhealthy here, in Lillback's descriptions, but his taxonomy is certainly helpful.[13]

Catechisms, for instance, sprang up across Reformation lands. Faithful ministers developed catechisms to train the youth of their churches. In Lausanne, Pierre Viret introduced his new *Catechism* (1558) with a telling reference to the widely available new resources: "[M]any would esteem this humble labor as superfluous and wholly unprofitable—seeing that there are

---

[11] Beeke and Ferguson, *Reformed Confessions Harmonized*, 232. The language "in his hands" is reminiscent of requirements for rulers in Deut 17, emphasis added.

[12] Peter Alan Lillback, "Confessional Subscription among the Sixteenth Century Reformers," in *The Practice of Confessional Subscription*, ed. David W. Hall (Lanham: University Press of America, 1995), 33–66.

[13] I do not, here, engage (or necessarily endorse) Lillback's larger argument about the trajectory of confessional changes, but his categories of confessional application are useful.

so many good catechisms which have been made in our time, and in all languages . . ." Viret believed that his catechism will find use as a briefer, clearer and more foundational work. His overarching goal was clear: he wanted men to "fulfill their duty as true fathers of their family, teaching their children the fear and admonition of the Lord from their youngest age."[14]

Some catechisms simultaneously served multiple purposes. *The Heidelberg Catechism* (1563), a remarkable production in the Palatinate of Frederick III, was designed to serve three specific functions. It would be a *catechetical* standard, to train the youth in the Christian faith, a *homiletical* standard, serving as a systematic preaching guide, and a *doctrinal* standard, committing the Palatinate to a winsome and experiential version of Reformed doctrine.[15]

The famous *New England Primer* included two catechisms.[16] One was Massachusetts Puritan John Cotton's *Spiritual Milk for American Babes: Drawn out of the Breasts of Both Testaments.* The other was the *Westminster Shorter Catechism.* American school children throughout the colonial period learned a theocentric and doxological answer to the big teleological question of life. Question 1: "What is the Chief End of Man?" Answer: "Man's Chief End is to Glorify God and to Enjoy Him Forever."[17] The *Westminster Shorter Catechism* became a beloved standard, providing a reliable theological foundation in both Congregational and Presbyterian circles. The Catechism "would introduce children to precise information that society agrees upon . . . [as] Catechisms are especially good for affirming traditions of knowledge." Everybody, Rick Kennedy explains, "is affirming out loud and in the same rhythm what everybody already knows."[18]

---

[14] Viret, *The Catechism of Pierre Viret (1558),* ix–x; Viret states, "I have also thought that there can be no harm in many people writing on the same matters. For some have one manner of teaching which is more suitable for some, and others, for others."

[15] Lyle Bierma, "The Purpose and Authorship of the Heidelberg Catechism," in *An Introduction to the Heidelberg Catechism: Sources, History and Theology,* ed. Richard A. Muller (Grand Rapids: Baker, 2005), 50–51.

[16] *New England Primer Enlarged* (1727). In addition to John Cotton's Catechism and the *Westminster Shorter Catechism,* the *New England Primer* included the historic symbols of the faith: the Lord's Prayer, the Apostles' Creed, and the Ten Commandments.

[17] Pierre Viret's Catechism begins with a similar question: "What is the chief purpose why God created man in His likeness and image?" Answer: "To be worshipped and honored by him." *The Catechism of Pierre Viret (1558),* 3.

[18] Rick Kennedy, *The First American Evangelical: A Short Life of Cotton Mather* (Grand Rapids: Eerdmans, 2015), 10.

Reformed Confessions also required some obligations for citizens, or church members, or at least ministers and church officers. It is one thing to establish a confessional standard, and it is something quite different to maintain it for a mass of people over time. Thus, as we have observed in confessional churches since the reformation, confessional subscription was fluid and highly contested.

Confessional Subscription

Subscription (literally, "to write beneath" or to sign) is a method of receiving and embracing a Confession, officially done at ordination, and, perhaps, literally done on other, ceremonial occasions. The Scottish reception of the Westminster Standards is instructive regarding the question of subscription.[19] The Westminster Standards were clearly considered derivative and subordinate. They were accepted only after careful review, discussion, and ratification. In approving the *Westminster Confession of Faith* in 1647, the Scots noted the review criteria: it was "most orthodox," it was "most agreeable to the word of God," and it had "nothing contrary to the received doctrine, worship, discipline and government of this Kirk [Church]."[20] Among other things, some authority was assigned to the settled practice, customs and usages of the historic Scottish Presbyterian church. The same adoption language (agreement with Scripture and Kirk's "received doctrine, worship, discipline and government") is also used for the *Westminster Larger* and *Shorter Catechisms*.[21] Human confessional statements, then, were not of equal authority with Scripture. The standards had to be judged "agreeable to" or "most agreeable to" the Word of God before they had any official authority.

There were some concerns with the *Westminster Confession of Faith*, however, regarding polity and politics. The "expressly declared" reservation on polity reads: "the not mentioning in this Confession the several sorts of

---

[19] By "Westminster Standards," I refer to the *Westminster Confession of Faith, Westminster Larger Catechism, Westminster Shorter Catechism, Westminster Directory for the Public Worship of God,* and *Westminster Form of Government and Presbyterial Ordination.* Reformers often applied the Bible to multiple areas of doctrine, worship and government. For the Reformers and their heirs, the Bible was the regulative standard for doctrine, worship, and government. This corresponded well with the traditional three offices of Christ—prophet, priest, and king. It also corresponded to the marks of the true church—involving Word, sacrament, and discipline.

[20] "Act approving the Westminster Confession of Faith," in *The Westminster Confession of Faith* (Glasgow: Free Presbyterian Publications, 2001), 17.

[21] "Act approving the Larger Catechism," in *Westminster Confession of Faith,* 126; "Act approving the Shorter Catechism," in *Westminster Confession of Faith,* 286.

ecclesiastical officers and assemblies, shall be no prejudice to the truth of Christ in these particulars, to be expressed fully in the Directory of Government."[22] In short, the lack of Presbyterian references in the *Confession* couldn't pass without Scottish comment or reservation. Regarding politics, the Scots declared that the Confession's language [Chapter 31, Article 2] regarding the magistrate's power applied only to "Kirks not settled." While the Civil Magistrate had some authority in religious matters, churches and assemblies must be free to meet "by the intrinsical power received from Christ, as often as is necessary for the good of the Church so to assemble, in case the Magistrate, to the detriment of the Church, withhold or deny his consent...."[23] In short, Scottish Presbyterians repudiated Erastianism, emphasized the Kirk's autonomous sphere of sovereignty, and carefully interpreted the application of the *Confession*.[24]

Scots in similar fashion approved the *Directory for the Publick Worship of God* (1645), approving it "according to the plain tenor and meaning thereof."[25] They mentioned one concern, however, about the Lord's Supper, which "mentioneth the communicants sitting about the table or at it, be not to be interpreted as if, in the judgment of this Kirk, it were indifferent..." Recommended seating arrangements for the Lord's Supper had occasioned much debate at the Westminster Assembly. While the Scots could accept the compromise language ("about" or "at"), they could not let the language pass without notice and expressly reserved the right to continue their historic practice (*at* the table).[26]

---

[22] "Approving the Westminster Confession," 17; The fuller statement reads: "But, lest our intention and meaning be in some particulars misunderstood, it is hereby expressly declared and provided, That the not mentioning in this Confession the several sorts of ecclesiastical officers and assemblies, shall be no prejudice to the truth of Christ in these particulars, to be expressed fully in the Directory of Government."

[23] "Approving the Westminster Confession," 17.

[24] Erastianism, commonly attributed to Thomas Erastus, that saw the monarch or civil authorities as having jurisdiction over the church.

[25] "Preface to the *Directory for the Publick Worship of God*," in *Westminster Confession of Faith*, 372. In April 1973, Westminster Presbytery (having seceded from the PCUS and prior to the formation of and reception into the PCA) used similar adoption language: "we do sincerely receive and adopt these Westminster Standards, in the plan sense of the words according to the intentions of the Westminster Divines as our statement of faith..." Quoted in Frank J. Smith, *The History of the Presbyterian Church in America*, 2nd ed. (Lawrenceville, GA: Presbyterian Scholars Press, 1999), 248.

[26] "Preface to the *Directory for the Publick Worship of God*," in *Westminster Confession of Faith*, 372. In Scotland, communicants would literally gather at tables in special sacramental celebrations of the Lord's Supper. See Leigh Eric Schmidt, *Holy Fairs: Scottish Communions and American Revivals in the Early Modern Period* (Princeton: Princeton University Press, 1989).

The Scottish Kirk also approved the *Form of Government and Presbyterial Ordination*, but had concerns about ecclesiastical polity. They reserved the right of further debate and discussion "as God gives further light." One issue involved church office—specifically the office of Teacher (and the Teacher's power to administer the sacraments). The other issue, and one which would convulse the Church of Scotland in the eighteenth century, was "the distinct rights of presbyteries and people in the calling of ministers…"[27] Despite initial reservations, the Church of Scotland was well pleased with the Westminster Standards. The 1711 Ordination Formula required an enthusiastic embrace of the Confession. New ministers were to answer in the affirmative this question: "Do you sincerely own and believe the whole doctrine contained in the Confession of Faith … to be founded upon the Word of God; and you do you acknowledge the same as the confession of your faith; and will you firmly and constantly adhere thereunto…."[28]

Subscription Equivocation

Confessional commitments started sliding in the eighteenth century, and Scotland was no exception. The introduction to a 1719 reprint of the *Westminster Confession* stated:

> The first and most noisy argument [against] all creeds . . . that they are in their own nature an arbitrary and tyrannical invasion upon the natural rights of mankind whereby every man hath a title to judge for himself and not to be imposed upon by the determinations of others, whether private persons or councils and churches. . . . Besides, 'tis alleged that 'tis contrary to our avowed principle, That the Scriptures are the only rule by which we are to try all opinions, and determine all controversies….[29]

Confessional subscription, confessional critics argued, undermined central Reformation principles of *sola Scriptura* and liberty of conscience.

---

[27] "Act…Concerning Kirk-Government and the Ordination of Ministers," in *Westminster Confession of Faith*, 396.

[28] J. Ligon Duncan, "Owning the Confession: Subscription in the Scottish Presbyterian Tradition," in Hall, *Confessional Subscription*, 77, 82. Some contend that this 1711 ordination formula imposed "an absolute commitment" to confessional standards, "that allowed no reserve or qualification, written or mental."

[29] Lillback, "Confessional Subscription," 34.

By the middle of the eighteenth century, Presbyterians in Scotland were deeply divided between Moderate churchmen (liberal) and the Popular Party (evangelical).[30] *Ecclesiastical Characteristics* (1753), by John Witherspoon, was a masterpiece of religious satire of the era.[31] The book was written from the perspective of a "Moderate" churchman giving advice to a neophyte pastor, coaching him in the ways of liberalism and apostasy. Witherspoon's *Ecclesiastical Characteristics* includes "Maxims" with an elaboration on each point. Maxim III, for instance, reads:

> It is a necessary part of the character of a moderate man, never to speak of the Confession of Faith but with a sneer; to give sly hints, that he does not thoroughly believe it; and to make the word *orthodoxy* a term of contempt and reproach.

Witherspoon's protagonist continues:

> Upon this head some may be ready to object, That if the Confession of Faith be built upon the sacred Scriptures, then, change what will, it cannot, as the foundation upon which it rests remains always firm and the same. . . . [But] who are the persecutors of the inimitable heretics among ourselves? Who but the admirers of this antiquated composition, who pin their faith to other men's sleeves, and will not endure one jot less or different belief from what their fathers had before them! It is therefore plain, that the moderate man, who desires to enclose all intelligent beings in one benevolent embrace, must have an utter abhorrence at that vile hedge of distinction, the Confession of Faith.[32]

---

[30] John Witherspoon, *A Serious Apology for the Ecclesiastical Characteristics* (1763), in *The Works of the Reverend John Witherspoon*, ed. H. Rondel Rumburg (Harrisonburg, VA: Sprinkle Publications, 2005), V:246. John Witherspoon argued that these divisions were by both theology and polity: "[W]hat first induced me to write, was a deep concern for the declining interest of religion in the church of Scotland, mixed with some indignation at what appeared to me a strange abuse of church-authority ..."

[31] The full title of Witherspoon's work is *Ecclesiastical Characteristics; Or, the Arcana of Church Policy: Being an Humble Attempt to Open the Mystery of Moderation, Wherein is Shown a Plain and Easy Way of Attaining to the Character of a Moderate Man as at Present in Repute in the Church of Scotland.*

[32] John Witherspoon, *Ecclesiastical Characteristics* (1753), in *The Works of the Reverend John Witherspoon*, ed. H. Rondel Rumburg (Harrisonburg, VA: Sprinkle Publications, 2005), V:196–98. Witherspoon's Moderate recommends, "Nothing is more easy than for them to keep themselves wholly ignorant of what it contains; and then they may, with a good conscience, subscribe it as true, because it ought to be so" (page 198).

Witherspoon nicely frames the questions of confessional adherence and subscription. Confessionalists require complete subscription because, they believed, the Westminster Standards were built on timeless scriptural truths. Moderates argue that evangelicals followed an old-fashioned code, "pin their faith to others," and persecute all who disagree.

Witherspoon's book prompted outrage in Scottish ecclesiastical circles, but American Presbyterians loved it.[33] American Presbyterians had adopted the Westminster Confession of Faith in 1729. Although some reservations were allowed concerning the role of the Civil Magistrate, there was considerable agreement on the nature of confessional authority and subscription. Virginia's Hanover Presbytery, established 1755, is an excellent case study. Ministerial candidates subscribed the "substance" of the Westminster Standards. Samuel Davies, Hanover's leading minister, posed a series of ordination questions:

> Do you receive the Westminster confession of Faith as the confession of *your faith*? . . . And do you purpose to explain the Scriptures agreeable to the *substance* of it? Do you receive the directory for worship and government as composed by the Westminster Assembly, as agreeable to the word of God, and promise to conform to the *substance* of it?[34]

Three things stand out here. The Westminster Confession is "received" as the ordinand's own. A full range of Westminster documents is subscribed (*Confession, Directory, Form of Government*)—in addition to the catechisms. Candidates promise to "conform" to the "substance" of the confessional

---

[33] Witherspoon refused to be despondent about Scotland's spiritual declension, arguing that God could still revive the Church of Scotland. "Nothing is impossible to the power of God. I add that the most remarkable times of the revival of religion in this part of the united kingdom, immediately succeeded times of the greatest apostasy, when 'truth' seemed to be 'fallen in the street...' [Isa 59:14]" "This was the case immediately before the year 1638 [National Covenant]. Corruption in doctrine, looseness in practice and slavish submission in politics had overspread the church of Scotland; and yet, in a little time, she appeared in greater purity and greater dignity than ever [before or since]. Let no Christian, therefore, give way to desponding thoughts. We plead the cause that shall at last prevail. Religion shall rise from its ruins; and its opressed state at present should not only excite us to pray, but encourage us to hope for its speedy revival." John Witherspoon, *Serious Apology for the Ecclesiastical Characteristics* (1763). *Ecclesiastical Characteristics* was largely responsible for Witherspoon being called to the presidency of the College of New Jersey [Princeton] in 1768.

[34] Samuel Davies, "Qualifications for the Ministerial Office: The Manner of Ordination," *Sermons of the Rev. Samuel Davies* (Presbyterian Board of Publication, 1854; repr., Soli Deo Gloria, 1995), III:525–26. Davies preached the sermon on July 13,1758, in Virginia. Emphasis in the original.

standards.[35] (These in turn beg larger subscription questions—of "receiving," "conformity," and "substance.")

Samuel Davies was astonished at the differences in Presbyterian subscription (and orthodoxy) during his 1754 trip to Great Britain. The situation was so bad that evangelical Presbyterians and their Calvinistic Baptist friends would frequent one coffee house, Davies wrote, "rather than associate with their Presbyterian Brethren of Socinian sentiments..." at another.[36] One liberal Presbyterian told Davies with a "sneer" that "he was no friend to Subscriptions."[37] English Presbyterians, a horrified Davies noted, "have universally, as far as I can learn, rejected the Tests of Orthodoxy, and require their Candidates at Ordination, only to declare their Belief in the Scriptures."[38]

Another liberal minister specifically inquired of Davies about strictness of colonial American Presbyterians. He "told me he heard we would admit none into the ministry without subscribing the Westminster Confession. . . ."[39] Davies explained, "We allowed the candidate to mention his objections against any Article in the Confession, and the Judicature judged whether the Articles objected against were essential to Christianity; and if they judged they were not, they would admit the Candidates, notwithstanding his Objection." "He seemed to think," Davies continued, "that we were such rigid Calvinists, that we would not admit an Armenian [sic] into Communion, etc. Alas! For the laxness that prevails here among Presbyterians."[40] The lessons Davies learned were fascinating. English

---

[35] The language of "substance" was used by Jonathan Edwards, who at the same time was exploring a call in Scotland. John Erskine, a Scottish evangelical leader, asked if Edwards could "sign" and "submit" to the Westminster Confession of Faith. Edwards affirmed that, "As to my subscribing to the substance of the Westminster Confession, there would be no difficulty: and as to the Presbyterian government, I have long been perfectly out of conceit with our unsettled, independent, confused way of church government in this land. And the Presbyterian way has ever appeared to me most agreeable to the Word of God, and the reason and nature of things, though I cannot say that I think that the Presbyterian government of the Church of Scotland is so perfect that it can't in some respects be mended." Jonathan Edwards to John Erskine (June 5, 1750), in *Letters and Personal Writings* (Works of Jonathan Edwards Online Vol. 16), ed. George S. Claghorn, 355.

[36] George Pilcher, *The Reverend Samuel Davies Abroad* (Urbana: University of Illinois Press, 1967), 65.

[37] Pilcher, 64. The man asked if the College of New Jersey [Princeton] would admit an Arminian, Arian, or Socinian—since the Charter stated "that Persons of all Denominations to have equal advantages of Education." Davies's exasperation is clear, as he notes that Mr. [Gilbert] Tennent went among "the honest Independents" at the Amsterdam Coffee House. (Because Davies was the more irenic and diplomatic of the two colonial ambassadors, he often worked with marginal supporters.)

[38] Pilcher, 84.

[39] Pilcher, 84. The exchange, recorded in Davies's diary, took place March 19, 1754.

[40] Pilcher, 84. Davies was on a fund-raising trip. Liberal Presbyterians were unlikely to support the collegiate efforts of their confessionally strict trans-Atlantic brethren.

Presbyterians had largely abandoned confessional orthodoxy and sub-scription (or "religious tests"). Americans seemed far more confessional. Virginia Presbyterians, in Davies's explanation, might allow some confes-sional reservations—determined on a case-by-case basis by the Presbytery.[41] It is one thing to establish a confessional standard or subscription prac-tice. It is another thing to keep it. Subscription debates have continued in American Presbyterian circles—most recently in the Presbyterian Church in America in the 1990s. All denominations with firmly held doctrinal standards will have questions about how to preserve these standards and deal with exceptions.

Conclusion

Thirty-five years ago, I was pastor of a small Bible church in northern Min-nesota. I was perplexed by a disagreement with one of the elders, an old church patriarch, in a Sunday School class, over the inerrancy of Scripture. I pointed out that we were committed to the doctrine—and that it was the first point of the Statement of Faith posted on our church bulletin board. The man's response was unforgettable: "Oh, that. I put it together. We just copied it from somewhere!" Like Witherspoon's Moderate, the errant elder immediately claimed that the Statement of Faith was but a copied standard.

So, how do we preserve the faith? Many of us have great affection for the doctrinal truths of the Protestant Reformation. How do we preserve, promote, and perpetuate these truths? How does the faith become personal for each generation? John Witherspoon may frame the question as well as anyone. We do not want to "pin" our faith "to other men's sleeves"—or just copy it from somewhere. We love Reformation truths and standards, believing they are founded on the enduring truths of God's Word.

Doctrinal truths must be anchored in Scripture, and in this commit-ment confessions and creeds must not replace the Word of God. However, as has been argued, churches should make good use of faithful confessional and catechetical statements to train children and congregations, precisely

---

[41] One subsequent instance of confessional latitude in Hanover Presbytery involved Archibald Alexander and Conrad Speece. Alexander notes that in 1797–1799, he "fell into doubt respecting the authority of infant baptism." He further notes, "We also communicated to Presbytery the state of our minds, and left them to do what seemed good in the case; but as they believed that we were sincerely desirous of arriving at the truth, they took no steps, and I believe made no record." See James Alexander, *The Life of Archibald Alexander, DD,* chap. 9 (1854; repr., Harrisonburg, VA: Sprinkle Publications, 1991), 204–5.

because they affirm biblical truths.[42] Confessional standards must be required for training and screening ministers and church officers. Churches do not become weaker when they emphasize a clear, succinct, and robustly biblical doctrine. Indeed, the apostle Paul stresses that the inspired Scriptures are "profitable for doctrine" (2 Tim 3:16 KJV).

Bibliography

Alexander, James. *The Life of Archibald Alexander, DD*. 1854. Reprint, Harrisonburg, VA: Sprinkle Publications, 1991.

Beeke, Joel, and Sinclair Ferguson. *Reformed Confessions Harmonized*. Grand Rapids: Baker, 1999.

Davies, Samuel. *Sermons of the Rev. Samuel Davies*. 1854. Reprint, Soli Deo Gloria, 1995.

Dennison, James T. Jr., ed. *Reformed Confessions of the 16th and 17th Century in English Translation*. 4 vols. Grand Rapids: Reformation Heritage, 2008–2014.

Edwards, Jonathan. *Letters and Personal Writings*. Edited by George S. Claghorn. Jonathon Edwards Collection at Yale University. http://edwards.yale.edu.

Hall, David W., ed. *The Practice of Confessional Subscription*. Lanham, MD: University Press of America, 1995.

Herron, Alasdair I. C. "Calvin and the Confessions of the Reformation." *HTS Theological Studies* 70, no. 1 (June 2014):1–5. http://www.scielo.org.za/scielo.php?script=sci_arttext&pid=S0259-94222014000100013.

Hindson, Ed, and Dan Mitchell, eds. *The Popular Encyclopedia of Church History*. Eugene, OR: Harvest House, 2013.

Kennedy, Rick. *The First American Evangelical: A Short Life of Cotton Mather*. Grand Rapids: Eerdmans, 2015.

Muller, Richard A., ed. *An Introduction to the Heidelberg Catechism: Sources, History and Theology*. Grand Rapids: Baker, 2005.

Pilcher, George. *The Reverend Samuel Davies Abroad*. Urbana: University of Illinois Press, 1967.

Viret, Pierre. *The Catechism of Pierre Viret (1558)*. Translated by R. A. Sheats. Lausanne: Zurich Publishing, 2017.

Witherspoon, John. *The Works of the Reverend John Witherspoon*. Edited by H. Rondel Rumburg. Harrisonburg, VA: Sprinkle Publications, 2005.

---

[42] See chapter 8 in this volume by Joseph Pipa, "The Confessing Church."

10

The Legacy of the Heidelberg Catechism

ADRIAAN C. NEELE

In considering the legacy of Reformation confessions, catechisms, and preaching, this chapter will examine the Heidelberg Catechism of 1563, which was a manual of instruction for the Christian faith, written amid sixteenth-century politics, pedagogy, and preaching and bequeathed to us by the Reformed churches of Europe.[1] The purpose of this chapter is to primarily consider whether or not the Heidelberg Catechism should continue to find use in churches, homes, and centers of theological education, and if so, why.[2]

Since it was written, the popularity and usefulness of the Heidelberg Catechism throughout the history of the church cannot be questioned. It has been claimed that the Heidelberg Catechism "has circulated more widely than any other books except the Bible, Thomas à Kempis's *The Imitation of Christ*, and John Bunyan's *Pilgrim's Progress*."[3] Thus, many would

---

[1] The Heidelberg Catechism is divided into 129 questions and answers, which, for the sake of instruction, have been divided into 52 Lord's Days.

[2] The author acknowledges with much gratitude James O'Brien for his insightful comments and editing of this essay. See Kevin DeYoung's blog on reasons to read the Heidelberg Catechism, https://www.thegospelcoalition.org/blogs/kevin-deyoung/five-reasons-to-read-the-heidelberg -catechism-this-year/.

[3] Joel Beeke and Sinclair Ferguson, *Reformed Confessions Harmonized* (Grand Rapids: Baker, 1999), x. In addition to this, it is noteworthy that the 450th anniversary of the Catechism, in 2013, was widely commemorated and celebrated around the globe—in particular in Australia, Brazil, Canada, Germany, Hungary, the Netherlands, the United States and South Africa, by those who understand themselves to be rooted in the Protestant Reformation of the 16th century. Thus, it is not a catechism purely useful for one time and place, but useful for global Christendom, especially for those of a reformed heritage.

readily affirm the ongoing value of the catechism, noting its personal and most devotional nature, more so than any of the Reformation-era creeds and confessions. In short, for many, the theology of the Heidelberg Catechism is time tested and tradition approved, providing sufficient reason why this catechism should continue to be taught.

Despite its popularity, asking why we should adhere to a text written in a different context, culture, and time is a reasonable question. How can a catechism created in a uniquely contextualized location of history produce a product that can timelessly convey the Christian faith in a way that is recognizable, biblically founded, and relevant to the present? It is to these concerns that we will turn our attention, to provide an answer for the pedagogy and preaching of the Christian faith in the church, the home, and the school.

Context of the Heidelberg Catechism

When the Heidelberg Catechism was written in 1563, religious reformation had already been occurring within the Palatinate for many years. During the early years of the Protestant Reformation, in the 1520s, some reformed-minded leaders began to call for change. Heidelberg was a university town, and some of the faculty at the University of Heidelberg began to teach from a Protestant perspective. Wenzel Strauss, one of the preachers at the main church, the Heiliggeistkirche, for example, was not afraid to preach that salvation could only be attained by true faith in Christ.

The elector at the time, Frederick II, was open-minded about the Reformation, so, in 1546, he promoted some religious reforms in the Palatinate. However, though Elector Frederick II was an influential man, he was not nearly as powerful as the emperor, Charles V, who was staunchly Roman Catholic. After years of religious conflict between Protestants and Roman Catholics, and despite Roman Catholic and political opposition, the Peace of Augsburg was signed in 1555. This decree allowed each local prince to decide the religious direction of his region, including the Palatinate—the region around Heidelberg. This policy was summed up in the Latin phrase, *cuius regio, eius religio* (loosely translated, "whoever [rules] the region, he [decides] the religion").

The following year, 1556, Frederick II was succeeded by Otto Henry, a stronger supporter of the Reformation. Not only did Henry introduce a new church order, he also promoted the use of the Württemberg Catechism for education, along with other means for the instruction of his people in the Christian faith. He also sent a church visitation team around to all the local congregations to determine the actual, spiritual state of affairs in his territory. The results of the visitation (or survey) were not encouraging. Ministers were not well trained; congregations were not well-fed with the Word; and superstitions and false traditions were more prominent than the knowledge of Scripture and holy living. Elector Otto Henry was eager to change all that and he made a good start. Schools were started that not only taught in Latin but also in the German language. At these German schools both boys and girls had three main components in their curriculum: reading, writing, and ... catechism! However, Henry's noble efforts were cut short when he died only three years after becoming elector. In 1559, then, it was left to the new elector, Frederick III, Otto Henry's nephew, to continue what his uncle had begun.

The Lord's Supper Controversy

No sooner than Frederick III began advancing the work of reformation, he had to deal with a heated controversy. The disagreement was over the doctrine of the Lord's Supper. On one side of the dispute was Tilemann Heshusius, a professor at the University of Heidelberg who also served as a preacher in the main church of Heidelberg, the Heiliggeistkirche. Heshusius was a staunch defender of the Lutheran view of the Lord's Supper. On the other side was Wilhelm Klebitz.[4] He was a student at the University and a deacon in the church, and promoted a more Reformed view of the Lord's Supper. The dispute between these two men, professor and student, became so bitter and so public it was even addressed from the pulpit. Finally, Frederick III decided, for the peace and well-being of the church, the clash between these two men had to stop. He consulted with Philipp Melanchthon, the German Reformer, who was the close friend and collaborator of Martin Luther.

---

[4] See *Klebitz, Wilhelm (auch Klebiz, Klebitius)*, in: Controversia et Confessio Digital. Herausgegeben von Irene Dingel. <http://www.controversia-et-confessio.de/id/ab7d166d-324f-4e0f-9039-7e7c2851e077>.

Melanchthon responded to Frederick that same year (1559) in a letter, entitled "An Advice on the Controversies on the Lord's Supper."[5] Melanchthon hoped, first, that his letter might put the church at ease, saying, "We must care for the uniting of our churches by mediating advice."[6] Thus, the unity of the church, as well as mediating between the Lutheran and Reformed positions on the Lord's Supper, was of great importance to Melanchthon. Second, he stated in his letter, "I put to the most glorious Elector the proposal that he orders both competing parties to keep silent, so that there is no split in the tender church ... and I would wish that the contenders of both parties keep away."[7] Frederick acted decisively on this advice and dismissed both professor Heshusius and Klebitz, sending them off to find another place to live. Thirdly, Melanchthon advised the elector to "agree on one form of wording" on the doctrine of the Lord's Supper. He wrote, "and in this controversy it would be best to stick simply to the words of Paul: 'the bread which we break, is the communion with the body of Christ.'"[8] Thus, the German Lutheran Reformer suggested that a uniform and agreeable wording be chosen to define the doctrine, but also, and more importantly, that they follow Scripture closely in formulating the doctrine. Fourth, and lastly, Melanchthon concluded his rather brief letter to Frederick III by writing, "This strife of both parties must be forbidden." How? "[That] one and the same formula is useful." If "formula" (*forma*) is to be understood not only of a form of words but a formula that is an authoritative statement of faith, such as the Lutheran *Formula of Concord* (1577), then Melanchthon's advice to the elector deals not only with the Lord's Supper controversy in Heidelberg and the Palatinate but is also an implicit commissioning of a unifying doctrinal document for the churches. His closing sentence may point to such a conclusion: "I also hope that at

---

[5] The argument that follows is indebted to Wim Janse, "Calvin's Doctrine of the Lord's Supper," *Perichoresis* 10, no. 2 (2012): 137–63; Erik A. de Boer, "Philipp Melanchthon's *Iudicium de controversia Coenae Domini* (1559) to the Palatine Elector Frederick III," *Reformation & Renaissance Review* 17, no. 3 (2015); Philip Melanchthon, *Epitome renovatae ecclesiasticae doctrinae ad ill. Prin. Hessorum* ([Wittenberg], 1524); Philip Melanchthon, *Epistola Philippi Melanchthonis, ad Johannem Oecolampadium de Coena Domini* (Haganoae, 1529).

[6] Melanchthon, *Iudicium de controversia Coenae Domini*, "moderatis consiliis coniunctionem nostrarum Ecclesiarum foveamus." See for document source and translation, de Boer, "Philipp Melanchthon's Iudicium" n72.

[7] Melanchthon, n47.

[8] Melanchthon, n32.

some point in time all these controversies of these times will be discussed in a faithful Synod."[9]

That synod of the Palatinate took place in January 1563 at Heidelberg. The synod accepted the Heidelberg Catechism, which contained a preface written by Elector Frederick III. Frederick heeded Melanchthon's advice by developing a doctrinal statement that would help achieve his aim of unifying and solidifying the Reformation in his territory. This catechism would fill a basic need within the curriculum to train the future leaders of the Palatinate in sound Reformation doctrine.

The historical context and content of the preface answers this need. In times when ministers are not well trained, congregations are not well-fed with the Word, schools and education are in disarray, when there is the unsystematic teaching of doctrine, and superstitions and traditions are more prominent than the knowledge of Scripture and holy living; in times when too many people grow up without the fear of God and the knowledge of his Word; when many people have no knowledge of Christian doctrine, yet many maintain that they are Christians; in times of doctrinal controversy and confusion—the church needs tools for grounding its theological mooring. This was the context in which the Heidelberg Catechism was born—to address the educational culture of the sixteenth-century Palatinate. The Heidelberg Catechism provided an answer for Frederick's two aims: First, it presented a solidified and systematic instruction in Christian doctrine, according to the Word of God, which answered a need for a uniform method of catechetical instruction in the church, a need expressed already in 1529 in Luther's preface to his Small Catechism. Second, it provided a means to promote the unity of the church in his region.

These purposes of Frederick's day highlight similar considerations of why this legacy of the Reformation should be used today for teaching and preaching Christian doctrine, and for the unification of the church.

Prolegomena of the Heidelberg Catechism

The *Heidelberg Catechism* became a single catechetical tool replacing other means of instruction of Christian doctrine, thereby solidifying the teaching of the church. Second, it became a preaching guide for pastors and

---

[9] Melanchthon, *Iudicium de controversia Coenae Domini, Responsio,* "Opto etiam, ut aliquando in pia synodo de omnibus controversiis horum temporum deliberetur." Cf. de Boer, "Philipp Melanchthon's Iudicium" (last sentence *Responsio.*).

preachers. Last, it offered a form of unity in the church through confessional unity. The question arises immediately, what is taught in this 450-year-old manual of instruction of the Christian faith? To answer the question, let us consider the structure and content of the Heidelberg Catechism and conclude with some observations and remarks.

The Structure of the Heidelberg Catechism

Zacharius Ursinus (1534–1583), one of the authors of the Heidelberg Catechism,[10] began his university lectures in systematic theology in 1562 with preliminary questions, which he placed under the heading "Prolegomena." The prolegomena of a systematic theology usually address methodological questions dealing with the nature, task, and structure of theology. Ursinus's Prolegomena begins with the question: What is the doctrine of the church? He answers,

> The doctrine of the church is the entire and uncorrupted doctrine of the law and gospel concerning the true God, together with his will, works, and worship; divinely revealed, and comprehended in the writings of the prophets and apostles, and confirmed by many miracles and divine testimonies; through which the Holy Spirit works effectually in the hearts of the elect, and gathers from the whole human race an everlasting church, in which God is glorified, both in this, and in the life to come.[11]

The word "doctrine" derives from the Latin *doctrina*, which simply means teaching. The teaching of the church is "the entire and uncorrupted doctrine of the law and gospel." The "law-gospel" distinction is characteristic of Luther and Ursinus's teacher, Philipp Melanchthon. The content of this doctrine of the law and gospel concerns "the true God, together with his will, works, and worship." Where does one find this teaching about God, his will, his work, and how to worship him? According to Ursinus, it

---

[10] A unique feature of the Heidelberg Catechism, however, is that the two structures—Misery/Deliverance/Gratitude and, Creed/Commandments/Sacraments/Prayer have been woven together into one seamless instruction of the Christian faith. This feature is absent in Luther's *Small Catechism* (1529), Calvin's *Geneva Catechism* (1545), and Beza's *Confessio* (1559), though it is also present in Ursinus's *Small Catechism* (1562). Similarly, Ursinus's lectures on the Heidelberg Catechism consist of three parts: Misery, Deliverance, and Gratitude.

[11] Zacharius Ursinus, *Explicationum catecheticarum absolutum opus, totiusque theologiae purioris quasi novum corpus, Davidis Parei opera extrema recognitum*, trans. G. W. Williard (Neostadii Palatinorum, 1600), 1.

is found in Scripture. How does one come to embrace and believe in this teaching about God, his will, his work, and worship? He answers: "through which [that is the Word] the Holy Spirit works effectually in the hearts of the elect and gathers from the whole human race an everlasting church, in which God is glorified, both in this, and in the life to come."[12]

Further on in the Prolegomena, Ursinus raises the question: "What are the various methods of teaching and learning the doctrine of the church?" He answers, in a way suited to a university setting:

> The method of teaching and studying theology is three-fold: *The first* is the system of catechetical instruction, or that method which comprises a brief summary and simple exposition of the principal doctrines of the Christian religion, which is called catechizing.
>
> *The second method* is the consideration and discussion of subjects of a general and more difficult character, or the Common Places (*Loci Communes*), as they are called, which contain a more lengthy explanation of every single point, and of difficult questions with their definitions, divisions, and arguments.
>
> *The third method* of the study of theology is the careful and diligent reading of the Scriptures or sacred text. This is the highest method in the study of the doctrine of the church.[13]

Some may argue that Ursinus's method seems backward, with Scripture as the final piece of the list. However, any problems are removed when we understand the context in which Ursinus was writing these things. There can be no question that the Reformers, Ursinus included, were deeply committed to *sola Scriptura* and, therefore, based all their teachings on the interpretation of Scripture. Indeed, he explicitly states in his lectures that the content of the catechism must be derived from Scripture.

However, in this section of his Prolegomena, Ursinus is not addressing how doctrine is formulated. Rather, he is addressing the best way to educate ordinary Christians in a uniform, orthodox understanding of the Christian faith, which will promote unity in the church. To get people up to speed in what the Bible teaches, he recommends the Heidelberg Catechism. While the Scriptures are clear on the main points of Christian doctrine, there are passages that can be misinterpreted. We should remember

---

[12] Ursinus, 2.
[13] Ursinus, 12.

that some heretics claim to base their teachings on the Bible. Catechetical and theological training does not replace the study of the Bible, nor should it subvert that teaching. Rather, it gives the fruit of centuries of study of the Bible in condensed form, so that those who are just learning the faith will not be led astray in their understanding or reading of Scripture. Thus, for Ursinus, while a good catechism and systematic theology arise out of the careful study of the Bible, they also lead back to Scripture. The Heidelberg Catechism provided a means to promote the unity of the church by solidifying the teaching of the Christian faith in the church, but also, and very importantly, it is intended as the first method for learning those teachings.

If the purpose of the Heidelberg Catechism was to promote church unity, how should it be taught? Ursinus answers the question concerning structure of the catechism this way:

> The catechism of which we shall speak in these lectures consists of three parts. The first treats of the misery of man, the second of his deliverance from this misery, and the third of gratitude, which division does not, in reality, differ from those who divide catechetical instruction into five parts, because all the parts which are there specified are embraced in these three general heads.[14]

The use of catechisms has a long history in the Christian church. The five sections mentioned above were the central components of any catechizing throughout the centuries. Even the Early Church Father Hippolytus of Rome (170–235) commented, "We have set down these things [Creed] in order that those who have been well taught by our exposition may guard that tradition ... and remain firm [against] that backsliding or error which was recently invented through ignorance."[15] The ancient church instructed its candidates for membership to memorize the Apostles' Creed (and in some places the Lord's Prayer also). The concern was not only that the catechumens should tightly grasp orthodoxy, but that they should live out the faith into which they were being inducted. And so, the teaching of the Creed, Ten Commandments, and Our Father, as well as seven Sacraments, became part of the medieval instruction of faith confirmed at the Fourth

---

[14] Ursinus, 17.
[15] Geoffrey J. Cuming, ed. and trans., *Hippolytus: A Text for Students*, Grove Liturgical Studies (Bramcote: Grove Books, 1987), 8.

Lateran Council in 1215.[16] Luther also refers to the place and priority of catechism in the preface to his own:

> In the first place, let the preacher above all be careful to avoid many kinds of or various texts and forms of the Ten Commandments, the Lord's Prayer, the Creed, the Sacraments, etc. On the contrary, he should adopt one form, adhere to it, and use it repeatedly year after year .... This was well understood by our blessed fathers (the Church Fathers) for they all used the same form of the Lord's Prayer, the Creed, and the Ten Commandments. Therefore we, too, should [imitate their diligence and be at pains to] teach the young and simple people these parts.

In summary, when Ursinus refers, in his lectures of 1562, to the Decalogue (Ten Commandments), Apostles' Creed, Baptism, Lord's Supper, and Lord's Prayer, he reflects a long-standing trajectory of catechetical instruction in the church. Ursinus says that the writings concerning the church's doctrine are either Divine or Ecclesiastical. The Divine writings are "such as have been written by the Prophets and Apostles, who were immediately inspired by God. Under this head we may include the canonical books of the old and new Testaments. These alone are simply and divinely inspired as to their words and thoughts and are alone worthy of credit. They are, therefore, the rule of all other writings."[17]

Ecclesiastical writings, such as the Creeds and Confessions, "were written in the name and consent of the whole orthodox church [that is the early church], and were received and approved by the church, such as the Apostles' Creed. Catechisms belong to this latter class of writings."[18] Ursinus asserts that all the parts [that is the Creed, Commandments, Sacraments, and Lord's Prayer] are specified in the three general heads, which are the misery of man, the deliverance from this misery, and gratitude.[19] We see then another structure in the catechism, one that has been central to the teaching of Christian doctrine throughout the ages, cultures and historical context. There is a trajectory in the teaching of Christian doctrine through the ages from ancient places around the Mediterranean, throughout the

---

[16] There is an inscription on a fourteenth-century baptismal font in England: "Pater Noster, Ave Maria, Criede, Leren ye childe yt is nede" (Our Father, Hail Mary, Creed, teach the children is needed).

[17] Ursinus, *Explicationum catecheticarum,* 159.

[18] Cuming, *Hippolytus,* 10.

[19] Ursinus, 17.

European continent and the British Isles, to the Palatinate of 1563; from the Old Testament (Ten Commandments) and New Testament (Lord's Prayer, Sacraments), through the Early Church (Apostle's Creed) into the time of the Protestant Reformation, and the Heidelberg Catechism—a trajectory and continuity of the teaching of the Apostles' Creed, Sacraments, Ten Commandments, and the Lord's Prayer. In a time of theological controversy, catechetical confusion, and political struggle, the authors of the Heidelberg Catechism did not write this catechism merely out of a concern for the administrative unity of the church. They did not create something entirely new out of their own ideas. Rather, they returned to and continued the catholicity of teaching the doctrines of the church and its classically formulated theology as expressed in the Apostles' Creed, and from the Scripture, as found in the Decalogue, the Pater Noster (Our Father), and the institution of the Sacraments.

Content of the Heidelberg Catechism

Now we can begin to explain the essential teachings of the Heidelberg Catechism. At the end of his lectures on Prolegomena, Ursinus asks, "What is the design of the catechism, and of the doctrine of the church?" The word translated "design" here, in the original Latin publication is *scopus*—that is, the purpose or scope of the work that determines the interpretation of the doctrine of the catechism. He answered, "The design of the doctrine of the catechism is our comfort and salvation. What this only comfort is, to which it is the design of the catechism to lead us, will be explained in the first question."[20]

Turning to the catechism proper, we find that Q1 and Q2 belong to the "prolegomena" of the catechism. Q1 establishes its scope or design. It asks, "What is your only comfort in life and death?" Why is the question of comfort placed and discussed first in the catechism? Why doesn't this catechetical instruction begin with: Do you believe? Are you a Christian? Do you have faith? Ursinus stated, at the conclusion of his lecture on Prolegomena, that "comfort and salvation" is the purpose of the catechism. The question of comfort is placed and treated first, he says, because it not only embodies the purpose, but also the substance of the catechism. When we consult the original Latin edition, it states that the question of "consolation" is treated

---

[20] Ursinus, *Explicationum catecheticarum*, 20.

first because it is the *summa totius catechism,* the total sum of the catechism; the entire content of the catechism is summed up in the word *consolatio.* Comfort is the hermeneutical key to open and understand the explication of the Christian doctrine found in the Heidelberg: comfort in a time of political struggle, doctrinal and confessional confusion and unrest, and a time when superstitions and traditions caused fear and anxiety. But these are not Ursinus's reasons, as he explains in his exposition of Q1:

> This, therefore, is that Christian comfort, spoken of in this question of the catechism, which is an only and solid comfort, both in life and death—a comfort consisting in the assurance, of the free remission of sin; of reconciliation with God, by and on account of Christ, and a certain expectation of eternal life, impressed upon the heart by the holy Spirit through the gospel, so that we have no doubt but that we are the property of Christ, and are beloved of God for his sake, and saved forever, according to the declaration of the Apostle Paul (Rom. 8:35): "Who shall separate us from the love of Christ? Shall tribulation, or distress."[21]

Thus, Ursinus rises *above* the occasion of the time, historical context, and culture with its conflicts of political and religious struggle between the Roman Catholic Emperor Charles V and the Protestant states, such as the Palatinate (where there was doctrinal strife between the Lutheran and Reformed concerning the Lord's Supper); and personal conflict between Professor Heshusius and student and deacon Klebitz. The Heidelberg Catechism aims for a higher conflict, with sin—sin that stands between God and humanity—and offers a comfort that consists in the assurance of pardon: the remission of sin, and of reconciliation with God, by and on account of Christ, by the Holy Spirit through the gospel.

The historical context and culture, with its conflicts, was in need of consolation and comfort. But ultimately, for Ursinus, one has to rise above the temporal and natural struggles and come to grips with the eternal and spiritual strife. "In this most severe and dangerous conflict, which all the children of God experience, Christian consolation remains immoveable, and at length concludes: therefore Christ, with all his benefits, pertains even to me."[22]

---

[21] Ursinus, 22.
[22] Ursinus, 25.

Concluding his lecture, he asks: Why is this comfort necessary?

From what has been said, it is clearly manifest that this comfort is necessary for us; First, on account of our salvation, that we may neither faint nor despair under our temptations, and the conflict in which we are all called to engage, as Christians. And secondly, it is necessary on account of praising and worshipping God; for if we would glorify God in this, and in a future life, (for which we were created,) we must be delivered from sin and death; and not rush into desperation, but be sustained, even to the end, with sure [comfort] consolation.[23]

Therefore, for Ursinus, to enjoy this comfort in life and death (Q2) it is necessary to know the following information: how great my sins and misery are (Part I); how I may be delivered from all my sins and misery (Part II, which contains the teaching of the Apostles' Creed, and Holy Sacraments); and how I shall express my gratitude to God for such deliverance (Part III, wherein the Ten Commandments and the Lord's Prayer are taught). So structure and the essential content (*summa totius*) come together in the opening questions—the prolegomena of the Heidelberg Catechism—declaring what the teaching of doctrine must be in the church. This catechetical teaching is divided in 52 Lord's Days or 129 questions and answers. This method of teaching, Ursinus remarked, "is of the greatest importance to all, because it is equally necessary for all, the learned as well as the unlearned, to know what constitutes the foundation of true religion."[24]

Moving toward a conclusion, I want to first highlight a few key doctrinal aspects of the Heidelberg Catechism to broaden the assessment of this legacy of the Reformation.

Trinitarian Theology in the Heidelberg Catechism

First, this catechism is Trinitarian in its theology. The person and work of the Father and the Son are clearly present: for example, reference to God the Father is found in over fifteen questions or answers, and that in the triad of the catechism—misery, deliverance, and gratitude. The references to God the Son, Christ, Christ Jesus, and Jesus are numerous—the centrality of the person and work of Christ or Christo-centrality is certainly

---

[23] Ursinus, 25.
[24] Ursinus, 10.

an important orientation of the catechism. It may seem that the person and work of the Third Person of the Trinity, the Holy Spirit, has a meager presence in the catechism, with only one question devoted to him. QA53: "What do you believe concerning the Holy Ghost? A. First, that he is true and coeternal God with the Father and the Son; second, that he is also given me, to make me by a true faith, partaker of Christ and all his benefits, that he may comfort me and abide with me for ever." This has led to the comment that, in the Catechism, one finds only the barest outline of Christian teaching about the Holy Spirit and, therefore, the Catechism's discussion of the doctrine of the Holy Spirit is deficient for our day.[25] However, a closer look at the entire catechism will reveal that any such accusation is unjustifiable. The person and work of the Spirit in the Heidelberg Catechism shows that the doctrine of the Holy Spirit is integrated into the overall structure and essential content of the catechism. Does not the prolegomena of the catechism provide in QA1 the overall theme and teaching of the catechism as being the comfort Christians derived from the work of Christ, the providential care of the Father, *and* the work of the Spirit in assuring us of eternal life and producing within us heartfelt gratitude? The Spirit, then, is of the essence of the catechism's teaching. Does not the catechism teach in QA3–11 that the only way out of the situation of the guilt and misery of sin is to be "born again by the Spirit of God"?—which is the Spirit's work in regeneration. Does not QA21 teach that a true faith is "created in us by the Holy Spirit"? Is not the final section of the catechism QA86–129 organized around the theme of who renews a justified sinner after the image of Christ in the life of gratitude—the life of sanctification? In QA115, for obeying the Ten Commandments, the catechism urges us to look to Christ first—"but also to pray to God for the grace of the Holy Spirit to renew us after God's image." QA116 asks why a Christian needs to pray. The answer is "because prayer is the most important part of gratitude … and because God gives his grace and Holy Spirit to those who pray to him." One could find many more references to the Holy Spirit; thus, the Heidelberg Catechism contains an extensive discussion of the person and work of the Spirit. This teaching on the Holy Spirit in the catechism, then, was a biblical corrective to the excesses of the "Enthusiasts/Anabaptists" of

---

[25] Eugene P. Heideman, "God the Holy Spirit," in *Guilt, Grace, and Gratitude: A Commentary on the Heidelberg Catechism,* ed. Donald J. Bruggink (New York: Half Moon Press, 1963), 112; "[I]n that the biblical concept of evangelism and mission as being essential to the ministry of the Spirit…"

the mid-1600s, and also serves as a corrective to the Pentecostalism and Charismatic theology of our time. In summary, with the attention it gives to the person and work of God the Father, God the Son, and the work of the Holy Spirit, the catechism is Trinitarian in its theology.

Law and Gospel in the Heidelberg Catechism

Second, consider the Catechism and its use of the law (Ten Command-ments). Sixteenth-century Protestant theology taught that there are three basic uses of God's moral law (*lex moralis*), as contained in the Ten Com-mandments: civil use (*usus politicus sive civilis*), which is the law serves the commonwealth or body politic as a force to restrain sin; pedagogical use (*usus elenchticus sive paedagogicus*), which is the use of the law also shows people their sin and points them to mercy and grace outside of themselves in Christ; and normative use (*usus didacticus sive normativus*), which is the use of the law for those who trust in Christ and have been saved through faith apart from works. It "acts as a norm of conduct, freely accepted by those in whom the grace of God works in Christ through his Word and Spirit."[26]

It has been asserted that the third use of the law (the didactic or nor-mative use) is a Reformed distinctive, in particular that, in the Heidelberg Catechism, the commandments are expounded in Part III (gratitude) as part of the thankfulness we owe God. Such assertion is debatable. First, the catechism does not use the term "uses of the law." The part on gratitude or thanksgiving was also found in Lutheran catechisms of the time. Moreover, the language "third use of the law" comes from Philip Melanchthon and was used widely by Reformed writers in the classical period. Others have said that Calvin thought of the third use as the pedagogical use (while also showing people their sin and pointing them to Christ). This is confusing and not very helpful. In his 1559 *Institutes* Calvin wrote: "The third and principal use, which pertains more closely to the proper purpose of the law, finds its place among believers in whose hearts the Spirit of God already lives and reigns"[27]

How, then, does the Heidelberg Catechism provide for the uses of the law? A close reading shows that the catechism begins with the second use

---

[26] On the threefold use of the law, I followed "The Uses of the Law," Reformed Reader (blog), March 30, 2009, accessed January 17, 2018, https://reformedreader.wordpress.com/2009/03/30/the-uses-of-the-law/.

[27] John Calvin, *Institutes,* 2.7.12.

of the law, the "pedagogical" use whereby sinners are driven to Christ (See Lord's Days 2–4). Here, the catechism explains the law as a taskmaster, a pedagogue, a teacher, referring to Rom 3:20 in Q3. Furthermore, one detects the third and normative use of the law in Lord's Days 32–52 (questions 86–129) in Part III, which is about the Christian life, lived by grace, in union with Christ, as adopted sons and daughters, out of gratitude to God.[28] The question then arises, where does one find the civil use of the law in the catechism? The catechism is explicit on the pedagogical and normative uses, but not the civil use of the law, perhaps because it was widely understood in the sixteenth century that the magistrates (government) were bound to uphold God's law in civil life.[29] Calvin understood the civil use of the law flowing out of the normative use: a life of gratitude regulates a society of Christians. The last word on this issue has not yet been spoken. But there is present in the catechism provision for at least two of the law's uses—the pedagogical and normative.

Silences of the Heidelberg Catechism

In the environment that led to the Catechism, Frederick III wanted unity within the church. Following Melanchthon's advice, he did not see the need to speak beyond Scripture, but was willing to allow for catechismal silence when needed, and when practices or theologies were not clearly delineated in Scripture. Topics where the Heidelberg Catechism is silent include the doctrines of predestination, the covenant, and the Lord's Supper.

The doctrine of predestination. Heidelberg includes two passing references to election: in A52, "take me with all the elect to himself in heavenly joy"; and A54, that the church is "a community elected to eternal life." Nevertheless, no one question is devoted specifically to election, reprobation, predestination, double predestination, or limited atonement. Is it for

---

[28] The denial of the third use of the law is called *antinomianism*, which, according to R. Scott Clark, is widespread in American (and perhaps other) evangelical circles. Cf. "Law, Gospel, and the Three Uses of the Law (2)," The Heidelblog: Recovering the Reformed Confession, https://heidelblog. net/2013/07/law-gospel-and-the-three-uses-of-the-law-2/.

[29] Another possibility is that there were people who wanted to reinstitute the civil law in Protestant territories. Calvin referred to such "theonomists" as "seditious" in Bk. 4 of the *Institutes*. Since the Reformed rejected the wholesale implementation of the civil law, it may be that Ursinus left it out because it was not relevant to the scope of the Heidelberg Catechism, the education of the ignorant. The use of the civil law—that is, how to implement its "equity"—would not be a subject for ordinary believers.

the sake of doctrinal harmony that these are not mentioned? Is this an attempt at bridging the gap between the Lutheran and Reformed parties by not addressing controverted issues in a document that was intended to bring about unity in the church?

The doctrine of the covenant. The followers of Zwingli and the followers of Calvin each had their own understanding of the doctrine of the covenant. Their discussion was related to the terminology of sign and seals of the covenant, key words from Rom 4:11 that were hotly debated among the Lutherans and the Reformed in the sixteenth century.

The doctrine of the Lord's Supper. The catechism was written in a time of great disagreement over the doctrine of the Lord's Supper, perhaps the most pertinent catechetical controversy of the era. The crucial issue was how exactly the outward physical signs are connected to the spiritual blessing they signify. Calvin wrote in his *Short Treatise on the Lord's Supper* (1541), that the bread and wine "are as instruments by which our Lord Jesus Christ distributes" his body and blood to us. QA75 of the Heidelberg Catechism states that the Lord's Supper "reminds and assures the believer ... as surely as I receive from the hand who serves and taste with my mouth the bread and cup of the Lord ... so surely he nourishes and refreshes my soul."[30] What is striking here is that nothing is said about when and how this exactly happens; no reference is made to the elements as "instruments" or "means," language which Ursinus does not hesitate to use in his Small and Large Catechisms. Furthermore, Zwingli and Bullinger could be quite specific about the relationship between the sign and the thing signified in their expositions on the Lord's Supper. In Zwingli's particular understanding, the bread and wine were not "instruments," as Calvin stated, but merely a commemorative visual analogy. But here also, the Heidelberg Catechism is silent. In short, the catechism is nonpolemical and irenic on the doctrine of the Lord's Supper.

Conclusion

Whether the Heidelberg Catechism should continue to find use in homes, churches, and centers of theological education can be answered in the affirmative. The structure and content of the Heidelberg Catechism distinctively teaches, according to Ursinus, the doctrines of the church. Written

---

[30] Ursinus, *Explicationum catecheticarum*, 516.

and published in a time of theological controversy and confessional confusion, it was an integral part of a much-needed reform of religion and education. The catechism returned to and continued in the trajectory of the historic catholic tradition for teaching the main doctrines of the church: the exposition of the Creed, Sacraments, Commandments, and the Lord's Prayer. Why continue to use a 450-year-old catechism? Because it speaks pointedly and profoundly to the perennial truths of the gospel, and is a teaching manual of Christian instruction in the Reformed Protestant faith tradition.

Bibliography

Beeke, Joel, and Sinclair Ferguson. *Reformed Confessions Harmonized.* Grand Rapids: Baker, 1999.

Bruggink, Donald J., ed. *Guilt, Grace, and Gratitude: A Commentary on the Heidelberg Catechism.* New York: Half Moon Press, 1963.

Cuming, Geoffrey J., ed. and trans. *Hippolytus: A Text for Students.* Grove Liturgical Studies. Bramcote: Grove Books, 1987.

De Boer, Erik A. "Philipp Melanchthon's *Iudicium de controversia Coenae Domini* (1559) to the Palatine Elector Frederick III." *Reformation & Renaissance Review* 17, no. 3 (2015): 245–65.

Janse, Wim. "Calvin's Doctrine of the Lord's Supper." *Perichoresis* 10, no.2 (2012): 137–63.

Klebitz, Wilhelm. Controversia et Confessio Digital. Herausgegeben von Irene Dingel. <http://www.controversia-et-confessio.de/id/ab7d166d -324f-4e0f-9039-7e7c2851e077>.

Ursinus, Zacharius. *Explicationum catecheticarum absolutum opus, totiusque theologiae purioris quasi novum corpus, Davidis Parei opera extrema recognitum.* Neostadii Palatinorum, 1600.

11

Luther and Calvin's Theology of Preaching

BENJAMIN B. PHILLIPS

Contemporary preaching is heir to one of the most significant legacies of the Protestant Reformation, yet it is a mistake to think the Reformers reintroduced preaching to the church. The church of the Middle Ages loved preaching. The universities trained preachers, and the university sermon was the high point of medieval rhetoric. Preaching orders, such as the Franciscans and the Dominicans (the Order of Preachers), mobilized to take preaching into the cities and villages of Europe.

As significant and widely appreciated as preaching was, however, the theology and liturgy of the Roman Catholic Church subordinated preaching to the Eucharist as the center of Christian worship. Ritual observance was more important than Luke's admonishment, "He who has ears to hear, let him hear!" (14:35 NASB). The altar occupied the focal point of the cathedral and chapel, while the pulpit stood to the side. The sacrament, not the sermon, was central.

The great contribution of the Reformers to the practice of preaching is that they returned it to the primacy it enjoyed in the New Testament church. More significant, however, is the rationale they articulated in their own books, commentaries, and especially in their sermons for the primacy of preaching. The Reformers rethought the very nature of preaching and its purpose in God's economy of salvation.[1] This project was more than

---

[1] Hughes Oliphant Old, *The Reading and Preaching of the Scriptures in the Worship of the Christian Church*, vol. 4, *The Age of the Reformation* (Grand Rapids: Eerdmans, 2002), 1.

pragmatic; it was theological. Looking to Scripture to develop a theology of preaching led the Reformers to conclusions that are as stunning today as they were in the sixteenth century: the sermon is nothing less than the spoken Word of God, through which the triune God speaks to create faith that converts sinners and sanctifies saints. This high view of preaching should be reaffirmed and celebrated by the heirs of the Reformation today.

To appreciate and appropriate the Reformation legacy of preaching today, it helps to see their claims in the polemic context of the early- and mid-sixteenth century. Martin Luther and John Calvin, the most influential and prolific of the Reformers, were concerned to combat two threats to the primacy of preaching in Christian worship: the Roman Catholic insistence on the supremacy of the Eucharist, and the Spiritualist denial that the Holy Spirit works through external instruments, such as preaching.

Sermon vs. Sacrament

The Reformers' theology of preaching stands in contrast to the Roman Catholic focus on the Eucharist. Despite the significant interest in preaching within the pre-Reformation church, the homily remained subordinate to the altar in the Roman mass. It was the bread and wine, the Eucharistic host, that was venerated as the means by which Christ becomes present in the church. Their own high view of communion not withstanding, the Reformers' theology of preaching challenged the supremacy of the Eucharist, justifying and ensuring the Reformation's legacy of the supremacy of the pulpit for Christian worship.

Preaching as the Kerygmatic Presence of God

Unlike the Roman Catholic Church, Martin Luther saw preaching as the primary means by which God manifested his presence in Christian worship. Hughes Oliphant Old refers to Luther's view as an assertion of the "kerygmatic presence of Christ."[2] Luther adduced this principle from Luke 10:16, "The one who hears you hears me, and the one who rejects you rejects me" (ESV).[3] Because God works in this way, Luther could say "Christ

---

[2] Old, *Preaching of the Scriptures*, 40.

[3] Martin Luther, "Second Sunday after Easter: Third Sermon: John 10:11–16; 1523," in *The Sermons of Martin Luther: The Church Postils*, 8 vols., ed. John Lenker, trans. John Lenker et al. (Grand Rapids: Baker, 1995) 3.60–61. (Hereafter cited as *SML*, vol.page); *D. Martin Luthers Werke: kritische Gesammtausgabe*, 121 vols. (Weimar: Hermann Bohlaus Nachfolger, 1883–2009), 21.330. (Hereafter cited as *WA*, vol.page.)

speaks" to those who hear his Word proclaimed.[4] The implication of these assertions for Luther was that God has linked the presence of Christ with preaching in a way that paralleled his view of Christ's presence in the elements of communion.[5]

The presence of Christ in the spoken word of the sermon was the true source of its power. Without his presence in the preaching event, preaching would be useless, even if it were doctrinally and rhetorically sound.[6] Christ's presence in preaching was also important for Luther because it allows Christ to be present in the whole world at once, a feat not possible while Christ walked on earth.[7] Here again, the kerygmatic presence of Christ in preaching parallels Luther's belief in the real presence of Christ in the sacraments.

Like Luther, Calvin saw preaching as the primary manifestation of the presence of Christ in worship. Preaching serves to admit the hearer into the presence of God and so earns the right to be called the kingdom of God.[8] By bringing the hearer into the presence of God, preaching also allows the listener to hear Christ's voice in the preaching of the gospel.[9]

The affirmation of the kerygmatic presence of Christ grounded a high view of the sermon itself for both Reformers, just as the Roman Catholic claim of transubstantiation led to a high view of the physical elements of the Eucharist. Luther insisted that it is the "external Word and preaching"[10] which manifests the presence of Christ, not only the internal or subjective response to the sermon. As a result, Luther exhorted his listeners to believe that when hearing the Word preached, they should not view it as the words of a man, but as the Word of God himself.[11] Calvin agreed that Christ

---

[4] Luther, "Day of Christ's Ascent into Heaven: Third Sermon: Mark 16:14–20," *SML* 3.238–39; *WA* 21.407.

[5] Luther, "Third Sunday in Advent: Matthew 2:2–10," *SML* 1.94; *WA* 10 I/2.154.

[6] Luther, "Third Sermon: John 10:11–16," *SML* 2.397; *WA* 21.324.

[7] Luther, "Day of Christ's Ascent into Heaven: Mark 16:14–20; 1523," *SML* 3.183–84; *WA* 12.556.

[8] John Calvin, *Commentaries on the First Book of Moses, Called Genesis*, trans. John King (Grand Rapids: Eerdmans, 1948), *Genesis* 28:17, 117–18. (Hereafter cited as, *Genesis*, chapter:verse, page); *Calvini Opera* 59 vols in *Corpus Reformatorum* vols. 29–88. (Berlin: C. A. Schwetschke und Sohn, 1863–1900), *CO* 21/*CR* 51.394. (Hereafter *CO*, vol./*CR*, vol. page).

[9] John Calvin, *Calvin's New Testament Commentaries*, ed. David Torrance and Thomas Torrance, trans. A.W. Morrison, repr. ed. (Grand Rapids: Eerdmans, 1960–1965). (Hereafter cited as *CNTC*: book, chapter:verse, page), *Ephesians* 5:14, 201–2; *CO* 51/*CR* 79.219.

[10] Luther, "Pentecost Tuesday: Second Sermon: John 10:1–11; 1543," *SML* 3.388; *WA* 21.502.

[11] Luther, "Sunday after Easter: Third Sermon: John 19:20–31; 1540," *SML* 3.397; *WA* 49.149.

comes down by the external preaching of the Word[12] and approaches the hearer in his Word.[13]

Such a high view of the sermon demanded a high view of preachers as well. The great responsibility of the Roman Catholic priest was to handle the elements of the Eucharist. But the preacher supersedes the sacramental celebrant, for the preacher did not merely reenact the atonement, as Roman Catholics taught. Instead, he became the agent through which Christ speaks to the people today. Luther taught that, "It is a glory which every preacher may claim, to be able to say with full confidence of heart: 'This trust have I toward God in Christ, that what I teach and preach is truly the Word of God.'"[14]

Calvin also understood that to see the sermon as the spoken word of God was to affirm that God speaks through the voice of the preachers.[15] Calvin used Philip as an example of the way in which God honors preachers. He noted that God chose to speak through Philip and only used the angel to send Philip on his mission. Thus Calvin affirmed that "the voice of God sounds in the mouth of men . . . , while angels hold their peace."[16]

Preachers, then, are instruments of Christ in the present moment. They are ministers through whom God speaks to the world today.[17] Yet human preachers are never the primary focus for the Reformers. Preachers neither reenact the incarnation nor the atonement through their preaching. God and the preacher remain distinct as Divine Agent and human instrument. While they taught that "Christ acts by his ministers in such a manner that he wishes their mouth to be reckoned as his mouth, and their lips as his lips,"[18] the Reformers also insisted that God alone is the authority and deserves credit in preaching.[19] For both Luther and Calvin, God is the true Preacher. The primary focus remains on God, who speaks "by man's

---

[12] Calvin, *CNTC: Acts* 7:20, 184–85; *CO* 48/*CR* 26.140.

[13] John Calvin, *Commentary on the Book of the Prophet Isaiah*, trans. William Pringle (Grand Rapids: Eerdmans, 1948), *Isaiah* 50:2, 50; *CO* 37/*CR* 65.216–17.

[14] Luther, "Twelfth Sunday after Trinity: 2 Corinthians 3:4–11," *SML* 8.227; *WA* 22.215.

[15] Calvin, *CNTC: Acts* 10:44, 317–18; *CO* 48/*CR* 26.250–51.

[16] Calvin, *CNTC: Acts* 8:31, 246–48; *CO* 48/*CR* 26.191–92.

[17] Luther, "Second Sunday after Easter: John 10:11–16; 1523," *SML* 3.29; *WA* 12.538.

[18] Calvin, *Commentary on the Book of the Prophet Isaiah*, *Isaiah* 11:4, 381; *CO* 36/*CR* 64.240.

[19] Calvin, *CNTC: Acts* 9:6, 261–62; *CO* 48/*CR* 26.203–4.

mouth"[20] and "employ[s] the ministry of his servants, [so that] he speaks to us by their mouths."[21]

Transcending the Table: Soteriology and the Theology of Preaching

The Reformers' conviction that God is present in preaching made the sermon the equal of the sacrament. Yet the Reformers also developed a critical insight about the relationship between preaching and salvation that elevated preaching above the Eucharist. Their theology of preaching indicates the unique value of the ministry of the Word as the means through which salvation by grace alone through faith alone is accomplished.

Preaching, for the Reformers, was always, at its heart, the proclamation of the gospel.[22] Luther held that it was through "the voice of the gospel, or the hearing of faith in Christ preached" that God brought justification to people.[23] The Word of God alone produces saving faith in people. Proclamation of the gospel was thus essential to the conversion of the sinner in a way that the sacrament could not be. The sacrament was of no benefit to the unconverted, being reserved for those already in the fellowship of the church. Preaching, however, not only benefited Christians, it also converted unbelievers. Luther recognized the connection between preaching and salvation in Paul's assertion that "faith comes from hearing, and hearing by the word of Christ" (Rom 10:17 NASB). Luther took Paul to mean that the oral proclamation of the gospel is what summons forth saving faith in the hearts of sinful people.[24]

Luther can be taken to mean that conversion requires preaching in the narrow sense of formal proclamation of the gospel by an ordained minister in the setting of Christian worship. Calvin, however, was also careful not to limit God to using preaching in this formal sense as his sole instrument of producing faith. In commenting on Romans 10:14–17, Calvin stated that one cannot take the meaning of the passage to be that God can or does use only preaching. Paul did not intend "to prescribe a law for the distribution

---

[20] Calvin, *CNTC: Acts* 3:8, 93–94; *CO* 48/*CR* 26.64–65.

[21] Calvin, *Commentary on the Book of the Prophet Isaiah, Isaiah* 40:27, 235–36; *CO* 37/*CR* 65.27; cf. Calvin, *CNTC: 1 Timothy* 3:15, 230–32; *CO* 52/*CR* 50.288–89.

[22] Old, *Preaching of the Scriptures*, 5.

[23] Luther, "Lectures on Galatians," *LW* 26:206; *WA* 40 I.333.

[24] To be sure, the Reformers affirmed that communion does, in some sense, "proclaim" the gospel. Yet in this capacity communion did not convert, but rather affirmed and strengthened those who had received the oral proclamation in faith.

of grace."[25] God could, and, Calvin implied, sometimes does, produce faith through other forms of the ministry of the Word. Yet Calvin did agree that human preaching is the common instrument that God in his sovereignty has chosen to produce faith.[26] Here again, the external, audible preaching is the "instrument by which God draws us to faith."[27] Thus, the apostles and the preachers who follow them speak with the promise that God will proclaim the gospel through them.[28]

The power of preaching was also taken to expand beyond the conversion of individuals. Taken together, the conversion of individuals through the preaching of the gospel meant that preaching was the very voice of God in gathering the church, "so the same voice shall sound everywhere, that those which are far off may come and join themselves to you."[29] Quantitatively, preaching converts sinners and gathers them into the body of Christ. Qualitatively, God uses preaching to restore the world from death to life,[30] to produce faith,[31] to save the godly,[32] and to motivate Christians to obedience.[33] Preaching calls the church into existence, increasing its size through conversion and its holiness through sanctification.

Moreover, Calvin saw preaching as having the power to "extirpate the tyranny of Satan." He believed that Christ had commanded preaching with this very end in view—the ruin of Satan.[34] Luther also understood preaching to be the tool of God for expanding his kingdom.[35] Establishing and expanding the kingdom of God necessarily meant an attack on Satan's realm, so Luther also taught that preaching overthrows the devil

---

[25] Calvin, *CNTC: Romans* 10:14, 230–31; *CO* 49/*CR* 77.204–5.

[26] Calvin, *CNTC: 1 Corinthians* 3:6, 69–70; *CO* 49/*CR* 77.349–50.

[27] Calvin, *CNTC: John* 17:20, 146–47; *CO* 47/*CR* 75.354–55.

[28] Calvin, *Institutes of the Christian Religion, 1559*, trans. Ford Lewis Battles, Library of Christian Classics, vols. 20–21 (Philadelphia: Westminster, 1960). (Hereafter cited as *Institutes*, book.chapter.section), 4.11.1; *CO* 2/*CR* 30.891–93; cf. Calvin, *Commentaries on the Twelve Minor Prophets*, trans. John Owen (Grand Rapids: Eerdmans, 1950). (Hereafter cited as, book, chapter:verse, page), *Haggai* 1:2; *CO* 44/*CR* 72.85–86; Calvin, *Commentaries on the Book of the Prophet Jeremiah and the Lamentations*, trans. John Owen (Grand Rapids: Eerdmans, 1950), *Jeremiah* 32:33, *CO* 39/*CR* 67.30–31; Calvin, *CNTC: Philemon* 10, 396–97; *CO* 52/*CR* 80.36–37.

[29] Calvin, *CNTC: Acts* 2:39, 82–83; *CO* 48/*CR* 26.54–55.

[30] Calvin, *Genesis* 8:23, 38.

[31] Calvin, *CNTC: Romans* 10:17, 232–33; *CO* 49/*CR* 77.206–7.

[32] Calvin, *CNTC: Acts* 10:44, 317–18; *CO* 48/*CR* 26.250–51.

[33] Calvin, *CNTC: Acts* 3:8, 93–94; *CO* 48/*CR* 26.64–65.

[34] Calvin, *Harmony of the Gospels: Luke* 10:18, 18; *CO* 45/*CR* 73.315; cf. Calvin, *Institutes*, 1.14.18; *CO* 2/*CR* 30.129–30.

[35] Luther, "Epiphany: Matthew 2:1–12; 1522," *SML* 1.355; *WA* 10 I/1.601.

and his kingdom.[36] This view of preaching would serve later Reformed post-millennial eschatology, where it is the preaching of the gospel that will finally usher in the millennial kingdom.

The Reformers understood preaching to be the means appropriate to bringing about salvation by grace alone through faith alone. Unlike the Eucharist in the Roman Catholic mass, the external preaching of the gospel summons forth faith in the hearts of unbelievers who hear. Thus, preaching not only supports and enables conversion and sanctification, preaching causes conversion and sanctification. Preaching becomes a divinely efficacious offensive weapon, expanding the kingdom of God against the tyranny of Satan.

The theology of preaching developed by Luther and Calvin demonstrates a clear concern to elevate the sermon above the sacrament in Christian worship. The Reformers boldly asserted the presence of God in preaching, describing it as the living voice of God speaking through the mouths of men. They characterized the spoken Word of God, most often conveyed through preaching, as uniquely efficacious for the gracious creation of saving faith. Though they continued in varying ways to affirm the presence of Christ in the elements of the table, their theology of preaching grounded their primary development in relation to the role of preaching in the Roman Catholic Church. No longer was the sermon secondary to the sacrament. For Protestants, preaching now stood at the center of Christian worship. The pulpit took center stage, standing over the communion table.

Sermon vs. Spiritualism

The Protestant Reformation's critique of the Roman Catholic Church developed in many different directions, resulting in the splintering of the movement. Reformers found the need not only to attack the Roman Catholic Church, but also to argue against each other. The Spiritualist movement criticized the magisterial Reformers for remaining bound to externals in worship (i.e., formal rituals of worship, such as baptism, communion, preaching, etc.). In contrast, they claimed the Holy Spirit only works directly inside the individual. Caspar Schwenckfeld, for example, argued the inner Word of the Holy Spirit was received independently of

---

[36] Luther, "Lectures on Galatians," *LW* 26.14; *WA* 40 I/1.53; cf. Luther, "Pentecost Monday: Second Sermon: John 3:16–21," *SML* 3.367; *WA* 21.493.

the external Word (Scripture or preaching).[37] The disjunction of inner and outer Word developed among the Spiritualists into the elevation of the inner Word over the Scripture. External, mediated forms of the Word (both Scripture and preaching) were set aside in favor of the internal, unmediated "inner light."[38] First Luther,[39] and later Calvin,[40] reacted to these claims by vehemently insisting on the unity of the Spirit and the Word.

The Speech of the Spirit through the External, Spoken Word

The Reformers' Trinitarianism led them to expect that if Christ speaks through preaching, then the Holy Spirit is also working and speaking in the sermon. To say the Holy Spirit works in the external preaching of the gospel means it can be said that the Holy Spirit preaches.[41] Luther's belief in the working of the Spirit in the oral preaching of the gospel led him to the conclusion that oral preaching is a necessary tool of the Spirit in conversion. The preaching that creates faith allows the entrance of the Spirit into the heart.[42]

Luther was concerned to avoid the Spiritualist error of denigrating external preaching as unnecessary.[43] He taught that preaching is the tool of the "government of the Holy Spirit" by which Christ rules through "the external Word alone, which the Holy Spirit will preach."[44] Luther based this understanding on the promise of Jesus in John 16:8, that the Spirit would convict the world of sin, righteousness, and judgment. Luther taught the

---

[37] William Gilbert, "The Radicals of the Reformation," chap. 15 in "Renaissance and Reformation" (unpublished manuscript, 1997), accessed online February 3, 2018, http://vlib.iue.it/carrie/texts/carrie_books/gilbert/15.html.

[38] Justo Gonzalez, *A History of Christian Thought*, vol 3., *From the Protestant Reformation to the Twentieth Century* (Nashville: Abingdon, 1987), 98–99.

[39] Luther preached against "those fanatics who seek to receive, and dream of having, the Holy Spirit without the oral word." Martin Luther, "Twelfth Sunday after Trinity: 2 Corinthians 3:4–11," *SML* 8.227; *WA* 22.215.

[40] John Calvin, *Commentary on the Book of the Prophet Isaiah, Isaiah* 59:21, 271; *CO* 37/*CR* 65.351–53.

[41] Luther, "Fourth Sunday after Easter: Third Sermon: John 16:5–15; 1523," *SML* 3.143; *WA* 21.361; cf. Luther, "Sunday after Christ's Ascension: Second Sermon; John 15:6–16:4," *SML* 3.256–58; *WA* 21.425–26.

[42] Luther, "Nineteenth Sunday after Trinity: Second Sermon: Matthew 9:1–8; 1529," *SML* 5.225; *WA* 29.580–81.

[43] Luther, "Pentecost: Third Sermon: John 14:23–31," *SML* 3.300; *WA* 21.445.

[44] Luther, "Fourth Sunday after Easter: Third Sermon: John 16:5–15; 1523," *SML* 3.134–35; *WA* 21.354.

Spirit would bring about this conviction through "an oral Word or an office of preaching, called the Word of God."[45]

Calvin agreed the Spirit works in the external preaching of the gospel but preferred to emphasize the idea that the Holy Spirit empowers the preacher.[46] No human being is qualified to preach and thus speak for God unless God himself "clothes him with his Spirit, to supply his nakedness and poverty." As a result, the "heavenly Spirit" must empower the preachers of the gospel.[47] For this reason, and because preaching is the primary instrument the Spirit uses to create spiritual fruit, Calvin could call preachers "ministers of the Spirit."[48]

Ultimately for Calvin, the external preaching is necessary because God has chosen to reveal Himself only through the external reality of the Church and its preaching. As a rule, "the Spirit does not teach any but those who submit to the ministry of the Church."[49] Thus, the Reformers' emphasis on the work of the Spirit through the sermon formed a decisive rejection of the Spiritualist abandonment of all externals in worship. Whatever else might be challenged as mere human ritual, the presence and activity of the Spirit in preaching ensured its rightful place in Christian worship.

The Whisper of the Spirit in the Inner Ear of Hearers

The Reformers taught that the Holy Spirit converts and sanctifies through preaching, yet preaching does not always reach the heart and become accepted in faith.[50] This apparent "failure" would seem to contradict the claim that preaching is the place where the voice of Christ and the Holy Spirit is heard, the instrument of God to summon forth faith that converts and sanctifies. Yet where their Spiritualist opponents saw weakness and foolishness in preaching, the Reformers saw a spiritual defect in those who "have ears but do not hear" (Jer 5:21 NASB).

Luther taught that the refusal of those who hear the sermon to receive the external Word illustrates the need for its "true interpreter," that is, the illuminating and convicting work of the Holy Spirit.[51] It is not enough that

---

[45] Luther, *SML* 3.134–35; *WA* 21.354.

[46] Calvin, *CNTC: Acts* 10:44, 317–188; *CO* 48/*CR* 26.250–51.

[47] Calvin, *Harmony of the Gospels, Luke* 24:49, 243; *CO* 45/*CR* 73.818–199.

[48] Calvin, *CNTC: Acts* 10:44, 317–88; *CO* 48/*CR* 26.250–51.

[49] Calvin, *Commentary on the Book of the Prophet Isaiah, Isaiah* 54:13, 271; *CO* 37/*CR* 65.292–93.

[50] Luther, "Pentecost: Third Sermon: John 14:23–31," *SML* 3.330; *WA* 21.445.

[51] Luther, "Easter Monday: Second Sermon: Luke 24:13–36," *SML* 1.281; *WA* 21.230.

Christ is preached; Luther concluded the Spirit must not only preach the Word to us externally but also "enlarge and impel us from within."[52] The Word of God is not weak; rather, it is the hearers who need help to hear rightly. For Luther,

> Something is needed in addition to [external] preaching; it is the Holy Spirit who is sent to impress preaching on the heart, so that it abides there and lives. If we are to possess it [salvation] the Holy Spirit must come and teach our hearts to believe and say: I, too, am one of those who are to have this treasure.[53]

Calvin shared much the same view as Luther of the need for the Spirit's internal work in preaching. The idea that the external word is powerless was, for Calvin, "delirious and even dangerous."[54] Yet external preaching is of no positive effect unless the Spirit touches the heart of the hearer.[55] It is only through the illuminating work of the Spirit inside the individual that he comes to effectual faith and enters the kingdom of God.[56]

Luther held that the power of the external Word was deeply hidden, and the listener must therefore experience it internally.[57] In addition to his understanding of the working of the Holy Spirit in external preaching, Luther added an equal emphasis on the internal preaching of the Spirit to the "inner ear."[58] The internal power of the Word is given and worked by the Spirit, whose office is to "write on the hearts of men."[59] Preaching, then, consists of two parts for Luther: the external, in which the Spirit comes and stands before the heart of the listeners, and the internal, where the Spirit stands in the heart and offers peace.[60] By connecting the internal work of the Spirit with his external work in preaching, Luther makes the salvific effects of the external preaching of man dependent on the internal preaching of the Spirit.[61]

---

[52] Luther, "Easter Sunday: Third Sermon; Mark 16:1–8," *SML* 1.253; *WA* 46.334.

[53] Luther, "Pentecost: Third Sermon; John 14:23–31," *SML* 3.305; *WA* 21.469.

[54] Calvin, *CNTC: Hebrews* 4:12, 62; *CO* 55/*CR* 83.49–52.

[55] Calvin, *CNTC: Acts* 25:18, 265–67; *CO* 48/*CR* 76.533–34.

[56] Calvin, *CNTC: Acts* 14:27, 20–21; *CO* 48/*CR* 76.334–35.

[57] Luther, "Second Sunday after Easter: John 10:11–16; 1523," *SML* 3.21; *WA* 12.530–31.

[58] Bernard Ramm, *The Witness of the Spirit: An Essay on the Contemporary Relevance of the Internal Witness of the Holy Spirit* (Grand Rapids: Eerdmans, 1959), 21.

[59] Luther, "Pentecost: John 14:23–31; 1522," *SML* 3.274–75; *WA* 12.568.

[60] Luther, "Sunday after Easter: John 20:19–31," *SML* 3.355; *WA* 10 I/2.228–30.

[61] Luther, "Pentecost: Third Sermon; John 14:23–31," *SML* 3.300; *WA* 21.445.

Calvin used the example of Lydia as one in whose inner ear the Spirit spoke. He emphasized the fact that the Spirit did so by the external Word. The internal working of the Spirit opened Lydia's heart so she could hear with understanding and faith the "external voice of the teacher."[62] The example of Lydia shows that, for Calvin, the external preaching does not need power added to it because of an inherent lack of power in the oral word. It is the hearer who is powerless to hear preaching with understanding and faith apart from the internal working of the Spirit.[63]

Both Luther and Calvin insisted that any apparent deficiency in the effects of true preaching was the result of the weakness of the hearers, not the impotence of the spoken word. Yet Calvin also observed that the oral proclamation of the Word of God is not powerless even when the effects of conversion or sanctification are absent.[64] The need for the Spirit to work on the heart did not render external preaching worthless. Calvin insisted that the preached word was always powerful, even in those for whom preaching is unfruitful. The oral proclamation of the gospel "inflicts a deadly wound on the reprobate, so far as to render them inexcusable before God."[65] Calvin thus added the argument that the power of preaching is seen in judgment as well as salvation. Nevertheless, he shared Luther's view that where the Spirit does illuminate the heart, there preaching may be said to have been effective (i.e., it has accomplished its positive, salvific work).

The Unity of the Spirit and the Word

The heart of the Spiritualist's position was that the Spirit spoke only through the inner light. This view divorced the Spirit's speech to the individual's inner ear from the Spirit's speech through Scripture and sermon. In effect, it used the need for and reality of the Spirit's inner work to dismiss the work of the Spirit through external instruments. To counter the Spiritualist view, the Reformers needed to offer more than the bald assertion that the Spirit uses preaching. To these assertions, they added

---

[62] Calvin, *CNTC: Acts* 16:14, 72–74; *CO* 48/*CR* 76.377–78.

[63] Thomas Henry Louis Parker, *The Oracles of God: An Introduction to the Preaching of John Calvin* (London: Lutterworth, 1947), 29.

[64] Calvin, *CNTC: Romans* 11:14, 247–48; *CO* 49/*CR* 77.219; cf. Calvin, *CNTC:1 Peter* 1:11, 239–41; *CO* 55/*CR* 83.217–18; *CNTC: 1 Thessalonians* 1:4, 335–36; *CO* 52/ *CR* 80.141–42; and *Harmony of the Gospels, Matthew* 6:10, 204; *CO* 45/*CR* 73.197–98.

[65] Calvin, *CNTC: John* 1:43, 39; *CO* 47/*CR* 75.33; cf. Calvin, *Harmony of the Gospels, Luke* 1:14–17, 9, *CO* 45/*CR* 73, 15–16.

an explanation of the way in which the Spirit connects the external and internal aspects of preaching.

Luther connected the Spirit and preaching by developing a sacramental view of the sermon. He held that God sends the Spirit through the oral word into the hearts of those who believe.[66] The power of the external Word functions as a conduit through which the Spirit enters the heart.[67]

Luther taught that the Holy Spirit does not exercise his work of converting and sanctifying apart from the Word and its oral proclamation.[68] Seeing the Spirit's work in preaching as the sole source of a saving knowledge of Christ allowed Luther to conclude that searching "here and there for special revelations or illuminations" is futile.[69] Thus, he rejected the Spiritualist divorce of Spirit and Word, insisting that the Spirit speaks only through the Word.

The difficulty with Luther's view of the work of the Spirit in preaching is that it makes preaching an *opus operatum*.[70] On the one side, it seems to make the preacher simply a passive tool for God's Word.[71] If isolated from his larger perspective, this would miss the ways in which the preacher is to be seen as an active agent. In that case, Luther would be wrongly taken to teach that God does what he does through the sermon independently of the preacher. On the other hand, the very mechanical nature of the way in which Luther relates the external and internal working of the Spirit in preaching also raises the possibility of the preacher having inordinate power over the Word. If God only reveals himself through preaching, then the preacher has gained control over the revelatory and salvific work of God.[72] This is particularly the case if preachers can claim that anytime they preach, they speak God's Word. To be sure, Luther himself affirmed neither view to the extreme consequences described here. Rather, seeing the sermon as

---

[66] Luther, "Lectures on Galatians," *LW* 26.188; *WA* 40 I.310–12; "Lectures on Galatians," *LW* 26.202, *WA* 40 I, 329; "Lectures on Galatians," *LW* 26.218, *WA* 40 I, 330.

[67] Paul Althaus, *The Theology of Martin Luther*, trans. Robert C. Schultz (Philadelphia: Fortress, 1966), 37.

[68] Luther, "Lectures on Galatians," *LW* 26.206; *WA* 40 I.333.

[69] Luther, "Pentecost: Third Sermon: John 14:23–31," *SML* 3.300; *WA* 21.445.

[70] A. Skevington Wood, *Captive to the Word: Martin Luther, Doctor of Sacred Scripture* (Exeter, UK: Paternoster, 1969), 45.

[71] Wood, 48.

[72] This is a major concern of Karl Barth in the theology of preaching he develops in his *Church Dogmatics*.

both divine speech and human speech is an example of his love of theological dichotomies.

Calvin agreed that the outward preaching of the gospel and the inward power of the Spirit operate together.[73] Scripture honors the external preaching so highly that one must not separate the Spirit from it.[74] Calvin identified separating the Spirit and the Word as the error of fanatics who disdain the outward preaching, and talk in lofty terms about secret revelations and inspirations. "But we see how Christ joins these two things together; and, therefore, though there is no faith till the Spirit of God seal our minds and hearts, still we must not go to seek visions or oracles in the clouds; but the Word, which is near us, in our mouth and heart (Rom 10:8)."[75] However, Calvin also argued that this does not mean,

> that the grace of the Holy Spirit and his influence are tied to preaching, so that the preacher can, whenever he pleases, breathe forth the Spirit along with the utterance of the voice… We are, then, Ministers of the Spirit, not as if we held him enclosed within us, or as it were captive—not as if we could at our pleasure confer his grace upon all, or upon whom we pleased—but because Christ, through our instrumentality, illuminates the minds of men, renews their hearts, and, in short, regenerates them wholly.[76]

In Calvin's view the Spirit is not bound to preach each time that the preacher preaches.[77] The resulting emphasis that Calvin placed on the relative freedom of the Spirit to do his internal work is a critical difference between Luther's and Calvin's theology of preaching. Calvin described preachers as ministers of the Spirit, not to suggest the sovereignty of the preacher over the Spirit, but rather to honor the work God does through preachers. Calling preachers ministers of the Spirit acknowledges that they are servants of what Christ and his Spirit do by speaking through preachers.

---

[73] Calvin, *CNTC: Romans* 8:30, 181–82; *CO* 49/*CR* 77.160–61; cf. Calvin, *Institutes* 2.2.20, *CO* 2/ *CR* 30.201–2. Since the Spirit does not necessarily work at the same moment as the outward preaching, he may choose to delay his working, as he sees fit. *CNTC: John* 14:25, 87–88; *CO* 47/*CR* 75.334–35.

[74] Calvin, *CNTC: Acts* 26:28, 283–84; *CO* 48/*CR* 76.547–49.

[75] Calvin, *CNTC: John* 15:27, 110–11; *CO* 47/*CR* 75.354–55; cf. Calvin, *Commentary on the Book of the Prophet Isaiah*, Isaiah 49:22, 39; *CO* 37/*CR* 65.210.

[76] Calvin, *CNTC: 2 Corinthians* 3:6, 41–43; *CO* 50/*CR* 78.39–41.

[77] Wood, *Captive to the Word*, 52.

Instead of Luther's sacramental process, the concept that connects the Spirit and the Word—the internal and external aspects of preaching—in Calvin's thought is the sovereign grace of God. Rather than being mechanistic, the connection is personal. God has chosen to associate the internal working of the Spirit with external preaching so he "may keep us in reverence of his Word."[78] The internal working of the Spirit in preaching is to be distinguished from the external preaching so that "we may not apply to men what ought to be ascribed to the efficacy of the Spirit."[79] Calvin taught that God works in this manner because he wants people to rest on the "internal power of the Holy Spirit," and not on "outward masks."[80]

Connecting the Preached Word to the Written Word

Perhaps the most troubling aspect of the Reformers' theology of preaching for contemporary evangelicals is how it may appear to disconnect preaching from the Scriptures. The way in which the Reformers placed the sermon above the sacrament would also seem to place the spoken word above the written Word. If divorced from the Scriptures, the practical effect of their view of preaching would make the preacher little different from that of Spiritualists' view of the believer illumined by the inner light. Each would be able to claim an unchecked authority for their pronouncements. Under the startling force of the Reformers' high view of preaching and the sermon, it can be easy for evangelicals today to forget these same Reformers' commitment to *sola Scriptura*.

Luther's high view of preaching certainly claimed the necessity of preaching for giving voice to the written Word of God. He observed that the original form of the word of God given through the prophets and apostles was oral. This oral word was not, for Luther, an inferior form of the Word of God, for which the written Word was to be the advanced form. Scripture was the source of post-apostolic preaching, but it also makes preaching necessary by its very nature.[81] That which is written must once again sound in the ears of hearers.

Luther taught that the unconverted could not understand Scripture until preaching was present. The need in Christendom was not for more

---

[78] Calvin, *CNTC: Acts* 10:44, 317–18; *CO* 48/*CR* 26.250–51.
[79] Calvin, *Commentary on the Book of the Prophet Isaiah, Isaiah* 54:13, 271; *CO* 37/*CR* 65.292–93.
[80] Calvin, *CNTC:1 Corinthians* 4:20, 101–2; *CO* 49/ *CR* 77.375–76.
[81] Althaus, *Theology of Martin Luther*, 72.

New Testament books but for an ever-greater number of faithful preach-ers.[82] Luther interpreted John 1:5, "the light shines in the darkness, and the darkness did not comprehend it" (NKJV), to mean the world was not able to understand or apprehend the light. The inadequacy of the world's ability to grasp the light required John to come and "bear witness" to this light. Sinners need preaching that exposes the message and meaning of the Scrip-tures in all ages because "the natural reason is not able of itself to apprehend it [the light], although it is present in all the world: the oral Word of the gospel must reveal it and proclaim it."[83] In his strongest assertion about the connection between the Scriptures and preaching, Luther claimed

> the church is a mouth-house, not a pen-house, for since Christ's advent that Gospel is preached orally which before was hidden in written books. It is the way of the Gospel and of the New Testament that it is to be preached and discussed orally with a living voice. Christ himself wrote nothing, nor did he give command to write, but to preach orally. Thus the apostles were not sent out until Christ came to his mouth-house, that is, until the time had come to preach orally and to bring the Gospel from dead writing and pen-work to the living voice and mouth. From this time the church is rightly called Beth-phage, since she has and hears the living voice of the Gospel.[84]

Faithful preaching allows the written Word to become oral again, to become alive in the mouths of the preachers.[85] In this way, Luther refused to disconnect preaching from the written Word or to make it secondary to the Scripture in its significance and power. Indeed, Luther almost seems to have made the power of Scripture dependent on preaching.

Luther clearly had an extremely high view of preaching and its neces-sity for the church. Yet his view of the origin of preaching conforms to his commitment to *sola Scriptura*. While Christ commanded his followers to preach and extend the range of the gospel,[86] he made them dependent on Scripture for their message. Scripture was written because of the "infirmity of the human spirit," which readily gives way to heresy, false teaching, and

---

[82] Luther, "Epiphany: Matthew 2:1–12, 1522," *SML* 1.371–72; *WA* 10 I/1.625.

[83] Luther, "Third Day of Christmas: John 1:1–14," *SML* 1.200–1; *WA* 10 I/1.215–16.

[84] Luther, "First Sunday of Advent: Matthew 21:1–9; 1522," *SML* 1.44; *WA* 10 I/2.48; cf. Luther, "Day of Christ's Ascent into Heaven: Mark 16:14–30; 1523," *SML* 3.183–84; *WA* 12.556.

[85] Wood, *Captive to the Word*, 90.

[86] Luther, "First Sunday in Advent: Matthew 21:1–9; 1522," *SML* 1.31; *WA* 10 I/2.34–35.

error, "giving the sheep of Christ poison in place of pasture." [87] The written Word exists to preserve the purity of the preaching and allows the sheep to protect themselves against the wolves, and even "to be their own guides when their false shepherds would not lead them into the green pastures."[88] This view answered the Spiritualists who rejected the necessity of the written Word. Preaching needs the Scripture as a river needs its source; without the written Word, there is no spoken word in the church.

The Reformers' Theology of Preaching Today

Martin Luther and John Calvin gave the church back its voice, preaching that is nothing less than the spoken Word of God. Though preaching had been important for the previous half century and more, it was often disconnected from the Scripture as its source and was always subordinate to the sacrament of the Eucharist at the heart of the mass. The Reformers not only made the sermon the center of Christian worship, they justified this move with deep reflection on the biblical teaching about preaching. In short, Luther's and Calvin's great achievement for preaching was a theology of preaching that elevated the sermon above the sacrament, demonstrated the fitness of preaching as the instrument appropriate to salvation that is *sola gratia* and *sola fide*, while also protecting the church from false teachers by binding preaching to the written Word, *sola Scriptura*.

The legacy of the Reformers' theology of preaching encourages preachers today that the foolishness of preaching is nothing less than the very wisdom and power of God. God is at work in and through those who faithfully give voice to the written Word. When preachers faithfully proclaim the written Word, the grace of God transforms the sermon into something more than merely a motivational talk or a persuasive oration. When the sermon says what the Scripture says, the triune God speaks to those who hear. Yet this is not the accomplishment of the preacher, however hard the preacher studies. It is the Holy Spirit who works through their studying to grant knowledge and spiritual understanding.

The power of biblically faithful preaching is evidence that it is the spoken Word of God. Preaching is in itself a judgment on those who refuse to hear, leaving them without excuse. Yet the greatest display of the power of the spoken Word is the fulfillment of its gospel mission. When the written

---

[87] Luther, "Epiphany: Matthew 2:1–12; 1522," *SML* 1.372; *WA* 10 I/1.627.
[88] Luther, *SML* 1.372; *WA* 10 I/1.627.

Word is faithfully proclaimed, God uses that spoken Word to create faith in hostile hearts, converting sinners. God also speaks through the sermon to sustain faith in the willing hearts of believers, sanctifying saints.

The sermon has this place in God's economy of salvation by the gracious will of God. Though the inner working of the Spirit is necessary to remedy the spiritual defect of fallen humanity, God is not bound to our preaching. He has not delivered his voice into our mouths to be under our control. Rather than the Holy Spirit being dependent upon preachers to be able to speak, preachers must appeal to the Spirit for aid in being faithful to the written Word.

Conclusion

The legacy of the Reformers' theology of preaching was, for hundreds of years, seen in the placement of the pulpit. No longer relegated to the side of the sanctuary, the holy desk was the primary focal point of worship, elevated above communion table and congregation. When the preacher ascended the stairs to that lofty height, the task was to speak nothing less than—and nothing other than—the Word of God. So great was the confidence of the Reformation's heirs in faithful preaching that they expected it to overthrow Antichrist and usher in the very kingdom of God.

Today, circumstances seem very different. Pulpits, where they are used at all, are small and unobtrusive. They are easily moved, so that the focus can shift to other points throughout the course of worship. Preachers often act as if preaching needs enhancement through rhetoric, technology, or even the tools of performance and entertainment in order be effective. Some churches have the resources, both financial and human, to achieve "excellence" in these areas. Most do not.

Celebration and appropriation of Luther and Calvin's theology of preaching does not require that we return to elevated and immovable pulpits. Nor does it even demand that we abandon all use of rhetoric and technological tools. It offers a cautionary tale; preachers should not be seduced by the thought that faithful preaching is weak and needs human help to succeed. They should not place their confidence in the arts and tools of men, nor fear their absence.[89] God speaks through preachers who faithfully

---

[89] My point is not that it is wrong to use rhetoric and technology, simply that preachers must keep their confidence in God who speaks through faithful preaching of the Word rather than allow it to become based in human efforts to achieve excellence.

give voice to the written Word. This is true in the large, wealthy church. It is true in the small, struggling church. Most importantly, the Reformers' theology of preaching offers profound encouragement. God still speaks today; the Spirit still moves. Those who preach the Scriptures faithfully are co-laborers with Christ who commissioned the preaching of the Word. While there are other forms of the ministry of the Word and other instruments that the Spirit uses, preaching is primary by the wisdom and grace of God. Do not be distracted or discouraged. Preach the Word!

Bibliography

Calvin, John. *Calvin's New Testament Commentaries*. Reprint edition, ed. David Torrance and Thomas Torrance. Grand Rapids: Eerdmans, 1960–1965.

_____. *Calvini Opera*. 59 vols. *Corpus Reformatorum*. Vols. 29–88. Berlin: C. A. Schwetschke und Sohn, 1863–1900.

_____. *Commentaries on the Book of the Prophet Jeremiah and the Lamentations*. Translated by John Owen. Grand Rapids: Eerdmans, 1950.

_____. *Commentaries on the First Book of Moses, Called Genesis*. Translated by John King. Grand Rapids: Eerdmans, 1948.

_____. *Commentaries on the Twelve Minor Prophets*. Translated by John Owen. Grand Rapids: Eerdmans, 1950.

_____. *Commentary on the Book of the Prophet Isaiah*. Translated by William Pringle. Grand Rapids: Eerdmans, 1948.

_____. *Institutes of the Christian Religion: 1559*. Translated by Ford Lewis Battles. Library of Christian Classics. Vols. 20–21. Philadelphia: Westminster, 1960.

Althaus, Paul. *The Theology of Martin* Luther. Translated by Robert C. Schultz. Philadelphia: Fortress, 1966.

Gilbert, William. *Renaissance and Reformation*. Unpublished manuscript, 1997. http://vlib.iue.it/carrie/texts/carrie_books/gilbert/15.html.

Gonzalez, Justo. *A History of Christian Thought*. Vol. 3, *From the Protestant Reformation to the Twentieth Century*. Nashville: Abingdon, 1987.

Luther, Martin. *Luther's Works*. Vols.1–30, ed. Jaroslav Pelikan. St. Louis: Concordia, 1955–1976.

_____. *Luther's Works*. Vols. 31–56, ed. Helmut Lehmann. Philadelphia: Muhlenberg, 1957–1982.

_____. *D. Martin Luthers Werke: kritische Gesammtausgabe.* 121 Vols. Weimar: Hermann Bohlaus Nachfolger, 1883–2009.

_____. *The Sermons of Martin Luther: The Church Postils.* Edited by John Lenker. Translated by John Lenker et al. 8 vols. Grand Rapids: Baker, 1995.

Old, Hughes Oliphant. *The Reading and Preaching of the Scriptures in the Worship of the Christian Church.* Vol. 4, *The Age of the Reformation.* Grand Rapids: Eerdmans, 2002.

Parker, Thomas Henry Louis. *The Oracles of God: An Introduction to the Preaching of John Calvin.* London: Lutterworth, 1947.

Ramm, Bernard. *The Witness of the Spirit: An Essay on the Contemporary Relevance of the Internal Witness of the Holy Spirit.* Grand Rapids: Eerdmans, 1959.

Wood, Skevington. *Captive to the Word: Martin Luther, Doctor of Sacred Scripture.* Exeter, UK: Paternoster, 1969.

12

The Legacy and Re-Formation of Reformation Preaching: A Cry for Renascence

KEVIN L. KING

The Reformation was a seismic event that shook Western Europe culturally, politically, economically, and religiously. Just as the landscape of the earth is reshaped after the clash of tectonic plates, the landscape of Christendom in Western Europe was reshaped. There was perhaps no greater reshaping than in the homiletical landscape. As much as the Reformation was a preaching for reform, it was a reform of preaching, says H. Oliphant Old in volume 4 of his magisterial series *The Reading and Preaching of the Scriptures in the Worship of the Christian Church*. This reform of preaching can be seen in at least three areas: (1) a shift from the *lectio selectiva* to the *lectio continua* (*sola Scriptura*), (2) a shift to a Christocentric preaching from moralistic preaching (*solus Christus*), and (3) a shift to a genre of preaching that can be characterized as prophetic (stepping into the social and political spheres of life).[1]

One cannot think of the major figures of the Reformation apart from their preaching. Whether in Wittenberg, Zurich, Basel, Strasbourg, Geneva, or in the forests or caves, the Reformation brought about a reform of preaching that had clearly definable characteristics, beginning with a return to the *lectio continua* of the Patristic Fathers.

---

[1] Hughes Oliphant Old, *The Reading and Preaching of the Scriptures in the Worship of the Christian Church,* vol. 4, *The Age of the Reformation* (Grand Rapids: Eerdmans, 2002), 2.

The first liturgical reform of the Reformation occurred January 1, 1519, at the Grossmünster in Zurich, Switzerland. A thirty-five-year-old priest, Ulrich Zwingli, who had just recently been elected to this prestigious pulpit as the *Leutpriester,* announced that on the following day, instead of following the selected reading of the liturgical calendar, he would begin with Matthew chapter 1 verse 1. Zwingli would continue this practice, following the pattern left by the great the fourth-century preacher John Chrysostom. Many Reformers were ardent students of the Patristic Fathers and were influenced by their approach to Scripture in preaching through the text, *lectio continua,* as opposed to having the sermon dictated by the liturgical calendar.

It is well known that Martin Luther, as the professor of biblical studies at the University of Wittenberg, lectured through the Psalms (1513–1515), Romans (1515–1516), Galatians (1516) and Hebrews (1517–1518).[2] Zwingli's study in the Scriptures and the Church Fathers is not as well known.[3] While a young parish priest in Glarus, who energetically threw himself into his pastoral duties, he also taught himself Greek and Hebrew. He was then able to read extensively among the Church Fathers, building an impressive library that contained the works of Ambrose, John Chrysostom, Gregory of Nazianus, Augustine, and the recently published folio volumes of Jerome. As if this were not enough, the young priest copied most of the Epistles of Paul in Greek and memorized them.[4] This facility for the original languages and a desire to prioritize the conventions of antiquity was common among the Reformers, as they adopted the cry of the Renaissance, "*ad fontes*" (back to the original sources).

The Reformers were reared in ecclesiastical environments that loved preaching. Contrary to the popular opinion that prior to the Reformation, preaching in the Church had ceased or diminished, the truth is, prior to the Reformation there was a lot of preaching, some of it very good. But much like the churches built over the centuries that displayed impressive,

---

[2] Robert Kolb, "Martin Luther: Preaching a Theology of the Cross," in *A Legacy of Preaching: The Life, Theology, and Method of History's Great Preachers,* vol. 1, *Apostles to the Revivalists,* ed. Benjamin K. Forrest et al. (Grand Rapids: Zondervan, 2018), 279–93.

[3] In this chapter, the author limits his discussion to the two first-generation Magisterial Reformers. Space limitations, along with the considerable attention given to John Calvin and the relatively minor attention that the preaching of Ulrich Zwingli has received, have contributed to this decision.

[4] Kevin L. King, "Ulrich Zwingli: Pastor, Patriot, Prophet, and Protestant," in *A Legacy of Preaching: The Life, Theology, and Method of History's Great Preachers,* vol. 1, *Apostles to the Revivalists,* ed. Benjamin K. Forrest et al. (Grand Rapids: Zondervan, 2018), 294–312.

often ornate, architectural features, preaching, especially in the high Scholastic period, had taken on similar characteristics, using language that spoke more to the concerns of the professors in the academy than to the concerns of the parishioners. [5]

Hughes Oliphant Old gives us a helpful summary of the thousand-year period that covers [the] medieval era. Medieval preaching can be characterized in six ways: 1) Medieval preaching is different from what it followed and what followed it. A way to visualize this variety is to think of Justinian's Hagia Sophia in Istanbul on one hand, and the Cathedral of Notre Dame in Paris on the other. With this kind of variety there was the awareness of the need for universality, as seen in the attempts of Justinian to codify the tradition and in Charlemagne's establishing a lectionary that could be used throughout his empire.[6] 2) With the fall of the Roman Empire and the subsequent rise in illiteracy, it was becoming more difficult to understand the Bible and interpret the meaning of Scripture. Contemplation of the Dionysian variety[7] became a viable option as the inaccessibility of Scripture grew. 3) The language barrier contributed to the difficulty of interpreting Scripture; few people could read Greek or Hebrew. Expository preaching as demonstrated in the Fathers was almost impossible. Allegory grew in popularity as the distance grew in time and in language proficiency.

The Scriptures were always read in the medieval liturgy and at times preached. However, instead of the context of Scripture being the basis for interpretation, the liturgy, as influenced by Dionysian mystical contemplation, began to be the basis for interpretation.[8] The liturgy developed a series of ceremonial symbols that were more easily understood by a largely illiterate population. Over time, the reading and preaching of Scripture gave way

---

[5] Old, *Preaching of the Scriptures*, vol. 4:1–2.

[6] Given the drastic architectural differences as in the two listed churches, there was a drastic difference sermonically in the preaching of the Patristic Church, Medieval Church, and the Reformation Church.

[7] "Contemplation of the Dionysian variety" is a mystical approach to God based on the writings of Dionysius the Areopagite. This approach makes two important assertions: (1) no one can know God comprehensively; (2) language, images, and symbols all have severe limitations when it comes to speaking about God. See Gregory Allison, *Historical Theology: An Introduction to Christian Doctrine* (Grand Rapids: Zondervan, 2011), 190–91. H. Oliphant Old contends that under the influence of Dionysius the Scriptures during the medieval period were interpreted in the liturgical context rather than the historical context. In time, the Scriptures were replaced by the liturgy and preaching was simply omitted. H. Oliphant Old, *The Reading and Preaching of the Scriptures in the Worship of the Christian Church*, vol. 3, *The Medieval Church* (Grand Rapids: Zondervan, 1999), xvi.

[8] See Old, *Preaching of the Scriptures*, vol. 4.

to the concerns and demands of the liturgical calendar. 4) Medieval preaching relied on and was determined by the liturgical calendar. Scripture was fitted in and conformed to the liturgical calendar and each Sunday would have its own feast, which necessitated that a specific topic be addressed in light of the concerns of that feast. Festal preaching that followed the liturgical calendar became the standard with few exceptions (notably Dominican preaching—as evidenced by Humbert of Romans and Franciscan preaching like that of Anthony of Padua). 5) Two styles of preaching, spiritual catechism and Lenten preaching missions, sought to enhance devotional life. Spiritual catechism was designed to deepen the religious life of the monastic community and Lenten preaching missions can be characterized as evangelistic preaching of sorts, used as a means to deepen the devotional life of the whole population from the thirteenth century to the end of the Middle Ages. 6) Medieval preaching developed its own particular rhetoric, with a classic sermon outline. Nothing is more medieval than for a sermon to have an elaborate introduction, conclusion, three-point outline (that may or may not be supported by the text), adorned with amusing, edifying stories called exempla to keep the attention of the listeners.[9]

The change in the sermon brought on by the Reformation was due to the influence and example of the Patristic Fathers. The effect of preachers' engagement with the biblical text itself, not filtered by the gloss[10] or the liturgical calendar, was a by-product of the attitudinal changes brought on by the Renaissance and humanism, including the major influence of Erasmus, the "Prince of the Humanists." An additional factor in the change of the sermon was the flourishing, seemingly explosive growth in access to and facility with the Greek and Hebrew texts of the Bible, made possible by the major technological innovation of the age, the printing press. By the time Luther and Zwingli started their ministries, more people could read than had been able to in the previous thousand years. Sermons were popular during the Middle Ages for a variety of reasons; chief among them was the dissemination of information and the public event that festal preaching became. People would be brought together for the feast and a sermon would be delivered. The reaction of the Reformers to this kind of

---

[9] Old, loc. 82–133 of 9178, Kindle.

[10] While there are varying definitions for a gloss, researcher Tristan Taylor describes "gloss" as "an umbrella term which covers annotations, translations, summaries and commentaries." Tristan Taylor, "What Is a Gloss? Part 1," *Medieval Codes* (blog), November 21, 2016, accessed September 6, 2018, http://www.medievalcodes.ca/2016/11/what-is-gloss-part-1.html.

preaching was that it had little if anything to do with the intended message of the biblical text. If Scripture were read at all in these situations, it would quickly be left behind and then a series of exempla would follow that would extol the virtue of the saint of the day or some hagiographical story of a figure of history or legend.[11]

Sola Scriptura: The Authority of the Word of God

The first liturgical reform of the Reformation took place in Zurich, Switzerland, where Zwingli, just thirty-five years old and the newly elected *Leutpriester*, announced his departure from the selected reading of the liturgical calendar. Instead, he would let the text itself, in this case Matthew's Gospel, determine the sermon to be preached that day. In this context, Zwingli's decision was a radical step. The practice of following the liturgical calendar had been in place for centuries. Nevertheless, Zwingli was convinced of the need for expositional preaching of the Bible. His first motivation for departing from tradition was an undeniable and incontrovertible belief in the authority and sufficiency of the Bible (*sola Scriptura*).

Zwingli's approach to preaching Scripture can be seen in his statement regarding his composition and later defense of the Sixty-Seven Articles, the first document to articulate theological principles of the Reformation.

> I, Ulrich Zwingli, confess that I have preached in the worthy city of Zurich these sixty-seven articles or opinions on the basis of Scripture, which is called *theopneustos* (that is inspired by God). I offer to defend and vindicate these articles with Scripture. But if I have not understood Scripture correctly, *I am ready to be corrected, but only from Scripture.*[12]

The Word of God has authority because it is the Word of God. Its authority is not established rationally nor ecclesiastically. It has a self-authenticating authority. A common objection at this point is that Zwingli is holding to a naïve biblicism. H. Oliphant Old refutes the objection:

> When one realizes, however, the high level of Zwingli's biblical scholarship, one can hardly look at it this way. Zwingli was an accomplished

---

[11] Old, *Preaching of the Scriptures*, vol. 3, loc. 82–133 of 9178, Kindle.

[12] Ulrich Zwingli, "The Sixty-Seven Articles," in *Confessions and Catechisms of the Reformation*, ed. Mark Noll (Grand Rapids: Baker, 1991), 39. Emphasis added.

scholar who knew the Scriptures in the original languages and had studied deeply in the Fathers. When such a man tells us that the Scriptures have a self-authenticating authority which outstrips the recommendation of the Fathers, the councils, or any other human authority simply because it is the Word of God, that cannot be tossed off as naïve enthusiasm.[13]

Zwingli makes this argument in his sermon "Of the Clarity and the Certainty of the Word of God," originally preached in summer 1522 to the nuns of the Oetenbach convent. Another aspect of Zwingli's view of *sola Scriptura* is that the Word of God "is the common property of the whole people of God . . . to nourish our faith."[14] In Zwingli's words, "There is nothing which can give greater joy or assurance or comfort to the soul than the Word of its creator and maker."[15] This nourishing effect is a result of the *imago Dei*. In humanity, there is a desire and an affinity for the Word of God; according to Zwingli, this is a constituent element of the image of God in all men, saved and unsaved. It is the spiritual air we breathe, in which life itself is based.[16]

Zwingli's belief in *sola Scriptura* was shared by other Reformers of the period. Luther also had a high view of Scripture: "The highest worship of God takes place in preaching the Word since God is worshiped when the gospel is preached, thanks is given, and all the sacrifices and worship of the Old Testament are fulfilled. In this form of worship, the neighbor is served and the image of God is formed in people, so that they die and come alive in order to be God-like."[17] Robert Kolb unpacks this for us:

> That appraisal of public preaching rested on his understanding of God as a person who is in conversation with his human creatures, a conversation that creates the community that links them to him and to each other. Luther regarded God's Word as the instrument or agent of his creative and sustaining will. As God had spoken the worlds into

---

[13] Old, *Preaching of the Scriptures*, vol. 4:48.

[14] Old, 48.

[15] Huldrych Zwingli, "Of the Clarity and Certainty of the Word of God," in *Zwingli and Bullinger*, ed. G.W. Bromiley, Library of Christian Classics (Philadelphia: Westminster, 1953), 68.

[16] King, "Pastor, Patriot, Prophet and Protestant," 294–312.

[17] WA26:110,15, WA28:3692.

existence in Genesis 1, so also his word of gospel in Jesus Christ created sinners anew, refashioning them into his children.[18]

In 1523, in his essay "On the Ordering of Worship in the Congregation," Luther expressed his concern over the lack of preaching in the Roman Mass. It was not until 1525 that he introduced his "German mass" in Wittenberg. In his reworking of the mass, every worship service included expository preaching. Luther not only taught at the university in Wittenberg, but preached there regularly and when he traveled. In the afternoon service in Wittenberg, he preached following the *lectio continua*. From 1522 through fall 1524 he preached through 1 Peter, 2 Peter, Jude, and Genesis.[19] Luther displayed his confidence in the authority and sufficiency of the Word of God when he returned to Wittenberg after his year in the Wartburg Castle:

> I opposed indulgences and all the papists, but never with force. I simply taught, preached, and wrote God's word; otherwise I did nothing. And while I slept, or drank Wittenberg beer with my friends Philipp [Melanchthon] and [Nikolaus von] Amsdorf, the word so greatly weakened the papacy that no prince or emperor ever inflicted such losses upon it. I did nothing; the word did everything.[20]

Zwingli's conviction of and confidence in the authority of the Word of God can be seen in his years as the Leutpriester at the Grossmünster. In his *Apologeticus Archeteles,* (August 22–23, 1522), Zwingli defended his pulpit practice to the Bishop of Constance who was investigating the "trouble" in Zurich:

> For three years ago now (to give you an account of the preaching I have done at Zurich), I preached the entire Gospel according to

---

[18] See Kolb, "Martin Luther; Preaching," 287. See also Robert Kolb and Charles P. Arand, *The Genius of Luther's Theology. A Wittenberg Way of Thinking for the Contemporary Church* (Grand Rapids: Baker, 2008), 131–59. Johann Haar, *Initium creaturae Dei. Eine Untersuchung über Luthers Begriff der "neuen Creatur" im Zusammenhang mit seine Verständnis von Jakobus 1,18 und mit seinem "Zeit"-Denken* (Gütersloh: Bertelsmann, 1939).

[19] Beth Kreitzer, "The Lutheran Sermon," chap. 2 in *Preachers and People in the Reformations and Early Modern Period*, ed. Larissa Taylor (Boston: Brill Academic, 2003), 47–48. H Oliphant Old observes that liturgical reforms in Wittenberg were finally established in 1526, but with a compromise. On Sunday mornings the lectionary Gospels and Epistles would be preached in their traditional forms. In the Sunday vespers and in the morning and evening services during the week there would be a *lectio continua* of the Old Testament and other biblical books. Old, *Preaching of the Scriptures*, vol. 4, 37.

[20] Kreitzer, 41.

Matthew, and at that time I had not even heard the name of those persons to whose faction you accuse me of belonging. I added the Acts of the Apostles to the Gospel immediately, that the Church of Zurich might see in what way and with what sponsors the Gospel was carried forth and spread abroad. Presently came the First Epistle of Paul to Timothy, which seemed to be admirably adapted to my excellent flock.[21]

These series of sermons would take Zwingli four years to complete: after finishing preaching through Matthew, he started with Acts and preached straight through Paul's Epistles to Timothy.[22] Zwingli continued preaching expositionally and by 1525 had worked his way through the New Testament (except for Revelation) and then turned to the Old Testament.[23]

Solus Christus: Christocentric Preaching

The second shift that is characteristic of the reform in the preaching of the Reformation is that it has a clearly discernable Christocentric emphasis. Luther and Zwingli both underwent conversion experiences that centered in the sufficiency of the atoning death of Christ. They were freed of the uncertainty and bondage that accompanied the works-based soteriology of Catholic theology. Luther's experience is well known but not as well known is how Zwingli came to Christ. In his own words he told how, after reading *Expostulation of Jesus with a Man Perishing through His Very Own Fault,* a poem by Erasmus, the light of the liberation and freedom that is in Christ enveloped his soul:

I shall not conceal from you, dearly beloved brethren, the manner in which I arrived at this opinion, the utterly sure conviction that we have no need of any mediator apart from Christ . . . I read a poem of that most learned man, Erasmus of Rotterdam, in which Christ

---

[21] Ulrich Zwingli, "Defence Called Archeteles . . . ," chap. 14 in *The Latin Works and the Correspondence of Huldreich Zwingli: Together with Selections from His German Works,* vol. 1: *1510–1522,* ed. Samuel Macauley Jackson, trans. Henry Preble, Walter Lichtenstein, and Lawrence A. McLouth (New York: G. P. Putnam's Sons, 1912), 238.

[22] Lee Palmer Wandel, "Switzerland," chap. 7 in *Preachers and People in the Reformations And Early Modern Period,* ed. Larissa Taylor (Boston: Brill Academic, 2003), 229–30.

[23] Timothy George, *Theology of the Reformers,* rev. ed. (Nashville: B&H Academic, 2013), loc. 3530 of 8602, Kindle. George comments that Zwingli did not preach through the book of Revelation because he doubted that it belonged in the canon.

pleads with men as to the reason why men are so stupid as not to seek all things in Him.[24]

Zwingli was unashamed and unabashed in this conviction that Jesus Christ was sufficient for salvation and sanctification. He writes in defense of his preaching:

> They will learn also that Christ, having been made a sacrifice once for all, has accomplished their salvation forever. This is the seed I have sown. Matthew, Luke, Paul, and Peter have watered it, and God has given it splendid increase, but this I will not trumpet forth, lest I seem to be canvassing my own glory and not Christ's. Go now and say that this plant (to come back to your point) is not of the Father in Heaven. I have not, I say, used any false nostrums or tricks or exhortations, but in simple words and terms native to the Swiss I have drawn them to the recognition of their trouble, having learned this from Christ himself, who began his own preaching with it.[25]

Zwingli's Christocentric conviction can be seen in the first four articles of the Sixty-Seven Articles that Zwingli composed in preparation of the First Zurich Disputation in 1523:

> 1. All who say that the gospel is nothing without the confirmation of the church make a mistake and blaspheme God.
>
> 2. The sum of the gospel is that our Lord Jesus Christ, true Son of God, has made known to us the will of his heavenly Father, redeemed us from death by his innocence, and reconciled us to God.
>
> 3. Therefore, Christ is the only way to salvation for all who have been, who are and who will be.
>
> 4. Whoever seeks or points out any other way to God is a murderer of souls and a thief.[26]

Luther also came to understand the central place of Jesus Christ in the salvific plan of God as he read the entire Bible from Genesis to Revelation. God has revealed Himself in and as the person [of] Jesus Christ.[27]

---

[24] Ford Lewis Battles, "Jesus Christ the sole mediator between God and man," *Hartford Quarterly* 5, no. 4 (1965): 67.

[25] Zwingli, *Latin Works*, 239.

[26] Zwingli, "Sixty-Seven Articles," 40.

[27] Kolb, "Martin Luther: Preaching," 279–93.

In his preparation for lectures and weekly preaching, he came to realize "the whole point of the Gospel is that God out of His love for us has given us his Son that we might be saved through faith in Him."[28] As Luther fleshed out his understanding of the sufficiency of Christ (*solus Christus*), he developed his *Postils*. The *Postils* were sermon helps for preachers who were expected to preach from the lectionary. In Luther's opinion, preaching that followed the lectionary was aimed at teaching people to do good works instead of preaching the gospel. Luther provided a Christocentric interpretative grid that assisted the preacher to take the text of the day, as determined by the lectionary, and make Christ the centerpiece of the sermon.[29]

A sermon that Luther delivered at Erfurt as he was on his way to Worms in 1520 typifies his Christocentric understanding of Scripture. The appointed reading for the day was John 20:19–31, the story of Jesus appearing in the Upper Room on the evening of the resurrection. To summarize briefly, Luther's exposition of the passage centers on the salvation that we receive in Christ and how, because of what Christ does in and through us, that salvation is lived out. It is not our works that free us from sin. It is the death of Christ that frees us. Luther referenced Paul's words in Romans 5, using Scripture to interpret Scripture, and he brought out the vicarious nature of the atoning death of Jesus Christ. He took great pains to draw out the difference in his teaching and the emphasis that papal authorities had been teaching. According to these authorities, keeping their rules—fasting, praying, and butter eating—and good works formed the bedrock of salvation.

"But I say that none of the saints, no matter how holy they were, attained salvation by their works. Even the holy mother of God did not become good, was not saved, by her virginity or her motherhood, but rather by the will of faith and the works of God, and not by her purity, or own works."[30]

Prophetic Preaching

The last shift I would like to discuss is what has been described as the prophetic preaching of the Reformation. Prophetic preaching, in this instance, is defined as a specific word, for a specific people, in a specific

[28] Old, *Preaching of the Scriptures*, vol. 4:5.
[29] Old, 4:13.
[30] Old, 10.

time. Luther and Zwingli both exhibited this element in their preaching. Prophetic preaching also has an occasional element to it. That is, there are specific occasions (i.e., cultural and political situations) that arise and demand a specific treatment at that specific moment in time. Some might associate prophetic preaching with the kind of preaching that Savonarola did in Florence. A statue of Savonarola is included in the Reformer's Park in Worms, Germany. The sculptor placed Savonarola at one of the four corners of the pedestal of Luther's statue, including him among the European pre-Reformers whose efforts helped pave the way for Luther.

In a sense, the whole Reformation may be termed prophetic since the basic elements of Luther's and Zwingli's theology of preaching were also present in the preaching of Wycliffe and Huss; however, the cultural, political, social, theological, and technological factors did not converge as they did at the beginning of the sixteenth century. Luther demonstrated prophetic preaching. Whether he was preaching expositionally through the Gospels or the Epistles, or in his catechetical sermons, his message included denunciations of the abuses of the Church and society of his day.[31] As the occasion(s) arose, whether it was the Roman Catholic Church, the peasants, the *Schwarmer*, or Karlstadt, Luther was quick to embrace his role as prophet and confront the abuses as he saw them. For he famously said in response to the question of whether he would recant his positions, "Do you recant or do you not?" Luther responded in German, "My conscience is a prisoner of God's Word. I cannot and will not recant, for to disobey one's conscience is neither just nor safe. God help me. Amen."[32]

Zwingli increasingly saw his role as the pastor of the Grossmünster in the model of the Old Testament prophet. In 1522, Zwingli resigned as the "people's priest" and was retained in Zurich as a preacher to the entire city of Zurich.[33] Just as Luther had denounced Johann Tetzel for his attempt to sell indulgences, likewise Zwingli confronted the Swiss Tetzel, Bernard Samson. Zwingli, preaching against Samson, said, "There were also false prophets among the people of Israel even as there will be false teachers among you. . . . In their greed for money they will trade on your credulity with sheer fabrications. . . ."[34] In the role of the shepherd/prophet, Zwingli

---

[31] Old, 7.

[32] Justo L. Gonzalez, *The Story of Christianity*, vol. 2: *The Reformation to the Present Day*, 2nd ed. (New York: HarperOne, 2010), 35.

[33] King, "Pastor, Patriot, Prophet, and Protestant," 8.

[34] King, 15.

saw himself as responsible not only to protect his flock but to feed his flock. Concerning whether to observe the fast or not, Zwingli preached, "If you want to fast, do so; if you do not want to eat meat, don't eat it; but allow Christians a free choice. . . . If you would be a Christian at heart, act in this way. If the spirit teaches you thus, then fast, but grant also your neighbor the privilege of Christian liberty . . ."[35]

Just as the Old Testament prophets thundered against idolatry, so did Zwingli. While not an iconoclast, nor an enemy of art, he prevented any substitution of the creature for the Creator. Later, the Council authorized the removal of the trappings of idolatry in the churches of Zurich.[36] His prophetic voice eventually abolished the mass in April of 1525.[37] Also, as a prophetic preacher, he opposed the mercenary system. When Cardinal Schinner came to Zurich to arrange for the recruitment of soldiers and while the Cardinal was in attendance in full vestments sitting just below the pulpit, Zwingli said, "And I could wish that one would declare the alliance with the Pope null and void and would send the treaty back with the messenger . . . Against a wolf one raised the hue and cry, but no one really opposed the wolves who destroyed most people."[38]

Conclusion: A Cry for Renascence

This chapter has identified at least three salient characteristics of the reform of preaching that took place in the preaching for reform that we call the Reformation. Preaching reforms included a return to the Patristic preaching of *lectio continua* and a shift away from moralistic preaching to Christocentric preaching; finally, the preaching of the Reformation contained an element of prophetic preaching. These changes occurred because of a conviction in and commitment to *sola Scriptura* and *solus Christus*. The biblical text is authoritative and sufficient for faith, practice, and especially preaching. Jesus Christ alone is sufficient for salvation. We stand on the shoulders

---

[35] King, 17.

[36] Old, *Preaching of the Scriptures*, vol. 4:51–52. The principle that Zwingli tried to apply was the restoration of biblical faith and practice. It is surprising, considering his considerable scholarly achievement, that he would retreat to a wooden biblicism on this issue. If the Bible did not expressly commend a practice, it was to be excluded in the worship service of the church. He excluded the playing of organs, the violin (which he played with expertise), and other uses of music as well. Even the Lord's Supper was not to be taken too frequently (he preferred four times a year), as anything that might take away from the hearing of the preached Word of God should be prohibited. Cf. Gonzalez, *Story of Christianity*, 61.

[37] George, *Theology of the Reformers*, Kindle.

[38] Zwingli, *Latin Works*, 69.

of those that have gone before us. They enable us to survey the landscape in a way they might not have been able to do. And yet, something must be wrong with the state of preaching in our day. In just a quick survey of recent and influential books on preaching in the last several years we can detect the authors' concern about the state of contemporary preaching.

In 2008, in the foreword to Albert Mohler's *He is Not Silent: Preaching in a Postmodern World*, John MacArthur writes,

> Clearly, preaching—specifically *biblical* preaching—is the main strategy God Himself ordained for church growth and for leading and feeding His flock. Naturally, it is the one strategy He has always truly blessed. It is remarkable, then, that over the past half century (or longer) evangelicals have devoted vast quantities of energy and resources to the invention of novel church-growth strategies that tend to discount biblical preaching.[39]

The last few decades have been a period of wanton experimentation in many pulpits. One of the most troubling developments is the decline and eclipse of expository preaching. In its place, some contemporary preachers now substitute messages intentionally designed to reach secular or superficial congregations—messages that avoid preaching a biblical text and thus avoid a potentially embarrassing confrontation with biblical truth.[40]

Although there are several possible reasons for this decline of expositional preaching, it will suffice here to list just a few. First, contemporary preaching suffers from a loss of confidence in the power of the Word. Second, contemporary preaching suffers from an infatuation with technology. Third, contemporary preaching suffers from embarrassment before the biblical text. Fourth, contemporary preaching suffers from an emptying of biblical content. Fifth, contemporary preaching suffers from a focus on felt needs. Sixth, contemporary preaching suffers from an absence of gospel.[41]

Mohler is not alone this assessment and apparently the passage of a few years did nothing to allay the concern he expressed. In 2010, in his introduction to *Text-Driven Preaching*, David Allen takes us to today's preaching pantheon that pays homage to various homiletical luminaries: there

---

[39] John MacArthur, foreword to Albert R. Mohler, *He is Not Silent: Preaching in a Postmodern World* (Chicago: Moody, 2008), 12.

[40] MacArthur, Kindle loc. 159–63, Kindle.

[41] Mohler, preface to *He is Not Silent*, loc. 170–232, Kindle.

you will find the statue of homiletical "creativity," also present is the "culturally relevant" homiletical statue, along with shrines to the "narrative," the "pop-psychology," the "topical," and even a statue to the "unknown preaching method." Allen saliently reminds the admirers of this last homiletical statue that this method is not "unknown." It was used by the earliest preachers of the apostolic era—expository preaching.[42]

In 2011, in the foreword to *Engaging Exposition*, David Platt recounts an evening in which a guest preacher was speaking in a church he attended. The speaker was popular and crowds came to hear him speak. Platt comments that right away, he had a clue something was not right, when the speaker started by saying that he forgot his Bible. The preacher continued to belabor the point that he had no idea what God wanted him to say on this night, but nothing ever came to his mind. The preacher concluded that maybe God simply did not have anything to say to the people on that night. And with that, the "preacher" walked off stage.[43] The authors of *Engaging Exposition* follow this story with their assessment of the current homiletical landscape:

> This book reflects a serious concern as well as certain nonnegotiable convictions the three us hold in common. We believe the church of the Lord Jesus Christ is at a critical point. A crisis is in our pulpits and this situation is critical. Seduced by the sirens of modernity, preachers of the gospel have jettisoned a word-based ministry that is expository in nature. . . . We have neglected preaching the whole counsel of God's Word. What has resulted? Too many of our people know neither the content nor the doctrines of Scripture. What is the fallout? Not knowing the Word, they do not love or obey the Word. If the Bible is used at all in preaching, it is usually included as a proof-text that is used out of context and has no real connection to what the Biblical author is saying. Many who claim and perhaps believe they are expositors betray their confession by their practice.[44]

Too much preaching today resembles medieval preaching or the preaching of the revivalists, rather than preaching inspired and modeled on

---

[42] David Allen, introduction to *Text-Driven Preaching*, ed. Danny Akin, David Allen, and Ned Mathews (Nashville: B&H Academic, 2010), 1.

[43] David Platt, foreword to *Engaging Exposition*, ed. Danny Akin, Bill Curtis, and Stephen Rummage (Nashville: B&H Academic, 2011), ix.

[44] Akin, Curtis, and Rummage, *Engaging Exposition*, 1.

Reformation preaching, which was modeled on Patristic preaching.[45] Too often churchgoers cannot find serious and substantive engagement with the books of the Bible within the walls of their churches. Instead, we find a new liturgical calendar, not designed by a denomination, but by the individual preacher, or the calendar of culture. Some may in fact exposit the text as they preach, but due to their calendar, the text for the sermon next week, will not follow this week's text in order, as the author intended when the text was inscripturated. This is not to say that there are not occasions that warrant a specific word, at a specific time from a specific text, for this is the essence of prophetic preaching. But the week-to-week diet of preaching that has been given to the church has been "written for our instruction" (1 Cor 10:11) and it is on this Word that we must feast.

Do we think God did not know the twenty-first century would materialize? Do we think God did not know changes in society and technology would occur? And do we not think God knew and knows our deepest need and that, as much as has changed in human history, we still struggle with the same things as our forebears? Those who hold to the omniscience of God must also hold to the conviction that God has spoken for today through his Word—but this Word must be preached!

The legacy of the Reform in preaching seems to be at low tide in our day, if the authors mentioned are correct. But as their writings attest, if you take the time to read them, the current situation does not have to be a lasting one. Maturation in the life of one pastor or one pulpit means a re-formation and reformation that carries forth the Word of God to ears that need to hear and eyes that need to see. The author has the privilege of teaching preaching and expectantly and prayerfully believes the Lord will bless us, and like-minded and sister institutions, with a renascence (the revival of something that has been dormant) of preaching that embodies and encapsulates the characteristics of the preaching of the Reformation, preaching that proclaims the truth, instead of preaching that trifles with the truth. Preaching that fosters faith, instead of preaching that leads to a faith that fizzles before the finish. Preaching that tells of the unmerited grace of the Father, instead of preaching that grovels at the altar of self-achievement. Preaching that exalts the Savior, instead of preaching that makes excuses for him. Preaching that makes no apologies, no excuses, no equivocation, and

---

[45] Akin, Allen, and Mathews contend in *Text Driven Preaching* that this would be better labeled apostolic preaching.

has no hesitation in declaring his glory in creation, his glory in the church, and his glory in the ages to come forever and ever. Amen!

Bibliography

Akin, Danny, Bill Curtis, and Stephen Rummage, *Engaging Exposition* Nashville: B&H Academic, 2011.

Akin, Danny, David Allen, and Ned Mathews, eds. *Text-Driven Preaching.* Nashville: B&H Academic, 2010.

Battles, Ford Lewis. "Jesus Christ the sole mediator between God and man." *Hartford Quarterly* 5, no. 4 (1965): 67.

Bromiley, G. W., ed. *Zwingli and Bullinger.* Library of Christian Classics. Philadelphia: Westminster, 1953.

George, Timothy. *Theology of the Reformers.* Rev. ed. Nashville: B&H Academic, 2013.

Gonzalez, Justo L. *The Story of Christianity.* Vol. 2, *The Reformation to the Present Day.* 2nd ed. New York: HarperOne, 2010.

King, Kevin L. "Ulrich Zwingli: Pastor, Patriot, Prophet and Protestant." In *A Legacy of Preaching: The Life, Theology, and Method of History's Great Preachers.* Vol. 1 of *Apostles to the Revivalists,* ed. Benjamin K. Forrest et al. Grand Rapids: Zondervan, forthcoming.

Kolb, Robert. "Martin Luther: Preaching a Theology of the Cross." In *A Legacy of Preaching: The Life, Theology, and Method of History's Great Preachers.* Vol. 1 of *Apostles to the Revivalists,* ed. Benjamin K. Forrest et al. Grand Rapids: Zondervan, 2018.

————. *Martin Luther and the Enduring Word of God.* Grand Rapids: Baker Academic, 2016.

————, and Charles P. Arand. *The Genius of Luther's Theology: A Wittenberg Way of Thinking for the Contemporary Church.* Grand Rapids: Baker, 2008.

Kreitzer, Beth. "The Lutheran Sermon." In *Preachers and People in the Reformations and Early Modern Period,* ed. Larissa Taylor. Boston, Brill Academic, 2003.

Mohler, Albert R. *He is Not Silent: Preaching in a Postmodern World.* Chicago: Moody, 2008.

Old, Hughes Oliphant. *The Reading and Preaching of the Scriptures in the Worship of the Christian Church.* Vol. 3, *The Medieval Church.* Grand Rapids: Eerdmans, 1999.

_____. *The Reading and Preaching of the Scriptures in the Worship of the Christian Church.* Vol. 4, *The Age of the Reformation.* Grand Rapids: Eerdmans, 2002.

Platt, David. Foreword to *Engaging Exposition,* ed. Danny Akin, Bill Curtis and Stephen Rummage. Nashville: B&H Academic, 2011.

Potter, G. R. *Huldrych Zwingli: Documents of Modern History.* New York: St. Martin's Press, 1977.

Taylor, Tristan. "Medieval Codes: What is a Gloss? Part 1." *Medieval Codes* (blog), November 21, 2016. http://www.medievalcodes.ca/2016/11/what-is-gloss-part-1.html.

Wandel, Lee Palmer. "Switzerland." In *Preachers and People in the Reformations and Early Modern Period,* ed. Larissa Taylor, 221–48. Boston: Brill Academic, 2003.

Zwingli, Ulrich. *The Latin Works and The Correspondence of Huldreich Zwingli: Together with Selections from His German Works.* Vol. 1, *1510–1522,* edited by Samuel Macauley Jackson, trans. Henry Preble, Walter Lichtenstein, and Lawrence A. McLouth. New York: G. P. Putnam's Sons, 1912.

_____. "The Sixty-Seven Articles." In *Confessions and Catechisms of the Reformation,* ed. Mark Noll. Grand Rapids: Baker, 1991.

Part IV

CELEBRATING THE LEGACY OF THE MISSIONS AND MARTYRS OF THE REFORMATION

13

The Mangled Narrative
of Missions and Evangelism
in the Reformation

RAY VAN NESTE

O ver the past century, many of the books dealing with the history of Christian missions have declared, with varying degrees of certainty, that the Protestant Reformers were derelict in their duty to spread the Gospel throughout the entire world.[1] Writers have accused the Reformers of both inactivity and indifference. This thesis has become an unverified certainty among the popular audience. However, is this a fair assessment of what the Reformers did and taught? In this chapter, I will trace the history of this deleterious account of the Reformers in regard to missions and evangelism, critique the methodology of this view, and present the writings and actions of three Reformers: Martin Luther, Martin Bucer, and John Calvin, to show the missional ventures of the Reformers.

A Negative Interpretation

The Reformation has long been considered by Protestants as a great spiritual revival and doctrinal renewal of the church. Nevertheless, some writers have argued that the Reformers failed to grasp the missionary imperative of the church and have even accused the Reformers of leading the church astray. This view appears to originate with German missiologist Gustav Warneck

---

[1] A version of this article has been published as "The Mangled Narrative of Missions and Evangelism in the Reformation," *Southeastern Theological Review* 8, no. 2 (Fall 2017): 3–27.

(1834–1910), a pastor and missions enthusiast whom many regard as the father of Protestant missiology. In his influential survey, *Outline of the History of Protestant Missions from the Reformation to the Present Time*, Warneck stated although the conclusion was "painful," nevertheless it is clear that Luther and Calvin's "view of the missionary task of the church was essentially defective."[2] Warneck concedes that Luther preached the gospel earnestly himself, but "nowhere does Luther indicate the heathen as the objects of evangelistic work."[3] Furthermore, Luther "never gives an intimation from which it can be inferred that he held direct mission work among the heathen to be commanded."[4] Warneck concludes, "The mission to the heathen world had no interest for [Luther] or his fellow-labourers."[5]

What evidence does Warneck produce to ground such a conclusion? He acknowledges the many obstacles confronting any worldwide effort by Protestants in the sixteenth century, including persecution, lack of contact with "heathen" nations, lack of infrastructure, and inability to travel to newly discovered lands since Catholic countries (e.g., Spain and Portugal) held sway over the oceans. Still, Warneck faults the Reformers for not lamenting such limitations, suggesting that if they really wanted to reach such faraway areas, there would be indications in their writings of strong yearnings to break through these obstacles to mission.[6] Instead, according to Warneck, we find among the Reformers no idea or activity of missions "in the sense in which we understand them today."[7]

According to Warneck, faulty theology caused the Reformers' defective perception of the imperative of missions. He specified three problematic ideas. First, Warneck says Luther believed the apostles had fulfilled the Great Commission so it no longer applied to the church of his time. However, Warneck acknowledges that Bucer and Calvin did not believe this. Second, Warneck says the Reformers' doctrine of election kept them

---

[2] Gustav Warneck, *Outline of the History of Protestant Missions from the Reformation to the Present Time* (Edinburgh: J. Gemmell, 1884), 17. Three of Warneck's ten German editions were translated into English in 1884, 1901, and 1906.

[3] Warneck (1884), 12.

[4] Warneck, 16.

[5] Warneck, 18.

[6] Gustav Warneck, *Outline of the History of Protestant Missions from the Reformation to the Present Time*. Authorized translation from the seventh German edition, ed. George Robson (New York: Revell, 1901), 8–9. The various editions of this book remain consistent in the critique of the Reformers. I drew the first several quotes from an earlier edition because Warneck's points were made more succinctly there.

[7] Warneck (1901), 9.

from sensing any missionary duty. Even though Bucer and Calvin did not think the Great Commission was fulfilled, their belief that the work of salvation was God's work meant there was no human responsibility for the work of missions. Third, the eschatological views of the Reformers inhibited missionary thinking. "Luther and his contemporaries were persuaded that the end of the world was at hand, ... so that no time remained for the further development and extension of the kingdom of God on the earth."[8]

Warneck's negative representation has been echoed by others through the years. Kenneth Scott Latourette says the Reformers were indifferent to the task of world missions due to their faulty theology, though he does not mention election specifically.[9] Herbert Kane marvels that "spiritual forces released" in the Reformation failed to produce *any* missionary activity, and he blames the same three points of theology that Warneck lists.[10] Stephen Neill finds "exceedingly little" interest in missions from the Reformers.[11] Neill says little about the reasons for this deficiency, but does comment that the Reformation churches did not feel that missions was obligatory. William Hogg says the Reformers "disavowed any obligation for Christians to carry the gospel."[12] Michael Nazir-Ali charges the Reformers with abandoning the responsibility of world missions and blames this on their understanding of election and the idea that the Great Commission no longer applied.[13] According to Ruth Tucker, during the Reformation "the urgency to reach out to others was not seen as a top priority," and she suggests the Reformers did not acknowledge the responsibility to evangelize those without the gospel.[14] She also roots this problem in faulty theology. Gordon Olson says the Reformers did "virtually nothing to advance the cause of

---

[8] Warneck, 16.

[9] Kenneth Scott Latourette, *A History of the Expansion of Christianity* (New York: Harper, 1937), 27. Latourette focuses on Luther but does not quote Luther on any of these points. He simply cites Warneck as proof.

[10] J. Herbert Kane, *A Concise History of the Christian World Mission: A Panoramic View of Missions from Pentecost to the Present* (Grand Rapids: Baker, 1978), 73.

[11] Stephen Neill, *A History of Christian Missions*, 2nd ed. (New York: Penguin Books, 1991), 189.

[12] William Richey Hogg, *Ecumenical Foundations: A History of the International Missionary Council and its Nineteenth Century Background* (New York: Harper, 1952), 1–2. Hogg cites Warneck as his support.

[13] Michael Nazir-Ali, *From Everywhere to Everywhere: A World View of Christian Witness* (Eugene, OR: Wipf & Stock, 2009), 43.

[14] Ruth Tucker, *From Jerusalem to Irian Jaya: A Biographical History of Christian Missions* (Grand Rapids: Zondervan, 2004), 20. According to Tucker, only in the eighteenth century did Protestants begin "acknowledging their responsibility to evangelize those without the gospel" (98).

world evangelization," and he blames the Reformers' theology, mentioning the same three points as Warneck.[15] Johannes Verkuyl blames the Reformers' lack of missions activity on their belief that the Great Commission no longer applied, but he does not reference election or eschatology.[16] Justice Anderson, in a standard mission textbook, attributes the Reformers' lack of missionary zeal to a misunderstanding of the Great Commission and eschatology.[17]

This negative interpretation of the Reformers appears commonly in more recent, popular theological writings as well.[18] Clearly, Warneck's argument took root. Few of these works present their own primary source research on the topic. They simply cite or allude to Warneck or to someone who has followed him. Rarely is there evidence of Warneck being read critically. Typically Warneck's view of the Reformers is simply asserted or assumed as one of the proven facts of historical scholarship. However, this raises the question of whether Warneck was correct or even if he has been properly understood. Thus, we now turn to critical interaction with Warneck, particularly how he defined missions and his appraisal of the Reformers' theology.

---

[15] C. Gordon Olson and Don Fanning, *What in the World Is God Doing?: Essentials of Global Missions: an Introductory Guide* (Lynchburg, VA: Global Gospel Publishers, 2013), 103.

[16] Johannes Verkuyl, *Contemporary Missiology: An Introduction,* trans. Dale Cooper (Grand Rapids: Eerdmans, 1987), 18–19.

[17] Justice Anderson, "Medieval and Renaissance Missions (500–1792)," in *Missiology: An Introduction to the Foundations, History, and Strategies of World Missions*, ed. John Mark Terry, Ebbie Smith, and Justice Anderson (Nashville: B&H, 1998), 194–95. Anderson, like several other free church authors, says the connection between state and church in the Magisterial Reformers hindered missions since a state church's mission is confined to national interests. But this fails to account for the missionaries sent out from Geneva to various countries throughout Europe.

[18] For example, Ed Stetzer writes, "The church that 'reformed' lost touch with the God who sends, and the mission of the church suffered." Ed Stetzer, *Planting New Churches in a Postmodern Age* (Nashville: B&H, 2003), 23. Missions professor Alton James says, "The Reformers' theology had little or no room for missions activity" and "a faulty theology served as a hindrance to the early Protestant Church being involved in missions." R. Alton James, "Post-Reformation Missions Pioneers," in *Discovering the Mission of God: Best Missional Practices for the 21st Century*, ed. Mike Barnett and Robin Martin (Downers Grove, IL: IVP, 2012), 251, 252. David Allen refers to the "general consensus" that the Reformers had almost no missionary vision. David Allen, "Preaching for a Great Commission Resurgence," in *Great Commission Resurgence: Fulfilling God's Mandate in our Time*, ed. Chuck Lawless and Adam Greenway (Nashville: B&H Academic, 2010), 286n6. In an essay in his highly influential textbook, *Perspectives on the World Christian Movement*, Ralph Winter says Christians of the Reformation era sent no missionaries, "did not even talk of mission outreach," and did "not even try to reach out." Ralph D. Winter, "The Kingdom Strikes Back: Ten Epochs of Redemptive History," in *Perspectives on the World Christian Movement: A Reader*, 4th ed., ed. Ralph D. Winter and Steven C. Hawthorne (Pasadena, CA: William Carey Library, 2009), 224..

Warneck's Definition of Missions

In popular theological literature and conversation, a common assumption is that the Reformers had no concern for the salvation of souls or the preaching of the gospel. However, this is not what Warneck argued at all. In fact, he concedes that the Reformers were effective in Christianizing Europe and, in this sense, the Reformation "may be said to have carried on a mission work at home on an extensive scale."[19] Warneck also concedes that Luther encouraged any who were taken captive by the Turks (a real threat in the sixteenth century) to be prepared to be a gospel witness to their captors. Luther urged Christians in that situation to faithful living and witness that they might "convert many." This would appear to be significant mission-mindedness but Warneck dismisses it as simply "the spirit of Christian testimony" rather than proper "missionary work" since it resulted from the scattering of persecution rather than the systematic sending out of missionaries.[20] Elsewhere Warneck quotes a long excerpt from an Ascension Sunday sermon of Luther's where he described how the gospel would go out to the whole world "sped ever farther by preachers hunted and persecuted hither and thither into the world." This, however, cannot be understood as an interest in world missions, Warneck says, because there is "no reference to any systematic missionary enterprise."[21] These are just two examples of many that show that Warneck is operating with a very narrow, even anachronistic, view of missions. To be reckoned as "missions" Warneck believes, it must be a systematic work, preferably by an institution outside the church that consistently sends missionaries to previously unevangelized areas.[22] As a result, Warneck completely discounts numerous mission-minded statements made by various Reformers because they do not call for the establishment of a missions agency. For example, Martin Bucer's rebuke of Christians for their attitude towards Jews and Turks is diminished because "there is little trace of earnestness as to how one may win their souls to Christ our Lord." Bucer prays for church leaders who will

---

[19] Warneck, *History of Protestant Missions* (1901), 8.
[20] Warneck, 15. Yet, the original spread of the gospel in Acts resulted from an outbreak of persecution.
[21] Warneck, 14.
[22] See also Klaus Detlev Schulz, *Mission from the Cross: The Lutheran Theology of Mission* (St. Louis: Concordia, 2009), 45–46. Schulz describes Warneck's conception of mission this way: "Warneck promotes a sociological and organizational concept of mission that encourages a 'sending' pursued deliberately by an institution, such as a mission society or a core group of individuals, and that works in geographic terms of leaving one territory for another, preferably across an ocean." Schulz, 46.

help the church labor for the salvation of Jews, Turks, "and all unbelievers to whom they may ever have any access." Warneck concedes that this
sounds like "a direct summons to missions," but it only appears so since
Bucer neglects to say anything about "instituting missions."[23] What Warneck means by this is clarified later when he faults Bucer for failing to see
the need to devise an "institution for the dissemination of Christianity."[24]

Warneck fails to find any evidence of mission activity or thinking in
the Reformers essentially because he has defined "missions" in accordance
with what he and others were doing in the nineteenth century.[25] His arguments merely prove that the Reformers were not participants in a nineteenth-century missions agency. But they do not prove that the Reformers
had little or no concern about the worldwide spread of the gospel or the
salvation of people from all over the world.[26]

This begs the question of a proper definition of "missions." Such a
definition is an ongoing topic of debate among contemporary missiolo-
gists. David Bosch warns against defining mission "too sharply and too
self-confidently." He states, "Ultimately, mission remains undefinable; it
should never be incarcerated in the narrow confines of our own predilec-
tions."[27] Instead of defining missions, he expounds the various elements
of missions. He clearly believes that missions involves taking the gospel
to a world in need, preaching, planting churches, discipling and meeting
needs in Jesus's name.[28] Bosch argues there is no theological basis for distinguishing "foreign" and "domestic" missions. He refers to the myth "that
travelling to foreign lands is the *sine qua non* for *any* kind of missionary
endeavor and the final test and criterion of what is truly missionary," and
says this idea has been demolished.[29] Bosch's survey suggests that modern

---

[23] Warneck, *History of Protestant Missions* (1901), 18.

[24] Warneck, 19.

[25] Jean-François Zorn has shown that the word "mission" was first used in regard to global gospel
outreach in the sixteenth century by Roman Catholics. This is why this specific term is not used by the
Reformers – it was a new term coined by those in opposition to them. Jean-François Zorn, "Did Calvin
Foster or Hinder the Missions?" *Exchange* 40, no. 2 (2011): 179–81.

[26] The charge that Warneck has anachronistically formulated his analysis is also made by Robert
Kolb, "Late Reformation Lutherans on Mission and Confession," *Lutheran Quarterly* 20, no. 1 (2006):
26. For a thorough critique of Warneck's conception of "mission" see Elias Medeiros, "The Reformers' Commitment to the Propagation of the Gospel to All Nations from 1555 to 1654" (PhD diss.,
Reformed Theological Seminary, 2009), especially 15–111.

[27] David Bosch, *Transforming Mission: Paradigm Shifts in Theology of Mission*, 20th Anniversary ed.
(Maryknoll, NY: Orbis, 2011), 9.

[28] See his table of contents as well as his closing comments on p. 519.

[29] Bosch, 10.

missiology has turned away from the narrow definition that governed Warneck's analysis. At the core, missions is the church joining in the mission of God to bring people into fellowship with himself by gospel proclamation, church planting, discipleship, and living out the ethical implications of the gospel.[30]

Warneck's Assessment of the Reformers' Theology

Even if Warneck's definition of missions is too restrictive, is there truth to the claim that the Reformers' theology kept them from seeing and embracing the missional mandate of Scripture? We will take up each of the three points of theology Warneck and others have listed as problematic.

First, did the Reformers teach that world missions was no longer an obligation for the church? Calvin explicitly rejects this idea in his commentary on Matt 28:20: "It ought likewise to be remarked, that this was not spoken to the apostles alone; for the Lord promises his assistance not for a single age only, but *even to the end of the world.*"[31] Furthermore, lecturing on Mic 4:3, Calvin stated, "The kingdom of Christ was only begun in the world, when God commanded the Gospel to be everywhere proclaimed, and … at this day its course is not as yet completed."[32] Whatever one thinks of Calvin's theology or mission involvement, he certainly did not teach that the Great Commission had been fulfilled in the apostolic era.[33]

Neither is it true that Luther taught that the day of missionary obligation had passed.[34] Writing on Matt 22:9, Luther stated, "This [time for missions] is not yet completed. This era continues so that the servants go out into the highways. The apostles began this work and we continue inviting all. The table will be full at the advent of the last day and when the

---

[30] This is similar to the definition suggested by Justice Anderson, that missions refers to "the conscious efforts on the part of the church, in its corporate capacity, or through voluntary agencies, to proclaim the gospel (with all this implies) among peoples and in regions where it is still unknown or only inadequately known." Justice Anderson, "An Overview of Missiology," in *Missiology: An Introduction to the Foundations, History, and Strategies of World Missions*, ed. John Mark Terry, Ebbie C. Smith, and Justice Anderson (Nashville: Broadman & Holman, 1998), 2. See also Bruce Ashford, ed., *Theology and Practice of Mission: God, the Church, and the Nations* (Nashville: B&H Academic, 2011).

[31] John Calvin, "Commentary on a Harmony of the Evangelists," in *Calvin's Commentaries*, 22 vols., trans. W. Pringle (Grand Rapids: Baker, 1984), 17:391.

[32] Calvin, "Commentary on Micah," in *Calvin's Commentaries*, 14:265.

[33] Part of the problem with this misrepresentation of the Reformers is that later readers expect the Reformers to speak of missions from the same texts modern readers do (e.g., Matt 28:19–20).

[34] John Warwick Montgomery stated, "To attribute such views to Luther is, however . . . to fly directly in the face of the evidence." John Warwick Montgomery, "Luther and Missions," *Evangelical Missions Quarterly* 3, no. 4 (1967): 193–202.

Gospel has been made known in the whole world."[35] He also stated, "It is necessary always to proceed to those to whom no preaching has been done, in order that the number [of Christians] may become greater."[36] In contrast to Warneck's accusation that Luther thought there was no need to take the gospel further because it had already reached the whole world via the apostles, Luther said,

> Their preaching went out to the whole world even though it has not yet reached the whole world. This outcome has begun and its goal is set though it is not yet completed and accomplished; instead, it shall be extended through preaching even farther until the Day of Judgment. When this preaching reaches all corners of the world and is heard and pronounced, then it is complete and in every respect finished and the Last Day will also arrive.[37]

Luther anticipates that people "will be sent by God among the nations as preachers and thus draw many people to themselves and through themselves to Christ."[38] Luther specifically called for the gospel to be taken to the Bohemians, the Russians, and the Muslim Turks.[39] Within a short time after his death, Luther's disciples had set out on mission work to all of these groups.[40] And these men, like those sent to other parts of Europe, went out knowing they were likely to be executed.

Second, did the Reformers' doctrine of election prevent them from doing mission work? Warneck says that since Luther saw salvation as a work completely of God's grace, he did not think a "human missionary agency"

---

[35] WA 17/1:442.46ff., cited in Ingemar Öberg, *Luther and World Mission: A Historical and Systematic Study with Special Reference to Luther's Bible Exposition* (St. Louis: Concordia, 2007), 134. Werner Elert has a helpful discussion of how Luther's comments have been misunderstood as suggesting the era of world mission closed with the apostles. Werner Elert, *The Structure of Lutheranism*, trans. Walter A. Hansen (St. Louis: Concordia, 1962), 386.

[36] Cited in Elert, *Structure of Lutheranism*, 389.

[37] Luther, "Ascension Sermon, May 29, 1522," WA 10/3:139.17–140.16. Cited in Volker Stolle, *The Church Comes from All Nations: Luther Texts on Mission* (St. Louis: Concordia, 2003), 24. See also Luther's "Sermon on Titus 2:11–15, Christmas Postil, 1522," WA 10/1.1:21.3–23.14 (cited in Stolle, 98–99) where he clearly says the work of taking the gospel to the whole earth is not yet completed.

[38] Luther, *The Prophet Zechariah Expounded*, LW 20:305–6. Cited in Stolle, 97.

[39] Warneck also critiques Luther's idea of world mission by saying Luther thought the mandate was simply that the gospel be preached to all people, not that they would necessarily believe. Warneck is bothered that "the Reformer [Luther] does not understand the progress of the Gospel through the whole world in the sense that Christianity would become everywhere the ruling religion, or that all men would be won to believe the gospel." Warneck, *History of Protestant Missions* (1901), 13.

[40] Öberg, *Luther and World Mission*, 498–99.

was part of God's plan.[41] He asserts the same of Bucer and Calvin. For proof he simply cites one statement by Calvin without context: "We are taught that the kingdom of Christ is neither to be advanced nor maintained by the industry of men, but this is the work of God alone; for believers are taught to rest solely on His blessing."[42] Later writers often make this same assertion, citing the same quote without context or any mention of where it is found.[43] It is a strong statement, but anyone familiar with Calvin's writings will recognize his affirmation that salvation and the advance of God's kingdom ultimately depend on God alone. However, even a cursory reading of Calvin will show that he also strongly emphasizes human responsibility as well as recognizing that God works through means.[44] For example Calvin states that the "gospel does not fall like rain from the clouds, but is brought by the hands of men," and God "makes use of our exertions, and employs us as his instruments, for cultivating his field."[45] Warneck does not demonstrate how Calvin's understanding of election hindered missions. Neither do later writers. It is assumed that the doctrine of election "made missions appear extraneous if God had already chosen those he would save,"[46] or, "If God wills the conversion of the heathen, they will be saved without human instrumentality."[47] Yet, we have already seen various statements from Luther and Calvin that called on believers to proclaim the gospel so that people might be saved. Furthermore, if this doctrine made foreign missions moot, why did it not stifle mission work within Europe? Even Warneck concedes that this work in Europe was significant. Why would a belief in God's sovereignty prevent the Reformers from trying to evangelize overseas but not preclude them taking the gospel to France (or other areas of Europe) at the risk of their lives?

---

[41] Warneck, *History of Protestant Missions* (1901), 16. Once again Warneck sees missions only in terms of a sending "agency."

[42] Warneck, 20. I have not been able to find the source of this quote. In the books I have found, authors quote it without citation or simply cite Warneck.

[43] E.g., Kane, 74; Olson, 103.

[44] Jean-François Zorn, "Did Calvin Foster or Hinder the Missions?," 178, 184, is especially helpful on Calvin's emphasis on the necessity of means. See also David Calhoun, "John Calvin: Missionary Hero or Missionary Failure?" *Presbyterion* 5, no. 1 (Spring 1979): 18–20.

[45] Calvin, "Commentaries on the Epistle of Paul to the Romans," in *Calvin's Commentaries*, 19:399; "Commentary on a Harmony of the Evangelists," 16:121. Elsewhere Calvin also says the fact that ministers help rescue souls from death "ought to be no small encouragement for godly teachers to stir up the heat of their … desire, when they hear that they call back miserable souls from destruction, and that they help those who should otherwise perish, that they may be saved." "Commentary upon the Acts of the Apostles," 19:98.

[46] Tucker, 97. See also page 20.

[47] Kane, 74.

Last, Warneck asserts that the Reformers did not believe there was much time for mission engagement since the world would end soon. Latourette, Kane, and Tucker all repeat this claim without any citations from Luther or any demonstration of how the idea shaped actions other than saying the Reformers (particularly Luther) did not think there was time for mission work. Warneck conceded that Luther nowhere says the imminent end of the age was a reason for not doing missions. Thus, this connection is merely a guess. Nevertheless, Warneck says the reason Luther never makes the connection is that even apart from his eschatology, Luther knew nothing of a duty for world mission.[48] So, Luther's eschatology kept him from missions, and we know this because even though we cannot link his views on eschatology and missions, Luther was ignorant of a missions duty anyway. This is a convoluted argument, and yet people have repeated it for over a century.[49]

Thus, all three areas of doctrinal critique fail. Whether or not one agrees with the specific doctrines in view, the arguments fail to prove either that these doctrines were held by the Reformers or that they hindered mission thinking or work.[50]

Evaluation of the Reformers Themselves

Now we must turn to the deeds and writings of three Reformers to see what evidence we find of missions involvement and evangelistic impulse. Since we have critiqued Warneck's narrow definition of missions, in the Reformers' words and deeds, we will now turn to the Reformers' active calling of people to faith in Christ and a concern for the gospel to reach the nations.

Mission within Christendom

One key problem in Warneck and those who follow him is their failure to recognize the missionary setting for Protestants in Europe in the sixteenth century. The gospel was largely unknown by the vast majority of people in Europe, and the Reformers labored to get this gospel message to as many people as possible. Calvin's preface to his *Institutes of the*

---

[48] Warneck, *History of Protestant Missions* (1901), 16.

[49] See Schulz, 51–52, for further refutation of the idea that Luther was certain of the imminent end of the world and that this hindered missions.

[50] It will not do to argue as Gordon Olson does that at least we know some people have used the doctrine of election to stifle mission endeavors. Practically every positive doctrine has been abused by someone over the years. Olson and Fanning, *What in the World?*, 104. The question in view is whether the doctrine hindered mission work in the Reformers themselves.

Christian Religion declares that his writing was intended to aid his fellow countrymen in France, "very many of whom I knew to be hungering and thirsting for Christ; but I saw very few who had been duly imbued with even a slight knowledge of him."[51] Calvin expounded the Scriptures to help people know Christ. One biographer says, "Calvin in Strasbourg or Geneva was also a missionary, an envoy."[52] Luther also said that many of the people who attended the church services "do not believe and are not yet Christians." Thus, he said, "the gospel must be publicly preached to move them to believe and become Christians."[53]

Scott Hendrix's *Recultivating the Vineyard: The Reformation Agendas of Christianization* has been particularly helpful in demonstrating the mission element involved in the Reformers' work in Europe.[54] His basic premise is that the "Reformers saw themselves in a missionary situation in which the faith had to be taught to a populace they judged to be inadequately informed."[55] The entire program of the Reformers was to re-evangelize their native lands. Calvin, for example, saw himself as a missionary, laboring "to turn nominal believers into real Christians."[56] Hendrix grants it took some time before full-fledged international mission work began in Reformation churches, but this developing outward reach was an organic result of Reformation ideas. "The Reformation's own sources state plainly how reformers saw their enterprise as a missionary campaign to renew and replant Christianity in European culture."[57] Nineteenth-century scholars working in a largely Christianized Europe could miss the fact that in the mind of the Reformers the majority of Europe in their day was in need of evangelization.[58]

---

[51] John Calvin, *Institutes of the Christian Religion*, trans. Ford Lewis Battles, Library of Christian Classics, vol. 20 (Philadelphia: Westminster, 1960), 9.

[52] Bernard Cottret, *Calvin: A Biography*, trans. Wallace McDonald (Grand Rapids: Eerdmans, 2000), 138.

[53] Luther, "German Mass," LW 53:62–64. Cited in Stolle, *From All Nations*, 44.

[54] Scott Hendrix, *Recultivating the Vineyard: The Reformation Agendas of Christianization* (Louisville: Westminster John Knox, 2004).

[55] Hendrix, 172.

[56] Hendrix, 95. Hendrix also cites the revised preface of the 1559 edition of the *Institutes* where Calvin says, "God has filled my mind with zeal to spread his kingdom and to further the public good" (88).

[57] Hendrix, 163–64. Theodor Bibliander (1509–1564), was a biblical scholar from Zurich who, according to Hendrix, was probably the best informed among the Reformers about Islam. He published a book on how Christians should respond to the Turks; he also published the first printed version of the Koran in Latin. He "emphasized that God willed all peoples, including Muslims, to be saved" (166–68).

[58] Today we can also easily miss that in the sixteenth century a variety of distinct cultures and people groups existed within what is now the boundary of a single country.

The training and sending out of pastors that occurred in Geneva and Wittenberg should be understood as an essential element of the Reformers' missionary campaign. The missionary zeal of these pastors is underscored by the fact that many or most of the areas to which they went were hostile, so they went out at the risk of their lives. Under Calvin's leadership, Geneva became "the hub of a vast missionary enterprise"[59] and "a dynamic center or nucleus from which the vital missionary energy it generated radiated out into the world beyond."[60] Protestant refugees from all over Europe fled to Geneva; they came not merely for safety but also to learn from Calvin the doctrines of the Reformation so they could return home to spread the true gospel. The registers of the Venerable Company of Pastors in Geneva record numerous people sent out from Geneva during Calvin's time to "evangelize foreign parts."[61] The records are incomplete, and eventually, due to persecution, it became too dangerous to record the names of those sent out, although it numbered more than 100 in one year alone. Bruce Gordon refers to the sending of such a large number of missionaries into France the "most audacious missionary effort" undertaken by the Genevan church.[62] By 1557 it was a normal part of business for the Genevan pastors to send missionaries into France. Robert M. Kingdon called it a "concentrated missionary effort."[63] Philip Hughes notes that Geneva became a "school of missions" that had as one of its purposes "to send out witnesses" who would take the gospel "far and wide." Hughes describes Geneva as "a dynamic centre of missionary concern and activity, an axis from which the light of the Good News radiated forth through the testimony of those who, after thorough preparation in this 'school,' were sent forth in the service of Jesus Christ."[64]

---

[59] Raymond K. Anderson, "Calvin and Missions," *Christian History*, 5 no. 4 (Fall 1986): 23.

[60] Philip E. Hughes, "John Calvin: Director of Missions," in *The Heritage of John Calvin: Heritage Hall Lectures 1960–1970*, ed. John H. Bratt (Grand Rapids: Eerdmans, 1973), 45. Portions of this section of the essay are taken from Ray Van Neste, "John Calvin on Missions and Evangelism," *Founders Journal* 33 (1998): 15–21.

[61] Alister McGrath, *A Life of John Calvin, a Study in the Shaping of Western Culture* (Oxford; Basil Blackwell Ltd., 1990), 182. Cf. Philip Hughes, ed. and trans., *The Register of the Company of Pastors of Geneva in the Time of Calvin* (Grand Rapids: Eerdmans, 1966), 308.

[62] Bruce Gordon, *Calvin* (New Haven: Yale University Press, 2009), 312. Calhoun states, "The degree of commitment of Calvin and the pastors of Geneva to this missionary outreach is nothing less than amazing." David Calhoun, "John Calvin: Missionary Hero or Missionary Failure?," 28.

[63] Robert M. Kingdon, "Calvinist Religious Aggression," in *The French Wars of Religion, How Important Were Religious Factors?*, ed. J. H. M. Salmon (Lexington, MA: D. C. Heath, 1967), 6.

[64] Hughes, *Register*, 25. See also Michael A. G. Haykin, "John Calvin's Missionary Influence in France," *Reformation and Revival* 10.4 (Fall 2001): 35–44.

Zorn suggests that Calvin developed a "missionary theology for Europe."[65] For good reason, Hendrix concludes, "The Reformation was a missionary campaign that envisioned a renewed Christian society in Europe."[66]

There is no need to discount the words and deeds of the Reformers in regard to the evangelization of their neighbors and neighboring lands, as Warneck did. Given the persecution they faced and the difficulty of travel, we should commend their work. Critics also seem to miss the fact that Germany, for example, did not become a unified nation until later in the nineteenth century, so Protestant preachers were quite often crossing national lines, engaging with "other countries," according to the thinking of the time. Let us then turn our attention to a sampling from the writings of Luther, Bucer, and Calvin, as representative Reformers, to see the attention given to concern for the salvation of others.

Luther (1483–1546)

Although it does not seem to have been picked up in most evangelical missions textbooks, substantial attention has already been given to Luther's comments on evangelism and world mission. Volker Stolle's *The Church Comes from All Nations: Luther Texts on Mission* gleaned significant sections from Luther where he advocates for the task of taking the gospel to all people.[67] Robert Kolb hailed Stolle's work as "more historically sensitive" than Warneck, and it "demonstrates Luther's interest in the spread of the Christian faith."[68] Werner Elert has also drawn from the rich resources of Luther's mission-oriented comments to demonstrate Luther's concern for mission, noting how his concept of mission differed from (and was healthier than) Warneck's view.[69]

Ingemar Öberg, in his *Luther and World Mission: A Historical and Systematic Study with Special Reference to Luther's Bible Exposition*, demonstrated thoroughly Luther's drive to get the gospel to all people.[70] Robert Kolb commended Öberg's work stating that he had mined a "wide variety

---

[65] Zorn, "Did Calvin Foster or Hinder the Missions?," 178. Zorn's article is perhaps the best one on Calvin and missions.

[66] Hendrix, *Recultivating the Vineyard*, 174.

[67] Stolle, *From All Nations*.

[68] Kolb, "Lutherans on Mission," 40.

[69] Elert, *Structure of Lutheranism*, 385–402.

[70] Ingemar Öberg, *Luther and World Mission: A Historical and Systematic Study with Special Reference to Luther's Bible Exposition* (St. Louis: Concordia, 2007).

of sources within Luther's writings with great care and acumen."[71] As a result, Kolb said, Öberg showed the wealth of insights to be found in Luther's writings "for sound mission thinking."[72]

There is no need or space for restating all that Stolle, Öberg, and Elert have gleaned from Luther, but in what follows I will draw some examples from their work and my own observations to demonstrate Luther's evangelistic and missionary concern.[73] Luther's correspondence, alone, was a missionary endeavor as he wrote to people all over Europe urging gospel truths and counseling leaders and others in how to advance the cause of Christ.[74] Furthermore, Luther taught his people to pray for the conversion of unbelievers and for the gospel to be preached over the whole world. In his brief work written to teach his people how to pray he instructs them to meditate on each petition of the Lord's Prayer, turning that into specific prayers. Luther provides an example of how one might pray from each petition, and in the first three petitions he explicitly prays for the conversion of unbelievers.[75]

This evangelistic concern can also be seen in Luther's exposition of the Lord's Prayer in his Large Catechism. Discussing the second petition, "Your kingdom come," Luther explains that it teaches us, among other things, to pray that the kingdom "may gain recognition and followers among other people and advance with power throughout the world." Later in the same question he says this petition teaches us to pray both that believers might grow in the kingdom and that "it may come to those who are not yet in it." Concluding he writes, "All this is to simply say: 'Dear Father, we pray Thee, give us thy Word, that the gospel may be sincerely preached throughout the world and that it may be received by faith and work and live in us.'"[76] People who pray regularly for the conversion of people around the world

---

[71] Robert Kolb, foreword to, Öberg, *Luther and World Mission,* viii.

[72] Kolb, foreword, viii. See also John Warwick Montgomery, "Luther and Missions," *Evangelical Missions Quarterly* 3, no. 4 (1967): 193–202.

[73] Schulz, *Mission from the Cross,* 46–47 n3, lists more works that highlight the mission emphasis in Luther's writings.

[74] For a fascinating graphic display of the geographic distribution of Luther's correspondence, see Ernest G. Schwiebert, *Luther and His Times: The Reformation from a New Perspective* (St. Louis: Concordia, 1950), 4. Plass calls Luther's correspondence "a missionary influence, as was the University of Wittenberg." Ewald M. Plass, *What Luther Says, An Anthology* (Saint Louis: Concordia, 1959), 958.

[75] Martin Luther, *A Simple Way to Pray,* trans. Matthew C. Harrison (St. Louis: Concordia, 2012).

[76] Luther, *Larger Catechism,* 2.51–54; in Theodore G. Tappert, *The Book of Concord: The Confessions of the Evangelical Lutheran Church* (Philadelphia: Fortress, 1959), 427–28.

are a mission-minded people. Pastors who teach their people to pray this way are mission-minded pastors.

As noted previously, Warneck conceded that Luther "with all earnestness" urged "the preaching of the gospel, and longs for a free course for it" but said "nowhere does Luther indicate the heathen as the objects of evangelistic work."[77] However, preaching on Matt 23:15, Luther says, "The very best of all works is that the heathen have been led from idolatry to God."[78] Furthermore, the conversion of the "heathen" was a significant theme in a number of Luther's hymns, including this one based on Psalm 67:

> Would that the Lord would grant us grace,
> With blessings rich provide us,
> And with clear shining let his face,
> To life eternal light us;
> That we his gracious work may know,
> And what is his good pleasure,
> And also to the heathen show,
> Christ's riches without measure
> And unto God convert them.[79]

Another hymn of Luther's based on Mark 16:15–16 and Luke 24:46, says,

> Christ to all his followers says: Go forth
> Give to all men acquaintance
> That lost in sin lies the whole earth,
> And must turn to repentance.
> Who trusts and who is baptized, each one
> Is thereby blest forever;
> Is from that hour a new-born man,
> And thenceforth dying never,
> The kingdom shall inherit.[80]

In another hymn, based on Simeon's song in Luke 2:28–32, Luther also taught his people to embrace world evangelization.

---

[77] Warneck, *History of Protestant Missions* (1884), 12.

[78] Cited in Plass, *What Luther Says*, 957. Also in Elert, *Structure of Lutheranism*, 390.

[79] LW 53:234, cited in Öberg, *Luther and World Mission*, 496. Öberg provides other examples as well.

[80] Cited in Öberg, 496.

It was God's love that sent you forth
As man's salvation,
Inviting to yourself the earth,
Ev'ry nation,
By your wholesome healing Word
Resounding round our planet
You are the health and saving light of lands in darkness;
You feed and lighten those in night
With your kindness.
All God's people find in you
Their treasure, joy and glory.[81]

Luther's hymns were central to the piety of Christians who embraced his teachings. These hymns were sung by families and at work, thus significantly shaping the thinking and lives of the people.[82] The inclusion of such explicit mission themes in these hymns is significant.

Luther is abundantly clear about the duty of believers, not just magistrates or official clergy, to share the gospel with others. He says "one must always preach the Gospel so that one may bring some more to become Christians."[83] Furthermore, "It would be insufferable for someone to associate with people and not reveal what is useful for the salvation of their souls."[84] Indeed, Luther says, "If the need were to arise, all of us should be ready to die in order to bring a soul to God."[85] Luther recounts his own conversations with Jews where he sought to demonstrate Jesus is the Messiah and to call them to faith.[86] Luther states, "It is certain that a Christian not only has the right and power to teach God's word but has the duty to do so on pain of losing his soul and of God's disfavor." Luther then answers

---

[81] "In Peace and Joy I Now Depart" (Lutheran Worship 185.3–4) "Lobgesang des Simeon" (Hymn of Simeon) 1524 Evangelisch-Lutherisches Kirchengesangbuch 310.3–4 WA 35:439.8–20. Cited in Stolle, *From All Nations*, 49–50.

[82] See, for example, Robin Leaver, *The Whole Church Sings: Congregational Singing in Luther's Wittenberg* (Grand Rapids: Eerdmans, 2017); and Christopher Boyd Brown, *Singing the Gospel: Lutheran Hymns and the Success of the Reformation* (Cambridge, MA: Harvard University Press, 2005).

[83] "Sermon on the Good Shepherd," 1523. WA 12:540.3–15. Cited in Stolle, *From All Nations*, 26.

[84] "Sermons on the First Book Of Moses," WA 24:261.26–262.11. Cited in Stolle, 16.

[85] Plass, *What Luther Says*, 2836.

[86] "Sermon on Jeremiah 23:6–8," November 25, 1526. WA 20:569.25–570.12. Cited in Stolle, *From All Nations*, 61. Luther's interaction with the Jews is too large a subject to delve into here. He urges gentleness toward them for the sake of evangelism in his early work. His later, harsh work is theologically, not racially, motivated, where in frustration he calls for punishments with the aim of drawing them to Christ. This is misguided evangelistic zeal with terrible consequences.

the objection that someone might raise that all are not ordained to the gospel ministry. He says that if you find yourself in a place where there are no other Christians, then one "needs no other call than to be a Christian …. It is his duty to preach and to teach the gospel to erring heathen or non-Christians, because of the duty of brotherly love."[87]

As Herbert Blöchle said, "Luther did not speak just on occasions and periodically to the questions about mission to the heathens. His entire theology is rather permeated by a 'missionary dimension.'"[88]

Martin Bucer (1491–1551)

As noted earlier, Warneck conceded some missionary interest by Bucer, even though Warneck did not discuss Bucer's book, *Concerning the True Care of Souls,* which is filled with evangelistic pathos and exhortation. In this book Bucer even rebukes the church for failing to mount a more serious missionary endeavor to the "Jews and Turks" and says that the current threat from the Turks is God's judgment for their failure.[89]

Bucer calls for earnest, zealous evangelistic labor. To pastors he says, "True carers of souls and faithful ministers of Christ are not to miss anyone anywhere out with the word of salvation, but diligently to endeavor to seek out all those to whom they may have access in order to lead them to Christ our Lord."[90] Bucer calls for perseverance in sharing the gospel with people who do not readily accept it: "Faithful members of Christ are not to give up lightly on anyone."[91] In fact, Bucer says, "One should be so persistent with people [in calling them to faith] that to the evil flesh it seems to be a compulsion and urgent pressing."[92] For Bucer, zealous missionary work is rooted in God's desires and stirred by the example of Paul:

---

[87] *The Right and Power of a Christian Congregation*, 1523. LW 39:309–10. Cited by Stolle, *From All Nations*, 21. Additional examples of Luther's theology of missions are referenced throughout Stolle's work, particularly pages 20, 23, and 43. See also *Sermons on 1 Peter,* first ed., 1523. WA 12:318.25–319.6; *Exposition of the Fourteenth and Fifteenth Chapters of the Gospel of St. John*, LW 24:87–88; and *German Mass*, LW 53:62–64.

[88] Quoted in Schulz, *Mission from the Cross*, 48.

[89] Martin Bucer, *Concerning the True Care of Souls*, trans. Peter Beale (Carlisle, PA: Banner of Truth, 2009), 87. Hendrix also notes that in spite of the known difficulty and dangers "a sixteenth-century mission to the Turks was nonetheless supported by Erasmus, Luther, Bullinger and Bibliander." Hendrix, *Recultivating the Vineyard*, 168.

[90] Bucer, 76. "Carers for souls" is Bucer's typical phrase for pastors, even though a term for "pastor" was available.

[91] Bucer, 78.

[92] Bucer, 78.

> He [God] desires that they should be sought wherever they are scattered, and sought with such seriousness and diligence that one should be ready to be all things to all men, as dear Paul was [1 Cor. 9:22], and even to hazard one's own life, as the Lord himself did, so that the lost lambs might be found and won.[93]

Bucer affirmed God's sovereign election of souls to salvation, but did not see this as conflicting with energetic missionary enterprise:

> But it is not the Lord's will to reveal to us the secrets of his election; rather he commands us to go out into all the world and preach his gospel to every creature. . . . The fact that all people have been made by God and are God's creatures should therefore be reason enough for us to go to them, seeking with the utmost faithfulness to bring them to eternal life.[94]

Combining the pastoral care noted previously and evangelistic zeal, Bucer prayed, "May the Lord Jesus, our chief Shepherd and Bishop, grant us such elders and carers of souls as will seek his lambs which are still lost."[95]

John Calvin (1509–1564)

Contrary to the impression or assumption of many, Calvin exhibited deep evangelistic concern.[96] Refugees came to Geneva, fleeing persecution, with many coming to be trained to return to their countries as gospel preachers. Pete Wilcox states, "Even if not all of those who attended Calvin's lectures were missionaries in training, the majority were caught up with him in an evangelistic enterprise."[97]

In 1556, Calvin and his fellow ministers helped support the first mission endeavor to target the New World, with a group sent to Brazil.[98] Warneck discounted this as a mission endeavor because he questioned Calvin's

---

[93] Bucer, 78.

[94] Bucer, 77.

[95] Bucer, 193.

[96] Indeed, Benoît could state of Calvin, "From the outset his theological work is an effort of evangelization and of witnessing." J. D. Benoît, "Pastoral Care of the Prophet," in *John Calvin, Contemporary Prophet*, ed. Jacob Hoogstra (Grand Rapids: Baker, 1959), 51.

[97] Pete Wilcox, "Evangelisation in the Thought and Practice of John Calvin," *Anvil* 12, no. 3 (1995): 212.

[98] Cf. R. Pierce Beaver, "The Genevan Mission to Brazil," in *Heritage of John Calvin*, ed. John H. Bratt (Grand Rapids: Eerdmans, 1973), 55–73; Kenneth J. Stewart, "Calvinism and Missions: The Contested Relationship Revisited," *Themelios* 34, no. 1 (2009): 63–78.

involvement or sympathy and doubted whether the aim was really to evangelize indigenous people or just to provide religious services for the European settlers. However, we have a good account of the Genevan church's actions in the personal journal of Jean de Léry, a member of the church in Geneva. A man seeking to establish a French colony in Brazil sent a letter to Calvin and the Genevan church asking for ministers of the gospel to accompany the settlers. According to de Léry the letter specifically asked for preachers and other people "well instructed in the Christian religion" so that they might teach the other Europeans and "bring savages to the knowledge of their salvation."[99] The firsthand account we have of the event makes the missionary element of the endeavor crystal clear. Furthermore, the response of the church to this request is striking. De Léry records, "Upon receiving these letters and hearing this news, the church of Geneva at once gave thanks to God for the extension of the reign of Jesus Christ in a country so distant and likewise so foreign and among a nation entirely without knowledge of the true God."[100] This is not the response of a church that has no heart for missions, a church concerned only with stabilizing itself. Rather, this is the result of teaching and preaching that held up the responsibility to proclaim the gospel to all people.[101] Here we see the longing for opportunity to engage in world missions that Warneck says is missing.

Warneck also said the Brazil mission does not qualify as a mission endeavor because it did not last long enough. It is true that through treachery the effort came to an end. However, obedience and not success has always been the call. While the Brazil mission was still ongoing, a letter was sent to Calvin from one of the missionaries. He described the difficulties of their evangelistic efforts but said, "Since the Most High has given us this task, we expect this Edom to become a future possession of Christ."[102] Not only was this clearly a mission endeavor, the missionaries themselves persevered in a most difficult task buoyed by confidence in a sovereign God.

What kind of preaching led to a church that had such missionaries as these and that responded so jubilantly to mission possibilities despite the difficulties? Calvin's sermons have been too much neglected by scholars,

---

[99] Beaver, 61.

[100] Beaver, 61.

[101] Beaver says Calvin was not in Geneva when the church decided to send these ministers. Beaver, 61. However, Wilcox corrects this point showing that Calvin was in Geneva and, thus, included among the celebrants. Wilcox, "Evangelisation," 216.

[102] Beaver, "Genevan Mission to Brazil," 64.

but there we find the type of exhortation and prayer that would propel evangelistic activity as he regularly and earnestly urged his people to seek the salvation of the nations.[103] For example, preaching on Deuteronomy, Calvin said, "If we have any kindness in us, seeing that we see men go to destruction until God has got them under his obedience: ought we not to be moved with pity to draw the silly souls out of hell and to bring them into the way of salvation?"[104] In his sermons on 1 Timothy, preached in the year leading up to the Brazilian mission, Calvin regularly concludes with a prayer for the salvation of the nations.[105] He tells pastors God has made them ministers for the purpose of saving souls and thus they must labor "mightily, and with greater zeal and earnestness" for the salvation of souls.[106] Even when people reject the salvation offered to them, Calvin tells pastors they must continue to "devote" themselves to this evangelistic work and "take pains" in calling people to faith so they might "call as many to God as they can." Calvin urges, "We must take pains to draw all the world to salvation."[107]

Calvin expounds Paul's call to pray "for all men" (1 Tim 2:1 KJV) with application to the church's missionary responsibility to the world: "Call upon God and ask him to work toward the salvation of the whole world, and that we give ourselves to this work both night and day."[108] Throughout this sermon Calvin calls for fervent prayer and persistent action for the salvation of souls, urging his people to "have pity and compassion on the poor unbelievers."[109] He tells his people, "The greatest pleasure we can do to men is to pray to God for them, and call upon him for their salvation."[110] It is no surprise, then, that at various places in these sermons Calvin speaks of the salvation of our neighbors as being "dear to us."

This evangelistic compassion is rooted in the character and action of God, as Calvin states in his sermon on 1 Tim 2:3–5:

---

[103] Parker provides a moving description of Calvin's preaching and its power. T. H. L. Parker, *Calvin's Preaching* (Louisville, KY: Westminster John Knox, 1992)

[104] John Calvin, *Sermons on Deuteronomy*, trans. Arthur Golding (London, 1583; facsimile repr., Edinburgh: Banner of Truth Trust, 1987), 1219. From a sermon on Deuteronomy 33.

[105] John Calvin, *John Calvin's Sermons on 1 Timothy*, ed. Ray Van Neste and Brian Denker, 2 vols. (Jackson, TN: CreateSpace, 2016). For more on Calvin's evangelistic prayers, see Elsie McKee, "Calvin and Praying for 'All People Who Dwell on Earth,'" *Interpretation* 63, no. 2 (April 2009): 130–40.

[106] John Calvin, *Sermons on 1 Timothy*, 2:133.

[107] Calvin, 2:141.

[108] Calvin, 1:156.

[109] Calvin, 1:156.

[110] Calvin, 1:159.

Let us mark first of all when the Gospel is preached to us that it is just as if God reached out his hand (as he says by the prophet Isaiah, Isa. 65:2) and said to us, "Come to me." It is a matter which ought to touch us to the quick, when we see that God comes to seek us, and does not wait until we come to him, but shows that he is ready to be made at one with us, although we were his daily enemies. He seeks nothing but to wipe out all our faults and make us partakers of the salvation that was purchased for us by our Lord Jesus Christ. And thus we see how worthily we have to esteem the Gospel, and what a treasure it is.[111]

Some have said that the ministry of the Reformers was concerned only with teaching further the Christians who were in their midst. These sermons demonstrate how wrong this is about Calvin. He stated, "It is not enough for us to teach other men faithfully, unless we have a zeal to edify and care for the salvation of all men."[112] He tells his congregation that believers "must draw their neighbors to God in such a way that they must go with them."[113] Specifically speaking to pastors, Calvin encourages them to ask, "'Why has God placed me here?' To the end that church should increase more and more, and the salvation of men be always sought for."[114]

Some have argued that Calvin's view of predestination prevented any evangelistic impulse. But notice that Calvin is not inhibited from calling all who hear him to Christ. "So often as we preach the doctrine of salvation, we show that God is ready to receive all who come to him, that the gate is open to those who call upon him, and to be assured that their inheritance is prepared for them there above, and they can never be deceived of it."[115] Commenting on James 5:20, Calvin also states,

> To give food to the hungry, and drink to the thirsty, we see how much Christ values such acts; but the salvation of the soul is esteemed by him much more precious than the life of the body. We must therefore take heed lest souls perish through our sloth, whose salvation God puts in a manner in our hands. Not that we can bestow salvation on

---

[111] Calvin, 1:193.
[112] Calvin, 1:130.
[113] Calvin, 2:130.
[114] Calvin, 2:127–28.
[115] Calvin, 2:388.

them; but that God by our ministry delivers and saves those who seem otherwise to be nigh destruction.[116]

In fact, Calvin strongly rebukes those who lack evangelistic concern:

So then let us mark first of all that all who care not whether they bring their neighbors to the way of salvation or not, and those who do not care to bring the poor unbelievers also, instead being willing to let them go to destruction, show plainly that they make no account of God's honor. ... And thus we see how cold we are and negligent to pray for those who have need and are this day in the way to death and damnation.[117]

Rather than someone who was merely concerned with organizing the new Protestant church or for deeper teaching, we find in Calvin a true shepherd who cares for his people and yearns for the salvation of souls.[118] As he stated, "We cannot bestow our lives and our deaths better than by bringing poor souls who were lost, and on their way to everlasting death, to salvation."[119]

Conclusion

In his history of Christian missions, Stephen Neill says, "When everything favorable has been said that can be said [about the Reformers' commitment to mission], and when all possible evidences from the writings have been collected, it amounts to exceedingly little."[120] This brief article has shown this to be untrue, and I have not been able to include the large number of quotes others have cited in the writings of the Reformers on this topic. It is time for the narrative to change. The evidence is ample; the conclusion is clear. The charge of apathy regarding missions among the Reformers is common but unfair. If we reject an anachronistic, narrow, unscriptural definition of missions, it is obvious that the Reformers were significantly mission minded and present to us a largely untapped resource for mission strategy, especially as the West is once again increasingly devoid of the

---

[116] John Calvin, "Commentaries on the Catholic Epistles," in *Calvin's Commentaries*, 22 vols., trans. W. Pringle (Grand Rapids: Baker, 1999), 22:361.

[117] Calvin, *Sermons on 1 Timothy*, 1:201.

[118] See also Michael A. G. Haykin and C. Jeffrey Robinson Sr., *To the Ends of the Earth: Calvin's Missional Vision and Legacy* (Wheaton: Crossway, 2014).

[119] Calvin, *Sermons on 1 Timothy*, 1:297.

[120] Neill, *History of Christian Missions*, 189.

gospel. They did not launch full-blown overseas mission projects as later Christians would, but that is due to the limitations of their time and not due to a lack of concern for missions.[121] Indeed, their work laid the foundation for the later expansion of world mission endeavor. Rather than denigrating these forebears, we need to examine their work afresh to see what lessons they may have for us in this hour of great need for gospel advance.[122]

Bibliography

Allen, David. "Preaching for a Great Commission Resurgence." In *Great Commission Resurgence: Fulfilling God's Mandate in our Time*, ed. Chuck Lawless and Adam Greenway, 281–98. Nashville: B&H Academic, 2010.

Anderson, Justice. "An Overview of Missiology." In *Missiology: An Introduction to the Foundations, History, and Strategies of World Missions*, ed. John Mark Terry, Ebbie Smith, and Justice Anderson, 1–17. Nashville: Broadman & Holman, 1998.

_____. "Medieval and Renaissance Missions (500–1792)." In *Missiology: An Introduction to the Foundations, History, and Strategies of World Missions*, ed. John Mark Terry, Ebbie Smith, and Justice Anderson, 183–98. Nashville: Broadman & Holman, 1998.

Anderson, Raymond K. "Calvin and Missions." *Christian History*, 5, no. 4 (Fall 1986): 23.

Ashford, Bruce, ed. *Theology and Practice of Mission: God, the Church, and the Nations*. Nashville: B&H Academic, 2011.

Beaver, R. Pierce. "The Genevan Mission to Brazil." In *The Heritage of John Calvin*, ed. John H. Bratt, 55–73. Grand Rapids: Eerdmans, 1973.

Benoit, Jean-Daniel. "Pastoral Care of the Prophet." In *John Calvin, Contemporary Prophet*, ed. Jacob Hoogstra, 51–67. Grand Rapids: Baker, 1959.

Bosch, David. *Transforming Mission: Paradigm Shifts in Theology of Mission*. 20th Anniversary ed. Maryknoll, NY: Orbis, 2011.

---

[121] Scharpff was correct: "Luther was a man of his times. For this reason and for reasons already mentioned elsewhere, evangelism could not be carried on as we do today. Nonetheless, Luther no less than the modern evangelist, appealed directly to the individual and invited him to decision." Paulus Scharpff, *History of Evangelism: Three Hundred Years of Evangelism in Germany, Great Britain, and the United States of America* (Grand Rapids: Eerdmans, 1966), 12.

[122] Schulz seeks to tease out some of these lessons and states, "It would be a fatal mistake to ignore the fundamental contributions that this period [the Reformation] has brought to the Church and her mission." Schulz, *Mission from the Cross*, 67.

Brown, Christopher Boyd. *Singing the Gospel: Lutheran Hymns and the Success of the Reformation*. Cambridge, MA: Harvard University Press, 2005.

Bucer, Martin. *Concerning the True Care of Souls*. Translated by Peter Beale. Carlisle, PA: Banner of Truth, 2009.

Calhoun, David. "John Calvin: Missionary Hero or Missionary Failure?" *Presbyterion* 5, no. 1 (Spring 1979): 16–33.

Calvin, John. *Calvin's Commentaries*. Translated by W. Pringle. 22 vols. Grand Rapids: Baker, 1984.

_____. *Institutes of the Christian Religion*. Edited by John T. McNeill. Translated by Ford Lewis Battles. 2 vols. Philadelphia: Westminster, 1960.

_____. *Sermons on Deuteronomy*. Translated by Arthur Golding. Reprint ed. Edinburgh: Banner of Truth Trust, 1987.

_____. *Sermons on 1 Timothy*. Edited by Ray Van Neste and Brian Denker. 2 vols. Jackson, TN: CreateSpace, 2016.

Cottret, Bernard. *Calvin: A Biography*. Grand Rapids: Eerdmans, 2000.

Elert, Werner. *The Structure of Lutheranism*. Translated by Walter A. Hansen. St. Louis: Concordia, 1962.

Gordon, Bruce. *Calvin*. New Haven: Yale University Press, 2009.

Haykin, Michael A. G. "John Calvin's Missionary Influence in France." *Reformation and Revival* 10, no. 4 (Fall 2001): 35–44.

_____, and C. Jeffrey Robinson. *To the Ends of the Earth: Calvin's Missional Vision and Legacy*. Wheaton: Crossway, 2014.

Hendrix, Scott. *Recultivating the Vineyard: The Reformation Agendas of Christianization*. Louisville: Westminster John Knox, 2004.

Hogg, William Richey. *Ecumenical Foundations: A History of the International Missionary Council and Its Nineteenth Century Background*. New York: Harper, 1952.

Hughes, Philip E. "John Calvin: Director of Missions." In *The Heritage of John Calvin*, ed. J. H. Bratt, 40–54. Grand Rapids: Eerdmans, 1973.

_____, ed. and trans. *The Register of the Company of Pastors of Geneva in the Time of Calvin*. Grand Rapids: Eerdmans, 1966.

James, R. Alton. "Post-Reformation Missions Pioneers." In *Discovering the Mission of God: Best Missional Practices for the 21st Century*, ed. Mike Barnett and Robin Martin, 250–66. Downers Grove, IL: IVP, 2012.

Kane, J. Herbert. *A Concise History of the Christian World Mission: A Panoramic View of Missions from Pentecost to the Present.* Grand Rapids: Baker, 1978.

Kingdon, Robert M. "Calvinist Religious Aggression." In *The French Wars of Religion, How Important Were Religious Factors?*, ed. J. H. M. Salmon, 6–11. Lexington, MA: D. C. Heath, 1967.

Kolb, Robert. "Late Reformation Lutherans on Mission and Confession." *Lutheran Quarterly* 20, no. 1 (2006): 26–43.

Latourette, Kenneth Scott. *A History of the Expansion of Christianity: The First Five Centuries.* New York: Harper, 1937.

Leaver, Robin. *The Whole Church Sings: Congregational Singing in Luther's Wittenberg.* Grand Rapids: Eerdmans, 2017.

Luther, Martin. *A Simple Way to Pray.* Translated by Matthew C. Harrison. St. Louis: Concordia, 2012.

McGrath, Alister. *A Life of John Calvin, a Study in the Shaping of Western Culture.* Oxford; Basil Blackwell, 1990.

McKee, Elsie. "Calvin and Praying for 'All People Who Dwell on Earth.'" *Interpretation* 63, no. 2 (April 2009): 130–40.

Medeiros, Elias. "The Reformers' Commitment to the Propagation of the Gospel to All Nations from 1555 to 1654." PhD diss., Reformed Theological Seminary, 2009.

Montgomery, John Warwick. "Luther and Missions." *Evangelical Missions Quarterly* 3, no. 4 (1967): 193–202.

Nazir-Ali, Michael. *From Everywhere to Everywhere: A World View of Christian Witness.* London: Flame, 1990.

Neill, Stephen. *A History of Christian Missions.* 2nd ed. New York: Penguin, 1991.

Öberg, Ingemar. *Luther and World Mission: A Historical and Systematic Study with Special Reference to Luther's Bible Exposition.* St. Louis: Concordia, 2007.

Olson, C. Gordon, and Don Fanning. *What in the World Is God Doing?: Essentials of Global Missions: An Introductory Guide.* Lynchburg, VA: Global Gospel Publishers, 2013.

Parker, T. H. L. *Calvin's Preaching.* Louisville: Westminster John Knox, 1992.

Plass, Ewald M. *What Luther Says: An Anthology.* Saint Louis: Concordia, 1959.

Scharpff, Paulus. *History of Evangelism: Three Hundred Years of Evangelism in Germany, Great Britain, and the United States of America*. Grand Rapids: Eerdmans, 1966.

Schulz, Klaus Detlev. *Mission from the Cross: The Lutheran Theology of Mission*. St. Louis: Concordia, 2009.

Schwiebert, Ernest G. *Luther and His Times: The Reformation from a New Perspective*. St. Louis: Concordia, 1950.

Stetzer, Ed. *Planting New Churches in a Postmodern Age*. Nashville: B&H, 2003.

Stewart, Kenneth J. "Calvinism and Missions: The Contested Relationship Revisited." *Themelios* 34, no. 1 (2009): 63–78.

Stolle, Volker. *The Church Comes from All Nations: Luther Texts on Mission*. St. Louis: Concordia, 2003.

Tappert, Theodore G. *The Book of Concord: The Confessions of the Evangelical Lutheran Church*. Philadelphia: Fortress, 1959.

Tucker, Ruth. *From Jerusalem to Irian Jaya: A Biographical History of Christian Missions*. Grand Rapids: Zondervan, 2004.

Van Neste, Ray. "John Calvin on Missions and Evangelism." *Founders Journal* 33 (1998): 15–21.

Verkuyl, Johannes. *Contemporary Missiology: An Introduction*. Translated by Dale Cooper. Grand Rapids: Eerdmans, 1987.

Warneck, Gustav. *Outline of the History of Protestant Missions from the Reformation to the Present Time*. Edinburgh: J. Gemmell, 1884.

_____. *Outline of the History of Protestant Missions from the Reformation to the Present Time*. Authorized translation from the seventh German edition by George Robson. New York: Revell, 1901.

Wilcox, Pete. "Evangelisation in the Thought and Practice of John Calvin." *Anvil* 12, no. 3 (1995): 201–17.

Winter, Ralph D. "The Kingdom Strikes Back: Ten Epochs of Redemptive History." In *Perspectives on the World Christian Movement: A Reader* ed. Ralph D. Winter and Steven C. Hawthorne, 209–27. 4th ed. Pasadena, CA: William Carey Library, 2009.

Zorn, Jean-François. "Did Calvin Foster or Hinder the Missions?" *Exchange* 40, no. 2 (2011): 170–91.

◇ **14** ◇

The Word of God as Missional Tinder of the Reformation[1]

JOHN D. WOODBRIDGE

*"Is not my word like fire, declares the Lord,
and like a hammer that breaks the rock in pieces?"*[2]
Martin Luther's Citation of Jeremiah 23:29

Martin Luther, like Augustine and the author of Hebrews (e.g., 4:12), was committed to the authority and power of the Word of God. This power in, of, and from the Word of God formed the basis for the missional endeavors and convictions of the early Reformers. Luther himself said, "I simply taught, preached, and wrote God's Word; otherwise I did nothing … the Word did everything."[3] And elsewhere, "First of all, you need to know that the holy scripture is the kind of book that makes the wisdom of all other books into foolishness, since none of them teaches about eternal life except this alone."[4] The wisdom of God's Word given to man in the pages of Scripture was the foundation for all of Luther's action, conviction,

---

[1] Permission granted by Crossway publishers [editor Justin Taylor] to cite portions of pages from article, John D. Woodbridge, "The Authority of Holy Scripture Commitments for Christian Higher Education in the Evangelical Tradition," *Christian Higher Education Faith, Teaching and Learning in the Evangelical Tradition*, eds. David S Dockery and Christopher W. Morgan (Wheaton: Crossway, 2018) in present essay: p. 72, "The Authority…" and p. 16 of present essay; pp. 74–75, "The Authority…" and pp. 18–19 of present essay.

[2] Martin Luther, *Luther's Works Volume 25: Lectures on Romans, Glosses and Scholia* (St. Louis: Concordia, 1972), 415.

[3] Martin Luther, "Eight Sermons at Wittenberg, 1522: The Second Sermon, March 10, 1522, Monday after Invocavit."

[4] Martin Luther, *Luther's Spirituality*, ed. Philip Krey and Peter Krey (New York: Paulist Press, 2007), 122.

261

and reformation. Without the Word, he would not have withstood railing critics, whether the Holy Roman Emperor, kings, or princes. But because of the Word, he stood strong when all the power of the papacy accosted him. He believed: "The Bible is alive, it speaks to me; it has feet, it runs after me; it has hands, it lays hold of me."[5] This Word of God was the power of the Reformation as the Holy Spirit used the revealed, inspired, inerrant, and authoritative Word to accomplish the purposes and plans of God (Isa 55:11) that his name might be known in Jerusalem, Judea, Samaria, and to the ends of the earth (Acts 1:8).

In 1530, Luther explained the source of the Reformation's power to undermine the indulgence system, which he viewed as "an abomination." Luther clearly indicated that the Word of God and not his own effort had afforded the spiritual power to subvert the indulgence system:

> If our Gospel has done nothing else than release men's consciences from the shameful abomination and idolatry of the indulgences, that alone would be enough to show that it was the Word and power of God. For the whole world must admit that no human wisdom could have done this, since no bishop, no chapter, no monastery, no doctor, no university, not I myself, in short no human reason, understood or knew this abomination; still less had any knowledge how to check it or attack it.[6]

Consequently, one of the most important missional teachings of the Protestant Reformation was this: Based on biblical teaching and in accord with the instruction of Luther, Calvin, and other Reformers, many evangelical Christians likewise depended missionally on the power of the gospel (Rom 1:16), the power of the Word of God (Heb 4:12), and the power of the Holy Spirit (Luke 11:13). Like Luther and Calvin, they realized that based solely on their own strength, they were incapable of obeying the Great Commission, reforming the churches, loving God with all their hearts, souls, and minds, and loving their neighbors as themselves. Neither their intellectual acumen, nor money, nor education, nor good intentions, nor any other factor provided them with the sufficient spiritual capital or

---

[5] Martin Luther, *Table Talk of Martin Luther*, ed. Thomas Kepler (New York: World, 1952; repr., Mineola, NY: Dover, 2005; first published in German in 1566), Section 1.

[6] Martin Luther, "Exhortation to the Clergy of Augsburg (1530)," in *Works of Martin Luther* (Grand Rapids: Baker, 1982), 4:336–37.

power to do so. Rather, they understood the reality of Jesus's statement, "You can do nothing without me" (John 15:5).

The focus of this chapter is indeed the legacy of the missional movements of the Protestant Reformation—in the sixteenth century and beyond.[7] In his own day, Luther identified the missional goal of Christians as their obedience to Christ's Great Commission. Reflecting on John 20:21 and Christ's charge to his disciples, Luther wrote,

> In this way the Lord desires to say: You have now received enough from me, peace and joy, and all you should have, for your person you need nothing more. Therefore, labor now and follow my example, as I have done, so do you. My father sent me into the world only for your sake, that I might serve you, not for my own benefit, I have finished the work, have died for you and given you all that I am and have; remember and do ye also likewise, that henceforth ye may only serve and help everybody, otherwise ye would have nothing to do on earth. For the faith ye have enough of everything. Hence, I send you into the world as my Father has sent me; namely that every Christian should instruct and teach his neighbor, that he may also come to Christ . . . By this...all Christians are commanded to profess their faith publicly and also to lead others to believe.[8]

Luther thought the missional advance of the Reformation was directly dependent on the Holy Spirit's unleashing of the power of holy Scripture. He described this unleashing as the "great things" the Word had done. As we look back through the story of the Reformation, we will see how the Word of God empowered the missional spread of the gospel that Martin Luther found in his reading of God's Word.

Interpreting the Protestant Reformation

Historians have often neglected Martin Luther's own perception or belief that the missional impact of the Reformation issued from the power of the Word of God and gospel preaching and teaching. Instead, historians have proffered a wide variety of theological, sociological, or

---

[7] For an influential study of the various uses of the word "mission" in church history, see David J. Bosch, *Transforming Mission Paradigm Shifts in Theology of Mission*, 20th Anniversary ed. (New York: Orbis, 2011).

[8] Cited in Charles L. Chaney, "Martin Luther and the Mission of the Church," *Journal of the Evangelical Theological Society* 13, no. 1 (Winter 1970): 31.

ecclesiastical interpretations regarding the purpose, origins, and/or results of the Reformation.

1. The Protestant Reformation simply should have never taken place. According to leading ecumenicist thought, the Protestant Reformation constituted a tragedy by fracturing Christendom and provoking religious disunity.[9]

2. The Protestant Reformers became swept up in an allegedly "unintended" Reformation that ultimately spawned modern-day skepticism and secularization.[10]

3. The Reformation's most significant impact stemming from the spirit of Calvinism was to give birth to modern-day capitalism.[11]

4. The Protestant Reformation represented a paltry and insignificant movement when compared to the rise and influence of modern science.[12]

5. Protestantism was a game-changer movement and is "the faith that made the modern world."[13]

6. There was not a single reformation, but several Reformations, principally a Protestant Reformation and a Roman Catholic Reformation.[14]

7. The Protestant Reformation's missional impact was nonexistent. The Reformers allegedly did not engage in missional action or have a concern for evangelistic outreach beyond their own geographical settings. According to Warneck, it was the Pietists who launched the missions movement.[15]

---

[9] Multiple scholars, both Protestant and Roman Catholic, have made this claim.

[10] Brad S. Gregory, *The Unintended Reformation: How a Religious Revolution Secularized Society* (Cambridge: Belknap Press of Harvard University Press, 2015).

[11] Max Weber, *The Protestant Ethic and the Spirit of Capitalism: and Other Writings*, ed. and trans. Peter Baehr and Gordon C. Wells (New York: Penguin Classics, 2002).

[12] Herbert Butterfield, *The Origins of Modern Science 1300–1800*, rev. ed. (New York: Free Press, 1997).

[13] Alec Ryrie, *The Age of Reformation: The Tudor and Stewart Realms 1485–1603*, 2nd ed. (New York: Routledge, 2017).

[14] Carlos M. N. Eire, *Reformations: The Early Modern World, 1450–1650* (New Haven: Yale University Press, 2016).

[15] Gustav Warneck famously wrote, "We miss in the Reformers not only missionary action, but even the idea of missions, in the sense in which we understand them today [1881]. And this not only because the newly discovered heathen across the sea lay almost wholly beyond the range of their vision … but because fundamental theological views [eschatology and election] hindered them from giving their activity, and even their thoughts, a missionary direction." Warneck, *History of Protestant Missions* (1901), 8.

The list of assessments of the Protestant Reformation's origins and missional impact by respected historians will undoubtedly continue to expand beyond these proposals and conclusions. Several of these interpretations enjoy certain merit. They point out correctly that some Europeans did embrace Protestantism for nonreligious reasons—including social, political, nationalistic, and economic motivations. Other interpretations shelter serious deficiencies. In this chapter, we are not going to assess the validity of each, but instead add to the list by underscoring Martin Luther's own often-neglected perception of the Reformation. He perceived the "great things" of the Word of God, of Scripture, and of the gospel as having a missional impact on his contemporary society.

The Reformers' Perspectives: The Word of God as the Missional Tinder

Contrary to much Reformation historiography, which focuses largely on the social, political, and economic origins of the Reformation, Luther, Calvin, and their evangelical colleagues believed the essential thrust of the Protestant Reformation was doctrinal and spiritual and stemmed from obedience to Christ's Great Commission. More specifically, the Reformers were convinced that the inerrant Word of God inspired by the Holy Spirit, which speaks of Christ and his gospel, "did everything." By contrast, Luther said he did nothing. According to the Reformers, Scripture's divine power and gospel preaching accounted for much of the missional advance of the Protestant Reformation. The Reformers also believed Scripture should inform the world views of Christians—thinking about who God is, sin and salvation, devotions, preaching, evangelistic outreach, loving care for others, education, politics, law, money, natural philosophy or science, the liberal arts, music and other domains. In a word, this proposal suggests that the "missional" impact of the Reformation was remarkably expansive and extensive. Birthed principally in scriptural gospel teaching and preaching, the Reformation's missional impact fueled significant evangelistic, educational, and ecclesiastical initiatives in Europe and beyond for centuries to come.

Three considerations must be examined to support this thesis. For many historiographers the proverbial "elephant in the room" is whether or not the Protestant Reformers had interest in "missional initiatives" as this concept is understood today. This is a widely repeated thesis originating from the teaching of missiologist Gustav Warneck. In a definitional gambit, Warneck contended that the Reformers could not be legitimately deemed advocates of missional activities because they allegedly did not pursue foreign missions such as the ones Warneck witnessed in his own day—the late nineteenth century. Second, we will reflect upon a brief portion of Luther's personal biography, specifically considering the reasons Luther embraced *sola Scriptura, sola gratia,* and *sola fide,* and finally, we will reflect on the missional initiatives Luther believed flowed quite naturally as entailments from the Reformation *solas.* Specifically, we will focus on Luther's views of the missional entailments of the doctrines of *sola Scriptura* and *sola fide* as they relate to Christian education.

The Missional Reformation

In making a case for our proposal, we must first consider the controversy regarding the use of the word "missional" as it related to the Reformation. For some commentators, our subject today—the missional impact of the Reformation—is simply a nonstarter concept. It is rendered purposeless by Warneck's definitional argument that most of the Magisterial Reformers—Luther, Zwingli, and others—had no "missional" interests: that is, they did not engage in foreign missions, the plumb-line definition of "missional" according to the missiologist. These commentators claim that, whereas Anabaptists engaged in evangelism, a number of the Reformers believed that Christ's Great Commission in Matthew 28 applied only to the immediate generation of Christ's disciples and not to later generations of Christians like the Protestant Reformers.

Adding support to Warneck's interpretation, Franklin Littell, a distinguished historian, boldly claimed, "'[W]hen Luther referred to a mission to the heathen world, he was almost always referring to the so-called Christian world. "We have among us too many Turks, Jews, heathen, non-Christians, with both public false teaching and exasperating, scandalous life."'"[16] Littell believed this statement by Luther confirms that the Reformer lacked concern for foreign non-Christians or foreign-mission initiatives outside of Europe. However, Professor Littell did heuristically acknowledge that Luther was "missional" regarding Europe. The historian

---

[16] Cited in Glenn S. Sunshine, "Protestant Missions in the Sixteenth Century," *The Great Commission Evangelicals and the History of World Missions,* ed. Martin Klauber and Scott M. Manetsch (Nashville: B&H Academic, 2008), 12.

simply could not overlook overwhelming evidence to this effect. Luther, with his two-kingdom theology, hoped in conjunction with the backing of the evangelical princes, city officials, and clergy to witness the advance of the gospel in Europe through preaching, catechetical instruction, creation of schools, Bible translations, and other forms of Christian education. Luther did in fact engage in "missional" initiatives directed toward Europeans, since he believed that Europe was desperately gospel bereft.

We are by no means defrauding a responsible use of the word "missional" by arguing that Martin Luther and his evangelical colleagues engaged in missional activity in bringing the gospel to many of their contemporary Europeans. But did Luther have a wider concern for foreign missions? In parrying the charge that the Reformers were not interested in foreign missions, Professor Glenn Sunshine sagely points out that the Reformers could not have easily engaged in overseas missions, due to the geo-political hegemony Roman Catholics exercised over large portions of Europe. Sunshine writes,

> The best explanation for the lack of foreign missions is simply the Protestants' lack of access to mission fields. Put simply, for most the sixteenth century, Catholic powers such as Spain, Portugal, and the Italian city-states had trading connections and colonies in Asia, Africa, and the New World, while the Protestant powers did not. So while Catholics were able to engage in extensive missionary activity around the globe in the sixteenth century, Protestants had little opportunity to do so until later. In the few instances where they did have access to mission fields, the Protestants were involved in cross-cultural evangelism.[17]

This contextual reality helps explain the limited number of Protestant overseas mission enterprises such as the one undertaken by Huguenot Admiral Coligny to Brazil in 1556. This would also explain John Calvin's missional initiative in sending young French pastors back into his native, neighboring France from Geneva. This would provide a context for the Roman Catholic Bellarmine's retrospective boast that Roman Catholics had been very successful in converting heathen overseas, but that heretics—understand "Protestants"—failed.

---

[17] Sunshine, 14.

If the Reformers focused their missional efforts on local or nearby geographical venues, does this mean they had no interest in the spread of the gospel worldwide? In an intriguing 1985 article, "Was Luther a Missionary?", Eugene Bunkowske marshals a persuasive case that Luther did in fact evidence a deep longing to witness the gospel spread through the entire world.[18] For example, Luther commented on Psalm 19:4:

> The days and nights will declare the glory of God and the works of His hands in the languages of all people and in all lands.... This was fulfilled as the apostles proclaimed the great deeds of God in many tongues and it continues to be fulfilled in the whole world, for the Gospel which was disseminated into various languages through the apostles continues to resound in those same tongues unto the ends of the world.[19]

Bunkowske contends that Luther believed the Great Commission applied to Christians in his own day. On Psalm 45:14, Luther commented,

> The Apostles teach about Christ. The Prophets teach about Him too. The teachers, bishops, pastors and ministers who baptize, who administer the Sacraments—all are led to Christ that they may believe and serve in faith in our Lord Jesus Christ, each one in his own way.... So if I am a teacher of the Gospel, I do the same thing that Paul and Peter did.[20]

He also said, "Now if all heathen are to praise God ... they must know Him and believe in Him.... If they are to believe, they must first hear His Word.... If they are to hear His Word, then preachers must be sent to proclaim God's Word to them."[21]

Moreover, Luther in his early career attempted to evangelize Jews in Germany and the Turks of the Balkans. He urged German prisoners of war held by the Turks to be missionaries. They should "adorn and praise the Gospel and the name of Christ" which might "perhaps convert many."[22] After Luther's initial evangelistic efforts to Jews failed, the Reformer

---

[18] Eugene W. Bunkowske, "Was Luther a Missionary?," *Concordia Theological Quarterly* 49, nos. 2–3 (April/July 1985): 161–79.

[19] Bunkowske, 163.

[20] Bunkowske, 166.

[21] Bunkowske, 167.

[22] Bunkowske, 167.

tragically became very hostile to them.[23] Nonetheless, from author Bunkowske's reading, the thesis that Luther did not advocate or engage in missional initiatives with non-European or foreign horizons in mind is simply groundless. Through his use of the printed media, translation of the Bible, the wide-spread distribution of his Large and Small catechisms, his hymns, his teaching of students (nearly one third of the 16,000 theological students at Wittenberg between the years 1520 and 1560 were foreigners), Luther's desire to fulfill the Great Commission was manifest.[24] The weaknesses of the Warneck thesis suggest that it is not a reliable interpretation to inform our understanding of the relation between the Protestant Reformation and missions.

The **Solas** *of the [Missional] Reformation*

What factors led Luther to espouse the gospel of Jesus Christ (*sola gratia, sola fide*) as well as the final authority of Scripture (*sola Scriptura*)? This question brings us to the second consideration necessary for our proposal: a brief biographical sketch of Luther's spiritual pilgrimage, especially related to *sola Scriptura* and *sola fide*, to help us better understand his "missional thinking."

"'Reverend father, will you die steadfast in Christ and the doctrines you have preached?' 'Yes,' replied the clear voice for the last time. On February 18, 1546, even as he lay dying in Eisleben, far from home, Martin Luther was not to be spared a final public test, not to be granted privacy even in this last, most personal hour." So begins the account of Martin Luther's life in Professor Heiko Oberman's classic biography, *Luther: Man between God and the Devil.*[25] Intriguingly, Oberman inaugurates his study with this scene drawn from Luther's deathbed. Also intriguing is the final question and answer in Luther's life: "Will you die steadfast in Christ and the doctrine you have preached?" Please notice that Luther's last moments and thoughts focused upon his "preached doctrines." This poignant episode reinforces our sense of the importance of the role of doctrine in the Protestant Reformation and for Luther.

---

[23] Bunkowske, 170–71.
[24] Bunkowske, 167–71.
[25] Heiko A. Oberman, *Luther: Man between God and the Devil*, trans. Eileen Walliser-Schwarzbart (New York: Image Books, 1992), 3.

Oberman observed that Luther had undergone many public tests in his life. Perhaps the most significant of these had taken place twenty-five years earlier, in April 1521. At the Imperial Diet of Worms, Martin Luther (1483–1546) stood accused of heresy allegedly expressed in his writing. He appeared before young Charles V, the Holy Roman Emperor, prominent lords of the Empire and mighty clerics of the Roman Catholic Church. Luther boldly declared that the Bible is the only infallible authority and final arbiter for what he believed about Christ and the Christian faith. Asked to repudiate his books and theological convictions, Luther responded with these iconic words:

> Unless I am convinced by the testimony of the Scriptures or by clear reason (for I do not trust either in the Pope or in councils alone, since it is well known that they have often erred and contradicted themselves), I am bound by the Scriptures I have quoted and my conscience is captive to the Word of God. I cannot and I will not retract anything, since it is neither safe nor right to go against conscience. … May God help me. Amen.[26]

By arguing that both popes and councils had erred, Luther shook the authority of the Roman Catholic Church to its very foundations. Luther thereby took his stand on Scripture alone, which does not err.

In Luther's day, "standing for the Word of God" alone (*sola Scriptura*) could be very costly: imprisonment or martyrdom. As Luther left the Diet of Worms, Spanish soldiers chanted at him, "To the flames." After the Diet of Worms, Luther was forever an outlaw.

Nearly a decade earlier, in 1512, Luther had become a newly minted Doctor of Theology in his specialty—Scripture. As a Doctor of Holy Scripture, he taught the Bible at the University of Wittenberg. As early as 1514, he began criticizing the indulgence system. Sometime between November 1515 and September 1516, while preparing his lectures, Luther made a major exegetical discovery. It helped him to understand the doctrines of *sola gratia*—"unmerited grace"—and *sola fide*—salvation by faith alone—and ultimately *sola Scriptura*. He carefully exegeted Rom 1:17: "For in it [the Gospel] the righteousness of God is revealed." Luther's own words capture well his troubled mind-set when the discovery took place:

---

[26] Cited in John Dillenberger, ed., *Martin Luther Selections from His Writings* (New York: Anchor, 1962), xxiii.

I hated the expression "righteousness of God," for through the tradition and practice of all the doctors I had been taught to understand it philosophically, as the so-called "formal"—or, to use another word, "active"—righteousness through which God is just and punishes sinners and the unjust. But I could not love the righteous God, the God who punishes. I hated him. ... I was very displeased with God, if not in secret blasphemy, then certainly with mighty grumbling. ... I pondered incessantly, day and night, until I gave heed to the context of the words, namely: "For [in the Gospel] is the righteousness of God revealed, as it is written: 'The just shall live by faith.'" Then I began to understand the righteousness of God as a righteousness by which a just man lives as by a gift of God, that means by faith. I realized that it was to be understood this way: the righteousness of God is revealed through the Gospel, namely the so-called "passive" righteousness we receive, through which God justifies us by faith through grace and mercy. ... Now I felt as if I had been born again: the gates had been opened and I had entered Paradise itself.[27]

Luther's "new birth" not only changed the direction of his life but dramatically transformed his view of God the Father whom he had previously hated. Luther began to view God the Father not solely as a God who rightfully judges but as a heavenly Father who lovingly and providentially cares for his children. This accounts in some regards for Luther's own love for the Lord's Prayer. Because he now trusted his heavenly Father, he could pray with open heart that the Lord's will be accomplished in heaven and on earth. Luther later wrote that if we want to have a better understanding of who God the Father is, we should consider who Christ is. Why Christ? He is the mirror of God's loving heavenly heart. The Protestant Reformation's emphasis on God as a loving heavenly Father was a game changer for the way many Europeans thought about God. They had often envisioned God as a fulminating and vengeful tyrant—a thrower of lightning bolts. Luther himself had earlier received a couple of incoming bolts of lightning in a traumatic experience.

It took some time for Luther to grasp the entailments of *sola gratia* and *sola fide* and the implications of the doctrine of justification by faith alone. Luther became ensnarled in the indulgence controversy with Johann

---

[27]Oberman, *Luther*, 165.

Tetzel, who in a neighboring region was hawking indulgences with sensationally inflated claims: total forgiveness of your sins no matter how horrible the sins were. Luther believed he had to react to protect the honor of the church. Luther later acknowledged that at the time of the indulgence controversy, he was so loyal to the pope, he would have killed for him.

Luther was particularly vexed by Tetzel's claim: "A penny in the box, a soul out of purgatory." How could that conceivably be true, if Christ calls us to authentic repentance and if we are saved by faith alone? On October 31, 1517, Luther posted Ninety-Five Theses per university custom on the door of the Castle Church in Wittenberg. These theses criticized the indulgence system but also underscored the need for true repentance per Thesis One. Later Luther repudiated some of the Ninety-Five Theses, describing certain theses as "groveling concessions" to the papacy.

After posting the theses, Luther quickly emerged as a firebrand in Germany. Papal representatives met with him and tried to bring him back to a right state of Roman Catholic mind. The Dominican Sylvester Prierias, one of Luther's most perceptive critics, challenged him by saying, "Whoever says that the Church of Rome may not do what it is actually doing in the matter of indulgences is a heretic."[28] Elsewhere Prierias claimed, "He who does not accept the doctrine of the Church of Rome and pontiff of Rome as an infallible rule of faith, from which the Holy Scriptures, too, draw their strength and authority, is a heretic."[29] The battle between Tetzel and Luther had taken a dramatic turn—a contest between the authority of Scripture alone [*sola Scriptura*] as an infallible rule of faith versus the authority of the Church of Rome and the pope as an infallible, authoritative interpreter of the faith.

In 1520, Luther published a series of pamphlets that became instant best sellers, including "The Babylonian Captivity of the Church." The pamphlets probably sealed Luther's near-term fate. Luther's popularity was surging. He could no longer be mistaken as just another drunken German, who once sober would not be a troublemaker, as one pope had speculated or hoped. Luther was summoned to appear before the Holy Roman Emperor at the Diet of Worms in 1521. He came to the gathering, a believer in *sola gratia, sola fide* and *sola Scriptura*. He also came to it thinking he might never exit the Diet of Worms alive. Charles V kept his promise, but the

---

[28] Oberman, 194.
[29] Oberman, 193.

Holy Roman Emperor indicated in twenty-five days Luther would be officially condemned.

In God's good providence, Luther survived. Frederick the Wise, Luther's prince, arranged for him to be "kidnapped" and whisked away to the Wartburg Castle, where he assumed an alias name, grew a beard, began to translate the Bible into German and very famously threw an inkwell at the Devil. Luther very much believed the Devil existed. He also believed that the Devil was engaged in all-out war against God, the gospel, and Christians, and Martin Luther. The Edict of Worms proclaimed Luther a criminal and prohibited anyone from helping him under the penalty of death. All his books were banned. Now Luther was both a heretic and a criminal.

Sola Scriptura *and the Missional[!] Reformation*

Our third consideration is Luther's own perception of the missional impact of the Reformation. Luther provided a "report card" regarding the advance of the Reformation in his "Exhortation to the Clergy of Augsburg." This remarkable assessment written in 1530 reveals clearly that Luther was convinced that the missional impact of the Reformation since the Diet of Worms, nine years earlier, was not due to himself but to the "glorious fruit" of the Word of God. Indeed, Luther gave all credit for Reformation advances to the power of the Word of God and the gospel. On his own, he confessed, he would have been powerless to bring about any reforming advances. He made it very clear that an evangelical Reformation was desperately needed. Luther observed:

> Because I am now discussing the fact that people have forgotten [in 1530] what the world was like before my teaching began and are not now willing to admit that anyone did anything wrong, I must bring out again the old pretenses and picture to the clergy their forgotten virtue, so that they may see or recollect what the world would be like if our Gospel had not come. We, too, may see, to our comfort, what great and glorious fruit the Word of God has produced. We shall begin at the point where my doctrine began, that is, with the indulgences.[30]

---

[30] Luther, "Exhortation to the Clergy of Augsburg," 336.

Then Luther reviewed how the power of the Word of God and the gospel had challenged the indulgence system, the confessionals, penance, sale of masses, the ban and other disputed Roman Catholic practices.

In his analysis, Luther explained why the Reformation was so desperately needed:

> Everything was so upside down with discordant doctrines and strange new opinions that no one knew any more what was certain or uncertain, what it was to be a Christian or an un-Christian. The old doctrine of the faith of Christ, of love, of prayer, of the Cross, of comfort in affliction was overthrown; nay, in all the world there was not a doctor who knew the whole catechism—that is, the Lord's Prayer, the Ten Commandments and the Creed—to say nothing of understanding and teaching it, as praise God! it is now taught and learned even by the young children.[31]

Luther's comment about young children leads us to reflect more upon the missional impact of the Reformation regarding education. The Reformers preached justification by faith alone [*sola fide*] as taught solely in the infallible Word of God, Holy Scripture [*sola Scriptura*]. The Reformers were appalled that Roman Catholics had failed to place the gospel and Holy Scripture in the core of their educational curriculum. Luther thundered, "The universities need a sound and thorough reformation.... [N]othing could be more wicked, or serve the devil better, than unreformed universities." Luther indicated that "the young people of Christendom languish and perish miserably in our midst for want of the gospel, in which we ought to be giving them constant instruction and training."[32]

In 1520, Luther put the onus on the papacy for the miserable condition of Christian education: "Everything that the papacy has instituted or ordered is directed solely towards the multiplication of sin and error. ... Loose living is practiced there [the universities]; little is taught of the Holy Scripture or the Christian faith."[33] Luther urged that Scripture should be

---

[31] Luther, 348.

[32] See Luther's "An Appeal to the Ruling Class of German Nationality as the Amelioration of the State of Christendom," in Dillenberger, *Martin Luther: Selections*, 470–76. For a complementary discussion of Luther's view of Christian Education, consult: Woodbridge, "The Authority of Holy Scripture Commitments for Christian Higher Education in the Evangelical Tradition," *Christian Higher Education Faith, Teaching and Learning in the Evangelical Tradition*, eds. David S. Dockery and Christopher W. Morgan (Wheaton, IL: Crossway, 2018), I, pp. 71–76.

[33] Dillenberger, 470.

the basis of university education, "for Christian youth, and those of our upper classes, with whom abides the future of Christianity, will be taught and trained in the universities."[34]

Luther espoused a two-kingdom theory of society. He urged that both religious and public schools should emphasize teaching based on Holy Scripture. In 1537, he explained the reason Scripture should have such prominence:

> Therefore, you should immediately take no hope from your own reason and understanding. With them you will not reach eternal life. On the contrary, by such presumption you and others with you will plunge from heaven into the abyss of hell. . . . Instead, kneel down in your little room and pray to God with true humility and sincerity that God through the dear Son might give you the Holy Spirit, who will enlighten and direct you and give you understanding.[35]

Luther and other Reformers gave themselves over missionally to preaching sermons, drafting catechisms and books, and establishing schools which could promote a near-total rebuilding of contemporary education based on the teachings of Holy Scripture.[36] Luther recommended, "Above all, the foremost and most general subject of study, both in the higher and the lower schools, should be Holy Scriptures, and for the young boys the Gospel. And would to God that every town had a girls' school also, in which the girls were taught the Gospel for an hour each day either in German or Latin."[37]

---

[34] Dillenberger, 471.

[35] Luther, *Luther's Spirituality,* 122. For Luther's views of biblical authority, see Mark D. Thompson, *A Sure Ground on Which to Stand: The Relation of Authority and Interpretive Method in Luther's Approach to Scripture* (Eugene, OR: Wipf & Stock, 2006); Robert Kolb, "The Bible in the Reformation and Protestant Orthodoxy," in *The Enduring Authority of the Christian Scriptures,* ed. D. A. Carson (Grand Rapids: Eerdmans, 2016), 89–114; Scott M. Manetsch, "The Gravity of the Divine Word: Commentators and the Corinthian Correspondence in the Reformation Era," *Concordia Theological Quarterly* 81, nos. 1–2 (2017): 55–76.

[36] For a theology of education of the Reformers, see William M. Marsh, "Martin Luther: Education for the Preservation of the Gospel and Society"; Dongsun Cho, "Huldrych Zwingli: A Christian Humanist Educator"; Martin Klauber, "Philip Melanchthon: Christian Education in the German Reformation"; and Dustin Bruce, Timothy P. Jones, and Michael S. Wilder, "John Calvin: Teacher in the School of Christ," in *A Legacy of Religious Educators,* ed. Elmer Towns and Benjamin K. Forrest (Lynchburg, VA: Liberty University Press, 2016).

[37] Martin Luther, "An Open Letter to the Christian Nobility of the German Nation Concerning the Reform of the Christian Estate 1520," trans. Charles Michael Jacobs, in *Works of Martin Luther,* vol. 2 (Grand Rapids: Baker, 1982), 151–52.

"Teaching" the Word of God and the Missional Reformation

Historian Robert Kolb has described well the impact of Luther's educational reforms: "Luther's reorientation of the foundations of religious life, placing God's Word and biblical teaching at its center or as its foundation, exercised a transforming impact on both public teaching and individual lives, on the understanding of the liturgy and other rituals, on the office of pastor."[38] For Luther, the doctrine of *sola Scriptura* had definite missional educational implications. As for the common objection that education was too expensive, Luther countered, "If it is necessary, dear sirs, to expend annually such great sums for firearms, roads, bridges, dams and countless similar items, in order that a city may enjoy temporal peace and prosperity, why should not at least as much be devoted to the poor, needy youth, so that we might engage one or two competent men to teach school?"[39]

Luther argued that the doctrine of *sola fide* should free up money for education that would normally be spent on meritorious salvific works. Luther observed that whereas a German citizen was formerly "obliged to give up much money and property for indulgences, masses, vigils, endowments, testaments, anniversaries, mendicants, brotherhoods, pilgrimages, and other like humbug; but now that he is rid by the grace of God of all that robbing and giving, he ought, out of gratitude to God and for His glory, to give a part of that amount for schools in which to train the poor children, which would indeed be a good and precious investment."[40] Once again, Luther drew out a missional entailment from a "sola"—in this instance *sola fide*.

Luther's translation of the Bible into German [1534] likewise constituted a major impetus for the establishment of universal education. If people were to read God's Word, they must first have the requisite skills to do so. The push for universal education for boys and girls represented a major shift from the prevailing attitude toward education, generally reserving it for those who were going to become a priests, doctors, lawyers or civil servants.

---

[38] Robert Kolb, *Martin Luther and the Enduring Word of God; The Wittenberg School and its Scripture Centered Proclamation* (Grand Rapids: Baker Academic, 2016), 41.

[39] Martin Luther, "To the Councilmen of All Cities in Germany that They Establish and Maintain Christian Schools 1524," in *Works of Martin Luther*, 4:106.

[40] Luther, 4:106–7.

Luther knew the biblical languages well. He had engaged in the serious study of Hebrew. He rejoiced about the recent recovery of the knowledge of Greek in the West. It permitted Christians to have a more accurate understanding of the gospel than they could access from only consulting Jerome's Vulgate edition of the Bible: "No one knew what purpose God suffered the languages to be revived, until we now begin to see that it was for the sake of the Gospel, which He intended afterwards to reveal, in order to expose and destroy thereby the kingdom of anti-Christ.... In proportion then, as we prize the Gospel, let us guard the languages.... And let us be sure of this: we shall not long preserve the Gospel without the languages."[41]

Luther identified fathers in homes as key Christian educators. Fathers were to teach their children the catechism. After all, it encompassed the basics of the Christian faith. He asserted that unruly German youth had not apparently received proper catechetical instruction. Nor had they been taught to honor fathers and mothers. Luther went so far as to propose that young people should not be permitted to eat if they did not memorize the catechism. For Luther teachers in schools represented parents in instructing the young in the Christian faith.

As a Christian humanist, Luther recommended that schools should teach not only the Bible but also the liberal arts, the languages, and other disciplines. Luther observed, "For my part, if I had children and could accomplish it, they should study not only the languages and history, but singing, instrumental music, and all of mathematics."[42] Luther especially praised the study of history because it could provide readers with moral lessons. He wished he had been taught more of the liberal arts and poetry. He commended the Romans for the instruction they gave to young people in the liberal arts that prepared them for community service in government. Luther, the composer of a "A Mighty Fortress is Our God," very much reveled in music, calling it "the mistress of the soul." Luther, therefore, did not advocate that the Bible alone should be the sole subject studied in church schools or public schools. However, he did discount or reject any secular teaching if it contradicted Holy Scripture.

Melanchthon, Luther's colleague, became known as "The Preceptor of Germany." He famously developed principles for interpreting Scripture and encouraged a wise use of the liberal arts and humanities in creating an

---

[41] Luther, 4:114.
[42] Luther, 4:123.

educational curriculum for schools. But like Luther, Melanchthon believed Scripture and the gospel should remain at the center of Christian education. In an oration "On the merit of studying theology (1537)," Melanchthon wrote,

> Therefore, let me come to the point. Just as Paul says: "I am not ashamed of the Gospel of Christ" [Romans 1:16], so it is proper for all the faithful to be disposed in such a way that they love the word of God with all their heart, acknowledge that it is the highest of all God's favours, and respect with great piety its ministry, that is, the public office of teaching, bestow honour upon it, assist it for the sake of its calling, and defend and adorn it. This must be the chief concern of all the faithful.[43]

Schools should have as one of their principal goals the training of pastors who preach the gospel. In this light, Melanchthon urged princes to establish schools where students could be well trained for pastoral ministry.

Conclusion

Martin Luther urges us to remember that as believers we are all on a mission—Christ's mission for his church. Whether we are theologians or train conductors, nurses or notaries, we are to fulfill Christ's Great Commission as his messengers. All Christians have Christ's marching orders in the Great Commission. Luther writes,

> Therefore he [Jesus] says: You have now seen what kind of an office I have filled upon the earth, for which I was sent by my Father, that I should establish a spiritual kingdom ... and thereby to bring them that believe on me to eternal life.... Therefore I send you also forth in like manner to be my messengers ... to conduct the same office as I have ... filled, namely: to preach the Word you have heard and received from me.[44]

Luther believed the requisite power we need to preach the Word comes not from us but from God. Not only did Luther think the Bible taught this, but he testified that God's Word had done everything in his own reforming

---

[43] Philip Melanchthon, *Orations on Philosophy and Education,* ed. Sachiko Kusukawa (Cambridge: Cambridge University Press, 1999), 183.

[44] Cited in Chaney, "Mission of the Church," 31.

endeavors. In the second verse of "A Mighty Fortress is Our God," Martin Luther the hymn writer also reiterated the same point about our weakness: "Did we in our own strength confide, our striving would be losing, were not the right man on our side, the man of God's own choosing. Dost ask who that may be? Christ Jesus, it is he; Lord Sabaoth, his name, from age to age the same, and he must win the battle." In pursuing our mission, then, we should rely on the conjoined power of the Holy Spirit, the power of the gospel, and the power of Scripture in Christian preaching and witness. The Protestant Reformer William Tyndale, citing Heb 4:12, reminds us that the Word of God is indeed alive and amazingly powerful: "For the word of God is living and active and sharper than any two-edged sword, and piercing as far as the division of soul and spirit, of both joints and marrow, and able to judge the thoughts and intentions of the heart" (NASB). The apostle Paul reminds us that the gospel is the very power of God for salvation (Rom 1:16). Luther also urges us to meditate on the Word of God in order for us to live on mission:

> The teacher, however, fetching his doctrine from heaven, detests all the devoted endeavours of men, and gives this only true definition of blessedness which is wholly unknown to men:—that he is the "blessed" man who loves the law of God. It is, indeed, a short definition, but it contains a savour that is contrary to all human ideas, and especially human wisdom.[45]

Continuing in his commentary on Psalm 1, he says,

> This "will" [to meditate] is to be sought by us from heaven … by humble faith in Christ, when we are brought to despair of all strength in ourselves. And mark this well.… this man that is blessed, has his love, the law of the Lord, always in his mouth, always in his heart, and always (if he can) in his ear. For "he that is of God heareth God's words," John 8:47.[46]

And should we become intimidated by ominous demonic forces arrayed against us or falter on our mission through a sense of our own weakness and sin, Luther enjoins us to remember that God who is a "Mighty Fortress"

---

[45] *Martin Luther's Complete Commentary on the First Twenty-Two Psalms*, trans. by Henry Cole, vol. 1 (London: W. Simpkin and R. Marshall, 1826), 11–12.

[46] *Martin Luther's Complete Commentary on the First Twenty-Two Psalms*, 24–25.

is with us: "And though this world, with devils filled, should threaten to undo us, we will not fear, for God hath willed his truth to triumph through us. The Prince of Darkness grim, we tremble not for him; his rage we can endure, for lo, his doom is sure; one little word shall fell him." And when we draw close to finishing our race, having kept our eyes on Jesus, the author and finisher of our faith, may we joyfully declare as had Martin Luther, "I simply taught, preached, and wrote God's Word; otherwise I did nothing…. The Word did everything."[47] God's glory is our chief end, not our own.

Bibliography

Luther, Martin. *Martin Luther: Selections from His Writings.* Edited by John Dillenberger. New York: Anchor Books, 1962.

Luther, Martin. *Luther's Spirituality.* Edited by Philip Krey and Peter Krey. New York: Paulist Press, 2007.

Kolb, Robert. *Martin Luther and the Enduring Word of God; The Wittenberg School and Its Scripture-Centered Proclamation.* Grand Rapids: Baker, 2016.

Oberman, Heiko A. *Luther: Man between God and the Devil.* New York: Doubleday, 1992.

Strauss, Gerald. *Luther's House of Learning Indoctrination of the Young in the German Reformation.* Baltimore: John Hopkins, 1978.

Thompson, Mark D. *A Sure Ground on Which to Stand: The Relation of Authority and Interpretive Method in Luther's Approach to Scripture.* Eugene, OR: Wipf & Stock, 2006.

---

[47] Martin Luther, *Eight Sermons at Wittenberg, 1522*, "The Second Sermon, March 10, 1522, Monday after Invocavit."

15

Sola Scriptura and the Recovery of Bible Translation in Global Mission

EDWARD L. SMITHER

In late 1521 and early 1522, a young scholar and theology professor risked his life to translate the New Testament into colloquial German. Convinced that the Word of God had final authority in a believer's life and that every Christian possessed the ability to understand Scripture even without the aid of a priest or teacher, Martin Luther (1483–1546) modeled very practically the value of *sola Scriptura* through this translation exercise. Although Luther and other early Protestant Reformers were not directly involved in global mission,[1] the principle of *sola Scriptura* that they championed provided a theological foundation and fresh vision for Bible translation that invigorated the missionary enterprise.

In this chapter, I will argue that the value of *sola Scriptura* was the Reformation's greatest contribution to Protestant global mission and that the recovery of vernacular Bible translation as a central mission practice contributed to making the modern missions movement revolutionary. Following some preliminary thoughts on the vernacular principle and *sola Scriptura*, I will sketch out the work of key missionary Bible translators

---

[1] As Woodbridge and Van Neste have argued in their essays, Luther and Calvin and other sixteenth-century Reformers did care about the Great Commission and, in some cases, sent laborers to other lands. That said, their primary mission field was the church in Europe, and they did not personally engage in global mission. The most significant Protestant missionary movements emerge after the sixteenth century.

from the seventeenth to the twentieth century to show that Protestant mission has indeed been a mission of translation. I will conclude with some remarks on how *sola Scriptura* and the vernacular principle have shaped evangelical Protestant missions and how together they might offer guidance moving forward in twenty-first-century mission.

Pre-Reformation Vernacular Translation

Jesus did not write a book. Instead, "the Word became flesh and dwelt among us" (John 1:14). Andrew Walls writes, "Incarnation is translation. When God in Christ became man, Divinity was translated into humanity, as though humanity were a receptor language."[2] Building on this, the Gospels and New Testament books were not written in the heart language of Christ or the New Testament writers; rather, they were produced in *koine* Greek to insure the widest possible circulation and comprehension in the first-century Roman world. The New Testament in its original form was a translation. So we affirm with I. Howard Marshall that the NT books were "documents of a mission."[3] When the gospel expanded beyond the frontiers of the Greek-speaking world, the church intuitively continued translation, making Scripture available in Syriac, Latin, Armenian, Coptic, Gothic, and Ethiopic among other languages in the first six centuries.[4]

Lamin Sanneh identifies this central value of translating Scriptures into the world's heart languages as the vernacular principle. He refers to Christianity as a "vernacular translation movement" and that Christian mission is "mission by translation."[5] Sanneh argues, "Mission as translation affirms the *missio Dei* as the hidden force for its work. It is the *missio Dei* that allowed translation to enlarge the boundaries of the proclamation."[6] With the gospel moving across social and cultural boundaries, Sanneh concludes, "Scriptural translation rested on the assumption that the vernacular has a primary affinity with the gospel, the point being

---

[2] Andrew F. Walls, *The Missionary Movement in Christian History* (Maryknoll: Orbis, 1996), 27. See also Darrell L. Guder, "A Multicultural and Translational Approach," *The Mission of the Church: Five Views in Conversation*, ed. Craig Ott (Grand Rapids: Baker Academic, 2016), 28.

[3] I. Howard Marshall, *New Testament Theology: Many Witnesses, One Gospel* (Downers Grove, IL: IVP Academic, 2014), 34–35. See also Lamin Sanneh, *Translating the Message: The Missionary Impact on Culture* (Maryknoll: Orbis, 1989), 1.

[4] See Smither, *Mission in the Early Church* (Eugene, OR: Cascade Books, 2014), 91–108.

[5] Sanneh, *Translating the Message*, 7, 29.

[6] Sanneh, 31, 82.

conceded by the adoption of indigenous terms and concepts for the central categories of the Bible."[7]

While Bible translation went hand in hand with the mission of the church in the first six centuries, the church departed from this value at many points between the seventh and sixteenth centuries. This was largely due to an increasing Christendom mind-set and the elevation of Latin and Greek as acceptable languages for worship. Biblical products such as the Latin Vulgate—a fourth- and fifth-century revision of the Old Latin Bible—effectively squelched the energy and vision for vernacular translations.[8] These tendencies came to a head in the ninth century when Cyril (ca. 826–869) and Methodius (815–885) developed a Slavic alphabet and began translating the Scripture into Slavonic. Called before a regional church council at Vienna (ca. 866), the brothers confronted the trilingualist controversy (the belief that Latin, Greek, and Hebrew were the only acceptable languages for worship), arguing for the legitimacy of vernacular translation from both Scripture and historic Christian examples. Though opposed by Latin-speaking bishops in Eastern Europe, Cyril and Methodius's work continued because of support from the pope and some Slavic-speaking monarchs.[9]

Despite the Latin Vulgate's exalted position in the western Roman Catholic Church, some European Christians yearned to express their faith in the vernacular during the medieval period.[10] Though Bible translation projects eventually emerged in English, German, French, Italian, and Spanish, these efforts began because priests and teachers strived to make the Scriptures accessible to the theologically untrained. In some cases, monarchs and wealthy Christians used their influential positions to have parts of Scripture translated into their local languages. The Psalms—a central element of liturgy and the church's hymnbook—was most typically the first portion of Scripture to be translated into the vernacular.[11]

---

[7] Sanneh, 166. See also Walls, *Missionary Movement,* 26–33.

[8] See further Geoffrey Shepherd, "English Versions of the Scriptures before Wyclif," in *Cambridge History of the Bible,* vol. 2: *The West from the Fathers to the Reformation,* ed. G.W.H. Lampe (Cambridge: Cambridge University Press, 1969), 364–74.

[9] See further Edward L. Smither, *Missionary Monks: An Introduction to the History and Theology of Missionary Monasticism* (Eugene, OR: Cascade Books, 2016), 119–37.

[10] See further Lampe, *Fathers to the Reformation,* 2:338–491.

[11] See further G. Sujin Pak, "Scripture, the Priesthood of All Believers, and Applications of 1 Corinthians 14," in *The People's Book: The Reformation and the Bible,* eds. Jennifer Powell McNutt and David Lauber (Downers Grove, IL: IVP Academic, 2017), 33–34.

This trend toward vernacular worship in Europe was also resisted, especially in Germany and England. Many church leaders believed that, unlike Latin, a colloquial language such as English lacked a sufficient "cultural standing" and theological framework for conveying Scripture and sound doctrine.[12] They were convinced that preaching and reading Scripture in the vernacular would quickly lead to heresy. Sound doctrine depended on a priest trained in Latin who could tell the congregation what to believe. Rejecting these values (and angering the pope in the process), John Wycliffe (1320–1384) translated the Latin Vulgate into colloquial English before his death in 1384. In a fourteenth-century articulation of both *sola Scriptura* and the vernacular principle, Wycliffe claimed that church belief and practice should "conform to the practice of Christ and his followers as recorded in the Scriptures [Old and New Testaments] . . . these laws were open to the direct understanding of all men on the points most essential to salvation. For such understanding it was necessary that all men should be able to study the Gospels in the tongue in which they might best understand their meaning."[13]

Sola Scriptura and Sixteenth-Century Translation

Luther famously wrote, "Scripture alone is the true lord and master of all writings and doctrine on earth."[14] Unpacking how the Reformers understood *sola Scriptura,* Vanhoozer helpfully writes, "Scripture is supremely authoritative in (and over) the church. It is the final court of appeal for understanding the gospel—identifying Jesus as the Christ and saying what God was doing in Christ—or anything else that pertains to Christian faith and life."[15] On the relation between Scripture and tradition, Barrett adds, "*Sola Scriptura* acknowledges that there are other important authorities for the Christian, authorities who should be listened to and followed. But Scripture alone is our *final* authority."[16]

---

[12] See Shepherd, "Scriptures before Wyclif," 382, 387.

[13] Henry Hargreaves, "The Wycliffite Versions," in Lampe, *Fathers to the Reformation*, 2:392.

[14] Luther, *Defense and Explanation of all the Articles* (LW 32:11–12), cited in Matthew Barrett, *God's Word Alone: The Authority of Scripture* (Grand Rapids: Zondervan, 2016), 21.

[15] Kevin J. Vanhoozer, "Holy Scripture," in *Christian Dogmatics: Reformed Theology for the Church Catholic,* ed. Michael Allen and Scott R. Swain (Grand Rapids: Baker Academic, 2016), 51. See also Kevin J. Vanhoozer, *Biblical Authority After Babel: Retrieving the* Solas *in the Spirit of Mere Protestant Christianity* (Grand Rapids: Brazos, 2016), 111.

[16] Barrett, *God's Word Alone,* 23. See also Roland H. Bainton, "The Bible in the Reformation," in *Cambridge History of the Bible,* vol. 3: *The West from the Reformation to the Present Day,* ed. S. L. Greenslade (Cambridge: Cambridge University Press, 1975), 1–6.

What does *sola Scriptura* entail? First, Scripture is inspired. "What Scripture says, God says."[17] Second, the Word of God is perfect and without error. Luther wrote, "The saints could err in their writings and the sin in their lives, but the Scriptures cannot err."[18] Third, the Scriptures are sufficient for Christian faith and practice. One of a number of Reformed confessions to address this issue, the Belgic Confession (1561), stated, "We believe that those Holy Scriptures fully contain the will of God, and that whatsoever man ought to believe unto salvation is sufficiently taught therein."[19] Finally, the Scriptures are clear. "When God speaks, he intends to be heard and understood."[20] This last element relates closely to Luther's argument for the priesthood of the believer *(sola sacerdos)*. Every believer could read Scripture and grasp its meaning because of its clarity.[21]

During the sixteenth century, the early Reformers explicitly articulated the authority of Scripture, which the church fathers had expressed more implicitly.[22] A number of Reformers looked to Augustine of Hippo (354–430), who argued for biblical authority in his fourth- and fifth-century disputes with the Donatists. Arguing against the Donatists' appeal to the authority of earlier African bishops, Augustine wrote, "No one agrees with the catholic bishops if they are anywhere by chance mistaken in holding any opinion contrary against the canonical Scriptures of God."[23] Supporting his claims for *sola Scriptura*, Luther, previously a member of the Augustinian order, directly quoted Augustine's correspondence with Jerome (347–420): "I have learned to do only those books that are called the holy Scriptures the honor of believing firmly that none of their writers has ever erred."[24]

Building on Wycliffe's beliefs and actions about Scripture and the vernacular, Luther labored in 1521 and 1522 to produce a colloquial German New Testament. After his colleague Philip Melanchthon (1497–1560)

---

[17] Barrett, 24.

[18] Luther, *Misuse of the Mass* (LW 36:136–37) cited in Barrett, *God's Word Alone,* 40.

[19] Belgic Confession, article 7, cited in Barrett, *God's Word Alone,* 23–4. See also Thirty-Nine Articles (1563), article 6; Westminster Confession (1646), article 1.6; Vanhoozer, *Biblical Authority after Babel,* 114–15.

[20] Barrett, *God's Word Alone,* 29.

[21] See further, Mark Labberton, "Perspiscuity and the People's Book," in McNutt and Lauber, eds., *People's Book*, 225–37.

[22] See Vanhoozer, "Holy Scripture," 37.

[23] Augustine, *On the Unity of the Church*, 11.28. Also, Augustine, *On Baptism Against the Donatists*, 2.3.

[24] Luther, *Defense and Explanation of All the Articles* (LW 32:11–12), cited in Barrett, *God's Word Alone,* 40. See Augustine, *Letter*, 82.3.

checked the translation, 3,000 copies were printed and the first run sold out almost immediately. Luther worked continually to revise the German New Testament while also putting together a committee to complete translation of the Old Testament, which was realized in 1534. Luther's work practically demonstrated his theological value for *sola Scriptura* and his own conviction for the vernacular principle. Making use of the most up-to-date printing technology available, the German Scriptures were widely circulated and read by German lay believers who could understand Scripture's clear meaning in their colloquial language and grow in grace because of it.[25]

Many sixteenth-century European theologians emulated Luther's work and translated Scripture into the vernacular. Basil Hall writes, "There was a *preparatio evangelica* in the first quarter of the sixteenth century . . . the fruits of intensive study in the grammar and syntax of [Latin, Greek, and Hebrew]."[26] Erasmus (1466–1536) and others developed critical texts, which provided a foundation for colloquial translations. Over the course of the sixteenth century, translations appeared in Italian, French, Dutch, Czech, Danish, Swedish, Icelandic, and English.[27] In the preface to the 1515 Danish Scriptures, Christiern Pederson wrote, "Nobody ought to think that the Gospels are more sacred in one tongue than in another: they are as good in Danish or in German as they are in Latin."[28]

Due to government and church opposition, the French, Spanish, and English translations were developed elsewhere in Europe and the first French translations were published anonymously. William Tyndale (1494–1536) worked on the updated English Bible largely from hiding in Germany and Belgium, and completed drafts were smuggled back to the churches in England. Eventually, because of his work on the English vernacular Bible, and his more Protestant translation choices and theological commentaries, Tyndale was captured by Henry VIII's soldiers and executed in 1536.[29]

---

[25] See further Barrett, *God's Word Alone,* 51; also Hanz Volz, "German," in Greenslade, *Reformation to the Present Day,* 3:94–104; and M. H. Black, "The Printed Bible," in Greenslade, *Reformation to the Present Day,* 3:432–36.

[26] Basil Hall, "Biblical Scholarship: Editions and Commentaries," in Greenslade, *Reformation to the Present Day,* 3:38.

[27] See Greenslade, *Reformation to the Present Day,* 3:94–174.

[28] Noak, "Scandinavian Versions," in Greenslade, *Reformation to the Present Day,* 3:137.

[29] See Barrett, *God's Word Alone,* 58–61; also, Greenslade, "English Versions of the Bible," in Greenslade, *Reformation to the Present Day,* 3:141–47.

Bible Translation in Mission
(Seventeenth–Twentieth Centuries)

As Protestants began to slowly engage in global mission in the seventeenth and eighteenth centuries, the values of *sola Scriptura* and the vernacular principle were quite evident. Eric Fenn notes, "The written Scriptures were a means by which the gospel could lay hold of the minds and hearts of men and women, sometimes more effectively than by any word of [missionaries]." He continues, "Whereas the Catholic missionary sought to bring people into the Church so that there they might learn the Gospel, the Protestant missionary (whether layman or minister) sought to give people the Bible in the language they could read so that they might discover for themselves the truth of the Gospel and the Church might be born among them by the impact of the Word of God."[30] The Bible was the missionary's message and Protestant mission efforts continued to be mission through translation.

Seventeenth Century

Protestant missionary work followed on the heels of commercial and political expansion, particularly through the Dutch East India Company, into South and Southeast Asia in the seventeenth century. The Dutch founded a seminary in Indonesia, and sent out twelve ministers for the island nation, while some Dutch ministers became proficient in local Indonesian languages. Agents of the Dutch East India Company began translating the Gospels into Malay in 1629. They completed the New Testament by 1668 and the Old Testament by 1735. The Dutch also labored to translate the Scriptures into Formosan (Taiwan) Chinese by 1661.[31]

On top of his duties as a full-time Puritan minister, John Eliot (1604–1690) began ministering to the Algonkian people in the mid-seventeenth century, making him one of the first Protestant missionaries to North America. Through his preaching, some 3,600 Algonkian embraced the gospel by 1671. Convinced that these new converts could not grow spiritually in their native context, Eliot extracted them from their tribal communities and established praying towns for teaching, fellowship, and accountability.

---

[30] Eric Fenn, "The Bible and the Missionary," in Greenslade, *Reformation to the Present Day*, 3:383, 385.

[31] Fenn, 385.

Eliot learned Algonkian so well that he translated the Bible into the Native American dialect by 1663.

In 1698, the Church of England formed the Society for the Propagation of Christian Knowledge (SPCK), in part to distribute Scripture and Christian literature. This initiative was an early attempt to connect the Bible to the work of mission, which anticipated the work of the nineteenth-century Bible societies.[32]

Eighteenth Century

In 1705, the Pietist King Frederick IV of Denmark (r. 1699–1730) sent two German missionaries, Bartholomäus Ziegenbalg (1682–1719) and Heinrich Plütschau (1677–1752), to begin Protestant mission work in Tranquebar, the Danish-controlled areas of South India. Though they faced opposition from Danish merchants and even Danish clergy in established churches, Ziegenbalg and Plütschau mastered the Tamil language, culture, and thought to contextualize their Lutheran Christianity into Indian forms. Although they ministered in a communal society, they emphasized preaching the gospel and calling for individual conversions. They established schools to provide general education for their host people and theological seminaries to train and set apart national church leaders. Ziegenbalg completed the translation of the Tamil New Testament in 1714 and also began work on the Old Testament.[33]

Continuing Ziegenbalg and Plütschau's work, Christian Friedrich Schwartz (1726–1798) labored for nearly a half century in India. He mastered multiple Indian languages, including Tamil, Urdu, and Persian, and finished the translation of the Tamil Old Testament started by Ziegenbalg. He also strived to contextualize the gospel in the Indian context. Remembered for pursuing simplicity, Schwartz planted a church in Tanjore that grew to some 2,000 believers before his death.[34]

In 1722, the Danish-Norwegian Lutheran missionary Hans Egede (1686–1758) began ministering in Greenland. Laboring in a challenging context, Egede's primary approaches to mission were caring for the sick

---

[32] Fenn, 386.

[33] See Hans-Werner Gensichen, "Ziegenbalg, Bartholomäus," in *Biographical Dictionary of Christian Missions,* ed. Gerald H. Anderson (New York: Macmillan Reference USA, 1998), 761; and Hans-Werner Gensichen, "Plütschau, Heinrich," in Anderson, *Dictionary of Christian Missions,* 540–41.

[34] See Hans-Werner Gensichen, "Schwartz, Christian Friedrich," in Anderson, *Dictionary of Christian Missions,* 606–7; also Neill, *History of Christian Missions,* 198–200.

and ministering to children. Although Egede struggled to gain fluency in the Greenlandic Eskimo dialect, his son Paul mastered the language and excelled as a preacher. In 1766, Paul Egede (1708–1789) finalized translation of the Greenlandic New Testament.[35]

Nineteenth Century

Mission historian Kenneth Scott Latourette (1884–1968) called the nineteenth century the "great century" for Christian mission. Following on the heels of the Pietist movement in Germany, and evangelical revivals in North America and Europe, the early nineteenth century witnessed the rise of the modern Protestant mission movement, particularly through the rise of voluntary mission societies. The most recognized individual in this development was William Carey (1761–1834), the English shoemaker and part-time Baptist pastor who argued in his *Enquiry* that the church was the means for God's mission in every generation.

Along with other members of the British Baptist Missionary Society, Carey established a mission base at Serampore (West Bengal). Their key missionary strategies included evangelism, church planting, training indigenous pastors, education, and contextualizing Christianity. Though he lacked formal linguistic training, a key part of Carey's legacy in mission was working on Bible translation in thirty-six Indian languages, including complete Bibles in Bengali, Marathi, and Sanskrit; New Testaments in ten other languages; and Scripture portions in another twenty-three.

Unlike Carey, Henry Martyn (1781–1812) was trained in linguistics at Cambridge. Originally sent to India in 1806 as a chaplain for the British East India Company, Martyn served as an itinerant evangelist in India and Persia. Though he died prematurely at the age of thirty-one, he put his linguistics training to good use and translated the New Testament into Hindi, Persian, and Arabic.

In 1807, Robert Morrison (1782–1834), a member of the London Missionary Society, became the first Protestant missionary in China. After mastering Mandarin and Cantonese, Morrison went to work with the British East India Company as a translator. This afforded him the time to pursue his real passion, Bible translation. Morrison completed the New Testament in Chinese in 1813 and the Old Testament in 1819. Throughout

---

[35] See Fenn, "Bible and the Missionary," 385.

his missionary career, Morrison encountered resistance from both Chinese and Roman Catholic missionaries; his translations of Scripture were able to access many places he could not.

The London Missionary Society was founded in 1796 for mission in Tahiti and the Pacific Islands region, one of the most fruitful mission fields in the world in the nineteenth century. In 1817, John Williams (1796–1839) arrived in the Society Isles to serve with the LMS. Laboring in a violent South Pacific context where cannibalism continued, Williams had two innovative approaches—purchasing a ship to facilitate itinerant preaching throughout the thousands of Pacific Islands, and setting apart local evangelists for the work. He engaged Tahitian evangelists to reach Samoa, and later Samoan workers to evangelize Vanuatu. Despite enjoying more than two decades of successful ministry, Williams was attacked and cannibalized during a visit to Vanuatu in 1839. Williams translated the New Testament into Raratonga (Cook Islands) in 1824.

Bible translation was also a major focus of nineteenth-century evangelical mission in Africa. Robert Moffat (1795–1883), David Livingstone's (1813–1873) father-in-law, spent forty-eight years ministering in southern Africa. His mission approaches included establishing schools and planting churches. Though he spent little time studying African religions or culture, he mastered the Tswana language and completed translation of the entire Bible by 1857.

Korea remained closed to Protestant missionary influences until 1882 when King Kojong allowed educators and medical workers to enter his nation. However, since two of the four Gospels had already been secretly translated into Korean and smuggled into the country, the first Protestant missionaries entering the country met Koreans already waiting to be baptized.[36] Once Korea became officially opened to Christian mission in 1885, Bible translation continued, along with church planting and the establishment of hospitals and schools. A revival broke out in the country in 1906 and by 1910, over 30,000 Koreans were worshipping in Presbyterian and Methodist churches.

Another nineteenth-century phenomenon that pointed to the centrality of Bible translation in Protestant mission was the establishment of Bible societies. These organizations developed alongside mission

---

[36] See Fenn, 394.

societies.[37] The earliest example was the British and Foreign Bible Society, which started in 1804 with a vision to provide Bibles for Wales. However, with its aims being "the production and distribution of the Scriptures in the languages of the world," the scope of the BFBS quickly became global and included countries such as China.[38] Valuing the believer's ability to grasp and understand Scripture (*sola sacerdos*), groups such as the BFBS printed Bibles without extensive notes or commentaries. In many mission fields, the Bible societies worked closely with other missionary efforts (e.g., Carey and Martyn in India; Morrison in China) as Scriptures were printed, distributed, and sold.

In addition to the BFBS, the early nineteenth century saw Bible societies launch in Germany (1804), Russia (1812), the Netherlands (1814), Denmark (1814), and the United States (1816). The Dutch Bible Society formed to support mission work that had already started in Indonesia. The American Bible Society began with bases in 100 US cities and states and quickly expanded to South America and China. Over time, these Bible societies pooled their resources and networked into the United Bible Societies. These efforts also resulted in the opening of many national Bible society offices on mission fields in Africa, Asia, and Latin America.

Twentieth Century

Bible translation and distribution continued to be just as important in the "global" (twentieth) century as it had been in the "great" century. By 1921, there were some 160 Protestant printing presses at work printing Bibles and Christian literature, while many new Christian literature ministries were starting.

Though he was never directly involved in Bible translation, Samuel Zwemer (1867–1952) focused much of his ministry in the Muslim world on Bible and literature distribution. In one of his earlier assignments, Zwemer opened a Bible bookshop on the island of Bahrain. Zwemer also developed and distributed Christian tracts, which complemented his ministry of spiritual dialogue with Muslims and Muslim theologians. Although Zwemer focused his ministry on literate peoples, the vast minority of the Arab world in the early twentieth century, he remained convinced that the printed page functioned as a ubiquitous missionary.

---

[37] Fenn, 389–99.
[38] Fenn, 387.

Bible translation efforts accelerated to a new level when Cameron Townsend (1896–1982) founded the Summer Institute of Linguistics in 1934 and Wycliffe Bible Translators in 1942. Originally focused on translating Scripture for indigenous peoples in the Americas, SIL and Wycliffe's work quickly became more global in scope. Through the leadership of Kenneth Pike (1912–2000), a PhD in linguistics graduate from the University of Michigan, SIL and Wycliffe leveraged the twentieth-century advancements in the study of linguistics for Bible translation. Part of their work included publishing the *Ethnologue,* which provides up-to-date research on the world's more than 6,900 languages and dialects. Wycliffe has also pursued its Vision 2025 campaign: "that by the year 2025 a Bible translation will be in progress for every people group that needs it."[39] At the time of this writing, this includes over 1,600 global languages and dialects without a word of Scripture.

Conclusion

Bible translation has been a central component of Protestant and evangelical mission since the Reformation. Protestant missionaries preached salvation by grace alone (*sola gratia*) through faith alone (*sola fide*). They also asserted that believers possessed the skills to grasp, understand, and apply the teachings of Scripture (*sola sacerdos*). Their belief about the gospel was firmly based on the conviction that Scripture alone was the final authority for Christian faith and practice (*sola Scriptura*). Building on these convictions, it is not surprising that evangelical Protestant mission efforts have been characterized by a faithful commitment to make Scripture available in the vernacular.

Although Protestants were a bit slow to engage in global mission in the sixteenth and seventeenth centuries, evangelical renewal movements such as the Pietists and evangelical revivals in Europe and North America in the eighteenth and nineteenth centuries nudged the church to think globally and missionally. Commenting on the connection between these renewal movements and *sola Scriptura*, Fenn writes, "New spirituality . . . so closely connected with the recovery of biblical truth meant that the Bible moved into the centre of faith and practice again."[40] Having Scripture in

---

[39] "The Vision," Wycliffe Global Alliance, accessed August 4, 2017, http://www.wycliffe.net/vision2025.

[40] Fenn, "Bible and the Missionary," 387.

the vernacular led to more spirited preaching, which influenced the church to take on more indigenous forms.[41]

How have the Reformation value of *sola Scriptura* and the vernacular principle positively shaped global mission? First, because Scripture is authoritative and colloquial, the Bible has been able to go places missionaries cannot physically access. The gospel penetrated Korea in the late nineteenth century before missionaries ever arrived because of available translated Scriptures. Zwemer's work selling and distributing Scripture in the Muslim world, as well as later efforts by others to smuggle Bibles into Soviet bloc states were based on this conviction. Since 1994, millions of Bibles and other gospel materials have been distributed at European ports around the Mediterranean to Muslim travelers entering North Africa, which has resulted in many families and individuals embracing the gospel. Finally, at present, Bible distribution continues in the digital sphere as newly translated books are made available to unreached peoples through smartphone apps.

Second, vernacular Scriptures have corrected the cultural mistakes made by missionaries and paved the way toward indigenous, local forms of Christianity. As southern African believers have imbibed Scripture in their heart languages, the nineteenth-century civilizing messages of well-meaning European missionaries have been drowned out. Vernacular Scripture has also critiqued syncretistic patterns and rooted out the influences of non-Christian primal religions. Finally, translated Scriptures became the basis for local theology and worship forms.

Third, colloquial Scriptures have helped to influence local cultures for the gospel. When Cyril and Methodius developed the Old Slavonic alphabet, they gave Slavic peoples a vehicle in which to worship but also to express themselves culturally. Fenn adds, "The contribution of translation into the vernacular to the task of nation-building can hardly be overestimated. Even among those peoples who already possessed a great literature, the wide dispersion of the Christian writings in their languages has had an indefinable effect on the basic ideas and values in their culture."[42] No one

---

[41] See further Norman Sykes, "Religion of the Protestants," in Greenslade, *Reformation to the Present Day*, 3:183–84.

[42] Fenn, "Bible and the Missionary," 403.

doubts the influence of the King James Bible on English literature over the past four centuries.[43]

Finally, missionary Bible translation brought some indirect practical benefits to global peoples. In nineteenth-century Africa, Bible translation strategies were coupled with literacy campaigns.[44] Although the majority of global cultures are oral cultures, which should be celebrated and maintained, most would agree that the ability to read is also a useful skill opening the doors to increased educational and employment opportunities.

How do the principles of *sola Scriptura* and the vernacular principle lead the church forward in twenty-first-century Bible translation and mission? Bible translation has often been controversial. Tyndale's Protestant-leaning word choice in translation bothered the leadership of the English Roman Catholic Church. Nineteenth-century Protestant translators vehemently disagreed over how to translate "God" in the Chinese Scriptures. A lively debate continues today over how "God" and other theological terms should be rendered in idiomatic translations in Muslim languages.[45]

Bible translation is contextualization and the tricky tension between content and context must always be navigated. On one hand, we affirm and celebrate verbal plenary inspiration—that every word and syllable of Scripture is God speaking. On the other hand, we recognize that languages are constructed differently. Some languages function without abstract nouns; so concepts like *faith, propitiation,* and *grace* must be rendered concretely and idiomatically. We must also recognize the difficulties of conveying biblical ideas in languages where there has been no Christian tradition or where religious vocabulary (i.e., God, sin, grace) is common to other religions. Will we fall into the Latin-only trap of the medieval English church? Will we repeat Francis Xavier's (1506–1542) mistake of transliterating Portuguese religious terms into Japanese when dynamic equivalencies are hard to find?

How do we uphold the authority of Scripture in Bible translation moving forward? First, we must remember that because of the incarnation

---

[43] See further Leland Ryken, *The Legacy of the King James Bible: Celebrating 400 Years of the Most Influential English Translation* (Wheaton, IL: Crossway, 2011); also David Lyle Jeffrey, ed., *The King James Bible and the World it Made* (Waco, TX: Baylor University Press, 2011).

[44] Fenn, "Bible and the Missionary," 394–95.

[45] See further, Rochelle Cathcart Scheuermann and Edward L. Smither, eds., *Controversies in Mission: Theology, People, and Practice of Mission in the 21st Century,* Evangelical Missiological Society Series, no. 24 (Pasadena, CA: William Carey Library, 2016), 211–68.

of Christ, the Christian message (and its Scriptures) is imminently translatable. Second, because of the image of God in man, all languages are sufficient to house authoritative Scripture. Like Luther, we must continually revise vernacular Scriptures, especially as the church incorporates them in its life of worship. Third, because of the priesthood of the believer, we must trust local believers, who bear the image of God and who possess the Holy Spirit, to lead the way in translation. Fourth, Bible translation in the vernacular does not mean that teaching and discipleship ends. Rather, biblical teaching must continually be unpacked and clarified and international believers ought to play a role in this. Fifth, local Bible translations must always be informed and held accountable by the global church. As the global church sits at a roundtable with authoritative Scripture at the center, mutual affirmation and correction on matters of doctrine ought to continue. As Vanhoozer has recently written, "A mere Protestant practice of *sola Scriptura* constitutes a catholic biblicism."[46] Finally, the concrete (storytelling) nature of many global languages should be celebrated and leveraged in Bible translation. Since the primary genres of Scripture (history, poetry, song) are narrative, the Bible does lend itself to be rendered faithfully in concrete languages. Abstract terms (i.e., sin, forgiveness) might run the risk of being watered down or compromised over time, but a well told story remains intact and does not lose its power.

"We are dying from the deliciousness of these words." That's how a tribal elder in Papua New Guinea reacted when he first heard the words of John 3:16 read aloud in his heart language. What a beautiful example of faith that comes from hearing the word of Christ in the Scriptures (Rom 1:17). Over 1,600 global language groups are still without a word of Scripture in their language. By faith, this global famine for the word of the Lord will end soon and many millions will also begin to "die from the deliciousness" of the saving gospel.

Bibliography

Augustine. *On the Unity of the Church (De Unitate Ecclesiae)*. http://www.augustinus.it/latino/lettera_cattolici/index.htm

_____. *On Baptism Against the Donatists (De Baptismo contra Donatistas)*. http://www.augustinus.it/latino/sul_battesimo/index2.htm

---

[46] Vanhoozer, *Biblical Authority after Babel*, 146.

Bainton, Roland H. "The Bible in the Reformation." In *Cambridge History of the Bible*. Vol. 3, *The West from the Reformation to the Present Day*, ed. S. L. Greenslade, 1–37. Cambridge: Cambridge University Press, 1975.

Barrett, Matthew. *God's Word Alone: The Authority of Scripture*. Grand Rapids: Zondervan, 2016.

Black, M. H. "The Printed Bible." In *Cambridge History of the Bible*. Vol. 3, *The West from the Reformation to the Present Day*, ed. S. L. Greenslade, 408–75. Cambridge: Cambridge University Press, 1975.

Fenn, Eric. "The Bible and the Missionary." In *Cambridge History of the Bible*. Vol. 3, *The West from the Reformation to the Present Day*, ed. S. L. Greenslade, 383–407. Cambridge: Cambridge University Press, 1975.

Gensichen, Hans-Werner. "Ziegenbalg, Bartholomäus." In *Biographical Dictionary of Christian Missions*, ed. Gerald H. Anderson, 761. New York: Macmillan Reference USA, 1998.

————. "Plütschau, Heinrich." In *Biographical Dictionary of Christian Missions*, ed. Gerald H. Anderson, 540–41. New York: Macmillan Reference USA, 1998.

————. "Schwartz, Christian Friedrich." In *Biographical Dictionary of Christian Missions*, ed. Gerald H. Anderson, 606–7. New York: Macmillan Reference USA, 1998.

Greenslade, S. L. "English Versions of the Bible, 1525–1611." In *Cambridge History of the Bible*. Vol. 3, *The West from the Reformation to the Present Day*, ed. S. L. Greenslade, 141–74. Cambridge: Cambridge University Press, 1975.

Guder, Darrell L. "A Multicultural and Translational Approach." In *The Mission of the Church: Five Views in Conversation*, ed. Craig Ott, 21–40. Grand Rapids: Baker Academic, 2016.

Hall, Basil. "Biblical Scholarship: Editions and Commentaries." In *Cambridge History of the Bible*. Vol. 3, *The West from the Reformation to the Present Day*, ed. S. L. Greenslade, 38–93. Cambridge: Cambridge University Press, 1975.

Hargreaves, Henry. "The Wycliffite Versions." In *Cambridge History of the Bible*. Vol. 2, *The West from the Fathers to the Reformation*, ed. G. W. H. Lampe, 387–415. Cambridge: Cambridge University Press, 1969.

Jeffrey, David Lyle, ed. *The King James Bible and the World it Made*. Waco, TX: Baylor University Press, 2011.

Labberton, Mark. "Perpiscuity and the People's Book." In *The People's Book: The Reformation and the Bible*, ed. Jennifer Powell McNutt and David Lauber, 225–37. Downers Grove, IL: IVP Academic, 2017.

Marshall, I. Howard. *New Testament Theology: Many Witnesses, One Gospel*. Downers Grove, IL: IVP Academic, 2014.

Noak, Bent. "Scandinavian Versions," In *Cambridge History of the Bible*. Vol. 3, *The West from the Reformation to the Present Day*, ed. S. L. Greenslade, 135–40. Cambridge: Cambridge University Press, 1975.

Pak, G. Sujin. "Scripture, the Priesthood of All Believers, and Applications of 1 Corinthians 14." In *The People's Book: The Reformation and the Bible*, ed. Jennifer Powell McNutt and David Lauber, 33–51. Downers Grove, IL: IVP Academic, 2017.

Ryken, Leland. *The Legacy of the King James Bible: Celebrating 400 Years of the Most Influential English Translation*. Wheaton, IL: Crossway, 2011.

Sanneh, Lamin. *Translating the Message: The Missionary Impact on Culture*. Maryknoll: Orbis, 1989.

Scheuermann, Rochelle Cathcart, and Edward L. Smither, eds. *Controversies in Mission: Theology, People, and Practice of Mission in the 21st Century*. Evangelical Missiological Society Series, no. 24. Pasadena, CA: William Carey Library, 2016.

Shepherd, Geoffrey. "English Versions of the Scriptures Before Wyclif." In *Cambridge History of the Bible*. Vol. 2, *The West from the Fathers to the Reformation*, ed. G. W. H. Lampe, 362–87. Cambridge: Cambridge University Press, 1969.

Smither, Edward L. *Mission in the Early Church*. Eugene, OR: Cascade Books, 2014.

_____. *Missionary Monks: An Introduction to the History and Theology of Missionary Monasticism*. Eugene, OR: Cascade Books, 2016.

Sykes, Norman. "Religion of the Protestants." In *Cambridge History of the Bible*. Vol. 3, *The West from the Reformation to the Present Day*, ed. S. L. Greenslade, 175–98. Cambridge: Cambridge University Press, 1975.

Vanhoozer, Kevin J. *Biblical Authority after Babel: Retrieving the* Solas *in the Spirit of Mere Protestant Christianity*. Grand Rapids: Brazos, 2016.

_____. "Holy Scripture." In *Christian Dogmatics: Reformed Theology for the Church Catholic*, ed. Michael Allen and Scott R. Swain. Grand Rapids: Baker Academic, 2016.

Volz, Hanz. "German." In *Cambridge History of the Bible*. Vol. 3, *The West from the Reformation to the Present Day*, ed. S. L. Greenslade, 94–109. Cambridge: Cambridge University Press, 1975.

Walls, Andrew F. *The Missionary Movement in Christian History*. Maryknoll: Orbis, 1996.

Wycliffe Global Alliance. "The Vision." Accessed August 4, 2017. http://www.wycliffe.net/vision2025.

16

"Church under the Cross": Anabaptist Theology of Martyrdom

REX D. BUTLER

Within a few months after the first Swiss Brethren were baptized on January 21, 1525, Eberli Bolt became the first Anabaptist martyr.[1] Bolt was followed shortly by other Anabaptist leaders, including Felix Manz, Michael Sattler, Hans Hut, Balthasar Hubmaier, and George Blaurock, not to mention multitudes of their unsung followers. During the sixteenth century, Anabaptist martyrs, executed at the hands of other, so-called Christians, probably outnumbered their patristic forebears killed by Roman pagans during the first three centuries of the early church.[2] Understandably, then, martyrdom colored and shaped the theology of Anabaptists, and at the same time, their understanding of a God who sustains through hardship and persecution.

Martyrdom became the common denominator among the diverse sects and regions of the Anabaptist movement so that, despite other differences, a uniform theology of martyrdom developed. This chapter will explore

---

[1] May 29, 1525, Eberli Bolt, an Anabaptist lay preacher, was burned at the stake in Schwyz, Switzerland, by Roman Catholic authorities. Bolt is considered the first Anabaptist to die for his faith. William R. Estep, *The Anabaptist Story: An Introduction to Sixteenth-Century Anabaptism*, 3rd ed. (Grand Rapids: Eerdmans, 1995), 29.

[2] Justo L. Gonzalez, *The Story of Christianity*, vol. 2, *The Reformation to the Present Day* (San Francisco: HarperSanFrancisco, 1985), 56. Gonzalez's claim cannot be substantiated because statistics for martyrdoms of early Christians and Anabaptists are not verifiable. However, the number of Anabaptist martyrs has been estimated to be four thousand or more. Dave and Neta Jackson, *On Fire for Christ: Stories of Anabaptist Martyrs* (Scottsdale, PA: Herald Press, 1989), 18.

three great themes of this doctrine that emerged from Anabaptist writings. First, the history of God's people was seen as a path of martyrdom. Second, apocalyptic expectation was interpreted through their experience of persecution. Finally, Christian practices, such as baptism, confession, and defenselessness, were ordered within the framework of their theology of martyrdom.[3]

These themes were expressed through various genre of Anabaptist writings and in every regional tradition. The earliest doctrinal teaching seems to come from the Swiss Brethren through Conrad Grebel's appeal to Thomas Muntzer, dated September 5, 1524: "True believing Christians are sheep among wolves, sheep for the slaughter. They must be baptized in anguish and tribulation, persecution, suffering, and death."[4] The Anabaptist theologian, Balthasar Hubmaier, succinctly expressed the doctrine in his famous motto, "Truth is unkillable" (*Die Wahrheit ist untodtlich*).[5] From outside the Swiss tradition came such tracts as "Concerning the True Soldier of Christ" from the Philippite Brethren of Moravia[6] and the Dutch Menno Simons's *The Cross of the Saints,*[7] both writings heavily supported by biblical quotations.

So devoted were the earliest Anabaptists to Scriptural teaching, at first they banned singing by the gathered congregations in favor of preaching the Word of God.[8] "But the fulness of the hearts of their most severely persecuted leaders called for an orderly overflow in song,"[9] beginning even as early as Felix Manz. Although Anabaptist hymnody represented three regional traditions—Dutch (*Het Offer des Heeren*), Swiss (*Ausbund*), and Hutterite (*Die Lieder der Hutterischen Bruder*)—a common religious mood, the passion of martyrdom, gave all the hymns an integrated style and spirit. The majority of the hymns were composed by martyrs shortly before their

---

[3] Ethelbert Stauffer, "The Anabaptist Theology of Martyrdom," trans. Robert Friedmann, *Mennonite Quarterly Review* 19, no. 3 (1945): 187.

[4] Conrad Grebel, "Letter 63–To Muntzer," *The Sources of Swiss Anabaptism: The Grebel Letters and Related Documents*, ed. Leland Harder (Scottdale, PA: Herald Press, 1985), 290.

[5] This motto, which appears on numerous of Hubmaier's writings, is also translated, "Truth is immortal." *Balthasar Hubmaier: Theologian of Anabaptism*, trans. and ed. H. Wayne Pipkin and John H. Yoder (Scottdale, PA: Herald Press, 1989), 42n12, 77n10.

[6] Robert Friedmann, "Concerning the True Soldier of Christ: A Hitherto Unknown Tract of the Philippite Brethren in Moravia," *Mennonite Quarterly Review* 5 (1931): 87–99.

[7] Menno Simons, *The Cross of the Saints*, in *The Complete Writings of Menno Simons c. 1496–1561*, trans. Leonard Verduin, ed. John Christian Wenger (Scottdale, PA: Herald Press, 1956), 579–622; also titled *Of the Cross of Christ*.

[8] Grebel, "Letter 63," 286–88.

[9] Clarence Y. Fretz, ed., *Anabaptist Hymnal* (Hagerstown, MD: Deutsche Buchhandlung, 1987), iii.

deaths or about martyrs or persecution in general. Other hymns glorified historical witnesses of the past, foremost among them, Jesus Christ himself. These martyrs' hymns contained much of the theology of martyrdom.[10]

Besides doctrinal teachings and hymns, the Anabaptists left a profound source for understanding their thoughts on martyrdom in their chronicles, of which two outstanding examples are *The Chronicle of the Hutterian Brethren*[11] and the Dutch-Mennonite tome, *Martyrs Mirror*, whose full title revealed its complete purpose.[12] Whereas, the *Martyrs Mirror* started its narrative with the time of Christ, the *Hutterite Chronicle* detailed the entire history of God's people, beginning with Adam. Both chronicles thus connected Anabaptist martyrdom with the suffering of God's people throughout the history of this present age.[13]

The source materials of the Anabaptist theology of martyrdom revealed a unity among the diversity of traditions. The treatises, hymns, and chronicles, no matter their origin, all expressed the three doctrinal themes of history, apocalyptic expectation, and church practice.

Martyrdom and History

At the foundation of the Anabaptist theology of history was the identification of the true church of God with the suffering church. Moreover, the Anabaptists saw themselves as inheritors of the martyrs' tradition and, therefore, collected martyrs' stories from the past to inspire and encourage them along their way.

That the path of the faithful was a way of passion was proved by the Bible itself. According to the *Martyrs Mirror*, "Hence the whole volume of holy Scriptures, especially the Old Testament, seemed to be almost exclusively, a book of martyrs."[14] For this reason, Anabaptist historians began their martyrs' accounts in the beginning where they saw Abel as "a good example and a fair indication as to the way the righteous have always been offscourings and a prey to the unrighteous, and how they will continue to

---

[10] Stauffer, "Theology of Martyrdom," 184–85.

[11] *The Chronicle of the Hutterian Brethren*, vol. 1, trans. and ed. Hutterian Brethren (Rifton, NY: Plough, 1987).

[12] Thieleman J. van Braght, ed., *The Bloody Theater or Martyrs Mirror of the Defenseless Christians Who Baptized Only Upon Confession of Faith, and Who Suffered and Died for the Testimony of Jesus, Their Saviour, from the Time of Christ to the Year AD 1660*, trans. Joseph F. Sohm (Scottdale, PA: Mennonite Publishing House, 1950).

[13] Stauffer, "Theology of Martyrdom," 185–87.

[14] *Martyrs Mirror*, 13.

be that, even as the Scriptures testify sufficiently, and as daily experience plainly teaches."[15] These ancient stories culminated in the suffering of Jesus Christ, himself:

> As one may read of Abel, famed,
> Zacharias too—recall it well—
> And Daniel too, whom bad men framed
> So that he among fierce lions fell;
> So were the prophets treated all,
> Christ Jesus too—it is good to recall—
> Nor were the prophets spared this call.[16]

For the Anabaptists, the people of God were the people of Christ, and all who suffered martyrdom, from Abel onward, suffered under the "Cross of Christ," as expressed in this stanza: "From the beginning have all the saints; For the sake of Christ given their lives."[17]

Accordingly, as the martyrs suffered in Christ, so Christ suffered in them, the members of his body, "from the beginning until the present day."[18] To Christ, therefore, the Anabaptists accorded first place, "because He is the head of all the holy martyrs, through whom they all must be saved."[19] As the head and leader of the persecuted, Christ was the archetypal martyr, whose entire life, not merely his crucifixion, was characterized by the cross: "But His entrance into this world, as well as His progress and end, was full of misery, distress and affliction, indeed it may be said: He was born under the cross; brought up under the cross! He walked under the cross, and finally died on the cross."[20]

When confronting the question why, regarding the persecution of Christ and his church, the Anabaptists focused on the struggle between God and the Antichrist. "Because, wherever God wants to build his work, the Anti-Christ concentrates his destructive power, and wherever the light presses forward to victory, darkness once again gathers all its demonic

---

[15] Simons, *Cross*, 588.

[16] Menno Simons, "My God, Where Shall I Wend My Flight," trans. Leonard Verduin, in *Anabaptist Hymnal*, 16.

[17] "*Von Anfang sind die Heiligen all Umb Christi willen gestorben hie.*" *Lieder der Hutterischen Brüder*, 670, cited by Stauffer, 190 (translation mine).

[18] Simons, *Cross*, 597.

[19] *Martyrs Mirror*, 67.

[20] *Martyrs Mirror*, 67–68.

potency."[21] Thus, the hatred of the children of this world against the people of God was an expression of this cosmic contest. This concept revealed the essential dualism of Anabaptist theology: "As there are two different peoples, two different congregations and churches, the one of God and from heaven, the other of Satan and from the earth; so there is also a different succession and progress belonging to each of them."[22]

The causal answer to the question of persecution was only preliminary, however, to the teleological issues concerning both the death of Jesus Christ and the martyrdom of his faithful followers. Christ's work of salvation had a twofold purpose: "the end of Satan's rule and the beginning of the new era of grace."[23] From this point of view, the triumph of evil at the cross paradoxically led to the overwhelming victory of God and the indictment of Christ's persecutors. In the same way, the persecution of the martyrs resulted in their own exaltation and the ultimate defeat of their opponents.

> For even though in His first appearance He was sacrificed as an innocent lamb, and opened not His mouth, nevertheless the time will come when He will appear as a triumphant prince and a victorious king to bring judgment. Then will those who persecute us look upon Him whom they have pierced. Then will they cry aloud and exclaim: Mountains, fall on us, and hills, cover us. But you will leap and dance for joy like fatted calves of the stalls. Joy and exultation will never forsake you, for your king, your bridegroom and redeemer, Christ Jesus, will remain with you forever.[24]

Until the triumphant return of Christ and vindication of the martyrs, however, this age was entirely under the sign of the cross, when the enemy of Christ was directing his wrath upon the confessors of Christ. The confessors, though, followed the example of Stephen, the archetypal martyr, who, following in his turn the example of Christ, prayed for his executioners, "Lord, lay not this sin to their charge, for they know not what they do."[25]

Michael Sattler epitomized this attitude of forgiveness during his infamous torture and execution. According to an eyewitness account, Sattler suffered having his tongue cut and his flesh torn with red hot tongs.

---

[21] Stauffer, "Theology of Martyrdom," 191.
[22] *Martyrs Mirror*, 21.
[23] Stauffer, "Theology of Martyrdom," 192.
[24] Simons, *Cross*, 621–22.
[25] Simons, 594.

"Nevertheless, at first in the square and then again at the place of execution he prayed to God for his persecutors and also encouraged others to pray for them."[26]

Anabaptist attitudes toward their persecutors, however, were not totally without polemical overtones. In many of their writings, contemporary adversaries were associated with biblical villains: "Cain is again the proto-type; the city of Vienna, which saw burnings at the stake, becomes the new Sodom; the Catholic emperor Ferdinand is the new Pharaoh; Philipp II of Spain is the new Antiochus."[27] The Roman Church was identified as "Bab-ylon the great, mother of harlots and of every horror and atrocity on earth. She was drunk with the blood of the saints and the martyrs of Jesus."[28]

The Anabaptist struggle was not with Catholicism alone but also with the Lutheran and Zwinglian state churches, out of which God separated the true church.[29] "This the enemy of truth could not endure,"[30] so he brought persecution on the Anabaptists through magisterial Reformers such as Zwingli. The persecution, however, served to increase the church and spread the movement, while, at the same time, swelling the ranks of the martyrs.

Therein lay the purposes of the *Martyrs Mirror* and *The Chronicle of the Hutterian Brethren*: to preserve the memory of the myriad martyrs of their faith and to connect them historically to the "cloud of witnesses" recorded not only in the biblical accounts but also in church history through the centuries. That Anabaptists were familiar with Eusebius was obvious from trial accounts as well as the patristic references in both chronicles.[31]

Although the miraculous was exceptional in Anabaptist martyrology, an interesting link existed between Eusebius's account of Polycarp's mar-tyrdom and the executions of two Anabaptists. Citing a letter from the Church at Smyrna, Eusebius reported that, when Polycarp died in the fire, two wonders occurred: first, the flames rose up like a vaulted room while Polycarp's flesh shone like refined silver and gold; and second, the body was

---

[26] Klaus von Graveneck, "Report of Michael Sattler's Martyrdom," in *The Legacy of Michael Sattler*, trans. and ed. John H. Yoder (Scottdale, PA: Herald Press, 1973), 75.

[27] Stauffer, "Theology of Martyrdom," 195.

[28] *Hutterian Brethren*, 38.

[29] *Hutterian Brethren*, 43. According to research by Claus-Peter Clasen, *Anabaptism: A Social History, 1525–1618* (Ithaca, NY: Cornell University Press, 1972), cited by Estep, *Anabaptist Story*, 30n2, Roman Catholics were responsible for 84 percent of Anabaptist martyrdoms; Protestants, for 16 percent.

[30] *Hutterian Brethren*, 46.

[31] Stauffer, "Theology of Martyrdom," 187n26.

not consumed, and, when the executioner pierced the body with his sword, the stream of blood quenched the fire.[32] Compare this story with Wilhelm Reublin's account of Michael Sattler's martyrdom:

> His right hand could not be burned up, nor the heart, until the executioner had to cut it into pieces, and then the blood at first spurted high heavenward. In the night, many observed the sun and the moon standing still above the place of execution, three hours long, with golden letters written within. Such a bright light went out from them that many thought it was midday.[33]

In the same year as Sattler's death, Leonhard Keyser's execution also was attended by a miracle, according to the *Martyrs Mirror*. Keyser plucked a flower on the way to the bonfire and said, "Lord judge, here I pluck a flower; if you can burn this flower and me, you have justly condemned me; but, on the other hand, if you cannot burn me and this flower in my hand, consider what you have done and repent." Indeed, the executioners attempted to burn Keyser twice to no avail, and the flower did not even wither. Finally, they hewed his body into pieces, which still would not burn, so they threw them into the river.[34] The miraculous elements of these martyrdoms tied the sixteenth-century events to those of the earliest centuries of Christian persecution: in Eusebius's *Ecclesiastical History* as in the *Martyrs Mirror*, the path of the church is the history of the "church under the Cross."[35]

In a historical tour de force, the *Martyrs Mirror* detailed century by century proofs that "[t]he divine and heavenly church, which is the separated holy flock and people of God, originated upon earth at the beginning of the world; has existed through all the ages up to the present time; and will continue to the end of the world."[36] In the *Martyrs Mirror* and also in the *Hutterite Chronicle*, the story of the persecution of God's people served as an introduction to the martyrdom of the Anabaptists, who considered themselves surrounded by a new "cloud of witnesses":

---

[32] Eusebius, *The History of the Church from Christ to Constantine*, trans. with an introduction by G. A. Williamson (New York: Dorset Press, 1965), 173.

[33] Wilhelm Reublin, Report of Sattler's Trial and Death, in *The Legacy of Michael Sattler*, trans. and ed. John H. Yoder (Scottdale, PA: Herald Press, 1973), 76.

[34] *Martyrs Mirror*, 421.

[35] Stauffer, "Theology of Martyrdom," 182.

[36] *Martyrs Mirror*, 21.

These confessors of the faith—so many that they become like a new cloud of witnesses surrounding us, like a fiery pillar going before us in the night—these Christians, valiant for the truth of God, were condemned to torture and death in ways too numerous to describe. There were men and women, youths and girls, old and young, teachers and listeners. In them we see that God pours out his grace and strength in recent times as well as in days gone by.[37]

The testimony of Anneken of Rotterdam to her son was recorded in a hymn of the Swiss *Ausbund*: "I go on the way of the prophets, The path of the apostles and martyrs."[38] This path that the Anabaptist martyrs shared with their forebears in the faith was the way of the cross, and, throughout their travails, they never forgot that they followed Christ in their discipleship (*Nachfolge*) and that their tribulations lasted as long as they were in this world:

One new spiritual song in which a disciple of Christ pours out his heart,
So much grief for the sake of the Word has captured him;
The Lord answers him gently with a story,
How, in this world, it must be endured by him.[39]

At the same time, the discipleship of Christ was the imitation of Christ, to whose passion the follower must conform himself. George Blaurock, one of the original Swiss Brethren, composed a hymn that conveyed Anabaptists' expectations: "As He then has suffered Himself, as He has hung on the Cross, So it happens now to the saints—they suffer great pain."[40] Finally, for the disciple, the way of the cross led through death to ultimate glory. As another hymn from *Ausbund* said it: "The bride must, as the bridegroom, Enter through suffering into joy."[41]

---

[37] *Hutterian Brethren*, 221.

[38] *Ich gehe auf der Propheten Weg, Der Mertrer und Apostel Steg. Ausbund*, 110, cited by Stauffer, "Theology of Martyrdom," 195.

[39] *Ein neu geistlich Lied, darin sich ein Nachfolger Christi klagt, so ihn die Trubsal um des Wortes willen troffen hat; der Herr antwortet ihm sanftmutig, mit Erzahlung, wie es ihm in dieser Welt auch ergangen sei.* Hans Buchel, The "45. Lied," *Ausbund*, 247, cited by Stauffer, "Theology of Martyrdom," 195 (translation mine).

[40] *Wie er denn selbst gelitten hat, als er am Kreuz gahangen Also es jetzt den Frommen gaht, die leiden grosse Zwangen.* George Blaurock, *Ausbund*, 39, cited by Stauffer, "Theology of Martyrdom," 196 (translation mine).

[41] *Die Braut muss wie der Brautigam Durch Leiden in die Freud eingahn. Ausbund*, 128, cited by Stauffer, "Theology of Martyrdom," 197 (translation mine).

In conclusion, the cross informed the Anabaptist theology of history in two ways: first, the cross was central to all history; and second, the cross was the guiding principle for God's people throughout history.[42] "[D]ivine truth is unkillable. Even if it may for a time be imprisoned, scourged, crowned, crucified, and laid into a grave, it would nevertheless arise again victorious on the third day and reign and triumph forever."[43]

Martyrdom and Apocalyptic Expectation

This triumph of truth, Christ, and the Anabaptist cause, which was the theme of apocalyptic expectation, was awaited at the approaching end of history. The tribulation of the Anabaptists was not just one stage on the path of martyrdom through history, but actually the final stage, "the last act in the apocalyptic drama between God and Satan." Drawing upon the figures of Revelation, the Anabaptists characterized various of their opponents—pope, emperor, and Luther—as Antichrist or false prophet. The expectation of Christ as conqueror upon the white horse, smiting the Beast and the Harlot, comforted the saints awaiting that ultimate victory.[44]

In the meantime, the Anabaptists perceived that they were at a critical point in history when suffering, a sign of divine election, tested them as gold in fire. Their views regarding martyrdom matched the various forms of execution—drowning, fire, and the sword—with the intended purposes of God. First, though the executioners dubbed drowning as a "third baptism" for Anabaptists, Menno Simons observed that God was able to turn bitter into sweet, even death by water: "Love . . . is stronger than death. Many waters cannot quench it, many floods cannot choke it."[45] Second, for love's sake, the martyr offered his life as a sacrifice before God on the stake, "the altar of burnt offering,"[46] and God promised that, through his consolation, the sacrifice would be pure: "Indeed, Lord, you desire us to succeed, To make to you one pure sacrifice."[47]

Finally, the martyr's blood was considered a seed, following Tertullian, which bore fruit in new believers. An example of this truth was reported

---

[42] Stauffer, "Theology of Martyrdom," 197.

[43] Balthasar Hubmaier, "An Earnest Christian Appeal to Schaffhausen," *Balthasar Hubmaier: Theologian*, 42.

[44] Stauffer, "Theology of Martyrdom," 197–98.

[45] Simons, *Cross*, 619.

[46] Stauffer, "Theology of Martyrdom," 199.

[47] *Dass uns, Herr, mog gelingen, Dir ein rein Opfer darzubringen. Ausbund*, 235, cited by Stauffer, "Theology of Martyrdom," 199 (translation mine).

in the *Hutterite Chronicle*: Dietrich von Schonberg, burgrave of Alzey, after beheading and drowning hundreds of Anabaptist men and women, said, "What shall I do? The more I condemn and execute, the more of them there are."[48]

Thus, the teleological meaning in martyrdom was that death meant, in relation to Satan, victory over the victor. "No other concept found such a ready and general echo among the Anabaptists as this one of overcoming Satan by the extreme sacrifice."[49] The Christian, then, came to be thought of as a knight, a champion of truth, and the Christian life as warfare of the cross. Simons exhorted, "O soldiers of God, prepare yourselves and fear not! . . . Do battle! The crown of glory is prepared for you! Shrink not, neither draw back; for yet a little while and He that shall come will come and not tarry."[50] In the *Martyrs Mirror*, the persecuted were "soldiers under the bloody banner of Christ," and the cross, "the ensign of those who serve and follow Jesus Christ, the Captain of the faith."[51]

The godly protagonists, however, seek vindication of God's justice over the existing evil, for the ultimate questions deal with theodicy: "the last great problem of an apocalyptic interpretation of the contemporary world situation."[52] Leonard Schiemer [Schoener], a minister beheaded January 14, 1528,[53] left behind this admonition to console fellow sufferers:

> O Lord how long wilt Thou be silent with regard to this? How long wilt Thou not judge the blood of Thy saints? Therefore we have in all our distresses a comforting confidence in Thee alone, and in no other; neither have we consolation, rest or peace in the earth. But he that hopes in Thee shall never be confounded. . . . Eternal glory, triumph, honor and praise be unto Thee now and in all eternity, and Thy righteousness abide forever. All nations bless Thy holy name, through Christ, the coming righteous Judge of the whole world, Amen.[54]

---

[48] *Hutterian Brethren*, 74–75.

[49] Stauffer, "Theology of Martyrdom," 200.

[50] Simons, *Cross* 621–22.

[51] *Martyrs Mirror*, 357.

[52] Stauffer, "Theology of Martyrdom," 201.

[53] For a biography of Leonard Schiemer and a discussion of his theology, see Michael D. Wilkinson, "Suffering of the Cross: The Life, Theology, and Significance of Leonard Schiemer," in *The Anabaptists and Contemporary Baptists: Restoring New Testament Christianity*, ed. Malcolm B. Yarnell III (Nashville: B&H Academic, 2013), 49–64.

[54] *Martyrs Mirror*, 425. See also Leonhard Schiemer, "Thine Holy Place They Have Destroyed," *Anabaptist Hymnal*, 7.

With Schiemer, Anabaptists found two answers to the problem of theodicy: first, God will be true to himself (*sich selbst verwirklichen*); and, second, "God is more real than anything called 'world.'"[55] The apocalyptic paradox discovered by the Anabaptists revealed that martyrdom was not an end, but a beginning. "It was seen by Anabaptists as participation in the events of the End, and the fiercer the persecution, the nearer they were to the return of Christ and their glorious salvation."[56] Not until the number of martyrs is complete and the sin of God's enemies is full will God reveal his justice and bring his kingdom.[57]

Martyrdom and Christian Practice

The theology of martyrdom was "the crypt or hidden sanctuary of Anabaptist Christianity," but its adherents were concerned not only with philosophical issues but also with practical matters. Baptism, confession of faith, and defenselessness were external features that characterized Anabaptist practice.[58]

Baptism

When the Anabaptists revived the early church practice of baptism, they also revived the Pauline conception of baptism as death (*Tauftod*) and death as baptism (*Todestaufe*). *Protestation and Defense*, an early product of the Swiss Anabaptists,[59] stated that "whoever has baptism has been buried in the death of Christ."[60]

In other writings, the background was the saying of Jesus, "I have a baptism to be baptized with" (Luke 12:50 ESV). Before Anneken of Rotterdam was drowned on January 24, 1539, she delivered her testament to her son, Isaiah:

> My son, hear the instruction of your mother. . . . Behold, I go today the way of the prophets, apostles and martyrs, and drink of the cup of

---

[55] Stauffer, "Theology of Martyrdom," 203–4.

[56] Walter Klaassen, *Living at the End of the Ages: Apocalyptic Expectations in the Radical Reformation* (Lanham, MD: University Press of America, 1992), 68.

[57] Stauffer, "Theology of Martyrdom," 201–2.

[58] Stauffer, 205.

[59] Stauffer, writing in 1945, attributed *Protestation and Defense* to Conrad Grebel, but later scholarship recognized that the work came from Felix Manz, one of Grebel's inner circle. See Leland Harder, ed., *Sources of Swiss Anabaptism*, 311.

[60] *Wer den Tauf hat, der ist im Tode Christi gepflanzet worden.* Felix Manz, *Protestation and Defense*, cited by Stauffer, "Theology of Martyrdom," 205.

which they all have drank [*sic*]. I go, I say, the way which Christ Jesus
. . . Himself went, and who went this way and not another, and who
had to drink of this cup, even as He said: 'I have a cup to drink of,
and a baptism to be baptized with; and how am I straitened till it be
accomplished!' Having passed through, He calls His sheep, and His
sheep hear His voice, and follow Him whithersoever He goes . . . .

This way was trodden by the dead under the altar, who cry,
saying: Lord, Almighty God, when wilt Thou avenge the blood that
had been shed? . . .

[W]here you hear of the cross, there is Christ; from there do not
depart.[61]

In the *Martyrs Mirror*, the death of Christ himself was pictured dramatically as a baptism of sorts: "Concerning the end of His life, it was the
most miserable, for it was, so to speak, the day, when all the fountains of
the great deep broke forth over Him, and the floods of suffering overflowed
Him, to swallow Him up altogether."[62]

Following Jesus's terminology, Anabaptists developed baptismal language with which to inform their theology of martyrdom. Grebel warned
that Christians "must be baptized in anguish and tribulation, persecution,
suffering, and death."[63] The *Hutterite Chronicle* acknowledged the validity
of the "baptism of blood" for those who died before receiving the baptism
of water.[64]

Completing the Anabaptists' baptismal theology was their idea that the
Christian, through baptism, enters the way whose end is martyrdom. One
of the Anabaptist hymnwriters, Hans Betz, based this hymn on 1 John 5:8:

> Whoever receives baptism, to his hand comes
> The Cross, sorrow, and suffering.
>
> . . . .
>
> Three testimonies are intended for us here:
> The two one calls water and spirit,
> The third, blood, which is suffering.[65]

---

[61] *Martyrs Mirror*, 453–54.

[62] *Martyrs Mirror*, 68.

[63] Grebel, "Letter 63," 290.

[64] *Hutterian Brethren*, 223.

[65] *Wer den Tauff nimmt, zu Hand ihm kommt Kreuz, Trubsal und das Leiden. . . . Drei Zeugnisse sind uns hier beschieden, Die zwei man heisst Wasser und Geist, Der dritte, Blut, das ist Leiden.* Hans Betz, *Ausbund*, 608, cited by Stauffer, "Theology of Martyrdom," 207 (translation mine).

Another hymn further elaborated this idea: "Whosoever will enter into a covenant with God needs three witnesses in Heaven, Father, Son, and Holy Ghost, and three witnesses on earth, spirit, water, and blood. The first baptism is the baptism with the spirit, the second the baptism with water, but the third is the baptism with blood."[66]

Confession

The terms "testimonies" and "witnesses," are related to the next external practice of the Anabaptist church, confession. The confession of faith for the Anabaptists most closely resembled the conceptions from the early church, as they revived the old word, "confessor." Following the example of the *Acts of the Martyrs*, the *Martyrs Mirror* and *Hutterite Chronicle* included the testimonies of faith delivered by Anabaptists in their trial records.[67] Also included are letters from confessors such as Joos Kind, burned at the stake in 1553. Inquisitors came to him in prison to ask him about his faith:

> They asked me so much, that I said to them: "I have freely confessed my faith, and am ready to go alive into the fire for it; hence be content that you know my faith. . . . Do therefore to me what you please; for it is through the grace of the Lord that I have these members, and I am also ready to give them up by the grace of the Lord, yea, to present them for His holy praise."[68]

Many victims would testify on their way to their executions, witnessing to persecutors and spectators alike. On his way to the Limmat River, Felix Manz taught believers' baptism to his guards and then cried out, "Into thy hands, O Lord, I commend my spirit," as his arms and legs were bound.[69] The story of Michael Sattler has already been related, how, even with his tongue cut out, he prayed aloud for his tormentors and testified to the truth of his beliefs.

The authorities eventually sought to prevent such confessions of faith through a device called a tongue screw. One victim mistreated so cruelly

---

[66] Stauffer, "Theology of Martyrdom," 207. Sixteenth-century manuscripts of 1 John 5:7–8 would have included the reference to Father, Son, and Holy Ghost, which is not found in more recently discovered manuscripts and, therefore, is excluded from modern translations.

[67] See for example Michael Sattler's trial recorded in *Martyrs Mirror*, 416–18; and *Hutterite Chronicle*, 51–52.

[68] *Martyrs Mirror*, 541.

[69] Estep, *Anabaptist Story*, 47.

was Maeyken Wens, burned at the stake in Antwerp on October 6, 1573. On the day of her death, her oldest son, Adriaen, went to the site with his youngest brother Hans. He lost consciousness, however, at the sight of his mother's execution and remained so until after the consumption of her body. Hunting through the ashes, he was able to recover the tongue screw, which he kept with him as a reminder of his mother's faith, which was passed on through many generations.[70]

According to the *Hutterite Chronicle*, what the Anabaptists confessed by mouth, they testified by blood. The theology of martyrdom informed these confessions of faith, teaching that confessions were sealed with blood because they confessed to the truth. They confessed not only to the truth of their convictions, but also to the truth of their Christ, who is truth and was crucified for that reason. Furthermore, he rose invincible because he is truth. In sum, "in a world which shuts itself off from truth by every means, with contradiction and scholarly sophistication, with deafness and dullness, with overbearing and hatred . . . in such a world there is no other chance to bring truth to victory than through catastrophe."[71]

Defenselessness

The only possible response on the part of Anabaptists to such a "catastrophe" as persecution was defenselessness. The theological foundation for such a concept was "yieldedness, or resignation" (*Gelassenheit*), based on Jesus's commission to the disciples (Matt 10:5–42); his Sermon on the Mount (Matt 5–7); and his encouragement in the apocalyptic chapters of the Gospels to be steadfast in the face of tribulation (Matt 24:4–14). Anabaptists quoted these passages and their parallels often and interpreted them correctly as the call of Christ to his disciples to accept persecution without resistance and to avoid violence in religious matters. The highest example of this attitude was intercessory prayer on behalf of the persecutors.[72]

The concept of resignation was central to the thought of *Concerning the True Soldier of Christ*, a treatise composed by Hans Haffner of the Philippite Brethren in Moravia. The thesis—"A genuine soldier of Christ must have true resignation, and must mortify his own life" —was based on the

---

[70] *Martyrs Mirror*, 979–80.
[71] Stauffer, "Theology of Martyrdom," 210–11.
[72] Stauffer, 212.

truths found in Luke 9:23–26, 57–62. It is through resignation that the Christian soldier wins over the world, flesh, and the devil.[73]

One such soldier of Christ who exhibited the quality of defenselessness was Dirk Willems. Willems, fleeing a thief-catcher employed for the purpose of apprehending him, succeeded in crossing an icy stream. When the unfortunate pursuer broke through the thin ice, however, Willems returned to pull him out of the freezing water, thereby saving his life. Once on the shore, the thief-catcher wanted to free Willems, but the burgomeister insisted that he honor his oath and arrest him. As a result, Willems was apprehended and burned on May 16, 1569.[74]

The Anabaptists paid with their lives for their policy of resignation or defenselessness. They accepted their fate, however, recognizing that the peace of Christ had no place in this age, but only conflict and that the antidote to conflict was the yieldedness modeled by Christ on the cross. Between Calvary and heaven, the path of discipleship was strewn with tribulations, but the end, though it passed through martyrdom, was glorious victory.[75]

Conclusion

As martyrdom claimed the lives of countless Anabaptists, it became the central theme of their understanding of past, present, and future. Dominating the history of God's people was the cross of Christ, the banner under which even the Old Testament and intertestamental saints suffered as well as the heroes of the New Testament and church history. Christ's work of salvation on the cross wrought the end of Satan's rule and ushered in a new era of grace. Therefore, the persecution endured by the Anabaptists, whether at the hands of the Catholics, Lutherans, or Zwinglians, won victory for them and ultimately defeated their opponents.

The cross, therefore, powerful symbol and example of martyrdom, guided God's people from persecution in history to their apocalyptic expectations for the future. Those expectations included the triumph of truth, Christ, and the Anabaptist cause and the defeat of Satan and death. In the meantime, the Anabaptists struggled with the question of theodicy but found succor in two answers: God was true, and God was real.

---

[73] Friedmann, "True Soldier of Christ," 91.
[74] *Martyrs Mirror*, 741–42.
[75] Stauffer, "Theology of Martyrdom," 214.

Their confidence in the future impacted the Anabaptist framework that structured their lives in the present: baptism, confession, and defenselessness. In observing these "sacraments," they followed Christ in obedience, through martyrdom, to ultimate victory.

Nearly five hundred years later, the "Church under the Cross" endures, still awaiting the revelation of God's justice. The focal point of Christian suffering, however, has shifted from Europe to other parts of the globe, such as Communist North Korea and China, Muslim countries in the Middle East and Southeast Asia, "Hindu-only" India, and South America, where drug cartels are the enemies of Christ. Christians who suffer in the contemporary world are sustained by their own "theology of martyrdom."

Contemporary, persecuted Christians around the globe, have much to teach about suffering for Christ. And like the Anabaptists, their theology includes an apocalyptic emphasis. For example, a Chinese pastor prepared this message for Western Christians: "Take this back from us. *Everyone* is living in the book of Revelation, because we all are part of the persecuted church…. Wherever you go in this earth, you will be seduced by a false prophet, or coerced by a beast, into worshiping some idol that is not God. That is apocalyptic reality. Your worship is what you put your energy into. The only difference between you and us is that here it happened so brutally, we saw it so clearly; where you live, it happens so subtly, you cannot see it at all…. Please don't miss this—*you need our faith to find your own!*"[76] Indeed, the American church faces a very different situation. Here, no established church can call upon the resources of the state to enforce conformity and suppress dissension, as the Catholics and Magisterial Reformers did. But the postmodern, post-Christian culture that appears to dominate American society seeks to marginalize Christianity in a more subtle form of persecution. As evangelical Christians find themselves cast in the role of outsiders in America, we have opportunities to embrace a prophetic role similar to that of the Anabaptist "Church under the Cross." The Anabaptists' theology of martyrdom "focuses our attention on the need for the cross in the day-to-day call to follow Christ, providing a much-needed corrective to the cultural accommodation, weak

---

[76] Ronald Boyd-MacMillan, *Faith that Endures: The Essential Guide to the Persecuted Church* (Grand Rapids: Revell, 2006), 15 (emphasis his).

discipleship, and distortions of the Christian life that have infected many contemporary churches."[77]

To fulfill the Chinese pastor's urgent request to "find our own faith," American Christians need to access the faith of other Christian sufferers, whether our contemporary brothers and sisters around the globe or Anabaptists. Looking beyond our borders or even our own time to "see persecution,"[78] we must claim solidarity with Christian sufferers and embrace our status as the "Church under the Cross."

American Christians, however, unlike Anabaptists, have religious rights and freedoms, which we guard carefully, and rightfully so. At the same time, we need to engage our culture humbly, by practicing in a sense what the Anabaptists called "defenselessness." The Anabaptists held closely to Jesus's teachings on resignation (e.g., Luke 9:23–26), and if they were to speak to our context, they would call on us to respond winsomely in the face of perceived persecution and to avoid acrimony in our dialogues with critics. In every case, Anabaptists would admonish us to pray for those who oppose us. In light of Dirk Willems, who sacrificed his freedom and life to rescue his pursuer, we can do no less.

Bibliography

Primary Sources

Anabaptist Hymnal. Edited by Clarence Y. Fretz. Hagerstown, MD: Deutsche Buchhandlung, 1987.

The Bloody Theater or Martyrs Mirror of the Defenseless Christians Who Baptized Only Upon Confession of Faith, and Who Suffered and Died for the Testimony of Jesus, Their Saviour, From the Time of Christ to the Year AD 1660. Translated by Joseph F. Sohm Thieleman and edited by J. van Braght. Scottdale, PA: Mennonite Publishing House, 1950.

The Chronicle of the Hutterian Brethren. Vol. 1. Translated and edited by the Hutterian Brethren. Rifton, NY: Plough Publishing House, 1987.

Eusebius. *The History of the Church from Christ to Constantine*. Translated with an introduction by G. A. Williamson. New York: Dorset Press, 1965.

---

[77] Wilkinson wrote these words about Leonard Schiemer, but they apply as well to the Anabaptists in general and to the need for discipleship in the American church. Wilkinson, "Significance of Leonard Schiemer," 64.

[78] Roy Stults, "Start Seeing Persecution," *Christian History* 109 (2014): 33.

Grebel, Conrad. *The Sources of Swiss Anabaptism: The Grebel Letters and Related Documents*. Edited by Leland Harder. Scottdale, PA: Herald Press, 1985.

Hubmaier, Balthasar. *Balthasar Hubmaier: Theologian of* Anabaptism. Translated and edited by H. Wayne Pipkin and John H. Yoder. Scottdale, PA: Herald Press, 1989.

Reublin, Wilhelm. "Report of Sattler's Trial and Death." In *The Legacy of Michael Sattler*. Translated and edited by John H. Yoder. Scottdale, PA: Herald Press, 1973.

Simons, Menno. *The Complete Writings of Menno Simons c. 1496–1561*. Translated by Leonard Verduin and edited by John Christian Wenger. Scottdale, PA: Herald Press, 1956.

Von Graveneck, Klaus. "Report of Michael Sattler's Martyrdom." In *The Legacy of Michael Sattler*. Translated and ed. John H. Yoder. Scottdale, PA.: Herald Press, 1973.

Secondary Sources

Estep, William R. *The Anabaptist Story: An Introduction to Sixteenth-Century Anabaptism*, 3rd ed. Grand Rapids: Eerdmans, 1995.

Friedmann, Robert. "Concerning the True Soldier of Christ: A Hitherto Unknown Tract of the Philippite Brethren in Moravia." *Mennonite Quarterly Review* 5 (1931): 87–99.

Gonzalez, Justo L. *The Story of Christianity*. Vol. 2, *The Reformation to the Present Day*. San Francisco: HarperSanFrancisco, 1985.

Jackson, Dave, and Neta Jackson. *On Fire for Christ: Stories of Anabaptist Martyrs*. Scottsdale, PA: Herald Press, 1989.

Klaassen, Walter. *Living at the End of the Ages: Apocalyptic Expectations in the Radical Reformation*. Lanham, MD: University Press of America, 1992.

Stauffer Ethelbert. "The Anabaptist Theology of Martyrdom." Translated by Robert Friedmann. *Mennonite Quarterly Review* 19 (1945): 179–214.

Wilkinson, Michael D. "Suffering of the Cross: The Life, Theology, and Significance of Leonard Schiemer." In *The Anabaptists and Contemporary Baptists: Restoring New Testament Christianity*, edited by Malcolm B. Yarnell III, 49–64. Nashville: B&H Academic, 2013.

Appendix 1:

Latin Poetry

Theodoro Bezæ P.l. (pp. xiii–xiv)

1   *Qualis quae intonsi servat fastigia montis*
    Annosa et ramis procera ingentibus arbor
    Quam Notus et gelida decurrens Caurus ab Arcto
    Ictibus alternis quatiunt frustraque minantur
5   *Vicina vasto complentes murmure silvas*
    Illa immota suis alte radicibus haeret
    Praecipitesque Iouis turbati despicit iras,

    Sic animi sincera tui constantia, qua tu
    Iamdudum infecto pietatem niteris orbi
10 *Asserere, atque animis hominum depellere quicquid*
    Vana superstitio ritusque imitata profanos
    Induxit, sensim terras grassata per omnes.
    Non regum imperiis fracta est, non victa resedit
    Immeritis odiis, saevi aut formidine leti,
15 *Sed magis illa tuo sententia pectore inhaesit,*
    Aeternum invitis Christum celebrare tyrranis.

    Quid memorem egregias dotes? si forte libebit
    Carmine secretos Musarum insistere calles,
    Dignus qui aeterna cingaris tempora lauro,
20 *Praecipue Ausoniis, Graiis, Gallisque Camenis*
    Davidicos aptare modos, et nablia sacra
    Aggressus, sacri merito fers nomina vatis,
    Seu sanctas solio leges expandis ab alto,
    Consolando pios, vitiisque immanibus asper,

25 *Tullius et Suadae tibi cesserit ipsa medulla.*
    Nec minus ignoras, causas exquirere doctus,
    Quicquid Aristoteles, quicquid mens dia Platonis
    Extulit in lucem, atque pios depromis in usus.
    Nec vero ipse probas id quod gens barbara garrit,
30 *Docta sequi tenebras, et cassa vivere luce,*
    Et studia et Musas pietati offundere nubem,
    Sed veluti ridenti adamas circumdatus auro
    Purior apparet, maiori exitque nitore,
    Quam plumbi durive inclusus carcere ferri,
35 *Sic verae pietatis amor, sic incluta virtus,*
    Siquando docto resident in pectore, miros
    Edunt concentus, maioraque lumina pandunt.

    Salve ergo decus O patriae, quo vindice tandem
    Aethereum radiare iubar, pulsisque tenebris,
40 *Dulcia sentimus melioris commoda vitae.*
    Haec tibi pro tantis meritis, quae pignora nostri
    Sint animi, grato audemus suspendere voto.

To Theodore Beza, From a Reverent Reader

1   Atop a wooded mount, a guard stands firm
    Whose massive branches soar aloft, a tree
    'Gainst which the winter winds and summer storms
    Blow hard, yet even hurricanes blow vain:
5   Though through the forest round they raise a roar,
    That tree moves not, held high by well-fixed roots,
    And Jupiter's mad raging he ignores.

    Just so stands firm your heart, as war you wage
    For righteousness in lands long stained with sin,
10 To banish from men's hearts the creeping curse
    Of superstition, with its empty rites,
    The vanity that slowly choked the world.
    Your firm resolve is broken not by kings,
    By thoughtless hate, by violent threat'ning death,
15 But all the more unmoved, your soul stands sure
    And worships Christ while tyrants rage in vain.

Your virtues, if I may, now let me tell:
You tread with skill the Muses' secret paths,
And win the laurel crown of every age.
20   Indeed, in Latin, Greek, and even French
You tuned great David's lyre to sweetly play,
And justly earned the name of holy bard.
But greater still, you preach God's sacred word:
The saints are cheered, sin hides its ugly head,
25   And Cicero and Cethegus bow low.
Nor less praiseworthy is your learned love
For Aristotle's thought, for Plato's truth,
And how you make them serve for holy ends.
And yet you give no thought to pagan talk
30   That boasts of light but ends in darkest sin,
And eloquently stifles godliness.
Instead, as when a diamond fitly set
Shines even brighter in its nest of gold,
Yet dull appears when chained in lead or steel,
35   So godly love and virtue, when they rest
Within a learned heart, a well-schooled soul,
What harmony then rings, what light shines forth!

And so we hail our homeland's honored son,
Him by whose help at length we feel warm rays
40   Pierce through the dark and heav'nly joy bestow.
For all these gifts, we pray this poem may prove
A fitting thanks, a token of our love.

Psalmus II (pp. 5–7)

1   *Gentium furor unde tantus hic est?*
Sic frustra populos tumultuari?
2   *Sic reges properare concitatos?*
Sic una inque Deum inque praepotentis
Regis a Domino caput perunctum,
Facta haec impia principes movere?
3   *Horum nunc age, nunc iuvabit (aiunt)*
Diruptis semel evolare vinclis,
Et curvo iuga mox fugare collo.

4 *Sic illi. At Deus ex poli supremo*
   Ridens vertice spectat hos furores:
   Hasque terribiles ferocientium
   Minas omnibus excipit cachinnis.

5 *Donec horribili furore fervens,*
   Ipsos praecipiti furore fractos,
   Voce terreat intonans tremenda.

6 *At hunc (inquiet) in Sione Regem*
   Designavimus: hunc placet sacrati
   Nobis imperium tenere montis.

7 *Tunc ego intrepidus Dei perenne*
   Edictum memorabo, namque nobis
   Hæc vero pater est locutus ore,
   Tu mi Filius: (inquit) hac beata

8 *Luce te genui, ecquid est quod optes?*
   Posce tu modo. Nam tibi universas
   Concessum simul undiquaque gentes,
   Et laxi spatia obtinere mundi.

9 *En sceptro tibi ferreo licebit*
   Mentes conterere omnium rebelles:
   Idque tam facile ac labore nullo,
   Quam potest figulus rotata vasa
   Levi frangere, quum libebit, ictu.

10 *Ergo deposito furore tandem,*
   Reges nunc sapite, oro: principesque
   Qui vasti imperium tenetis orbis,

11 *Nunc Deum veriti colatis ultro,*
   Et vestro pariter Deo exhibete
   Mixtos laetitia e tremore cultus.

12 *Nunc amplexibus obviis receptum*
   Ipsius quoque filium fovete,
   Iram ne semel eius asperetis,
   Quae si vel semel arserit, necesse est
   Vos mox funditus interire totos.
   At contra, omnibus o modis beatos,
   Illos qui Domino Deoque fidunt!

Psalm 2

1   Nations rage! Where does such a madness come from?
    Why in vain are the peoples so in uproar?
2   Why do kings, so incited, hasten quickly?
    Why 'gainst God and together 'gainst the head of
    The great King, by the Lord with oil anointed,
    Godless deeds such as these do rulers foment?
3   Now! they say, now to what we've always wanted:
    Break their chains, and be free from them forever,
    Then stiff-necked, take their yoke and cast it from us!
4   Thus they speak, but the Lord from highest heaven
    Peers down, laughing, upon these angry ragings.
    Fearful threats such as these, so fierce and savage,
    Move him not: with a violent laugh he mocks them!
5   Not long thence will he steam with fearful furor,
    Those same men he will crush in headlong furor,
    His voice thundering, he will terrify them!
6   See, he'll say, I have placed in Zion this King,
    This one, seated upon my holy mountain,
    To him gladly I give to rule the nations.
7   Bold then, I will announce the Lord's eternal
    Ordinance, for to me he has revealed it.
    These things truly my Father's mouth has spoken:
    You, my Son, on this blessed day I bore you—
8   Tell me, pray, is there anything you wish for?
    Say the word, for to you belongs the cosmos:
    All peoples will be yours, in every nation,
    The wide world, to possess in all its fullness.
9   Here, a rod made with hardened iron so that
    You may crush all the heads of the rebellious,
    And that easily, and to you no trouble
    More than that which a potter makes when on the
    Wheel he breaks, as he wish, the pot with one blow.
10 Put off, therefore at last, your wild raging,
    Kings, be wise, now I pray, and all you princes
    Who hold sway over lands throughout the whole world,

11 Now fear God! Serve him willingly, and show him,
    As your God, fitting praise and veneration,
    Joy and trembling united in his worship!
12 Hands flung wide, on your knees come and surrender
    To his Son: him embrace and freely love him,
    Lest his wrath once you foolishly awaken,
    Which if once, should begin to burn, then you must
    Be destroyed, all of you, completely ruined.
    Even so, they with every good are gladdened,
    Who trust God, on the Lord alone relying!

Testimonies
of the Anabaptist Women
Martyred in the Reformation

BY CANDI FINCH, PhD

Little is known about Anabaptist women during this time, although over one-third of recorded Anabaptist martyrs were women. In fact, much of what is known has come to us through court testimonies and letters and hymns composed by them while imprisoned. These remarkable women showed maturity of their faith during trials and a deep understanding of Scripture; they displayed extraordinary courage and a steely resolve not to abandon their faith, knowing that a conversion to Anabaptism almost guaranteed a death by execution. Two of the most extensive records of women found in the *Martyrs Mirror* are of a widow named Weynken and Elizabeth Dirks, detailing their examination, torture, and execution. It is important to note how these women respond with Scripture when questioned regarding Catholic doctrine.

On the 15th of November, 1527, Weynken, daughter of Claes, was brought as a prisoner from the castle of Woerden near the Hague. On the 18th, Weynken was arraigned before the governor and the full council of Holland. There a woman asked her, "Have you well considered the things which my lords proposed to you?"

Ans. "I abide by what I have said."

Ques. "If you do not speak differently, and turn from your error, you will be subjected to an intolerable death."

Ans. "If power is given you from above I am ready to suffer." (John 19:11)

Ques. "Do you then, not fear death, which you have never tasted?"

Ans. "This is true; but I shall never taste death, for Christ says: 'If a man keep my saying, he shall never see death.' (John 8:51) The rich man tasted death, and shall taste it forever." (Luke 16:23)

Ques. "What do you hold concerning the sacrament?"

Ans. "I hold your sacrament to be bread and flour, and if you hold it as God, I say that it is your devil."

Ques. "What do you hold concerning the saints?"

Ans. "I know no other Mediator than Christ." (1 John 2:19)

Ques. "You must die, if you abide by this."

Ans. "I am already dead." (Gal 2:19)

Ques. "If you are dead, how can you speak?"

Ans. "The spirit lives in me; the Lord is in me, and I am in Him." (John 14:20)

Ques. "Will you have a confessor, or not?"

Ans. "I have Christ, to Him I confess; nevertheless, if I have offended any, I would willingly ask them to forgive me."

Ques. "Who has taught you this opinion, and how did you come to it?"

Ans. "The Lord, who calls all men to Him; I am also one of His sheep; therefore I hear His voice." (John 10:27)

Ques. "Are you alone called?"

Ans. "No; for the Lord calls to Him all that are heavy laden." (Matt 28:11)

After many like words Weynken was led back to prison. During the two following days she was entreated and tempted by various persons, namely by monks, priests, women, and her nearest friends. Among others, a woman came to her, prompted by sincerity, who commiserated her after this manner: "Dear mother, can you not think what you please, and keep it to yourself? Then you will not die."

Weynken replied: "Dear sister; I am commanded to speak, and am constrained to do so; hence I cannot remain silent about it."

Wom. "Then, I am afraid, they will put you to death."

Ans. "Though they burn me tomorrow, or put me into a bag, I care not; as the Lord has ordained it, so, it must be, and not otherwise; I will adhere to the Lord."

Wom. "If you have done nothing else I hope you will not die."

Ans. "As for me; it matters not; but when I come down from the hall, I cry bitterly; and it grieves me to see that these good men are all so blinded; I will pray the Lord for them."

Two Dominican friars also came to her, the one as a confessor, and the other as an instructor. The latter showed her the crucifix, saying, "See, here is your Lord and your God." She answered, "This is not my God; the cross by which I have been redeemed, is a different one. This is a wooden god; throw him into the fire, and warm yourselves with him." The other asked her in the morning of the day when she was to die, whether she would not receive the sacrament, adding that he would willingly administer it to her. She said, "What God would you give me? One that is perishable, and is sold for a farthing?" And to the priest or monk, who rejoiced that he had read mass that day, she said that he had crucified God anew. He said, "It appears to me that you have fallen unto error."

Weynken replied, "I cannot help it, my Lord and my God, to whom be eternal honor, praise; and thanksgiving (Rev 4:11), has thus given it unto me."

Ques. "What do you hold concerning the holy oil?"

Ans. "Oil is good for salad, or to oil your shoes with." (1 Tim 4:4)

In the middle of the week she was brought before the Court, and when she came into the hall, the monk went up to her, and held the crucifix before her face, saying, "Do recant before sentence is passed." But Weynken turned from the crucifix, saying, "I adhere to my Lord and God; neither death nor life shall separate me from Him." (Rom.

8:39) As she stood before the judge, the monk whispered into her ear, "Fall down upon your knees, and ask the Lord for pardon." She replied, "Be still: did I not tell you, that you should not draw me from my Lord."

The Dean of Naeldwijck, subcommissary and inquisitor, read the sentence, in Latin, from a document, and repeating it in Dutch, said briefly, that she was found to be in error with regard to the sacrament, and that she immovably adhered to it; hence he decided that she was a heretic, and delivered Weynken to the secular arm, with the protest that he did not consent to her death. He then retired from the council, together with his two associate ecclesiastics.

The chancellor immediately read, that she, as reported, had been found obstinate, which could not be passed by without punishment, and that she should be burnt to ashes; and all her property be confiscated... As they were leaving the council chamber, the monk said to her that she should call upon our Lady to intercede for her.

She replied: "Our Lady, is well content in God."

Monk: "Call upon her."
    Weynken: "We have Christ, who sitteth on the right hand of His Father; He prays for us." (Rom 8:34)

...On the scaffold...she assisted the executioners to put the powder into her bosom. She then went gladly, as though she were going to a marriage; and her face did not once show fear of the fire. The executioner began to strangle her, which when she felt it, she cast down her eyes and closed them, as though she had fallen into a sleep, and gave up the ghost, on the twentieth day of November, AD 1527.[1]

Weynken's testimony recorded over several days reveals a woman well versed in Scripture. She articulated her understanding of the sacraments, Jesus as the only mediator between God and humanity, submission to governmental authorities within biblical boundaries, and God's providence even over her suffering. She willingly accepted her death rather than recant her beliefs. Her bold witness to governmental and ecclesiastical authorities,

---

[1] Braght, *The Martyrs Mirror*, 422–24.

as well as other witnesses assembled to tempt her from her beliefs, stands today as a powerful example of how to remain moored to Christ and sound doctrine no matter the consequences.

Elizabeth Dirks was another Anabaptist woman of remarkable courage. Raised in a nunnery in East Friesland, she learned to read Latin and dedicated much of her time to reading the Scriptures. During this time period, often the only schooling available to women was through convent schools. This is how Katie Luther received her formative education before her father committed her to the nunnery for life. Like Katie Luther, Elizabeth Dirks became certain that monasticism was not the way taught in Scripture. With the help of milkmaids, Elizabeth escaped and became a follower of Menno Simons, an influential Anabaptist leader. Not surprisingly, Elizabeth started teaching other women, and her extensive biblical knowledge gained through study while in the convent proved to be invaluable.

In 1549, Catholic authorities arrested Elizabeth when they found her Latin Bible. Mistakenly, they thought she was the wife of Menno Simons. When they tried to get her to take an oath at her interrogation, she refused, saying Christ had taught that our yes should mean yes and our no mean no.[2] When the examiners asked her to betray those whom she had taught, she refused, instead encouraging them to ask her anything about her own faith and she would answer gladly:

Lords: "We shall make you so afraid, that you will tell us."

Elizabeth: "I hope through the grace of God, that He will keep my tongue, so that I shall not become a traitoress, and deliver my brother into death."

Lords: "What then do you hold concerning the house of God? Do you not regard our church as the house of God?"

Elizabeth: "No, my lords, for it is written: 'Ye are the temple of the living God; as God hath said, I will dwell in them, and walk in them.'" 2 Cor 6:16.

Lords: "What do you hold concerning our mass?"

Elizabeth: "My lords, of your mass I think nothing at all; but I highly esteem all that accords with the Word of God."

---

[2] *Martyrs Mirror*, 481.

Lords: "What are your views with regard to the most holy sacrament?"

Elizabeth: "I have never in my life read in the holy Scriptures of a holy sacrament, but of the Lord's Supper." (She also quoted the Scripture relating to this.)

Lords: "You speak from a spirit of pride."

Elizabeth: "No, my lords, I speak with frankness."

Lords: "What did the Lord say, when He gave His disciples the Supper?"

Elizabeth: "What did He give them, flesh or bread?"

Lords: "He gave them bread."

Elizabeth: "Did not the Lord remain sitting there? Who then would eat the flesh of the Lord?"

Lords: "What are your views concerning infant baptism, seeing you have been rebaptized?"

Elizabeth: "No, my lords, I have not been rebaptized. I have been baptized once upon my faith; for it is written that baptism belongs to believers."

Lords: "Do you not seek your salvation in baptism?"

Elizabeth: "No, my lords, all the water in the sea could not save me; but salvation is in Christ (Acts 4:10), and He has commanded me to love God my Lord above all things, and my, neighbor as myself."

Lords: "Have the priests power to forgive sins?"

Elizabeth: "No, my lords; how should I believe this? I say that Christ is the only priest through whom sins are forgiven." Heb. 7:21...

Afterwards she was again brought before the council, and led into the torture chamber, Hans, the executioner, being present. The lords then said, "We have thus long dealt with you in kindness, but if you will not confess, we will resort to severity with you." The Procurator General said, "Master Hans, seize her."

Master Hans answered: "Oh, no, my lords, she will voluntarily confess."

But as she would not voluntarily confess, he applied the thumbscrews to her thumbs and forefingers, so that the blood squirted out at the nails.

Elizabeth said, "Oh! I cannot endure it any longer."

The lords said, "Confess, and we will relieve your pain."

But she cried to the Lord her God, "Help me, O Lord, Thy poor handmaiden! For Thou art a helper in time of need."

The lords all exclaimed, "Confess, and we will relieve your pain; for we told you to confess, and not to cry to God the Lord."

But she steadfastly adhered to God her Lord, as related above; and the Lord took away her pain, so that she said to the lords, "Ask me, and I shall answer you: for I no longer feel the least pain in my flesh, as I did before."

Lords: "Will you not yet confess?"
Elizabeth: "No, my lords."

They then applied the screws to her shins, one on each.

She said, "O my lords, do not put me to shame; for never a man touched my bare body."[3]

Common practice at this time was to undress prisoners during torture; this was more disturbing to the women than the threat of torture. The executioner crushed Elizabeth's leg bones with screws until she fainted.

But waking up, she said, "I live, and am not dead."

They then took off all the screws, and plied her with entreaties.

Elizabeth: "Why do you thus entreat me? this is the way to do with children." Thus they obtained not one word from her, detrimental to her brethren in the Lord, or to any other person.

Lords: "Will you revoke all that you have previously confessed here?"
Elizabeth: "No, my lords, but I will seal it with my death."

Lords: "We will try you no more; will you voluntarily tell us, who baptized you?"

---

[3] *Martyrs Mirror,* 482.

Elizabeth: "Oh, no, my lords; I have certainly told you, that I will not confess this."

Sentence was then passed upon Elizabeth, on the 27th of March, 1549; she was condemned to death to be drowned in a bag, and thus offered up her body to God.[4]

Both Weynken and Elizabeth's final days were spent defending the faith and beseeching God to help them remain steadfast to the end. The ease with which biblical truth rolled off their tongues before inquisitors and executioners indicated a confidence in the authority and sufficiency of the Word of God.

---

[4] *Martyrs Mirror,* 482–83.

Editors and Contributors

Editors:

Kevin L. King
Professor of Homiletics and
   Historical Theology
Rawlings School of Divinity,
   Liberty University

Edward E. Hindson
Distinguished Professor of Religion
Founding Dean, Rawlings School
   of Divinity
Liberty University

Benjamin K. Forrest
Professor of Christian Education
Associate Dean, College of Arts
   and Sciences
Liberty University

Contributors:

Rex D. Butler
Professor of Church History and
   Patristics
John T. Westbrook Chair of Church
   History
New Orleans Baptist Theological
   Seminary

Stephen Brett Eccher
Assistant Professor of Church
   History and Reformation Studies
Southeastern Baptist Theological
   Seminary

Timothy George
Founding Dean, Beeson Divinity
   School
Samford University

Candi Finch, PhD

Nathan A. Finn
Provost
Dean of the University Faculty
North Greenville University

Benjamin P. Laird
Assistant Professor of Biblical Studies
Liberty University

John McKinley
Associate Professor of Theology
Talbot School of Theology, Biola
    University

Adriaan C. Neele
Professor of Historical Theology
Director, Doctoral Program
Puritan Reformed Theological
    Seminary
Research Scholar and Digital Editor,
Jonathan Edwards Center
Yale University

Paul Owen
Professor of Biblical and Religious
    Studies
Montreat College

Benjamin B. Phillips
Associate Professor of Systematic
    Theology
Director, Southwestern Baptist
    Theological Seminary
    Darrington Extension
Associate Dean, Southwestern
    Baptist Theological Seminary's
    Houston Campus

Joseph Pipa, Jr.
Professor of Homiletic and
    Systematic Theology
President, Greenville Presbyterian
    Theological Seminary

Roger Schultz
Professor of History
Dean, College of Arts and Sciences
Liberty University

Edward L. Smither
Professor of Intercultural Studies and
    History of Global Christianity
Dean, College of Intercultural
    Studies
Columbia International University

Michael Spangler
Minister
Orthodox Presbyterian Church

Ray Van Neste
Associate Professor of Biblical
    Studies
Director of the R. C. Ryan Center
    for Biblical Studies, Union
    University

John D. Woodbridge
Research Professor of Church
    History and Christian Thought
Trinity Evangelical Divinity School

Scripture Index

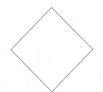

Name Index

Subject Index